JURA WINE

with local food and travel tips

WINK LORCH

Wine Travel Media

First published in Great Britain in 2014 by Wine Travel Media
174 Basin Approach, London, E14 7JS
Web: winetravelmedia.com

Second impression, 2015
Third impression, 2017
Fourth impression, 2020
Fifth impression, 2022

ISBN: 978-0-9928331-0-7

Main photography: Mick Rock, Xavier Servolle, Brett Jones
Designer: JD Smith
Editor and indexer: Patricia Carroll
Editorial assistant: Brett Jones
Cartographer: Quentin Sadler
Printed by: Dolman Scott Ltd

The town of Arbois viewed from the Curon vineyard.

CONTENTS

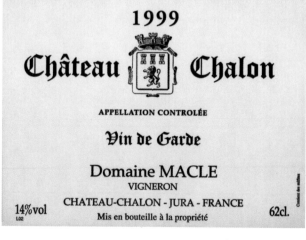

FOREWORD
RAYMOND BLANC OBE

You are about to embark on a magnificent journey to a very special place – be sure to pack a wine glass!

The Jura, it has to be said, is not on every traveller's must-visit list. This is a great shame because it is such a remarkable and stunning part of France. Those who visit tend to return.

I grew up in the village of Saône. The nearest town is Besançon, once a Roman city. The rugged, magnificent Jura Mountains are close by and the landscape is dramatic. Huge mountains

are layered with forests of *épicéas* (spruce trees) that are used to smoke the ham and the *saucisse de Morteau*, and provide the casing of the Mont d'Or cheese. Montbéliarde cows dot the mountainside and give their milk to create the famous local cheeses, such as Comté, Mont d'Or and many others.

During school holidays I'd go to summer camp in the mountains. The camp was in a forest of pines and was a place of absolute wonderment for my young mind. Streams and rivers gushed from the chalky mountains above, and waterfalls cascaded into large pools. The pools were an ice-cold bath for me but they were perfect for trout. I tried (without success) to learn the art of catching trout by hand, which starts with a gentle tickle of the underbelly of the fish. This is where we would also bathe. The trout of the Jura is divine upon a plate, and is in harmony on the palate when accompanied by an Arbois Chardonnay.

The Jura is one of the most unspoilt regions of France and one of our most ancient wine regions. We have our own *route du vin* which leads to the traveller's discovery of the most beautiful villages and towns such as Arbois, Poligny and Château-Chalon.

Along the way you will savour the world-beating, harmonious match of Vin Jaune with Comté and, of course, the morels. *Bon appétit.*

Jura Wine is written lovingly, and is a significant literary homage to one of my passions. Wink Lorch has devoted more than a decade of her life to its making, and I raise a glass to her.

That decade has not been dull, not one moment of it. Wink has been at the wine festivals; she has visited scores of wine producers – celebrated experts in their craft – and she has listened and learned, and tasted and then tasted once more, with a piece of delicious Comté cheese at her side.

In the pages that follow she shares her knowledge of the terroir and reveals the vinous secrets of Château-Chalon, Vin Jaune, Vin de Paille, Savagnin, Poulsard and Trousseau, and even Chardonnay and Pinot Noir.

Oh, how I wish I could have joined Wink on her travels, for this is my home, my region. The landscapes were the colourful backdrop to my childhood. This is where I fell in love with food and the perfect wine to go with it. I did not join Wink but this book does the trick – I feel as if I am there, at her side in the Jura.

Wink, why don't you pour while I fry the trout in a hot pan of foaming butter?

Born in Besançon, France, in 1949, Raymond Blanc is acknowledged as one of the finest chefs in the world, despite never having been formally trained. He opened his first UK restaurant, Les Quat'Saisons, in Oxford at the age of 28 and created the hotel and restaurant Le Manoir aux Quat'Saisons, synonymous with fine dining and hospitality, in 1984. The restaurant has held two Michelin stars for 30 years.

Opposite page: Raymond in the Jura during filming of his BBC2 TV series The Very Hungry Frenchman. *Left: At Le Manoir aux Quat'Saisons.*

INTRODUCTION

Like many wine students in the 1980s I was dimly aware of the Jura wine region and Vin Jaune. I probably first tasted Vin Jaune when I visited Henri Maire in the early 1980s, but I confess to remembering little except the impressive tasting room. I was doing a whirlwind tour of French wine regions at the time and suffering from information overload.

In the 1990s I started spending part of my year living in the mountains of Haute-Savoie, where I soon discovered Savoie wines and was keen to write about them. However, at that time Savoie was always linked with the Jura. My first serious commission arrived at the end of 1999, when I was asked to contribute a short

chapter on the wines of Savoie, Bugey and the Jura to *The global encyclopaedia of wine*, edited in Australia by Peter Forrestal. How could I refuse?

And so it was that in January 2000 I drove through the snow from Haute-Savoie to the Jura and spent a night in a hotel near Poligny, the only guest there. Dining alone, I chose a half-bottle of a mysterious local white to go with a classic main course of trout in a Vin Jaune and cream sauce. The wine was weird – just as the hotel owner, doubling as waiter, had warned me. The next day I made my

---

With vigneron Jacques Puffeney on a winter's day in Montigny-les-Arsures.

first serious visit to discover Jura wines in situ. In the course of a long day I visited each of the producer presidents of the four Appellation Contrôlée areas of the Jura. I started in the south with Alain Baud in AOC Côtes du Jura and could not have found a better or more patient teacher. Looking back at my notes, it is extraordinary how much information I garnered from him in less than two hours, tasting seven wines before 11am. After 20 years of studying wine, in the Jura I found that there was so much more to learn. That was the real start of my Jura journey and two years later, researching for my chapter in Tom Stevenson's *Wine Report*, I began to make my first exciting discoveries of Savagnin *ouillé*, Trousseau and extraordinary Chardonnays.

This book aims to fill a big information gap about Jura wines, the region they come from and the people who make them. Even up-to-date texts in French are hard to come by. Yet, having written this book, some things still remain a mystery in the Jura and who doesn't enjoy a mystery story? To me it remains completely fascinating that the smallest wine region of France is at once so intriguing and so completely different from any other wine region.

There seems to be a thirst among wine drinkers around the world, not only for Jura wines but also for the story behind them. When I began this project and decided that I would self-publish, my plan was loose – I did not expect to end up writing such a detailed book. This tiny wine region of France produces only 0.2% of the country's wines, yet there is so much to discover and explain. I hope you find enough to educate and inspire you about Jura wines and their makers.

Navigating the book

The book is divided into four main parts, starting with 'All about the wine' and continuing with 'History'. It is traditional to begin regional wine books with the history, but as so much Jura wine history is related to the history of Vin Jaune, the history is hard to appreciate unless you already know something about this wine and others in the Jura and how they are made. Unless you already know the fundamentals about Jura wines I strongly suggest reading about the wines first in Part 1, which is effectively the textbook part of the book. This is where you will find out about the AOCs, the climate, geology, grape varieties, viticulture, winemaking methods and much more.

One hundred producers are profiled in Part 3 'Places and people – the wine producers'. As well as their contact details you will find these producers' stories, together with information about how they work in their vineyards and make their wines. I believe that getting to know the people is the best way to know their wines, even before you taste them. Many European wine regions have complications – the intricate patterns of *premier* and *grand cru* vineyards in Burgundy or their equivalents in Piedmont, for example, or the plethora of German wine categories. As a wine lover you might not remember all the names of German *Prädikats* or Burgundy *lieux dits*, but you do tend to know what style of wine to expect. In the Jura that is far from the case. A range of 15 wines, each one quite different in terms of how it is made, is common in the Jura and 20–30 wines even in a small producer's range is not unusual. As these are ever-changing I have not listed each producer's wines, but there is an overview of the range in every profile,

9

with an indication of the wines I believe to be the most successful.

In Part 3 you will also find out more about the pretty wine towns and villages that dot each area of the Jura wine region. Each area has its own history and character, and of course the terroir is different too. For the most opinionated part of the book, read the last chapter of Part 3 about the future for the region.

Most Jura wines are better drunk with food and, if you have the chance to travel to the region, you will find almost nothing but regional food in the restaurants. Part 4, 'Enjoying the wines and the local food', gives an overview of the cheeses, most notably the famous Comté, so delicious paired with Vin Jaune, along with smoked sausages, Bresse chicken and other intriguing drinks, notably absinthe. This part also discusses how to serve the wines – some of the unusual Jura wine styles need to be handled differently from other wines. For those planning a visit to the region there is a short travel guide. Appendices follow, with AOC details and a glance at some wines made elsewhere inspired by the Jura. For reference there is a detailed glossary plus a guide to pronouncing all those key Jura words, from Jura itself to Savagnin, *ouillé*, Vin Jaune (of course) and many more.

The text has been hugely enhanced by the photographs and images – I chose each one to add something to the understanding of the region. The maps – incredibly hard to produce as source material is almost impossible to find – are the most detailed maps available for the Jura at present.

Omissions are inevitable as this tiny region offers such diversity, but there is more crammed into this one book, taking in all aspects of the wine region, than you will find anywhere else in any language. Any errors are my responsibility. If you do find an error, please contact me at wink@winetravelmedia.com.

By the banks of the River Cuisance in Arbois with photographer Mick Rock, who has just taken the photograph above, looking towards the Eglise St-Just.

Author's acknowledgements

This book could not have been written or published without the generous assistance of a large number of people to whom I give my heartfelt thanks. May I apologise now to anyone I have omitted.

First, those who supported the project financially through the Kickstarter campaign must be thanked for their faith in the project, which made me doubly certain that this book had to be written. They are listed separately on p. 350–1.

Specific individuals who helped to answer questions or check text are as follows:

For Part 1 ('All about the wines'): Michel Campy, Daniel Cousin and Gaël Delorme of Société de Viticulture du Jura, Professor Alex Maltman, José Vouillamoz and Monty Waldin. For Part 2 ('History'): Bernard Amiens, Mariëlla Beukers, Professor Kathleen Burk, Pierre Chevrier, Michel Converset, Roger Gibey, Jean-Paul Jeunet, Pierre Overnoy and Marie-Christine Tarby. Also to *World of Fine Wine* (*WFW*) for permission to use text first published in *WFW* Issue 35, 2012. For Part 3 ('Places and people'): all the producers profiled. For Part 4 ('Enjoying the wine and the local food'): Sue Style. For the appendices: Amanda Regan.

For general research help and image sourcing: Jean Berthet-Bondet, Christophe Botté and Sylvie Cambray of Fruitière Vinicole d'Arbois, Philippe Bruniaux, Caroline Campalto, Laurent Courtial and Aurélie Dupas of Rouge Granit, Baudoin de Chassey of Comité Interprofessionnel des Vins du Jura, Olivier Grosjean, Xavier Guillaume, Caroline and Patrice Hughes-Béguet, Daniel Keller, Christophe Menozzi, Stéphane Planche, Jennifer Russell, Xavier Servolle and Stéphane Tissot.

For help and encouragement on self-publishing and with the Kickstarter campaign: Susanna Forbes, Fiona Holman, Steve de Long (on whose original design the front cover of the book is based), Rob Lorch, Kathryn McWhirter, Will Mattos, Charles Metcalfe, Joëlle Nebbe-Mornod, Lyn Parry, Tom Stevenson and Arnold Waldstein, along with other wine bloggers on the Kickstarter videos. I also thank Raymond Blanc OBE for writing the foreword, as well as Jancis Robinson MW, OBE and Gerard Basset MS, MW, OBE for their kind comments endorsing the book.

Finally, my biggest thanks of all is reserved for those who in the past year have worked so tirelessly and patiently on this book, giving me unquestioned support whenever I needed it. *Jura Wine* is their book too. These are photographer Mick Rock and his wife Annie, editor Patricia Carroll, designer Jane Dixon-Smith and cartographer Quentin Sadler. And, by my side throughout this project, encouraging me always has been my partner Brett Jones, who made my travels, researches, self-publishing traumas and writing so much easier than they might have been.

ALL ABOUT
THE WINES

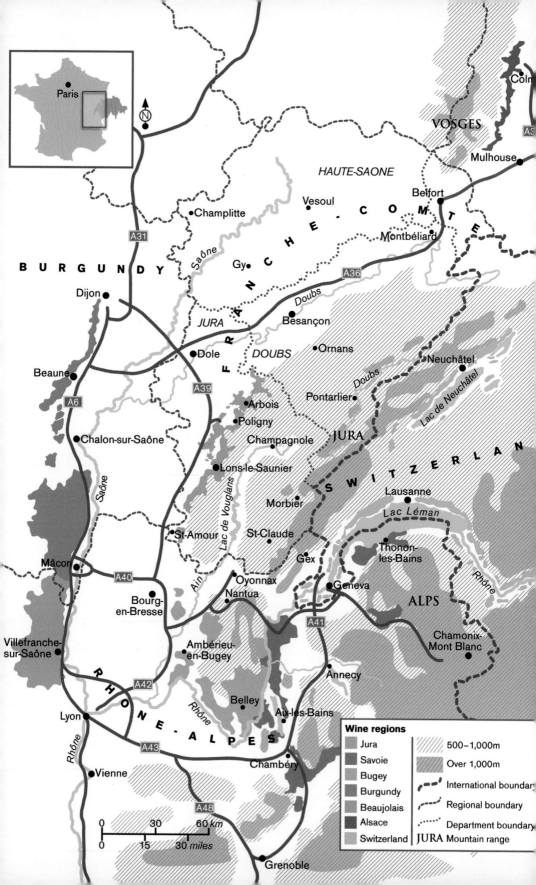

Paris

VOSGES

Coln

Mulhouse

HAUTE-SAONE

A31

Champlitte

Vesoul

Belfort

FRANCHE-COMTE

Montbéliard

BURGUNDY

Gy

A36

Saône

Dijon

JURA

Doubs

Besançon

A39

Dole

DOUBS

Ornans

Neuchâtel

Beaune

A6

Arbois

Pontarlier

Doubs

Lac de Neuchâtel

Poligny

Chalon-sur-Saône

Champagnole

JURA

Lons-le-Saunier

SWITZERLAND

Saône

Lausanne

Morbier

Lac Léman

Lac de Vouglans

St-Amour

St-Claude

Thonon-les-Bains

Mâcon

Ain

Gex

A40

Oyonnax

Geneva

Nantua

Rhône

Bourg-en-Bresse

ALPS

A41

Villefranche-sur-Saône

Ambérieu-en-Bugey

Chamonix-Mont Blanc

A42

Annecy

RHÔNE-ALPES

Belley

Rhône

Lyon

Aix-les-Bains

A43

Chambéry

Vienne

A48

Wine regions	
Jura	500–1,000m
Savoie	Over 1,000m
Bugey	International boundar
Burgundy	Regional boundary
Beaujolais	Department boundary
Alsace	
Switzerland	JURA Mountain range

0   30   60 km
0   15   30 miles

Grenoble

THE WINE REGION IN CONTEXT

The name 'Jura' is not only the name of the French department or political division in which the Jura wine region is wholly situated; it is also the name of the mountain range that divides France from Switzerland, northwest of the Alps. The Jura wine region of France is located on the lower foothills of the western slopes of the Jura Mountains in eastern France, just 80km due east of the Côte de Beaune in Burgundy, easily accessible from Dijon, Lyon or Geneva.

The Swiss city of Geneva lies at the southern end of the Jura Mountains, which stretch up through the canton of Bern almost to Basel at their northern reaches. Switzerland also has 'Jura wines', with a small production in the canton of the same name, but in a wider sense the Swiss wines of the canton of Neuchâtel are usually considered to be from the Jura, as the vineyards lie on the eastern foothills. Neither has much in common with French Jura wines. Another well-known drink-related Jura appears miles away – on the island of Jura in Scotland, which produces fine malt whisky, but there is no connection, even geologically. The word 'Jurassic' is famous throughout the world as the name for the period of geological time between 200 million and 145 million years ago. The name reflects the fact that rocks of this age were first

recognized in the Jura Mountains and the Jurassic period was named after them. It is believed that the name 'Jura' derives from Celtic languages – *Jor*, later transformed into *Joris* by the Romans, the Latin word for 'forest' or 'land of forests'.

The Jura department is within the greater political region of Franche-Comté and this book covers food specialities from the whole Franche-Comté region, rather than simply the Jura, and also includes a small section under producers discussing the few wines that are produced in the departments of Doubs and Haute-Saône to the north of the Jura, classified as Indication Géographique Protégé (IGP) Franche-Comté. Franche-Comté borders the region of Burgundy (Bourgogne) to its northwest and Rhône-Alpes to the south and southwest. To the east is Switzerland. Travel guides in English tend to focus on the name 'Jura' rather than 'Franche-Comté', even if they cover the whole region.

Previous page: Sunset with west- and southwest-facing vines below Château-Chalon and Menétru-le-Vignoble.

Left: About 400km or 250 miles southeast of Paris, the Jura wine region lies southwest of Alsace, east of Burgundy and north of the Savoie and Bugey wine regions. On the slopes below the First Plateau of the Jura Mountains, the vineyards are at altitudes similar to those in Burgundy and Alsace.

The Jura vineyard region

Today's vineyard area of around 2,100ha (about 0.3% of the total vineyards in France) is a fraction of that which existed in the 19th century, when it stretched further north into the Doubs and Haute-Saône departments and further south towards Bourg-en-Bresse. Although the vineyards are much more scattered in certain sectors than formerly, the area covered west–east, which reaches 5km at most, has shrunk less, for the simple reason that the vine can thrive only in certain conditions. Hence today's vineyards run for roughly 80km from Salins-les-Bains to south of Lons-le-Saunier, in a northeast to southwest strip between the Premier Plateau or First Plateau of the Jura Mountains to the east and the marshy Bresse plain to the west. This area is also known as the Revermont – the main part, sometimes called the Nord Revermont, is north of Lons-le-Saunier, and the smaller part, known as the Sud Revermont, lies to the south of Lons.

Unlike many wine regions, rivers are not a particularly significant influence on wine in the Jura, yet, as in Alpine regions, they gave rise to many industries that have kept the region economically alive – the salt, forestry and precision instrument industries in particular. The department of Jura is in the Rhône river catchment area and the most important Saône and Doubs rivers are tributaries of the Rhône. The Rhône au Rhin canal and the Doubs river run through the attractive town of Dole and its tributaries include the Loue, which was important historically for the salt industry. Tributaries of the Loue include the wonderfully named Furieuse running through Salins-les-Bains and the pretty Cuisance river tumbles through the town of Arbois. The gentle Seille river, which runs through the wine villages near Château-Chalon and also through Arlay, is a tributary of

North of the Poligny reculée, *Montbéliarde cows, whose milk is used for Comté cheese, graze on the flatland. The vineyards lie on the western slopes below the forest and the limestone cliff.*

the Saône and this attractive area is known as the Haute Seille. Most of these rivers have their sources in the Jura's distinctive geological *reculées* (blind or steephead valleys). The Jura is also known for its lake district, just southeast of the wine region, consisting of both natural and man-made lakes created mostly for the hydro-electric industry, another significant industry in the Jura, but now important for tourism.

Altitude

Contrary to popular belief, the Jura can hardly be regarded as a 'mountain vine-yard' even if its situation on the foothills of the Jura Mountains and the considerable steepness of several vineyards suggest it should be. Vineyard altitudes vary from around 220m up to 450m, more or less the same as the Alsace vineyards that lie on the Vosges foothills, and comparable with the finest *premier* and *grand cru* vineyards of the Côte d'Or in Burgundy at between 250m and 340m, which is the altitude at which the majority of Jura vineyards are situated.

The Jura wine region includes more than 100 communes (in France each commune – a town or village – has its own admin-istration with a mayor), all designated in the appellation rules, but only four real towns. From north to south these are the spa town **Salins-les-Bains** (often simply Salins); the real wine capital and home to Pasteur, **Arbois**; the home of Comté cheese, **Poligny**, an important thoroughfare to the Alps, and the departmental capital **Lons-le-Saunier** (simply Lons). To the north the attractive Jura town of **Dole**, once the capital of Franche-Comté (today the capital is Besançon in the Doubs department), is actually more populous than Lons and lies just to the north of today's wine region; in former times there were many vineyards in the so-called Pays Dolois or countryside surrounding the town, as well as around Besançon.

A snapshot of the wines

Bear in mind that the Jura wine region is only just larger than Margaux in Bordeaux and less than half of the whole of the Chablis area. Yet in both these regions only one style of wine is made – in the Jura almost every colour and style of wine is made, hence complications abound, but that is what makes the region's wines so endlessly fascinating. The chapters follow-ing in this part of the book will examine in detail all the aspects that Jura producers work with to make their wines: the appel-lation rules, the terroir, the grape varieties, the ways the grapes are grown and, finally, how the wines are made. This final chapter also attempts to describe how the myriad wine styles taste. To help you to understand various references in these chapters as you dip in and out, here is a summary.

Appellations: One regional appellation – Côtes du Jura, with three more specific geographical appellations: Arbois, L'Etoile and Château-Chalon. Two further appella-tions for Crémant du Jura sparkling wines and Macvin du Jura fortified wine.

Terroir: Vineyards primarily on the west-facing foothills of the Jura Mountains' Premier Plateau, on varied soils dominated by limestone and marl (clay-limestone) of varying colours. The climate is classified as northern semi-continental, with cold winters, warm summers and high rainfall.

Grape varieties: Two white varieties, Chardonnay and Savagnin, and three red varieties, Poulsard (or Ploussard), Pinot Noir and Trousseau, are permitted for AOC wines.

The wines: Dry whites (which may be oxidative, aged under yeast or classic), dry rosés and light reds are backed up by the so-called specialities, Crémant du Jura and other sparkling wines, Vin Jaune, Vin de Paille, Macvin and other liqueur wines.

How to get there

Travel connections to the Jura are easy by road. The A39 motorway runs just to the west of the vineyards and boasts two of the most interesting service stations I know in France. At the Aire du Jura you can visit a small museum with regularly changing locally inspired exhibitions and purchase decent regional food and wine in the shop. At the Aire du Poulet de Bresse you can admire the distinctive metal chicken sculpture outside.

By train, the high-speed TGV from Paris and elsewhere stops at Dole in the north and Bourg-en-Bresse to the south of the Jura. There are connections to both Lons-le-Saunier and Arbois but trains are infrequent. The Jura has its own small airport at Dole with some flights to England and elsewhere, but the nearest large airports are Geneva in Switzerland and Lyon St-Exupéry to the south, both around two hours' drive.

THE APPELLATIONS

There are four main geographical appellations in the Jura, all originally ratified in 1936 and 1937, the first years that the French Appellation d'Origine Contrôlée (AOC) rules came into force. In addition there are two appellations for specific wine types that were awarded later. All French wine AOCs have been incorporated into the European Designated Protection of Origin (DPO) system for food and drink, which in French is called Appellation d'Origine Protégée (AOP). The French wine industry has been allowed to retain AOC as a designation, but producers may use AOP if they wish. As there has been much confusion about this over the past few years, a few producers have adopted AOP on their labels, but most use AOC. This book will refer to AOC. An abbreviated version of the rules for each of these AOCs is included in the appendices.

The only permitted grape varieties for the AOCs in the Jura are Savagnin and Chardonnay (white) and Poulsard, Trousseau and Pinot Noir (red).

About 90% of wines from the Jura wine region are classified as AOC. The majority of those that are not AOC are from the relatively large number of privately owned vineyards in the region. Wines from outside the official Jura AOC geographical boundaries are labelled Indication Géographique Protégé (IGP), the European protection of origin standard that replaced the Vin de Pays category in France in 2009. The generic Vin de France category (previously Vin de Table) is also used for certain wines.

Detailed rules are included in Appendix 1, but the essentials are outlined here.

The decree for AOC Arbois wines in 1936 included the vineyards of Montigny-les-Arsures within the appellation.

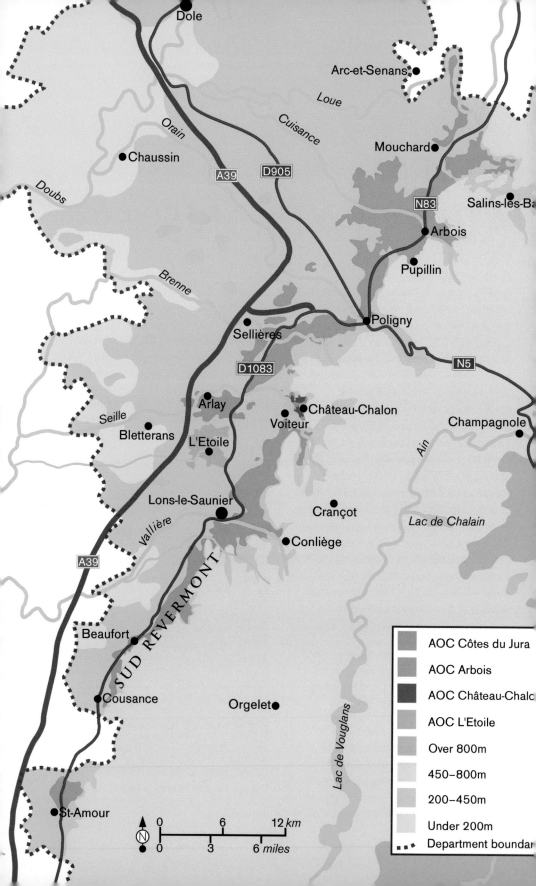

Dole

Arc-et-Senans

Loue

Cuisance

Orain

Mouchard

Chaussin

A39   D905

Doubs

N83   Salins-les-B.

Arbois

Brenne

Pupillin

Poligny

Sellières

N5

D1083

Seille

Arlay   Château-Chalon

Voiteur

Bletterans

L'Etoile

Champagnole

Ain

Lons-le-Saunier

Crançot

Lac de Chalain

Vallière

Conliège

A39

SUD REVERMONT

Beaufort

Cousance

Orgelet

Lac de Vouglans

St-Amour

0   6   12 *km*

N

0   3   6 *miles*

	AOC Côtes du Jura
	AOC Arbois
	AOC Château-Chalo
	AOC L'Etoile
	Over 800m
	450–800m
	200–450m
	Under 200m
····	Department boundar

AOC Côtes du Jura

Côtes du Jura is a regional AOC encompassing the whole of the Jura wine region, including the more specific village AOCs of Arbois, L'Etoile and Château-Chalon. In practice AOC Côtes du Jura is used mainly for wines from areas outside the larger Arbois AOC, including a small area north of Arbois between Champagne-sur-Loue on the border of the Doubs department and Salins-les-Bains, and the larger area south of Pupillin to Lons-le-Saunier and beyond in the Sud Revermont. The decree was ratified in 1937, one of the first AOCs in France to be designated. Even more so than the Arbois AOC, the proposed area originally planned would have allowed for many more hectares than are actually planted at present. Today it is hard to imagine what it would look like if the whole area was planted, but, with planting restrictions in force in Europe, any dramatic expansion towards its former glory is unlikely to happen. Along with wines from around the towns of Poligny and Lons-le-Saunier, well-known Côtes du Jura wine villages include Passenans, Voiteur, Le Vernois, Lavigny, Arlay, Gevingey and Rotalier.

All the Jura colours and styles of still wine may be made, including Vin Jaune and Vin de Paille, although white wines predominate under this AOC label.

AOC Arbois and AOC Arbois-Pupillin

Arbois was awarded its AOC in 1936 and is, in practice, the largest appellation in the Jura. The rules have changed several times, but the area has remained more or less the

In 2013 the region commissioned roadside signs for each of the four geographical AOCs.

same, covering much of the northern part of the Jura wine region around the town of Arbois, including the key wine villages of Montigny-les-Arsures and Pupillin. Since 1970 Pupillin has been entitled to its own appellation, Arbois-Pupillin, and growers in the Pupillin vineyards may choose which AOC to use, Arbois or Arbois-Pupillin.

As in Côtes du Jura, all the Jura colours and styles of still wine may be made, but 70% of the Jura's red wines are produced under the Arbois AOC. Technically growers in the Arbois AOC are allowed to use the Côtes du Jura appellation too, but this happens only if a producer owns vineyards in both appellations and wants to make a wine blended from both of them.

AOC Château-Chalon

The illustrious Château-Chalon appellation was awarded just a couple of weeks after

Left: The areas shown on the map indicating the extent of the various Jura AOCs are theoretical. Less than 2,000ha out of 11,000ha of AOC-designated land are actually planted.

The first AOC?

Arbois often claims to be the first AOC awarded in France in 1936. As far as I can tell, starting with an 'A' is all that can substantiate the claim that should more accurately be 'one of the first AOCs in France'. For the record, the first six AOCs in France were created on the same day, 15 May 1936, and were Arbois, Cassis, Châteauneuf-du-Pape, Cognac, Monbazillac and Tavel. It is, however, a credit to the historical importance of the quality of the wines of Arbois that it was in that earliest group.

that of Arbois in 1936. It is one of the most unusual AOCs in France. It is applicable to only one highly individual style of wine, Vin Jaune, and on paper it is also one of the most strictly monitored, with three stages of control: at the vineyards pre-harvest; as so-called 'base wine' before putting into barrel; and as Vin Jaune Château-Chalon before bottling. The AOC also includes vineyards in the nearby villages of Domblans, Menétru-le-Vignoble and Nevy-sur-Seille, but it depends greatly in all four villages on the particular exposition and soil whether the vineyards are categorized as Château-Chalon or Côtes du Jura. The former, currently with around 50ha of a potential 85ha planted, is of course almost all planted to Savagnin for Vin Jaune; the latter is mostly planted to Chardonnay. Savagnin deemed not good enough to withstand the ageing requirements for Vin Jaune must be sold as AOC Côtes du Jura, as are all wines from other grape varieties.

AOC L'Etoile

The L'Etoile appellation includes vineyards around the village of L'Etoile and three neighbouring villages. The original AOC was granted in 1937.

Only white wines may be made under the L'Etoile AOC, but this includes Vin Jaune and Vin de Paille, and the latter may include red grapes. Red or rosé wines made in this geographical area must be labelled under AOC Côtes du Jura. Traditionally L'Etoile was reputed for its sparkling wines, but since 1995 these have come under the Crémant du Jura AOC.

Château-Chalon's inspection committee

Château-Chalon is unique among AOCs. In regulations established in 1952 an inspection committee comprised of representatives of the INAO (who control the appellations nationally), the Société de Viticulture du Jura (SVJ), local wine laboratories, producers and négociants visit each parcel of vineyards shortly before harvest. In addition to checking whether there is sufficient sugar in the grapes, they also check how healthy the grapes are and their potential yield. Depending on the results, in extreme circumstances the producers of Château-Chalon may take a decision not to allow a vintage under the AOC – this happened in 1974, 1980, 1984 and 2001. In these years Savagnin from these vineyards had to be sold as AOC Côtes du Jura.

Key AOC rules for Vin Jaune

The rules for Vin Jaune under all the AOCs have changed little over the years and are based on the historical 'recipe'. The essentials are:

- Vin Jaune must be made 100% from the Savagnin grape.

- It must not be bottled until December six years after the harvest and must spend at least five years in barrel under a veil of yeast. (Being pedantic, the figure of six years and three months widely quoted as the minimum time a Vin Jaune spends in barrel under yeast is therefore not correct – see 'Vin Jaune - some secrets revealed', p.62.)

- It must be bottled in a *clavelin* bottle containing 62cl. Other sizes, particularly 37.5cl, may occasionally be seen in non-European countries, which are outside the jurisdiction of the INAO.

- It must not be sold before 1 January seven years after the harvest.

Key AOC rules for Vin de Paille

The rules for Vin de Paille under all the AOCs have been altered on several occasions and attract some controversy. There is a great temptation for producers to bend the rules when it comes to minimum/maximum sugar levels at pressing, oak ageing stipulations, alcohol levels and bottle dates. Increasing numbers of vignerons now produce wines from dried grapes outside these rules and bottle within the Vin de France category. This is a great shame for the region, as this speciality wine is highly valued – in my view the rules should be reviewed again with greater consultation among producers. Essentials for AOC wines are:

- Grapes must be hand-harvested.

- Only Chardonnay, Savagnin, Poulsard or Trousseau may be used and they must be dried on straw or in boxes, or suspended from rafters, for a minimum of six weeks in a well-ventilated room (fans may be used). No heating is allowed in the room.

Sales per AOC, 2012–13 (000 bottles)

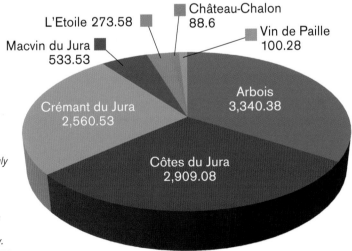

L'Etoile 273.58

Château-Chalon 88.6

Macvin du Jura 533.53

Vin de Paille 100.28

Arbois 3,340.38

Crémant du Jura 2,560.53

Côtes du Jura 2,909.08

The pie chart represents figures issued by the CIVJ showing producer sales figures for August 2012–July 2013. Sales of Vin Jaune are included in the figures for the AOCs of Arbois, Côtes du Jura and L'Etoile, whereas sales of Vin de Paille are shown separately.

- The sugar level of the grapes at pressing must be 320–420g/l.
- It must not be bottled until November three years after harvest, and must spend at least 18 months in barrel.
- The final wine must be a minimum of 14% alcohol (and minimum 19% potential alcohol including the residual sugar). This was reduced from 14.5% in the original AOC rules.

A selection of bottles for sale in Domaine Baud's tasting room and shop. Only the clavelin *bottle on the left is enshrined in AOC rules. Its use is obligatory for Vin Jaune, including Château-Chalon.*

AOC Crémant du Jura

One of the seven Crémant AOCs in France (possibly soon to be eight, with the expected addition of Savoie from 2015), the Jura joined the ranks in 1995 and follows the same basic production rules as the others. These include hand-harvesting, regulations for the types of press used, use of the traditional method with a minimum of nine months in contact with the second fermentation lees before disgorgement, and no sales allowed before 12 months after bottling.

The area covered is the same as for AOC Côtes du Jura. All five Jura grape varieties can be used for the base wine, but for white Crémant du Jura there must be a minimum of 70% Chardonnay, Pinot Noir and/or Trousseau, and for rosés a minimum of 50% red grapes. This means that Savagnin can never be more than 30% of the blend for white Crémant, which seems short-sighted considering the interesting quality potential and individuality of the grape.

AOC Macvin du Jura

Macvin du Jura is a 'liqueur wine', or fortified wine, which can be white, red or rosé. It was given its own AOC in 1991 and may be made from the juice or must of any

Vins de Liqueur

Macvin is one of only three Vins de Liqueur to be given an AOC in France, along with Pineau des Charentes (grape juice with Cognac) and Floc de Gascogne (grape juice with Armagnac). However, it is the only one that must be made with spirit distilled from grape *marc* rather than spirit distilled from wine. Outside the AOC rules there are several fortified wines made in the Jura labelled simply 'Vin de Liqueur', either made with Fine, the local brandy, or not aged for long enough to qualify for AOC, or according to age-old local recipes involving cooked and therefore concentrated must, or even with an addition of spices or fruit.

of the five Jura grapes grown in the same area as the regional Côtes du Jura AOC.

The grape juice (which may have just begun fermentation) is blended with one-third Marc du Jura, which has to have been aged for a minimum of 14 months. The *marc* (grape spirit) has to originate from the same producer but may be distilled on the premises or elsewhere. The final Macvin blend must be aged in oak for at least ten months, and the alcohol level must be between 16% and 22%.

IGP Franche-Comté

IGP Franche-Comté replaced Vin de Pays Franche-Comté in 2009 and it includes vineyard areas in the departments of Jura, Doubs, Haute-Saône and Territoire de Belfort. Various geographical names may be added when appropriate, including the departmental names of Doubs and Haute-Saône, and certain historic vineyard areas/villages, notably Coteaux de Champlitte and Gy. From 2015 wines from vineyards in villages within the Côtes du Jura AOC will no longer be allowed to use IGP Franche-Comté, so any wines not eligible for AOC must be sold as Vin de France. The category may be used for any colour of still wines, or for sparkling wines designated Vin Mousseux de Qualité. The list of permitted grape varieties includes those for the Jura AOCs and several others. However, rather sadly, few of the ancient Jura varieties are included.

Vin de France

This is technically the lowliest of legal categories for wine produced in France, but it is also the most flexible and, unlike Vin de Table, which it replaced in 2010, wines can state both grape varieties and vintage on the label. It is in use among several Jura producers for the following: Pétillant Naturel sparkling wines; late-harvest sweet wines; sweet wines from dried grapes that do not fit the Vin de Paille rules; wines made from unusual and/or ancient grape varieties; and for wines that fall into no other legal category.

On this label for Vignoble Guillaume in the Haute-Saône department, 'IGP' is not spelt out as 'Indication Géographique Protégé' – instead the old term 'Vin de Pays' is used.

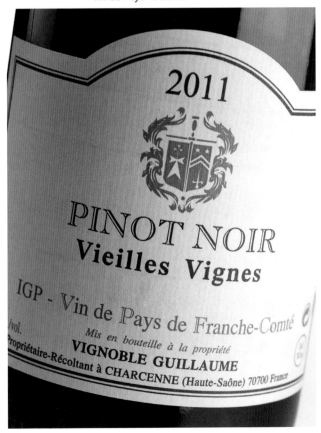

THE TERROIR
– GEOLOGY, SOIL TYPES AND CLIMATE

Great, interesting and individual wines are created by vignerons, who through their hard work and skill bring out the best from the meeting of a particular grape variety with a certain terroir. Many consider that the vigneron and even the cellar form part of terroir, but here I refer to terroir as the conditions in which the grapes are grown, shaped by the geology of the place. The vigneron is given no choice but to work with the weather, which might be different every year – note this is entirely different from the climate – and this could certainly be called the luck of the year. However, as everywhere else, the Jura vigneron can to a certain extent prepare for whatever the

Pupillin vineyard in springtime. Dark clouds threaten another downpour, the vines are just starting their growth, herbicide has been applied under the vine rows and cover crops have been planted between the rows.

weather presents, although no vigneron can control it.

Although I do not consider the Jura to be a mountain wine region, this does not mean that the Jura Mountains are not an influence – they are very much part of the terroir here. The vineyard region exists only because of the effects of the younger Alpine range of mountains pushing the Jura mountain range to the west towards the Bresse plain. The soils were created by this geological shift and the climate in the Jura is certainly influenced by the proximity of the mountains.

A little geology

Between about 230 million and 160 million years ago, during the epochs that geologists call the Late Triassic through to the Middle Jurassic, what is now the Jura region lay under the sea. Layers of sediment slowly accumulated, mainly of the marls (limey clays) and (towards the end of this interval) limestones that today give the distinctive soils of the Jura their basis. About 65 million years ago the land started emerging from the sea, and between about 35 million and 20 million years ago the so-called Bresse fault-line created the Bresse

The Jura's distinctive, heavy, hard-to-work grey marl soil in the hand of a vigneron.

basin. This fault also cut out what we now call the *reculées*, distinctive blind valleys, of which there are several in the Jura wine region, notably those found at Baume-les-Messieurs, Arbois and Poligny.

Some millions of years later, it was the formation of the Alps to the southeast that thrust the much older Jura Mountains several kilometres westwards towards the Bresse plain in a type of slippage that pushed up the sedimentary bedrock to form a series of folded layers, and created a series of plateaux. It was this more than anything else that created the conditions suitable for the vineyards between the mountains and

the Bresse plain. Over the millennia that followed erosion during different times of glaciation fashioned the topography still further, creating limestone hills and burying the lateral *reculées* still deeper. Many are the sources of the small rivers that cross the land here.

The vineyards are bordered to the east by the often wooded steep limestone cliffs that mark the edge of what we know today as the Premier Plateau or First Plateau (at an altitude of around 500m) of the Jura Mountains. Most of the vineyards lie on the slopes below these cliffs. The western boundary of the vineyard zone is the alluvial Bresse plain at 200–250m. In between one can also find distinctive small limestone hills (known here as *buttes*) that broke off from the plateau, providing not only the somewhat tortured landscape one sees in the Jura today, but also ideal conditions for vineyards on their southerly and southwesterly slopes and depressions. Both here and on the lower slopes below the Premier Plateau the subsoil is marl from the Late Triassic and Early Jurassic epochs (see diagrams on pp. 30–1).

Note that rocks of Early Jurassic age were traditionally referred to as 'Liassic', and because this term is still much used locally I am including it here and throughout the book. The limestones that commonly cap the Jura hills, formed during the division of Middle Jurassic time (about 170 million years ago), are termed 'Bajocian', and are consequently often called Bajocian limestone. (Technically, geologists refer to major time divisions such as the Triassic and Jurassic as 'periods', subdivisions such as the Early Jurassic as 'epochs', and further subdivisions such as the Bajocian as 'ages'.)

Glossary of Jura geology and soil terms

Listed here are the most common French geological terms used by Jura vignerons in their discussions and in their technical wine sheets.

- *Argile*: clay.

- *Bajocien*: Bajocian geological age, generally refers to the limestone formed at that time.

- *Béleminites:* fossils that look like small bullets, widely found in Château-Chalon and L'Etoile.

- *Calcaire:* limestone.

- *Calcaire à gryphées:* a limestone layer that appears in some vineyard sectors between grey Liassic marl and coloured Triassic marl – it's full of small oyster-like fossils.

- *Eboulis (calcaire):* scree or small stones, usually limestone-based.

- *Gravier gras* or *argile à chailles*: gravel or clay containing fragments of flint or other siliceous material.

- *Lias:* Liassic or Early Jurassic epoch.

- *Marne:* marl (clay-limestone), which comes in different colours, generally specified.

- *Marne grise:* grey (sometimes wrongly called blue) marl from the Liassic epoch. The most famous soil of the Jura.

- *Marnes irisés:* multi-coloured marls from the Triassic period.

- *Pentacrines:* star-shaped fossils (five-pointed fragments of crinoids) typically found in L'Etoile, Château-Chalon and nearby villages.

- *Schiste carton:* non-technical term for paper-like or crumbly shale, usually associated with grey or black marl from the Liassic epoch.

- *Trias:* Triassic period.

The principal soil types

North of Lons-le-Saunier, the vineyards that stretch out on the slopes below the limestone cliffs of the plateau are made up of very complex soil types, in particular clay or more specifically marl (clay with high calcium carbonate content). These marls are of various colours and compositions. Grey marl (often referred to as blue, wrongly according to geologist Michel Campy) was formed in the Liassic (Early Jurassic) epoch and appears either in the form of crumbly, layered, paper-like shale, or with small limestone chips mixed in – black marl also formed during this epoch. Rust-coloured shaly marl is from the Triassic period, and there are also so-called iridescent marls (red, green or grey) – the red tends to be warmer and therefore more suitable for red grapes. Clay from Triassic and Liassic times and scree of Bajocian limestone that has broken off from the cliffs appear in certain places.

L'Etoile and parts of Château-Chalon have many sea-fossils in their marl soils, particularly the distinct tiny star-shaped fossils that may have given L'Etoile its name. Limestone with oyster-like fossils (*gryphées*) also appears in parts of Arbois as well as in Côtes du Jura, and is much prized for Chardonnay, as is the dolomitic

Geomorphological block diagram of the Jura wine region

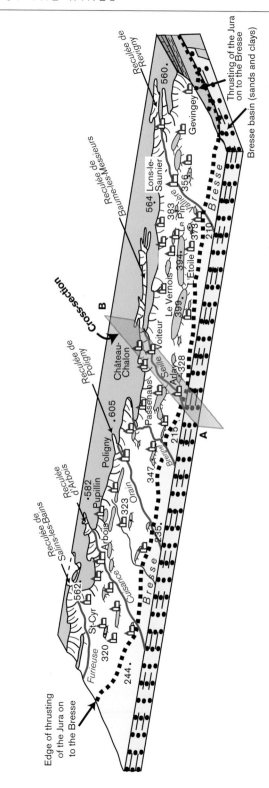

The eastern limit of the vineyard region is the limestone cliff (often wooded) of the Premier Plateau, with an altitude of 500–600m. Cut into the edge are the reculées. The reculées, the sources of the main rivers: Furieuse, Cuisance, Orain, Brenne, Seille and Vallière. The western limit is the Bresse plain, with an altitude of 210–240m.

Between these limits the vineyard zone appears as a series of hills, often parallel to the edge of the plateau. The tops of these hills reach 300–400m (320m at St-Cyr, 328m at Arlay, 394m at L'Etoile), overlooking the intermediate valleys which lie about 100m below. The altitude of this zone becomes lower close to the alluvial plain and the rivers running towards the Bresse.

The vineyard zone is relatively densely populated, with towns and villages dotted throughout.

Geological cross-section of the Jura vineyard region from Arlay in the west to Nevy-sur-Seille in the east

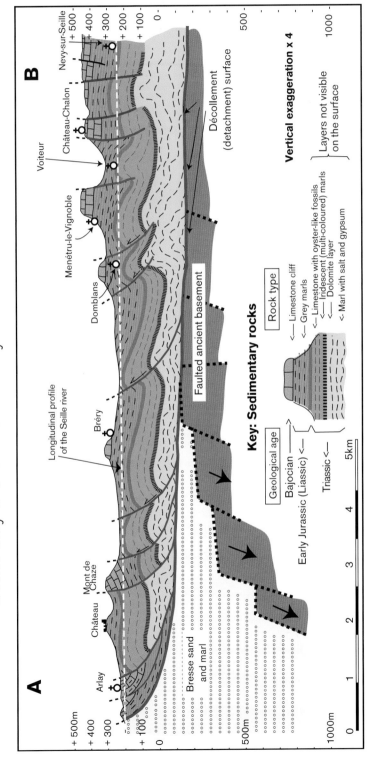

Key: Sedimentary rocks

Geological age

Bajocian
Early Jurassic (Liassic) <—
Triassic <—

Rock type

Limestone cliff
Grey marls
Limestone with oyster-like fossils
Iridescent (multi-coloured) marls
Dolomite layer
Marl with salt and gypsum

Vertical exaggeration x 4

} Layers not visible on the surface

Décollement (detachment) surface

Faulted ancient basement

Bresse sand and marl

Longitudinal profile of the Seille river

Helped by the plasticity of the salt- and gypsum-rich marl layer, the upper layer of the edge of the Jura Mountains detached and slipped towards the Bresse basin. During this thrusting process the land mass became separated into numerous fault blocks.

limestone that appears here and there.

The soils on the vineyard slopes on the small hills that have broken off from the main plateau and appear further west (as in L'Etoile and Arlay, for example) are extremely mixed. South of Lons in the Sud Revermont, the vineyards are even closer to the limestone cliffs of the Premier Plateau, giving less clay but more limestone from Bajocian times, although in places there are still outcrops of grey marl.

In practical terms for the Jura vigneron the dominant feature here is the water-retentive heavy marl that varies greatly in composition, sometimes with limestone stones on top, or marine fossils here and there. The marl can be as hard as a rock or very friable, yet despite this the grass and weeds thrive in this challenging climate, making it very hard work to manage the soils.

The other crucial consideration is that the soils are varied here, making certain soils more suitable for specific grape varie-

A display of gryphées *in the tasting room of Didier Grappe in St-Lothain. The oyster-like fossils are found in limestone-dominant soil, which is particularly prized for Chardonnay.*

ties (see p. 46). Having been an occasional sceptic on the amount of importance credited to what are often seen by the outsider as minor differences in soil types, in the Jura I have become convinced that the variations influence the wine flavours much more than in most wine regions.

A comparison of the geology between Burgundy's Côte d'Or and the Jura

I have often read that the Jura vineyards mirror those of the Côte d'Or and indeed it is a tempting assumption to make. Both vineyard regions run from northeast to southwest on either side of the Saône Valley and the Bresse plain, and the vineyards in the Côte d'Or predominantly face east, whereas those in the Jura face west, so there is a certain symmetry, but there this easy explanation must end.

The Côte d'Or vineyards lie on a series of vertical fault-blocks, each dominated by calcareous rocks from the Middle Jurassic period. The Jura vineyards are on undulating hillsides created by low-angle faults and folded layers formed when the Jura Mountains slipped towards the Bresse. This process brought to the surface mainly marl rocks from the Triassic and Liassic eras.

The differences in geology and soil types between the two regions can be generalized as follows: both have limestone and marls in abundance, but in the Côte d'Or around 80% of the base rock is limestone and 20% marl; in the Jura it is the other way around, with a base rock consisting of roughly 80% marl and 20% limestone.

Climate and weather

The climate can be termed as semi-continental or northern semi-continental. In wine terms this may be compared with Burgundy, Champagne or Alsace and equates to cold winters and warm summers. The French meteorological office summarizes the climate for the whole Jura department as 'high rainfall throughout the year (1,000–1,500mm), winters are tough, medium level of sunshine'. This certainly sums it up, though for the wine region, lying as it does on the lower mountain foothills, the detail is somewhat different, and naturally there are variations depending on each vineyard site. Climate statistics for the wine region are generally taken from the weather station close to the departmental capital, Lons-le-Saunier, at an altitude of 240m, the same level as the lowest vineyards, so this gives a reasonable average for the vineyard region.

Rainfall: Annual rainfall for the 30 years from 1972 to 2002 was 1,169mm per year and around 5% less during the decade from October 2002 to September 2012 at 1,093mm, but that followed a particularly wet decade, so there is no obvious pattern (see graph overleaf). During spring and summer excessive rain can present a problem to the vignerons. In 2013, for example, the rains in the first half of the year were so endless that for several months it was virtually impossible to plough the soils or mechanically weed because the vineyards were so wet. Rain around the period the vines flower is the most feared, as this will affect quantity. More unusual is persistent rain during summer, which provokes disease issues and of course if rain arrives around harvest time it can also present a problem.

Temperatures: The temperature average for 1972 to 2002 was just 10.8°C but for the decade from 2002 to 2012 it was a whole degree higher at 11.8°C (see graph overleaf). The decade included the heatwave year of 2003 with an average of 14.3°C, but the previous decade of 1992–2002 already indicated an average of 11.6°C. The midwinter months have stayed the same or have even been a touch colder, but spring has arrived sooner, with considerably warmer weather in March and April, and the important growing season for the vine has also been much warmer in recent years.

Sunshine: Whereas the vineyard region undoubtedly receives more than its fair share of rain through the year, and endless depressing misty days in the winter, this is the sunniest part of the Jura department, with 1,800–1,900 hours of sunshine each year, not much less than Burgundy.

Wind: The winds mostly come in from the south and west, the latter bringing the clouds that are drawn to the mountains, which block them, so the rain is emptied out on to the vineyards below. This is why the Jura receives so much more rain than Burgundy to the west. Snow is only an occasional winter visitor, but often vignerons will be pruning in a biting cold north wind known as 'la Bise'. La Bise sometimes arrives in summer too and can be a blessing if there is an oidium or rot (botrytis) problem in the vineyards, as it will dry out the grapes, sometimes saving the quality of the harvest. An occasional phenomenon is the arrival of continental warm east and southeast winds such as those that hit the region in the hot summer of 2003, and brought on ripening dramatically fast.

As in most northerly wine regions, the aspect of each vineyard is key to both its

Average monthly rainfall in Lons-le-Saunier 1972–2012 (millimetres)

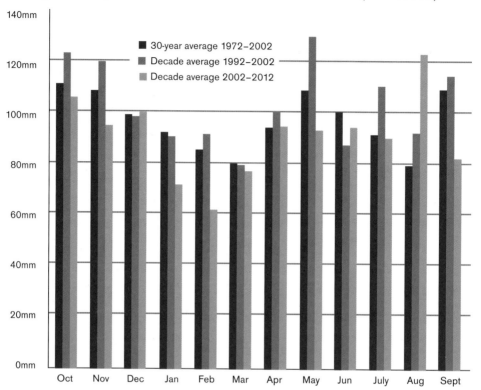

Average monthly temperatures in Lons-le-Saunier 1972–2012 (°Celsius)

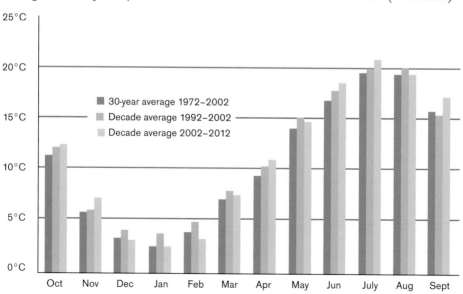

ripening pattern and its ability to withstand the effects of wind. In many Jura vineyards an element of protection is offered by the proximity of wooded cliffs above.

Weather hazards

Apart from the ever-present issue in the Jura of rain at the wrong time, as in most wine regions the most feared weather hazards are potentially damaging spring frosts and hailstorms. Cold winter temperatures have to drop below –15°C to damage the vines, so this is a rare occurrence. When it dipped to this level for a few days in February 2012, there was little reported damage. Spring frosts remain a regular threat, with little a vigneron can do to prevent them except ensure that the vines are not sited in frost pockets. Late spring growth is usually welcomed in the hope of avoiding frosts, which hit the early budders worst – Chardonnay, Pinot and Poulsard – rarely Trousseau or Savagnin.

In the winter of 2013, although frost was avoided, the late spring/early summer period was so cold, wet and cloudy that the vines were affected by a type of *coulure* known as *filage*. Due to lack of sunshine and photosynthesis the potential flowers fell to the ground before having a chance to form. This affected Savagnin and Trousseau in particular, especially in exposed, windy sites.

Hail takes no prisoners, here as everywhere. It tends to be random, arriving at any time during the spring or summer months, and with no specific vineyard sector more prone than any other. If it hits in spring after budding, but before flowering, a secondary growth may give some crop. However, when it comes in midsummer it can be devastating, stripping the leaves and shattering the developing berries, leaving them prone to rot. In extreme cases it can affect the wood or canes too, which means that the following year's potential harvest is affected. In recent vintages it has been a problem in different sectors during 2003, 2006, 2008 and 2009, usually causing losses of 20–50% in those vineyards hit, in rare cases even more.

The impact of climate change

The increase in average summer temperatures in the Jura vineyard area speaks volumes, but it does not tell the whole story about climate change, which is as much about the increasing unpredictability of the weather as the temperature and humidity changes. This has led to extreme uncertainty for vignerons. Planning must be much more last-minute for anything from export sales trips to holidays, because the vineyards may need urgent attention at any time.

That said, the extra warmth during the growing season in the Jura has brought average harvest dates forward, which means that less or – among many producers – no chaptalization has been needed, and for those who manage their vineyards well it has especially benefited the red grapes. I have noticed an improvement in the quality of the fruit in red wines since 2003, the heatwave year, partly through better vineyard work and lower yields, but also partly because in almost every year there has been more heat in the summer months than in previous years.

"Le plant de Ploussard
est un des plus estimés
du vignoble d'Arbois."
Louis PASTEUR

GRAPE VARIETIES

The Jura may have only five 'official' grapes accepted into the AOC regulations first established in 1936, but these five are very important in the history of grape varieties. Chardonnay and Pinot Noir are of course best known in Burgundy, but have been grown in the Jura for several centuries. The other three varieties, Savagnin, Poulsard and Trousseau, can now be described definitively as indigenous to the Jura wine region, indeed close to the primitive ancestors of *Vitis vinifera*, the wild varieties known as *Vitis sylvestris*. Before the arrival of phylloxera in the late 19th century there were many more grape varieties grown in the Jura in mixed vineyards, used as part of a blend. Today it is estimated that around 130ha of vineyards include varieties outside the big five for AOC; some are very rare indeed. Note that pre-phylloxera only about 10–15% of the grapes grown were white, for the simple reason that red wine was the popular colour of the day, considered the standard drink with meals.

In this chapter we explore the history and growing characteristics of these grapes in the Jura specifically. Accurate figures for how much of each variety is grown are hard to come by, but it is known that the area of Poulsard and Pinot Noir is declining, with Savagnin and especially Trousseau increasing. The choice of clone and rootstock is examined in more detail in the chapter on growing vines. The taste of the wines they produce is examined in the final chapter of this section on wine styles and how the wines are made.

Left: Not every grape variety has its own capital, but this old foudre *placed at the entrance of Pupillin is just one marker that this village is the capital of Ploussard or Poulsard. The Louis Pasteur quote states: 'The Ploussard vine is one of the most valued of the Arbois vineyards.' Right: Old Savagnin vine.*

White Varieties
Chardonnay

Chardonnay is the most planted variety in the Jura. It accounts for about 42% of the vineyard area, almost double that of Savagnin, though the percentage has been even higher, with as much as half of the Jura vineyards being planted to Chardonnay in the mid-1990s. Its importance should hardly be a surprise, given the region's proximity to Burgundy and the importance, quantity-wise, of Crémant du Jura, in which it plays such a significant part. However, I estimate (figures are not available) that, given that yields are higher for grapes for Crémant than for still wine, about half is used for sparkling and half for still white

wines and Macvin.

In old texts on the Jura a string of white grape varieties appears, a few of which, with advancing understanding of ampelographical methods, turned out to be variations of Chardonnay. This plethora of synonyms, often with names that led them to be confused with other varieties, includes most particularly Pineau Blanc, Melon or Melon d'Arbois in villages around Arbois and Dole in the north of today's Jura region, Gamay Blanc around Lons-le-Saunier, L'Etoile and the south, and Luisant in vineyards near Besançon in the Doubs and the Haute-Saône. Due to this profusion of names,

Melon à Queue Rouge

Confirmed as a natural variation of Chardonnay, the Melon à Queue Rouge (Melon with a Red Stalk) usually develops its distinctive red stalk close to ripening, although it can appear as early as just after flowering (see right). Sometimes there may even be some faint redness showing on the surface of the grape skin, giving rise to an old expression 'Les renards ont pissé dessus' or 'The foxes pissed on it.' As an alternative to the ubiquitous clones of Chardonnay, it is becoming increasingly prized and mass selection techniques are being used to perpetuate its existence. To date I know of at least six producers with Melon à Queue Rouge in their vineyards – Puffeney, Bacchus, La Pinte, Bornard, Crédoz and Ganevat – but there are many other vignerons with old vines where

Melon will be interspersed. When made on its own, nearly always from an old-vine selection, Melon à Queue Rouge shows a particular riper, softer and most attractive yellow fruit characteristic compared to the straight Chardonnays, though sometimes this can also be attributed to the low yields it produces.

The ubiquitous Chardonnay has been grown in the Jura for many centuries.

Chardonnay in the Jura is grown on many different soil types, something recognized increasingly by those producers who choose to vinify musts separately and bottle cuvées from different terroirs. It seems to suit almost all the variations of marls, although it is perhaps weakest on grey marl – in any case this soil type is generally reserved for Savagnin or Poulsard. Especially valued for fine, almost Burgundy-style Chardonnays are warmer hillside vineyards of marl covered in Bajocian limestone-rich pebbles or scree. The heavier clay-rich Liassic marls, which are so distinctively Jura, are also excellent for Chardonnay, and these soils seem to confer flavours that make many tasters comment on an oxidative character even when a wine is made in *ouillé* style (regularly topped up).

the history of when Chardonnay was first planted in the Jura is not confirmed, but it seems likely that it has been grown from the 14th century onwards due to the historical connections with Burgundy. Perhaps to protect Savagnin, already recognized as special and valuable, Chardonnay in its various guises was considered an inferior grape, and on several occasions risked being outlawed until 1774, when it was finally recognized for its quality. From then it went from strength to strength, especially for its use in sparkling wines, and in terms of geography most particularly prized in the vineyards around L'Etoile.

As a relatively early ripener, Chardonnay may be prone to late spring frost, and with thinner skins than the hardy Savagnin it is potentially more affected by oidium and subsequent grey rot, especially when allowed to crop high. In poor weather flowering can also be a problem, leading to a reduction in quantity. Despite this, today Chardonnay appears, as everywhere, to be one of the most reliable varieties. Much is harvested early for Crémant; for still wines it tends to be harvested after Pinot Noir, and often around the same time as Poulsard.

Savagnin

The rest of the wine world may have long fretted over whether Savagnin is related to Traminer and which came first, or whether their particular grape variety, known under a different name, was in fact the same as Traminer or Savagnin. But, meantime, in much of the local Jura wine literature dating back at least 150 years one can see

the Jurassiens as quietly confident that Savagnin was not only theirs by right, derived from a wild vine, but they also valued it as a very fine wine grape. Early ampelographers did indeed believe that it was at the very least related or perhaps even the same as Traminer, but many conjectured that it came from Austria or northern Italy. It

Some vineyards grow more than one variation of Savagnin, as here in Domaine Pignier's vineyard above Conliège. The picture shows tighter-bunched Savagnin Vert on the left and Savagnin Jaune on the right.

of it date back to the 14th or possibly the 13th century. Because its origins were not really understood, at some point it was thought to have come from Spain due to the fact that, like Sherry, it attracted a *flor*-type yeast on the surface of the wine (and also that Franche-Comté was at one time ruled by the King of Spain). It was always known as a strong, resistant variety that ripened very late, sometimes not until the first snows or frosts of winter. The ancients knew that in good years with sufficient crop they could make what was sometimes named a *vin de gelée* (picked after the first frosts) or a *vin de garde* (a wine to age), as Vin Jaune used to be named. Due to its thick skins (enabling it to withstand late picking), naturally high acidity and fascinating flavours, Savagnin is an extremely versatile and high-quality grape increasingly used today for a whole range of wine styles beyond the traditional Vin Jaune.

seems that the Jura's supreme confidence has been vindicated. Yes, DNA testing has confirmed that Savagnin is actually the same as Traminer (the better-known Gewürztraminer is an aromatic version) and yes, it originated in the Jura. Indeed in 2012 it was dubbed by the authors of *Wine grapes* as part of an exclusive group of 'founder varieties' and thus the parent, grandparent or ancestor of a whole host of other well-known grape varieties grown throughout Europe, not least the Jura's Trousseau.

The story of Savagnin, or Naturé as it is sometimes called, is inextricably linked with the story of Vin Jaune and earliest mentions

Around 23% of the Jura wine region is planted with Savagnin and if ever there was a perfect marriage between grape variety and soil or geology, the Jura has it with Savagnin. This variety loves the steep south-facing slopes of clay-rich marl soils, especially if they are deep and grey in colour. Being thick-skinned, it suffers rarely from mildew, and grey rot is only an occasional problem, with an often beneficial level of noble rot. It can suffer from *coulure* if the

Naturé – an ancient name

You will see Naturé on some labels, particularly of Arbois wines, and since the late 1990s, although not an official term, several producers have used Naturé to indicate a Savagnin *ouillé*, differentiating it from the more prevalent oxidative

Savagnin, aged like a Vin Jaune but for a shorter time. Naturé or sometimes Naturel are old names for Savagnin and can be found in many old texts referring to Arbois; even 19th- and early-20th-century English texts refer to it as Naturé.

weather is bad around flowering. Sadly, like Trousseau, it is proving to be badly affected by Esca and other fungal diseases affecting the wood.

There are several natural variations of Savagnin, most particularly Savagnin Vert (green) and Savagnin Jaune (yellow), although the latter is more prevalent. The yellow version gives more aromatic flavours; the green variety is particularly prized for its high acidity, an advantage for the long ageing of Vin Jaune, but also giving crispness to *ouillé* versions. Many producers like to work with a mix, especially for Vin Jaune. Savagnin Muscaté is a rare variation that exists in tiny quantities in the Sud Revermont, giving aromatic flavours somewhat reminiscent of Gewürztraminer (an aromatic mutation of Savagnin Rose), but the berry indicates that it is a sort of white-skinned Gewürztraminer.

Although flavours are beyond the scope of this chapter, it should be said that multiple texts erroneously describe the grape Savagnin giving wines that are distinctively nutty and spicy, classic descriptors for Savagnin wines that have aged under the veil of yeast destined to make Vin Jaune. Yet anyone who has had the chance to taste a Savagnin berry, or juice from the press, or better still drunk the Jura's *ouillé* Savagnin wines, knows differently – tangy citrus flavours dominate. This is a grape with a strong personality and I predict that now that the wine world is more secure in understanding this variety's origins and the fact that it is the same as Traminer (the non-aromatic form of course), and now that the Jura has a growing following, we are sure to see more planted around the world. Already there are Savagnins from Australia (from vines previously wrongly identified as Albariño) and from Canada's Niagara Peninsula (see Appendix 3). I believe there will be many more in future.

Red Varieties
Poulsard/Ploussard

Even if there is confusion over its name, Poulsard seems to be the indigenous Jura variety over which there is least confusion of place of origin, even though its parentage is not entirely clear. The latest ampelographical research shows that it has a likely parent–offspring relationship with the Valais grape Rèze, once grown as Petit Béclan Blanc in the Jura. Although much revered within the region and in evidence since the 14th century, until the 21st century there was never a whiff of fashion related to this variety, and never any interest on the part of other wine regions to lay claim to it. The only other established vineyard area for Poulsard is Cerdon, in the northern section of the Bugey region, just to the south of

The translucent Poulsard variety gives very pale red wines.

the Jura, where it is part of the blend for rosé sparkling wines made by the *méthode ancestrale*. As I write, all this is changing, as in the early teens of this century the wines of Poulsard seem to have garnered quite a following in New York and beyond, and there may even be a California Poulsard before too long.

Poulsard is the most planted red variety in the Jura, accounting for about 14% of the planted area, though not all is used for red wines. It is widely used for rosé too (and indeed many producers used to name the red wines rosé because of their pale colour and a few still do today – (see 'False rosés', p. 77). Poulsard is also an important variety for both Crémant Rosé (permitted in whites too) and for Vin de Paille, to which, once dried, it adds flavour complexity, acidity and an interesting colour. Both Crémant and Vin de Paille can cover up the difficulties of Poulsard – when badly handled the red wines can be reduced, acidic, harsh and lacking in fruit. Not only is the wine difficult,

this is a variety that is more challenging at every level to grow and make than even Pinot Noir. Yet the Jurassiens have persisted with Poulsard, even with its hugely variable yields, perhaps because when the weather behaves it can yield extremely highly, but also because it ripens earlier than the other two local grapes, Trousseau and Savagnin.

Poulsard is particular about soil, but is perfectly suited to the Jura's marls, especially the grey version, and even more so to the slightly warmer red marl. It is said that where Savagnin is happy Poulsard is happy too, and which variety a vigneron might plant is often due to the practicalities of the differing ripening dates, or even that a producer has more demand for one over the other. Vigneron Jacques Puffeney told me that, in the 1970s, he and others had some isolated vineyards of Savagnin which, as the last variety to ripen, were stripped by flocks of migrating starlings several years in a row. The only solution was to replant with the earlier-ripening Poulsard.

The sloe versus the Breton

Old texts from the Jura region dating to the 19th century become quite heated about the two designations, yet there seems little argument that the original name was Ploussard: Poulsard came later. The Ploussard name derives from older usages such as Plussâ or Peloussard in Arbois or Poligny, which in turn hark back to the local words *plusse* or *pelosse* for a wild variety of sloe, which had a pale purple skin resembling Ploussard. However, 18th-century texts showed the variety also named Pulsard in Lons-le-Saunier and it must have been from here that the name was picked up by a travel writer from Brittany, JM Lequinio, who men-

tioned Poulsard in his 1801 book, *Voyages dans le Jura* (Travels in the Jura). From then on the two names seem to have emerged, but in the 1936 AOC decrees Poulsard was named first and Ploussard, the more Jurassien name, came second. Today all the vignerons in the village of Pupillin, self-styled World Capital of Ploussard since 1991, use the Ploussard designation in AOC Arbois-Pupillin, as do several in AOC Arbois, though fewer in Côtes du Jura. Poulsard remains the key official name and this book will by default refer to it as Poulsard, unless referring to a producer in Pupillin or elsewhere who uses the Ploussard name.

Budding early makes it prone to spring frosts, it is highly sensitive to cold weather and subject to poor flowering, often suffers from *coulure*, and its thin skins cause it to be very prone to mildews and rot, as well as sunburn. Everything nature can throw at it seems to affect Poulsard, and it's no easier in the winery, but this quintessential Jura grape variety is nevertheless much loved in the region for the challenges it poses (a little like Pinot Noir elsewhere) and for the fact that, just like the naughty little girl, when it is good, it is very, very good.

Trousseau

The Jura is justly proud of the Trousseau variety, capable of producing its finest reds. Although the area is increasing, it accounts for only about 8% of total plantings. DNA testing has shown that Trousseau is either a parent or an offspring of Savagnin and thus almost certainly of Jura origin, yet much greater quantities of the same grape, under various names, have been grown on the Iberian peninsula for at least 200 years. In Portugal, as Bastardo, it is most prevalent, with over 1,200ha grown in the Dão, Douro (it is a permitted Port variety) and other regions, compared to around 150ha in the Jura. There is scientific proof that these varieties are identical, even though no one knows for certain how it arrived in Iberia. Yet some older Jura producers refuse to believe in the science, citing how different the wines are, about which there is no dispute, given the very different latitudes and climates. However, in California, where a handful of growers planted the variety some years ago inspired by the mix of grapes used for Port, more than one producer is attempting to make a Jura-style Trousseau (see Appendix 3).

The earliest-known mentions of Trousseau in Franche-Comté date from the 18th century and it became highly regarded, particularly to the north of Arbois around Salins-les-Bains and Montigny-les-Arsures. Today the village of Montigny is considered the capital of Trousseau, even if the villagers make less of a big deal about it than those in Pupillin do for Ploussard. In 2006 retired geologist Michel Campy, together with pedologist Christian Barnéoud, published a report based on geological and soil analysis of lands where Trousseau was growing throughout the region, combined with blind tasting. This report confirmed Montigny, with well-exposed slopes and outcrops of warm clay and flinty gravels, as the very best part of the Jura to grow Trousseau for deep, structured, age-worthy wines. However, it also identified other areas within the region that were perfectly suitable for growing Trousseau for lighter styles of easy-drinking wines.

Trousseau is a relatively hardy grape with

If allowed, Trousseau can be a very productive vine.

thick skins and, unlike Pinot and Poulsard, it is not affected by mildew, but as a vigorous variety it may be prone to grey rot if it is allowed to over-produce. It can often be affected by poor flowering and *coulure*. The variety requires warm sites, either on lower slopes or on the well-exposed, steeper and highest slopes, with warm, well-drained soils, such as gravel or stony topsoils over clays or clay-limestone bases. Unfortunately, like Savagnin, it is particularly prone to Esca and other wood infections. It is a late ripener, though some of this depends on the clone grown. Some producers will leave the hardy Trousseau hanging late for maximum ripeness, usually picking it at the same time as the late-ripening Savagnin. It loves an Indian summer.

Trousseau is used in tiny quantities for Crémant, Vin de Paille and Macvin, but is mostly reserved for reds. For me it is as a single-varietal red that it excels, becoming somewhat lost in red blends where it was traditionally used in the past. It would be good to see more Trousseau grown, especially since warmer summers and autumns have led to proper ripeness and there has been a better understanding of where and how to grow it, along with a realization of the need to control yields strictly.

Paying for the lady's trousseau

There are several explanations for the Trousseau name, most relating to the pyramid shape of the bunch of grapes, which seems *troussé*, or trussed up like a chicken. However, Lucien Aviet of Caveau de Bacchus insists that it is so called because many years ago vignerons would age their Trousseau wines, holding them back until their daughters got married, and then used these red wines to 'pay' for their daughters' wedding trousseaus (bottom drawer or hope chest). A natural variation of Trousseau is 'Trousseau à la Dame' ('Lady's Trousseau'), which is currently enjoying a revival, with growers choosing to plant mass selections, and an official clone has been developed. It gives a looser bunch and is very prone to *coulure*, so yields are very low (less than 20hl/ha on average), though when mixed in a vineyard with the naturally high-yielding 'normal' Trousseau this balances out well. It is liked today in particular for its more forward, open fruit, good for early-drinking styles. I am told the reason for its name 'à la Dame' is that its particularly sweet berries were known to be enjoyed by the ladies. Huh!

Pinot Noir

Although Pinot Noir has existed in the Jura probably for at least as long as Chardonnay, and is the second most planted red variety, it is very much the last variety most people consider when thinking about the Jura. Yet it has a most noble pedigree, being, ampelographically speaking, at the top of the tree, as an antecedent to many well-known varieties. In the Jura there are references in the archives of Château d'Arlay to it being planted as far back as the 13th century, when it was also referred to as Noirin or Noirien.

Pinot Noir has only relatively recently been used to make a single-varietal Jura red wine. Jura growers, traditionally fearful of not being able to produce as fine a wine as nearby Burgundy, mainly used Pinot as part of a red blend to which it added both colour and finesse. Whereas Pinot wines may be considered light-coloured in most regions, in the Jura it produces the deepest red of the three main varieties. It is authorized for use in both Crémant (white and rosé) and Macvin red or rosé, and is particularly in demand for the latter. However, it is the only one of the five Jura grapes not allowed for Vin de Paille, as its compact bunch is not so suitable for the drying process and the risk of rot is too great. Around 13% of Jura vineyards are planted with Pinot Noir today, a figure that appears to have increased steadily over the past couple of decades.

Pinot Noir ripens very easily in the Jura.

Pinot in the Jura is as fickle as everywhere, and may possibly be the Jura variety most affected by climate change, in both a positive and a negative way. On the positive side, the variety is more likely to ripen properly to give musts with a better sugar–acid balance than previously and this is reflected in the increase in single-varietal Pinots produced. On the negative side, as an early ripener (it is one of the first to be harvested along with Chardonnay), if Pinot is grown on particularly hot sites – yes, hot, even in the Jura – the berries have a tendency to shrivel very quickly after reaching full maturity. It is prone to grey rot if the weather is poor late in the growing season.

Traditionally there has been more Pinot Noir grown in the south of the region, especially on the better-drained Bajocian limestone soils of the Sud Revermont, and also in Arlay. Today, however, it seems to be planted all over the region, and most producers grow some, favouring well-drained soils, sometimes with a preference for gravels and stones on the topsoil.

Pinot Noir du Jura

There appears to exist an old selection known as Pinot Noir du Jura or sometimes Savagnin Noir, a variation of Pinot Noir de Bourgogne (the standard variety with its various clonal variations from Burgundy). According to Jean-Etienne Pignier, this will have adapted to the soils of the Jura over many centuries. Domaine Pignier grows some near Lons-le-Saunier and observes that it is less vigorous than standard Pinot, with bigger bunches but smaller grapes. The greatest difference, he says, is that it ripens about ten days later and the grapes taste less fruity but with plenty of rustic character. Ludwig Bindernagel of Le Chais du Vieux Bourg also has some old vines at Le Vernois.

Grape varieties and their preferred sites

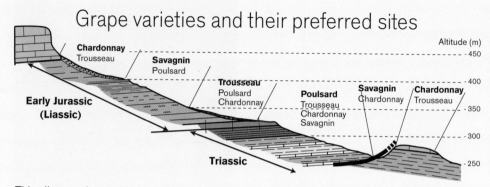

Altitude (m)

Chardonnay
Trousseau

Savagnin
Poulsard

Early Jurassic
(Liassic)

Trousseau
Poulsard
Chardonnay

Poulsard
Trousseau
Chardonnay
Savagnin

Savagnin
Chardonnay

Chardonnay
Trousseau

Triassic

450
400
350
300
250

This diagram is used as an illustration and does not represent reality. On the left is the limestone cliff of the Premier Plateau with the vineyard slope running down to the plain. On the right is a typical hillock (butte) such as that at Arlay or L'Etoile.

The grape variety at the top of each list in bold is the one most suited to the particular soil and altitude. Other varieties below may be grown there but are not the ideal choice; those at the bottom of the list in small type are the least suitable.

Pinot Noir is not included; it works well wherever Trousseau is suited. Chardonnay could be planted more or less anywhere except in the zone where Liassic (grey) marl dominates.

Below: This paper-like, crumbly grey marl, known as schiste carton, suits Savagnin perfectly.

Other almost-forgotten Jura grapes

Back when Charles Rouget wrote his amazing book on the vineyards and grape varieties of the Jura and Franche-Comté, *Les vignobles du Jura et de la Franche-Comté*, published in 1897, he identified nearly 40 main varieties grown, along with several minor varieties. Admittedly there was a much bigger surface area of vines, and a few of them turned out to be synonyms. However, after a steady decline since the heyday of plantings pre-phylloxera, many varieties vanished in a very short time once the five main varieties were designated for AOC in 1936/7. Those varieties that disappeared usually did so for good reasons, such as being poor or irregular ripeners, subject to the vagaries of the weather and to disease, or simply producing unpalatable wines with overly high acidity, etc.

The Société de Viticulture du Jura now has 51 varieties grown in three identical conservatories across the region, built up over a ten-year period from 2003. More than half of them are indigenous to the Jura. In addition, some of these varieties have been discovered by growers in old co-planted (mixed) vineyards around the region, and indeed a few producers are planting some rows experimentally. Among them are Jean-François Ganevat in the Sud Revermont, Domaine Pignier near Lons, Domaine de la Tournelle in Arbois and Domaines Ratapoil and Cavarodes, both north of Arbois. Many other producers have a few vines of rare varieties that they keep quiet about. Wines made from these varieties must be designated as either IGP or Vin de France, as they are not permitted under AOC rules. As in the past, they are made into wine as part of blends (often field blends), never as single-varietal wines, and are sometimes blended with one or more of the five classic varieties. Principal among these old varieties are: Argant, Gueuche Noir, Mézy, Enfariné, Petit and Gros Béclan (the latter is Peloursin) and Gamay (likely to be the same as in Beaujolais) (reds); Gueuche (also known as Foirard or the ubiquitous Gouais Blanc) and Poulsard Blanc (whites). Domaine Pignier will be trialling new plantings in 2014 of Rèze, Sacy Blanc and Peurion (whites), and Gueuche Noir, Corbeau and Peloursin (reds). Other varieties, such as the red Mondeuse Noire, originally from Savoie and known here as Maldoux, exist only in the conservatories, as far as I know.

Apart from curiosity, an interest in history and a wish to preserve biological diversity, there are other strong incentives for preserving and experimenting with these old grape varieties. First, with climate change and a better understanding of disease prevention, these varieties should not be as problematic as in former times, and some may even survive higher temperatures or drought better than the main five Jura varieties. They may need fewer chemical treatments, or perhaps resist certain diseases better. Finally, their characteristics may make them desirable to blend in with other varieties. For example, the variety Enfariné was notorious for its high acidity, but in warm years small amounts were blended with other varieties to provide greater acid balance, which is far preferable to adding tartaric acid corrections.

Below left: The entrance to the vine conservatory above Château-Chalon's Puits St-Pierre vineyards.

GROWING THE GRAPES

The Jura vineyards are often sited on steep slopes and based on heavy clay or marl soils; the weather is notoriously wet and cold in winter and spring, and may be extremely hot in midsummer. Then there are the other hazards to contend with, such as spring frosts and hailstorms. So, with nature seemingly stacked against you, why would anyone want to grow grapes in the Jura? And if you were a vigneron, wouldn't you want to take the easiest, least labour-intensive route? Often it's just the opposite. Bringing in healthy grapes has the same priority in making fine wine in the Jura as anywhere else and hard graft in the vineyard is what makes this possible.

As in all forms of agriculture, viticulture has changed dramatically in the past century due to technological advances: machinery performs essential tasks quickly and efficiently and chemicals ensure a consistently healthy and viable crop. But we are increasingly aware that these advances can pose complex environmental costs. Even if a few smaller growers in the Jura did manage to farm as they had done for generations, it would be naive not to acknowledge that most producers in the Jura, as elsewhere, went down the chemical route. Many producers chose to use chemicals because it made financial sense – predictably high yields of healthy grapes – and because they were unaware of the environmental downside. Some still think like this, especially as winegrowing is a very labour-intensive activity. French bureaucracy makes employing people both hugely expensive and time-consuming, and many vignerons find that fewer people than ever are willing to work in the Jura vineyards. The choice is usually stark – employ several temporary staff at high expense to remove leaves around the grape bunches to help them stay disease-free, or solve the problem by spending an hour on the tractor spraying the latest chemical preventative.

Yet, if asked, great vignerons will tell you that spending time in the vineyards is what they love more than anything else. Their faces light up when you say you would prefer to see their vineyards instead of the winery. The following are some of the aspects of growing vines in the Jura that need to be considered.

Planting vines: rootstocks, clones, mass selection, density and age

The Jura was relatively late in adopting clones, trialling them in the 1960s, particularly to combat fanleaf virus (something still present), so even today there are still old non-clonal vines available for mass (or massal) selections. However, as everywhere, today most of the vines planted in the Jura are clonal selections grafted on to phylloxera-tolerant rootstocks supplied by vine nurseries. There is only one vine nursery in the Jura, particularly favoured by many organic growers – Lahlou in Mesnay; others used include a couple in Savoie and the huge, internationally known Franche-Comté nursery Guillaume, which is based in Charcenne in the Haute-Saône, established after phylloxera hit in 1895.

In all but the most limestone-rich soils the recommended rootstocks are 3309 Couderc, which suits humid soils, and the high-quality, low-vigour 101-14 Millardet et de Grasset. Where limestone levels are too high SO4 used to be the rootstock of choice, but it is now known to be too vigorous, provoking *coulure* in Poulsard, for example. In soils with more than around 10% limestone recommended rootstocks are either the relatively new Fercal or 161-49 Couderc.

The main advantages of planting clones are their known characteristics in terms of vigour (the numbers of leaves and grape bunches are in balance), disease resistance, yield and time taken to ripen. The clones for Chardonnay and Pinot Noir are the same

The Trousseau à la Dame variation has looser bunches than others and is prone to millerandage or 'hen and chickens', where some berries do not ripen properly, thus reducing the crop. This can be a quality advantage, as Trousseau is naturally high yielding.

Trousseau vines planted in the 1950s at Domaine Dugois' Grevillière vineyard in Les Arsures.

as in Burgundy, although, bearing in mind the importance of Crémant du Jura, some growers choose earlier-ripening clones selected specifically for making sparkling wines. There have not been sufficient resources for the Société de Viticulture du Jura (SVJ) to develop many clones of the three Jura-specific varieties. In Poulsard there are now just two clones available and five exist for Trousseau (including a new one that is a Trousseau à la Dame clone). Four Savagnin clones are available, all ideal for potentially ageing wines oxidatively *sous voile*, with one in particular with even higher acidity, which ripens earlier and is particularly recommended for *ouillé* wines.

Organic growers, and most especially those working with biodynamic methods, try to use mass selection when replacing dead vines, replanting whole vineyards or planting new vineyards. They do this by taking cuttings from the strongest or most interesting old vines, either from their own plantings or occasionally from a friend's vineyard. They take the cuttings to their chosen vine nursery to graft on to rootstock and for the compulsory hot-water treatment,

which helps prevent grapevine yellows in particular (see 'The biggest disease threats today', p. 56). Mass selection is particularly interesting for propagating specific Savagnin variations, or for Melon à Queue Rouge (Chardonnay) or even Trousseau à la Dame, but can be used simply because a vigneron is particularly impressed with an old selection. The big advantage is that it encourages genetic diversity. More open to question and debate is whether the practice has a beneficial or non-beneficial effect on disease resistance in the vines.

Since 1992 the density at which vines must be planted in the Jura has been a minimum of 5,000 vines per hectare and over the past two decades wide spacing with densities of 2,000–3,000 vines per hectare (as introduced originally by Henri Maire in the 1960s) has been phased out, though not eliminated completely. You will still see some here and there, particularly around Gevingey in the Sud Revermont. In theory, growers with low-density plantings are supposed to plant a row of vines between each row to increase the density, but regional

Vigneron Benoît Royer of Domaine de la Cibellyne ploughs his steep, densely planted old Poulsard vineyard with his Comtois mare Kigali.

authorities may turn a blind eye if canopy management maintains a sufficiently high leaf canopy level, which to some extent compensates.

There is no official record of the average age of vines in the Jura, but in the time that I've been visiting the average age appears to have gradually increased, even if 5–10% of vines have to be replaced each year, due mainly to Esca. Although each year has seen new plantings, new vineyards represent only a small proportion partly because of the European policy of restricting planting rights. The 1960s and 1970s saw the big revival of the region, a period when many of today's producers' fathers turned from polyculture to specializing in vineyards, a process that was assisted by government aid for buying land. At the time of writing many vines planted in the 1960s and 1970s are still thriving, meaning a fair number of 40+-year-old vines.

Soil management

Grass and weeds grow like fury in the Jura due to the rainy, warm climate, so how to manage them to avoid competition with the vines for the necessary nutrients from the soils is a big challenge. The heavy soils are also a challenge and it is said that there is only a two-day window for ploughing between when it is too wet and when the clay soils dry out, becoming too rock hard to work. 'Working the soil' is the single most talked-about aspect by vignerons here: whether they plough; whether they let the grass grow or plant cover crops every other row and then mow; whether or not they use herbicide (weed-killer) and, if so, on a narrow strip along the vines or sprayed across the full width of the row. Of course those managing vineyards organically may not use any herbicide. However, these questions concern not only the broader environmental issues but also the risk of soil erosion due to the combination of relatively steep slopes, clay-heavy soils and high rainfall; another worry is that too much use of heavy machinery can over-compact the soil. Recently there has been a big increase in the use of *chenillettes* (mini-caterpillar tractors) for vineyard work, which are much lighter and gentler. In theory a horse is even better, and there has been a revival among some organic and other growers in using horses, particularly in steep vineyards with old, close-spaced vines, but this is very slow, hard work for both horse and human, and expensive as well.

The SVJ advocates working every other row and leaving grass in the second, and they say that today there is relatively little herbicide used in the region, although it is still visible in places. In Château-Chalon's vineyards, especially in the area of Sous Roche directly below the village, herbicide use is particularly obvious, which is a shame, but the combination of steepness and very rocky soils makes it extremely hard for ploughs to work the soil without breaking the machinery.

By eliminating herbicide, after just two years the presence of extra weeds forces the vine roots to go deeper, in turn helping the vines to find water in drought years and even possibly providing more minerality in the wines, as reported by some of the increasing numbers of even non-organic vignerons who have chosen this route. However, one possible side-effect of eliminating herbicide is a drop in the quantity of grapes during the first year or two. This happens because tractors ploughing out the weeds may also cut some of the vine's shallow feeder roots, which remain closer to the surface when herbicide is used.

Some chemical fertilizer is still used in the region, but most vignerons today use compost or manure, although a switch to this also plays a part in reducing yield initially. The SVJ is working on identifying the right cover crops to plant in order to help restructure the soils and ensure that valuable minerals needed by the vines are not washed away each time it rains.

Training and canopy management

Nearly all Jura vineyards are on wires these days, with either Single or Double Guyot training being the methods authorized in the AOC rules, although there are traditional variations, notably '*en courgée*', in which the canes are arched. A recent variation named Guyot Poussard is being used to help protect vines from Esca. Training single vines on stakes is used for plantings on steep slopes such as the revived vineyards of Stéphane Tissot at Clos de la Tour du Curon above Arbois, or on terraces such as those of Domaines Macle and Salvadori in the Puits St-Pierre vineyards below Château-Chalon.

The rest of the work in the vineyards from bud-rubbing at the start of the season to controlling the canopy and trimming or leaf plucking later on is no different to

After the winter pruning each vine must be tied to the wire.

anywhere else. In recent years green harvesting, or dropping the bunches pre-harvest, has been increasingly practised with reds in particular, especially Trousseau, which tends to carry a heavy crop.

Fighting disease

Apart from their choice of vine variety and clone, two disorders that vignerons can do nothing about are *coulure* and *millerandage*, which occur due to poor weather during and after flowering respectively. However, these so-called diseases can sometimes be a blessing in an over-productive variety like

Trousseau, though less welcome in Poulsard. In this wet climate cryptogamic (fungal) diseases such as mildews and rots are the biggest potential hazards that can ruin the crop. *Le mildiou* (downy mildew) is the most common hazard here and growers have to be vigilant about spray programmes – either chemical or Bordeaux mixture or a combination – to avoid its effects. Oidium (powdery mildew) is a problem in some years when it is warm and wet, though sulphur dusting can control or prevent it to an extent, but

The 1959 harvest in the Nouvelles vineyard above Arbois. Along with a pre-war Peugeot truck, oxen were still used for transport.

if it sets in this can trigger botrytis or grey rot, for which the only prevention is an anti-botrytis chemical spray, which is being used less and less in the region.

With spider mites under control, insecticide use has been almost eliminated for now, which makes the threat of grapevine yellows all the more ironic.

The harvest

As everywhere in France, there has been an increase in machine harvesting in the past 20 years in the Jura. As machine picking is currently forbidden for grapes for Crémant du Jura or Vin de Paille, nearly all producers, large and small, pick at least partly by hand. The growth of interest in whole bunch pressing for reds of course precludes machine picking, as this leaves the stalks behind. Even with the exclusive Vin Jaune, much will be from machine-picked grapes, especially as the Savagnin variety is so hardy and has thick skins. Machine harvesting has the advantage of speed (important when rain is due or grapes are in the process of rotting) and the ability to choose exactly when to pick, and if the most recent machines are used they do not damage vines as they used to – they even leave unripe and rotten berries on the vines. In particular, machine picking means not having to employ a team to pick once the Crémant harvest is over, which is a considerable saving in costs. The fact that grapes for Crémant are harvested first means that the timing can sometimes coincide with college students still being available for picking. Most organic producers do not pick by machine, even though it is not forbidden.

Organic growing

Somewhere between 13% and 15% of vineyards in the Jura are now run along certified

Savagnin grapes of Domaine de la Tournelle carefully harvested into small plastic crates and ready for transport to the winery in the village of St-Cyr-Montmalin beyond.

organic lines, among the highest proportions to be found in northern France, together with Alsace. Around 25% of producers who bottle their wines work in this way – an easy explanation for the discrepancy in figures is that more small producers work organically than large producers. In addition to these are vignerons who work organically but do not seek official recognition from one of France's half-dozen designated certification bodies (Ecocert being the best known). Why don't they? In most cases it is due to the cost of certification and/or not wishing to be categorized in this way; in a few cases it is because they wish to keep their options open in the event of a very difficult weather year, when they may choose to use a systemic chemical spray to save the harvest.

For several decades there were three or four small organically run vineyards, including those of Claude Buchot and Pierre

The biggest disease threats today

There are two big disease threats, both of which exist all over France and much of Europe, but as I write only one is not (yet) present in the Jura. Grapevine yellows (*flavescence dorée*), which is spread by a leafhopper, is on the doorstep in the Mâconnais, Burgundy. The leafhopper is widely present in the Jura and many people believe it's only a matter of time before the disease arrives. It is plant-borne, so the SVJ is working hard on prevention, insisting on hot-water treatment for all newly planted vines and checking young vines for symptoms. Under French law, as soon as symptoms of this brutal disease are noticed it must be reported and a programme of insecticide sprays undertaken by everyone within a certain geographical radius. There is no organic alternative, so organic producers would temporarily lose their certification, something that is causing much debate as to whether this is indeed the best approach to deal with the risks of the disease spreading. Should it arrive in the Jura, organic producers are resolved to fight the compulsory insecticide spray regime.

The second threat, which is actually a reality that vignerons have dealt with for at least ten years, is that from wood-borne fungal diseases, most especially Esca, which appears suddenly and kills vines from one season to the next. Incidences seemed to accelerate after the 2003 drought and, although it affects all varieties, Savagnin and Trousseau are among the most susceptible vine varieties in France. Hard to control, sadly, the most affected vines are those in the prime of life, aged between ten and 30 years. Gaps in the vines are visible everywhere – most producers report having to replace around 10% a year, which is a huge investment of time and money. Guyot Poussard training, which limits the exposed cuts in which the fungus can establish itself, is being advocated and used by some vignerons.

Overnoy, but in the 1990s three large (for the Jura) estates converted – La Pinte, Pignier and André et Mireille (Stéphane) Tissot, all now biodynamic. Most of the others have become certified since 2000; many of these are newly established vignerons who converted when they started. As evidence of the interest in organic viticulture here, in 2012 the agricultural college at Montmorot near Lons-le-Saunier became the first in France to offer a specific BTS (technical diploma course) in organic viticulture and winemaking.

The fundamentals of organic viticulture are simply that no use of synthesized chemicals is allowed in the vineyard, so no chemical fertilizer, herbicide (weed-killer), pesticide or fungicide is permitted. To combat the ever-present fungal diseases, the use of Bordeaux mixture is allowed, as is the use of elemental sulphur, both considered contact sprays. The biggest downside of the use of Bordeaux mixture is the amount of copper that leaches into the soil, especially as in a particularly wet region like the Jura these contact sprays can be washed away quickly and in some years have to be reapplied many times during the season. Organic growers are aware of the risk to the environment of high copper use

Jean-Etienne Pignier of biodynamic Domaine Pignier hoes between each vine.

that working with biodynamics properly requires staff in the ratio of one person per hectare, even if some of the time the staff will be involved in winery work. In this region I know only of Domaine Ganevat that works with this amount of labour. In another sense the adoption of biodynamic methods here should not be that surprising, given the region's proximity to Burgundy and even Alsace, where there are significant numbers of biodynamic producers and some similarities in soils and climate. Burgundy-based consultant Pierre Masson, who runs short courses in biodynamic methods, has a particular influence in the region.

The concept of trying to make the vineyard as self-sufficient as possible is fundamental to biodynamics. Compost made

(in fact they are permitted to use less than one-third that required in conventional farming) and are increasingly using herbal teas to combat disease.

Eliminating herbicide use across all vineyard holdings is fundamental, but is perhaps the biggest challenge in the Jura and is a key reason why more vignerons do not convert. There are many non-organic vignerons I have spoken to who use no chemicals at all except herbicide in a strip under the row of vines.

Biodynamic methods

The increase in Jura producers converting to biodynamic practices from either organic or even directly from conventional growing is interesting, as this method is usually associated with wealthier wine regions and wine producers who can afford both increased risk of lower crop levels and extra labour. Some people estimate

Bruno Ciofi, director of biodynamic Domaine de la Pinte, supervises the copper dynamizer used to mix homeopathic proportions of preparations to spray on the vineyards.

from vine prunings and *marc* is mixed with animal manure, which is then seeded with six medicinal plants (yarrow, chamomile, stinging nettle, oak bark, dandelion and valerian). When spread on the soil this strengthens both the vineyard and its vines, so both are better able to withstand diseases and inclement weather conditions. The two spray preparations 500 (horn manure to spray on the soil to help the vine roots) and 501 (horn silica to spray over the shoots and leaves to help grape ripeness and flavour) are essential to biodynamic farmers. Even organic growers who have not converted fully to biodynamics are using plant sprays in other preparations. Milk whey from the manufacture of goats' cheese is also proving popular. Mixed with Bordeaux mixture (along with elemental sulphur, this is permitted in biodynamic viticulture) and sometimes other plant preparations, it appears to make the spray more effective and longer-lasting, thus reducing copper use.

Those who follow biodynamics to the letter are guided by phases of the moon and other celestial cycles to determine when to perform certain vineyard activities. In the Jura, however, the vagaries of the weather make this particularly challenging. Including the three relatively large wine estates mentioned above, by 2013 there were eight estates, accounting for 130ha or over 6% of the Jura wine region, certified biodynamic and several more are using at least some biodynamic methods.

This isolated vineyard above Rotalier owned by Domaine Labet is ideal for organic farming as there is no risk of drift from neighbours' chemical sprays.

'Agriculture raisonnée' – a reasonable approach

The practice known as 'agriculture raisonnée', literally 'reasoned agriculture', also known sometimes as 'culture raisonnée' or 'lutte raisonnée' ('reasoned cultivation' or 'reasoned fight'), is often referred to as 'sustainable' or 'integrated' agriculture. Rather than spraying vineyards whether they need spraying or not, practitioners use detailed weather forecasts to predict potential attacks from pests and disease so that vineyards are sprayed only when absolutely necessary. Despite the somewhat confusing name, 'sustainable' can be a useful first step for growers who want to get off the chemical treadmill, and also allows the vineyard to gradually adapt to the new regime while staying economically viable for the grower. The approach has certainly led to a significant reduction in chemical use in recent years, but without certification and more importantly third-party checks, the word 'raisonnée', used by many growers to describe how they farm their vineyards, can be meaningless. More misleading is the term used by some less scrupulous producers that they are 'almost organic'.

Some growers take this reasonable approach further, and the region as a whole through the work of the SVJ has encouraged growers to take more care of the environment using more integrated and holistic methods. As well as limiting the spray programmes as described above, this includes reducing or eliminating the use of chemical fertilizers and the most noxious herbicides and pesticides, and also being more proactive in protecting the surrounding environment. In 2014 a group of Jura growers will join the organization Terra Vitis, a label that operates a code of practice and enforces traceability in order to protect the environment. This label takes a broader environmental approach, including aspects such as proper treatment and disposal of chemicals and water (for cleaning vineyard spray equipment, etc.) and recycling. It is hoped that the Terra Vitis programme will be a success and will be extended to include more producers.

Grassing down every few rows is a first step to a more environmentally friendly approach to viticulture. Here, on a sloping vineyard in Le Vernois, it helps to protect the vineyard from soil erosion.

HOW THE WINES ARE MADE AND HOW THEY TASTE

Philippe Bornard's cat seems curious about his non-AOC-designated Pétillant Naturel magnums.

One of the key reasons that new wine producers choose to set up in the Jura is that here, using just five different grape varieties, they have the opportunity and the challenge of making a plethora of different wine styles, most of them within appellation rules. This, however, is one of the key explanations for the complications of the Jura and what makes its wines at once intriguing and baffling.

In an average year the tiny Jura region produces only 10–12 million bottles (less than 0.2% of total French production). Just over a quarter is sparkling and the same amount red or rosé (official figures do not differentiate between them); this leaves around 38% for white wines, less than 4% for Vin Jaune, just 1% for Vin de Paille and 6% for Macvin.

Rest assured that many wines in the Jura are made just as they are anywhere else in the wine world, but the Jura specialities of Vin de Paille, Macvin and, above all, Vin Jaune are not; come to think of it, there are some pretty unusual ways of handling many of the whites and some reds too. That is partly what this chapter is about, explaining how the various wines are made in the Jura and how they taste.

Domaine de la Renardière uses the range of 'official' Jura bottles. From the left: Vin de Paille, red Jura, clavelin, *white Jura.*

Compared to many winemaking regions the Jura has a welcome lack of 'technological wines', by which I mean wines made to a recipe making maximum use of technological equipment and legally permitted additives. This does not, however, exclude many standard modern winemaking methods. Most wine producers have been trained in oenology (winemaking) at the local *lycée* (college), in Montmorot near Lons-le-Saunier, or in Beaune or Dijon in Burgundy. Some have experienced making wine elsewhere, but here more than anywhere there is a desire to let the unusual grapes and terroirs express the region, whether through wine styles from long ago, what has become traditional in the past 50 years, or through styles adopted more recently. There is a vibrant natural wine movement in the Jura (see 'The natural way', p. 74).

The distinctive Jura bottle shape, with its angular sloping shoulders and body slightly tapering at the base, comes from an original design made by La Verrerie de la Vieille Loye (see 'History', p. 97). In the 1930s it was adopted by the region for AOC wines, with the name 'Jura' embossed on it. However, it was nearly lost in the 1970s, as EU size standardizations meant reworking each mould and the main bottle manufacturer threatened to cease production because demand was too low. Larger producers stepped in to save it and today it is widely, but far from exclusively, used for reds and whites, and there is a half-bottle version as well. It is compulsory to bottle Vin Jaune in the *clavelin* and there are special bottles available for both Macvin and Vin de Paille.

This examination of the Jura's myriad wine styles starts with Vin Jaune, because understanding how this extraordinary wine is made and tastes is a key to understanding the other white wines of the region. I then explore in turn white wines; reds and rosés; sparkling wines; Vin de Paille; and Macvin. The first paragraph of these sections presents a brief overview of the wines. The winemaking methods and the taste of the wines are then described in some detail, a generalization across producers of course. The chapter 'Serving Jura wines' on p. 322 is useful to refer to for serving temperatures and tips on food matching for each style.

Vin Jaune – some secrets revealed

There is no voodoo magic involved in the making of the legendary, bone-dry, complex and extremely long-lived Vin Jaune (literally 'yellow wine'). However, the method seems to break all the rules of winemaking that we have understood since Pasteur's time. Before Pasteur, the making of Vin Jaune was probably a happy accident. White wine made from 100% Savagnin grapes is placed in a barrel and not moved or topped up for about six years. A layer of yeast called *le voile* ('veil') forms, similar to Sherry's *flor*, which protects the wine from extreme oxidation and gives it its particular nutty or spicy taste and richness. The amount that has evaporated from the barrel is said to be a reason for the compulsory use of the 62cl *clavelin* bottle.

Savagnin is picked fairly late, but only occasionally has a proportion of berries affected by noble rot (*Botrytis cinerea*). Ideally the potential alcohol should be about 13%, with chaptalization used in years when necessary (increasingly rarely), and the pH needs to be low (3.0–3.1) to give the acidity to withstand the years of ageing both in barrel and bottle. The wine is made as any other white wine, fermented to dryness with temperature control (but rarely very cool) in tank or sometimes *foudres*, and malolactic fermentation usually follows. Until this stage oxygen is kept at bay judiciously.

Most producers transfer the Savagnin wine into barrels in spring or early summer (April–July) during the year following vintage, but a few will delay until autumn or even the spring 18 months after harvest. I originally thought that the barrels were not entirely filled, and it is true that some producers leave 8–10 litres of ullage or air space, but others fill the barrels, allowing the wine to evaporate gradually and the layer of yeast to form. The amount of ullage space remains open to discussion. In the past more space was left, but it all depends on whether inoculated yeasts are used and where the barrels are to be aged – the warmer the storage environment, the less ullage space should be left in the barrel.

After a few weeks or months, a length of time that varies greatly, a layer of yeast, the *voile*, should appear on the surface

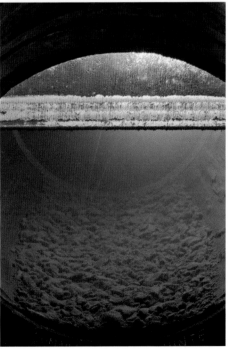

Above: Vin Jaune barrels ageing in a ventilated loft space above Stéphane Tissot's cellar. Below: A demonstration barrel at Domaine de la Pinte showing the thin grey layer of voile with yeast deposits at the bottom.

Natural versus cultured yeast

In the Jura as elsewhere, some producers choose indigenous yeast, which is naturally present on grape skins and/or in the cellar's atmosphere, for fermentation and some buy a cultured yeast from the local laboratory. Some will have a cultured yeast made for them by the laboratory from their own indigenous yeast. Biodynamic and natural wine movements forbid the use of cultured yeast, but one wonders how it is policed. Some people believe that, if a cultured yeast has been used at any time, it will remain in the cellar and dominate the fermentation process.

This issue is particularly important in the making of Vin Jaune, because some producers, for example Stéphane Tissot, believe that those who use a cultured yeast for their fermentation are less likely to get the important *voile* to establish itself naturally on the surface of the Savagnin barrels, although I know several who have no problems. Most believe it depends on the storage conditions for the Vin Jaune barrels, where the barrels come from and how they are cleaned, if at all. Many just keep Vin Jaune barrels full, not even cleaning between wines. It seems, however, that this is part of the mystery of Vin Jaune – there is no rhyme or reason.

Most of the large producers do routinely inoculate or seed (called *ensemence-* *ment* in French) a special yeast starter culture to establish the *voile*. It is said that about two-thirds of Vin Jaune produced is made with *ensemencement*, but in 2011 a few of the producers had an unusually high failure rate of barrels, when the wine turned into vinegar. They blamed the laboratory that supplied the yeast, but the lab proved them wrong. Since then discussions have been held on whether and how to clean the barrels, which might have been the cause for the failure, and whether this seeding should be used at all.

Ensemencement is subject to much vitriol, as it is deemed non-authentic and there are accusations that it can standardize Vin Jaune. However, tests have proved that there are no living yeasts left of the strain added two years after inoculation. In addition, blind tastings of young Vins Jaunes have rarely identified which were made with *ensemencement* and which without. However, experienced Jura sommelier Christophe Menozzi is not alone in believing that it does affect the taste, and he thinks that those inoculated do not taste nearly as good after a decade in bottle. There are few small producers who do not rise up in horror at the mere mention of it, as well as vehemently denying using the process.

Domaine Berthet-Bondet's semi-underground Vin Jaune barrel cellar. Each barrel has a guillette or tap used to extract a tasting sample from below the voile.

of the wine. The yeast strain is similar to Sherry's *flor*, consisting of various forms of *Saccharomyces*. Since the 1970s producers have had the choice of inoculating with cultured yeast (*ensemencement*) to establish the *voile* more quickly and, in theory, less riskily. The best-quality *voile* is grey and fairly thin, indicating a living and active yeast mixture – it can even be black. Once the *voile* has formed, its thickness and activity ebb and flow with the seasons.

The conditions in which the barrels are stored – either at ground level, partially underground, completely underground, in a loft, or simply upstairs – are crucial to the eventual quality of the wine. These locations create huge variables. Temperatures in a typical *cave à Vin Jaune* ('cellar' in the loosest possible term) in Arbois may vary from −5°C in winter to over 35°C if in a loft, whereas in Château-Chalon many producers favour conditions that vary only between about 10°C and 20°C. Indeed, many vignerons believe that the complexity of Vin Jaune is achieved partly by keeping the barrels in several different locations, all with different conditions. Everyone agrees that well-ventilated cellars are essential – windows or doors are left open and the barrels are rarely stacked on top of each

other without air space. Most agree that some temperature variation is useful and prefer fairly dry conditions, where the water content of the wine in the ullaged barrels evaporates slowly, concentrating other substances, including alcohol.

In the past, producers monitored the ageing process in each barrel by tasting, and some still do this by taking a sample from below the *voile* using a tap in the barrel known locally as a *dzi* or *guillette*. However, a technician from the official Jura wine laboratory also visits almost all Vin Jaune producers twice a year to take samples from every barrel of Savagnin destined for Vin Jaune, using a newly sterilized pipette for each barrel. A report is sent back, indicating the level of acetic acid (volatility or vinegar character) to ensure that it is not too high and checks that for the first few years the acetaldehyde (ethanal) level is rising. Both volatile acid and acetaldehyde are formed by the action of the yeast on the alcohol, and acetaldehyde is vital for Vin Jaune, the most important component for its distinctive taste. Depending on the laboratory reports, the producer then decides which barrels

The *clavelin* bottle

According to AOC rules Vins Jaunes must be bottled in the *clavelin* bottle, the only non-standard wine bottle size allowed under EU law. The *clavelin* is unusual in that the bottle size is 65cl (stamped on to the base of today's machine-made bottles), yet the official volume approved by the EU and marked on the label is 62cl. Château-Chalon has a special version with the name embossed on the *clavelin*.

Prevalent only since the early 20th century (see 'History', p. 97), the great marketing coup for the *clavelin* is that 62cl is said to be what remains of a litre of wine after evaporation during the years of ageing in cask *sous voile*. Certainly it makes the explanation easier, even if it's not exactly true. The usual loss can be less or more, depending greatly on storage conditions. Regulations in the USA do not allow the importation of this non-standard bottle, though it does find its way into the country by some circuitous routes. Some 37.5cl bottles of similar shape have been produced, but this is not, strictly speaking, allowed within the AOC rules, so cannot be sold within the EU, another complicated issue.

The distinctively shaped 62cl clavelin bottle is compulsory for all Vins Jaunes and AOC Château-Chalon has an embossed seal on its clavelins.

should be withdrawn from Vin Jaune ageing. Provided they are not spoilt, they are used for oxidative Savagnin white wine, or Chardonnay/Savagnin blends. If they are spoilt, the wines will be sent away either to vinegar manufacturers or for distillation. Most producers will deliberately select certain barrels for their oxidative ranges after two years or more.

Most Vins Jaunes vary from 13.5% to 15% alcohol, often on the higher side in Arbois (due to stocking barrels in lofts with wide temperature variations) and the lower side in Château-Chalon in particular. The level of acetaldehyde should end up at 350–600mg/l and does not increase once the wine is in bottle. On the other hand, sotolon, an aldehyde discovered in the 1970s and formed only in the presence of acetaldehyde, continues to develop during bottle ageing and is equally responsible for the *goût du jaune*, the typical taste of Vin Jaune.

All the publicity material and indeed any article or book I have ever read discusses the minimum six years and three months that Vin Jaune must stay in barrel under the veil before release – this specific length of time is a somewhat mythical, romantic figure. The following is the reality of how it works. From harvest to putting the wine into barrel is 8–18 months. There follows the minimum 60 months that the AOC requires the wine to stay in barrel *sous voile*. The earliest bottling is allowed in December six years after harvest and the earliest release is in January in the seventh year (or six years and three months) after harvest! So, for example, the 2007 vintage could have been put in barrel in July 2008, then blending of barrels could take place 60 months later in August 2013, bottling in December 2013 and sales from 2014. Many producers will leave their *jaune* in barrel for several months or occasionally years longer than this. Today the AOC laws insist on tasting approval tests (the *agrément*) for all Vin Jaune just before bottling. Château-Chalon instituted these tastings from 2004 for the 1997 vintage.

The taste of Vin Jaune

Is Vin Jaune indeed yellow? Well, in my experience young Vins Jaunes vary from pale yellow with a greenish tinge, through yellow-gold with hints of green, to positively amber. It all depends on how the wine

Sherry, Tokaji and Vin Jaune

Most wine drinkers outside France are more likely to have tasted a Fino or Manzanilla Sherry from Spain's Andalucía than a Vin Jaune. A lucky few may have tasted a Tokaji Szamarodni Dry from Hungary. These white wines all have one thing in common: after fermentation is complete they are aged in what is known as a 'biological way' under a layer or veil of yeast, which confers a special taste: many people's reaction to smelling and tasting a Vin Jaune for the first time is 'Oh, it's like Sherry.'

Sherry is made from Palomino grapes grown in a warm climate, but the really big differences from Jura's Vin Jaune are that Sherry is always fortified with spirit and that, although aged in barrel, it is aged in the solera system of fractional blending of different ages of Sherry, whereas Vin Jaune is always from one vintage. Even taking into account Sherry's solera system, Vin Jaune is aged for longer than most of the wine that is withdrawn for bottling from the Fino or Manzanilla soleras and on analysis normally contains considerably more sotolon.

Tokaji, from the Furmint grape, is made in northeast Hungary, and the rare Tokaji Szamarodni Dry style is closer to Vin Jaune than Sherry is. More oxidative Tokaji wines were made in the past, but only a very few post-Communist producers have revived the Szamarodni Dry style. The biggest difference from Vin Jaune is that the wines must be made from grapes affected by *Botrytis cinerea* (noble rot), and in addition the Tokaj cellars have a particular microorganism in the cellar atmosphere that forms part of the *voile*. Producers vary as to how long they age these wines under the veil, but, unlike Sherry, they are usually from a single vintage and not made in a solera system.

was made, especially how long and where it was stored (in other words how oxidative it really is), and how old it is (how long since it was bottled and in what conditions it was stored). Phew! All that for the colour, yet often the colour gives me a foretaste of what the wine will smell and taste like. If the colour tends to browning, the Vin Jaune may be too oxidized.

The aromas and flavours of Vins Jaunes are legion, including almost every section of an aroma wheel, ever changing with time in glass or open bottle, and to inexperienced tasters somewhat off-putting at first. From Arbois especially, the wines will be nutty – walnuts in particular, sometimes fresh walnuts (also known as green or wet walnuts), even hazelnuts. Vins Jaunes from other areas, especially Château-Chalon, will have a more earthy, even peaty or sometimes smoky or roasted coffee smell. Often there are aromas of spices – what the French call 'curry'. To clarify this, 'curry' in France is rarely like Indian curry or the international version of it. French curry powder is a mix of turmeric, coriander, cumin and cardamom, sometimes with ginger and fenugreek. Fenugreek is a spice associated with sotolon. Occasionally there may also be a candied (*confit* in French) lemon or even exotic fruit

character in the lighter styles, which show fewer of the nutty notes. As with all fine wines, it is complexity that counts and good Vins Jaunes will change quite dramatically in the glass as time goes on or in the bottle after opening and leaving somewhere cool for days, weeks or even months. A Vin Jaune where the oxidation has gone too far will have a rather heavy, dull, appley character. 'Maderized' is the technical term.

On the palate Vin Jaune is dry. In fact it appears shockingly bone dry, not only because it is always high in acidity but also because it really is dry – the *voile* manages to 'eat' every last drop of grape sugar. The high acidity is exacerbated by the oxidative effect, but then the flavours of the mid-palate kick in, sometimes nutty, sometimes candied fruit or spices, with the alcohol somehow holding the wine together, providing that it is not too high. By the second sip, especially if you are munching walnuts or Comté cheese, the acidity is not aggressive at all. It's worth feeling the texture of a Vin Jaune in the mouth, rounded out by those years of ageing. Not surprisingly, the finish on a Vin Jaune can be tremendously long. Check out the Vercel story ('History', p. 114) to read the tasting note of a 220-year-old Arbois Vin Jaune.

Green to gold – other whites

Whether from Chardonnay or Savagnin or a blend of the two, white wines in the Jura fall into two families. The first is called *sous voile*, *tradition* or *typé* in the local area. The wines are made in an oxidative style, with some exposure to oxygen during the maturation and may be aged as Vin Jaune is, *sous voile* or under the veil (layer) of yeast, with no topping up. The second style is known as *ouillé* or *floral* (*floraux* in the plural) and these are made in the same way as the vast majority of white wines around

the world. The word *ouillé* comes from *ouillage*, a technical term for the topping up of the tanks or barrels in which the wine ages. *Ouillage* is normally carried out regularly as the wine evaporates, to avoid any chance of oxygen coming into contact with the wine. In both families, where oak barrels are used they are almost always old oak that does not dominate the taste. All Jura whites are dry with high acidity, but their flavours are particularly dependent on which of these families of winemaking they come from.

The whites of all styles undergo the same process to begin with, varying only by producer. Some use whole bunch pressing in pneumatic presses, a few will lightly crush and partly destem before pressing. Fermentation temperatures are controlled, but in the Jura the tendency is for relatively high temperatures – up to 22°C is not uncommon. Malolactic fermentation nearly always takes place.

As everywhere, Chardonnay is a versatile grape for the wine producer, and in the Jura that versatility can be almost infinite, with the possibility of terroir selections, varying sizes and types of container for both vinification and ageing, the possibility

Left: Lucien and Vincent Aviet use the Jura bottle for their AOC Arbois white, although the label does not state the grape. Right: The old foudre *used for white wines by Domaine de Montbourgeau has a new wooden front and a stainless steel opening and tap.*

A plethora of white wine styles

Here is a list of the main variations of dry white wines in AOCs Arbois, Côtes du Jura and L'Etoile. Be warned that the labels rarely tell you which style is in the bottle, although a few use the terms shown below in brackets, either on front or back labels. Local Jura restaurants may also use these terms.

Chardonnay (*floral* or *ouillé*): tank or oak fermented, may be oak matured. Topped up. If fermented and aged in small barrels it may be referred to as being made in Burgundian style.

Chardonnay (*tradition* or *typé* or *sous voile*): tank or oak fermented, aged in barrel or foudre, not topped up. The *voile* may or may not be encouraged or form on its own, if so *sous voile* may be mentioned.

Savagnin (*ouillé*): tank or oak fermented, may be oak matured. Topped up.

Savagnin (*sous voile*): classic Savagnin, usually withdrawn early from Vin Jaune ageing.

Chardonnay/Savagnin (*floral* or *ouillé*): unusual topped-up blend.

Chardonnay/Savagnin (*tradition* or *typé*): usually 50–80% Chardonnay that may be of any of the Chardonnay styles above blended with 20–50% Savagnin made *sous voile*.

Oak barrels

I wouldn't mind betting that there are more old (4+ years) small oak barrels per litre of wine made in the Jura than almost anywhere, certainly for a region dominated by white wines. Nearly all the white wines are aged in oak, but, apart from during a few years at the turn of this century, there has been very little brand new oak used here. Almost all the barrels purchased are the 228-litre *fûts* or *pièces* from Burgundy (only occasionally do you see 225-litre Bordeaux *barriques*). They are bought sometimes directly from producers, with whom Jura vignerons may have become friendly while at wine college in Beaune for example, or they are purchased through the usual coopers.

The youngest purchased have usually contained two or three wines (i.e. two to four years old). Especially for Vin Jaune and oxi-dative whites, most people prefer to have barrels that have contained white wines in the past. Of course once barrels have been used for oxidative wines, they cannot be used for other wines, but many are kept in use for up to 50 years. For reds, many producers use small barrels for their Pinot Noir, but there is still quite widespread use of *foudres* (1,000 litres and larger), used also for whites by some too, and a very few are investing in oak fermenters for their reds. More and more oversized *pièces* of 300 litres or *demi-muids* that range from 350 to 600 litres are being purchased, especially as they can now be bought second-hand from Burgundy, where many producers started using them several years ago.

Foudres *and* fûts *used for both red and white wines in Jacques Puffeney's cellar.*

of oxidative methods, and/or blending with Savagnin. Whereas traditionally the Jura is usually associated with *sous voile* white wines, in Arbois most people claim that the tradition was always to make Chardonnay closer to Burgundy in style. From Pasteur's time, when it was understood that oxidation was an enemy of wine, in Arbois topping up the barrels would have been done, if not systematically then at least occasionally, with little oxidative character in the wines. On the other hand, making oxidative and *sous voile* Chardonnay is particularly traditional around Château-Chalon and in AOCs L'Etoile and Côtes du Jura.

On the whole Chardonnay is mostly fermented in tank (stainless steel, concrete or fibreglass) before being transferred to barrel or *foudre* for ageing. Ageing Chardonnay in *foudres* for between 18 months and four years continues among several producers – they may or may not top up the *foudre*, but with large volumes this makes less difference than with *fûts*. The *foudres* are considered to soften the high acidity levels found here and to bring out the terroir flavours.

When the secondary or malolactic fermentation takes place was traditionally a hit and miss affair. Indeed most did not know of its existence, or at least understand the process until the 1970s or even later, and in the Jura, as with other technical aspects of winemaking, many producers seem more relaxed about it than elsewhere. What will be, will be. Being a cool region with naturally high malic acidity in the grapes and thus the wine, malolactic fermentation is desirable to round out the taste and create more stability in the wine, but with low pH in the wines, when it happens depends partly on the weather, how much if any SO_2 is used, and the storage conditions (vinification cellars are often very cold in the Jura).

Since the late 1990s increasing numbers of Chardonnays have been made in what is referred to in the region as the 'Burgundian method', meaning that they are fermented in relatively new barrels and then left to age for 12–24 months, sometimes with lees stirring to give richer, more 'Burgundian' flavours.

Historically Savagnin was always considered to be the fine wine grape variety of the Jura, making wines to age (*vin de garde*, later known as Vin Jaune) when the year permitted it. It is hard to say when it became the usual practice for all Savagnin wines to be aged deliberately *sous voile* as potential Vins Jaunes, but this remained the norm until the mid-1990s, and today there are still many producers who only produce Savagnin this way. Very simply, these wines are withdrawn from Vin Jaune ageing after anything between 12 and 60 months *sous voile* (two to six years after harvest) and may be bottled directly. Some producers prefer to soften the taste by leaving them for a further period of non-oxidative ageing in tank or large barrels (now without the yeast veil and kept topped up).

However, Savagnin has proved that it too has great potential for producing an exciting range of white wine styles in a more conventional way. The earliest producer I know of who made Savagnin *ouillé* was Pierre Overnoy in the 1980s; Frédéric Lornet and Alain Labet also adopted this style in the mid-1990s. Many followed, though more in Arbois AOC than in the more traditional Côtes du Jura and L'Etoile AOCs. Methods are as varied as those for topped-up Chardonnay, with some using no oak ageing at all, others a year or two, or occasionally much longer, topped up in barrel or sometimes larger oak casks.

There are no official figures for how much Savagnin is made in the *ouillé* style. Estimates are 5–10%, but it is increasing slowly, especially among producers who export or who have strong sales outside Franche-

Comté. I believe that it is a style that has great potential for the future, providing that more producers start selecting at the vineyard stage which of their Savagnins are destined for *ouillé* and which for Vin Jaune. There are many site options and also options in variations of Savagnin (Jaune or Vert for example – see 'Grape varieties', p. 41). Considering that Vin Jaune itself accounts for a somewhat static 4% of sales and that the home market for the traditional *sous voile* styles is less certain to be maintained, it's worth treating the *ouillé* style as a serious quality product. Traditionalists in the area do not agree, and consider the style a threat to the Jura's tradition of unique *sous voile* wines. There is certainly an argument for a separate appellation for *ouillé* wines, both Chardonnay and Savagnin, but that will take too many years and no one will ever agree a name. Meantime, many producers, especially the younger ones, simply go ahead and make more *ouillé* styles if they have the market for them.

The taste of white wines

Almost all white wines from the Jura are dry (exceptions being the few late-harvest wines – see 'Savagnin late-harvest and ice wines') and relatively high in acidity, with alcohol ranging from 12% to 13.5%, only rarely higher.

The oxidative styles, whether blends or single-varietal wines, all have an intense colour, from greenish straw (especially Savagnins) to a deep gold, even amber. They share an aroma on the nose that may shock at first, almost reminiscent of a cut apple that has started to brown, and maybe nuts. All the Savagnins that have been aged *sous voile* are likely to be reminiscent of Vin Jaune, but not as complex or intense. Those Savagnins that have been bottled with three years *sous voile* or less (unless the vigneron is present you have to work it out based on the vintage date and when you purchased it) should still show some tangy citrus character mixed up with the characteristic nutty notes. These flavours all come through to the palate along with a richness in texture given by that time under the yeast veil – and it is this richness that in good wines balances the initial shock of high acidity. There is a subtle difference between those Chardonnays aged *sous voile* that become more reminiscent of Savagnin due to the high acetaldehyde content, and those few that are simply oxidative with no yeast veil influence. Oxidative blends are

Savagnin late-harvest and ice wines

There is no legal *vendange tardive* or late-harvest designation in the Jura, but, as Savagnin is such a late ripener, its thick skins allow it to be left on the vine late into the autumn until the first frosts. A handful of producers risk leaving a few rows of vines in years when the grapes look super-healthy and some of these may be partly affected by noble rot. The resulting wines are anything from off-dry through semi-sweet to lusciously sweet, sometimes oak-aged, sometimes not, usually filled into half-bottles using a fanciful name that often includes the word 'Novembre' ('November'), as that is when they are usually harvested. Technically most of these wines cannot be AOC, so are sold as Vin de France. The high acidity of Savagnin balances beautifully with the residual sugar and usually the citrus flavours of Savagnin emerge. Inevitably these wines are not made every year and only tiny quantities are available.

less distinct in character, varying hugely between those styles mentioned.

The non-oxidative Chardonnays vary every bit as much as their terroir, ageing methods and producers. I find that inexpensive Arbois Chardonnay, aged in either tank or *foudres*, has a vibrant yellow fruit skin nose, almost apricot or peach skin (even more so with those made from the Melon à Queue Rouge variation of Chardonnay) that suggests more ripeness than you discover on the palate, where the stony character and high acidity

Domaine Buronfosse Côtes du Jura Entre-Deux is a Savagnin ouillé *but you can't tell that from the label.*

cry out for food. Many, especially those that have spent 18 months or more in *foudres*, are intriguing. Some inexpensive Côtes du Jura are more like simple Mâcon Blanc, but many of the best producers here either go the oxidative route (as do almost all L'Etoile too) or the Burgundian route (as many do in the Sud Revermont).

The most exciting so-called Burgundy styles of Chardonnay, fermented and aged in smaller oak barrels, tend to reflect their terroir more distinctly, which is why most of the best producers in Arbois and Côtes du Jura have chosen to strike out with single-terroir cuvées. The type of oak and the maturation time make a difference, and producers of this type of wine are increasingly using lower sulphur levels and vinifying in a very reductive way (avoiding oxygen at all costs).

Even though experienced tasters can detect the differences in Chardonnays made from the two main terroir types, soils with more limestone and fossils trick some people into thinking the wine might be Chablis

or sometimes Côtes de Beaune, whereas, rather strangely, those from the heavier clay marls are often marked down as having an oxidative influence. The fact that these wines are actually made in the most reductive way possible gives credence to the much-disputed argument that soil types, minerals or terroir can be tasted. To me, the marl-based Chardonnays show a distinct nose of wet stone or indeed minerals, whereas in the Chardonnays from the limestone-based soils there is more of an elegant steeliness. On the palate these wines should be dry, elegant and, yes, mineral, often with extraordinary length and staying power. Test this ageing potential by leaving a bottle open somewhere cool for a few days – for a while, they get better and better. Vintages make a difference mostly in the ripeness of the fruit taste and in the acidity levels.

The growing numbers of delicious Savagnin *ouillé* wines vary from a very aromatic, fresh style full of tropical fruit to more stony, mineral styles with either lemon pith, skin or even lemon meringue pie coming up often in my tasting notes. This grape seems to absorb oak really well, and some oak ageing adds to the texture of the wines, giving finesse and length.

Finally, there are a few Chardonnay/Savagnin blends that are *ouillé* and in these I find it fascinating how, even with as little as 20% Savagnin, the characteristic citrus or aromatic character of Savagnin shows through the Chardonnay and these rare blends can make succulent, eminently drinkable wines.

The natural way

Several producers profiled in Part 3 work in the natural way, making 'natural wines', a term that is open to many interpretations: at the time of writing there are no definitive rules. Many, but not all, producers of organic or biodynamically farmed grapes adopt some or all of these natural practices. Conversely, a few who make wines in the natural way do not start with organic grapes.

All Jura producers I know who work in this way are entirely dedicated to these methods philosophically, and are convinced that the natural way will produce the best possible wine from their land and will continue to attract sufficient customers. So what is it?

In essence the natural way means that grapes are transformed into wine and bottled with as little intervention as possible, using very few or no additives in the cellar. Following the standard winemaking process through its various stages, the natural way uses – except for second fermentation yeasts for sparkling wines – only indigenous yeasts (see 'Natural versus cultured yeast', p. 64), no enzymes, rarely chaptalization or acidification (adding sugar or tartaric acid to grape juice), no malolactic bacteria and no preservatives, except sometimes low levels of sulphur dioxide (sulphites or SO_2 or in shorthand referred to as 'sulphur'). Most of the wines are clarified naturally by settling, using limited or no fining or filtration.

Some people define natural wine as being without added SO_2, but in reality there are very few producers who don't add any SO_2 throughout the process from grapes to bottle. However, increasing numbers use no SO_2 for their red wines, especially Poulsard. As they gain experience with working without SO_2, producers are adapting: for his whites Jean-François Ganevat has now stopped lees stirring in barrel to limit the risk of oxidation; for reds some use full or semi-carbonic maceration; and most producers will bottle retaining some carbon dioxide as protection. Whereas good hygiene should be paramount in all winemaking, it becomes even more vital when using the natural way.

The most important thing to understand is that producers working in other ways are not unnatural! Methods and additives mentioned above are not only legal within prescribed limits, but, if used correctly, they are routine, normal and proven to be no harm to health.

Here are my answers to a few common questions about the natural way:

- Do wines made in the natural way taste different? Yes, often.

- Do they taste more of their grape variety and/or terroir? No, mainly they do not, but that depends on what you believe those tastes are.

- Are they faulty or off in some way? Most are not, but there is a greater proportion of wines made in the natural way that are technically faulty. Among these wines you can find higher levels of volatility or vinegary smells in particular and some are prone to early oxidation.

- Can these wines age? The jury is out on this question. It depends on the style.

- Do they need different handling at home? Yes, they must be stored at a relatively low constant temperature. They are more likely to need decanting.

- Should you try these wines? Absolutely yes. The good ones offer wonderful purity of fruit and are eminently drinkable and enjoyable; the finest bring out the best of their grape and terroir too.

A bank of 420-litre clay amphorae in the winery of Stéphane Tissot, used for fermenting Savagnin or Trousseau on their skins, a method adopted by several producers working in the natural way.

Pink to purple – rosés and reds

All three Jura grapes – Poulsard, Trousseau and Pinot Noir – produce, in world terms, pale-coloured and light-bodied red wines, with oak usually kept to a minimum. As ever, the Jura manages to deliver a plethora of styles and in this category more than others market demands have an influence. Pale rosés, darker rosés, single-varietal reds, blended reds, more structured reds and fruity, early-drinking reds have all been in and out of fashion since the post-1960s revival of the Jura's vineyards. And the trends continue.

Unlike the whites, the vast majority of Jura reds are made to be bottled within a year. Traditional red winemaking methods used by most here entail: mechanical crushing and destalking; maceration with the skins in tank (stainless steel, cement or fibreglass) for 5–15 days (longer sometimes for Trousseau or Pinot) with regular pumpovers and occasionally punch-downs or *délestage* (rack and return); temperature control below 30°C; pressing; blending; and malolactic fermentation, sometimes in tank and sometimes in oak. Many red wines in

the Jura are matured simply in tank for a few months, others in large neutral oak *foudres*, and a few in small barrels.

The above explanation is about the majority of reds. As ever, there are a multitude of exceptions and most of the Jura's very best reds are indeed exceptions. I will mention just some of the most important variations to the traditional method outlined above.

Thin-skinned Poulsard needs particularly careful handling, with extraction of colour more important than tannins. This delicate grape is prone to reductive or animal flavours and, whereas traditionalists were either immune to these flavours or considered them part of the taste of 'terroir', most drinkers today are looking for a cleaner, more fruity character and softer tannins.

It is known that SO_2 inhibits oxidation, so if it is not used the wine will be less prone to reduction. But the wine still needs protection. Many Poulsard wines are now made without crushing and destemming the grapes, using whole bunches. These may then be put into a sealed vat saturated with carbon dioxide in a process called 'carbonic

Pierre Overnoy hand-destemming Poulsard grapes in the vineyards using the wooden crible. *This is a gentler way of destemming than a machine and ideal for keeping the berries uncrushed for carbonic maceration.*

red, requiring longer maceration to bring out the flavours and tannins from the skins. More than with other varieties the key is to keep the yields down and to bring in super-healthy grapes, rejecting any rotten grapes at harvest. Increasing numbers of small producers are reviving an older, gentler manual destemming method in the vineyards, using what is known locally as a *crible* – what looks like a wooden table with holes in it, placed on top of a large bin (some use this for Poulsard too). The bunches of grapes are tipped on to the table and rubbed very gently by hand, which frees the berries from the stems, allowing them to drop through the holes. The result is a pile of glistening black olive-like berries.

Cold maceration for a day or even several is practised by some producers with Pinot Noir, and sometimes with Trousseau as well. A few will even ferment in open-top barrels in which they can still punch down the cap of skins, sometimes even foot-treading; others prefer more gentle pumpovers. After pressing, some producers transfer their Trousseau and Pinot reds into barrels or *foudres* to complete fermentation and await malolactic fermentation. As to maturation, this varies from some traditionalists who might routinely mature in *foudre* for one to three years before bottling to those who experiment with every size of barrel, but with rarely more than 10% new oak.

Finally, red blends must not be forgotten. Whereas Poulsard and Trousseau have been made separately in the Arbois district for many decades, further south in the Côtes du Jura single-varietal reds have become widespread only since the 1990s. Blended reds are often made from Poulsard or Trousseau and Pinot Noir, or sometimes from all three varieties. Many will make these wines traditionally, picking all three varieties at the same time (despite different ripening

maceration', with intracellular fermentation taking place inside each grape berry. More often there may be a semi-carbonic maceration, as used often in Beaujolais, whereby some intracellular fermentation takes place, as well as some conventional fermentation without the vat being closed. The added advantage of keeping a wine in an atmosphere of carbon dioxide (CO_2) is that less or no SO_2 can be used because the CO_2 has a protective effect. Even with conventional fermentation methods it helps to maintain the wine in an atmosphere of CO_2 in tank after pressing, right up until bottling, and even bottling with some CO_2 helps. However, not all consumers like the fact that there might be a slight fizz in their red wine. Oak is rarely used for Poulsard.

Trousseau is regarded as a 'more serious'

False rosés – mostly Poulsard in disguise

By now you will know that the Jura likes to confuse. Even today there are some wine estates (mainly in southern Côtes du Jura where red wines are less prevalent) that market their Poulsard reds as rosés. From the 1950s to the 1990s, most estates sold a Rosé du Jura, in reality a red blend or even a single-variety Poulsard made like a red wine but with a short maceration of just three to ten days. The skins of the Poulsard grape are so thin that the colour remains pale.

When I first came across these wines I was really confused, because although the wines look like a dark rosé, and good ones have a bouquet of fresh red fruit, on the palate the albeit light but drying tannins gave the game away that these were in fact light red wines. The Henri Maire company uses the term 'Corail' for a Poulsard/Trousseau blend made in this way; even more confusingly, Corail is also used by Château d'Arlay for a wine made from a blend of all five Jura grape varieties, subject to a short maceration and three years' ageing in old oak. This replicates the way most small growers and families with a few rows of vines would have made wine in the 19th century and earlier, producing what we call a 'field blend'.

dates), so that the process is a blend from the beginning. Others will use more modern methods, vinifying each variety separately and blending a short time before bottling.

Today, alongside some oddities, Jura rosés have evolved like everywhere – made with direct pressing or using a short maceration on the skins, and bottled by May at latest. Most are made from Poulsard, though there are blends too. They are often marketed as 'rosé d'été' – summer rosé to be drunk during the warm summer days ahead – dry or off-dry, fresh and fruity.

The taste of red wines

Most red wines are shockingly pale and light in intensity, sometimes almost like a deep rosé (see 'False rosés'), with the three grapes Poulsard, Trousseau and Pinot Noir becoming progressively deeper in colour. Characteristic Jura acidity will show on these wines, and alcohol is usually 12–13%, rarely more and in some years less, especially among those who eschew chaptalization.

Poulsard wines can be a watery pale pinky red to a very light ruby, with a quickly browning edge. To me the quintessential Poulsard wine will have vibrant red fruit aromas, perhaps redcurrant jelly, or close to cranberry but not as intense, and occasionally lightly floral aromas. And then there are the other Poulsard wines that are 'reductive' (as it's known technically), almost feral and animal-like. A certain level can be acceptable, but more is unpleasant and tends to show through on the palate. If the nose was fruity, the palate on the first sip is shockingly dry, but there should be juicy, gluggable fruit behind and a lightly tannic structure. Poulsards made to age, from low yields and using longer maceration, develop more complex, spicy characters with time, sometimes lasting for decades. Others are adored for their youthful and exuberant fruit character. However, Poulsards made with full carbonic maceration can lose the characteristics of the grape and the region completely.

Trousseau gives pale ruby wines too. Only in warm vintages or at very low yields from old vines will you get a slightly deeper colour than this, but Trousseau retains a youthful colour longer than Poulsard. On the nose you can sometimes detect a stony or mineral character, especially from Arbois AOC, and there is usually dark red cherry or blueberry fruit along with woodland scents like mushrooms or occasionally a meaty character. These scents often reappear on the palate, especially the stony, mineral character in the best wines, allied with good structure and a weight that belies the pale colour. With age these wines fill out, seeming to become richer as well as more complex in flavour. Trousseau can be deceptively fine indeed, worth getting to know.

Pinot Noir occasionally seems like a paler imitation of Burgundy, but in the best there will be not only joyous red fruit but the stony mineral character that is so distinctive of the Jura. The blends vary greatly and only rarely show distinct red fruit character, as most of them are made in the traditional way with somewhat longer old wood ageing than the single-varietal wines. This often stamps out any freshness of fruit and leaves a character of warm leather and old cellars, reminiscent of Burgundies from another age.

Crémant and friends – a sparkling success

Of all the wine styles, Crémant du Jura, the excellent-value traditional-method sparkling wine that accounts for more than one in four bottles of Jura wine, is the most logical to explain. Most is white and *brut* in style, made from Chardonnay base wine, giving a fresh appley character with a little spicy yeastiness if longer lees ageing is used. Dry and off-dry Crémant rosés are also made.

There are several reasons why the region is ideal for producing base wines for high-quality sparkling wine production. These include its cool continental climate with a relatively late spring and long growing season and the clay-limestone soils, both factors giving high acidity. The availability of Chardonnay, proven to be an excellent sparkling base, is useful too. Less obvious is the fact that historically the region was close to La Verrerie de la Vieille Loye, once one of the most important producers of glass wine bottles, and which supplied Champagne with bottles strong enough to withstand the extra pressure. The tradition of sparkling wines goes back to the early 19th century.

Prior to 1995 the *mousseux* sparkling designation was incorporated into the various Jura appellations and, although the wines had to be made by the traditional method for the AOCs, Jura producers made many different styles, some even oxidative. Once the Crémant du Jura appellation was established it encouraged producers to lift their game and gave more consistency.

The Crémant appellation rules are strict and producers must declare which vineyard plots will be used for Crémant grapes to allow inspections to be made. Harvest is early and must be by hand into small boxes with perforations, followed by whole bunch pressing. Usually this is in either a traditional wooden Champagne press or a

A bank of computer-operated gyropalettes for riddling Crémant du Jura at La Maison du Vigneron, Crançot.

pneumatic (bladder) press, though the old Vaslins can be adapted for use by taking the chains out. A maximum of 100 litres of juice may be pressed from 150kg of grapes. Fermentation is usually in tank (though a couple of producers are experimenting with oak and some use traditional old *foudres*) and malolactic fermentation is standard practice, though not obligatory.

Having made their base wines, most small and medium-sized producers in the Jura will use an outside specialist service for some of the subsequent processes, in particular bottling and disgorgement. However, many handle the riddling themselves, either manually in *pupitres* or using manually operated or automatic gyropalettes if they have the space. Whether or not they store the bottles, producers are the ones to decide how long the wine remains beyond the minimum nine months required *sur lattes* or in contact with the second-fermentation lees before riddling and disgorgement. The decision is usually made according to stock

levels, though the best producers aim for at least 18 months *sur lattes*. Even using a service, producers decide on the final treatments, including the important level of *dosage* (the small amount of sugar added to wine to top up after disgorgement and before inserting the cork), and they may choose to supply their own.

As a side note, the Henri Maire company does produce Vin Fou Crémant du Jura, but most of its sparkling wines sold under the Vin Fou brand (see 'History', p. 118) are made from base wines sourced outside the Jura and made sparkling by the more industrial tank method, with a second fermentation in tank followed by filtration.

The taste of Crémant du Jura

Most white Crémant du Jura is 100% Chardonnay and is a delicate sparkling wine, often with an apple character, sometimes with brioche or leesy/yeasty notes, depending on

79

Pet Nats – another kind of celebration

Known as Pétillant Naturel (literally 'naturally sparkling'), or Pet Nat for short, these sparkling wines have been making a comeback here in the past few years, as they have in the Loire Valley and elsewhere. They are sold under the Vin de France (previously Vin de Table) category, as they do not fit into AOC rules. Pet Nats are made in the same way as the *méthode ancestrale* (a term used elsewhere for the AOCs Bugey Cerdon, Clairette de Die and Blanquette de Limoux), involving a single fermentation in bottle without any addition of yeast and sugar.

Pet Nats are made from any of the local grape varieties, but Poulsard is a particular favourite, giving a vibrant pinky-ruby frothy wine. The wines are filled into sparkling wine bottles before fermentation is complete and finish their fermentation in bottle. Once these sparkling wines are ready for sale, some vignerons sell them as they are, somewhat cloudy. Others clarify using the traditional method of riddling and disgorging. There are many variations on the methods used.

The biggest advocates are producers who work in the natural way. Without the addition of yeast for a second fermentation these could be considered the ultimate natural sparkling wines, celebrating the purity of fruit they are made from. The resulting sparkling wines are sometimes slightly cloudy, packed full of fruit on the nose; on the palate they are light, all-too-easy drinking (usually only around 9–11% alcohol) and very fruity, with soft bubbles, lacking any yeast autolysis flavours. Producers have great fun with labels and names on these delightfully frivolous wines.

the length of time on second-fermentation lees. Above all, along with a relatively soft bubble it has a lovely fresh acidity, but with plenty of ripe fruit to balance, and is rarely more than 12% alcohol. I have found many people who declare Champagne too acidic but who really enjoy Crémant du Jura. Does the tell-tale minerality or stony character of Jura Chardonnay show through? I believe it does with the best. There is a welcome trend for producers to use some Pinot Noir (the other Jura grapes less so) in their base wine blends and these sparkling wines tend to appear a little richer and more mouth-filling, often finer too, with a longer finish. Savagnin is all too rarely part of the blend, but can add interesting weight and character.

Brut is the most prevalent style, though some producers sell a sweeter *demi-sec* white too. The term *brut*, as everywhere, gives flexibility with the *dosage*, but wines are gradually becoming drier, especially for exports, and there are even a few *brut zéro* (zero *dosage*) Crémants, particularly among organic producers.

Production of rosé Crémant du Jura is increasing, with blends varying widely, but many are 100% Pinot Noir, which gives a lovely red fruit character. When Poulsard is used, its tendency to somewhat animally, reductive flavours needs to be checked. In general the rosés are somewhat less dry than the white Crémants.

Vin de Paille – let's take a straw poll

One of Jura's legendary specialities, Vin de Paille (literally 'straw wine') is made as AOC Arbois, Côtes du Jura or L'Etoile under strict rules that not all producers are happy with. Very small quantities are made, less than 1% of total Jura production, yet this is much more than was made historically, when it was a real rarity. From dried grapes of any of the Jura varieties except Pinot, Vin de Paille wines range from medium sweet to lusciously sweet, balanced by good acidity and a minimum of 14% alcohol, plus three years' ageing (including 18 months in wood).

The Vin de Paille grape mix varies widely between producers and vintages, with the commonest being a blend of one-third each of Chardonnay, Savagnin and Poulsard, with occasionally a little Trousseau. However, even 100% Chardonnay or 100% Savagnin Vins de Paille exist. For those who use the three it is said that Chardonnay gives the richness, Savagnin the freshness and Poul-sard a touch of colour and fruit character.

Grapes, often from old vines, are harvested by hand early in the harvest period, during or usually directly after the harvest for Crémant grapes. Selected bunches must be perfectly healthy with no trace of rot (note this is the opposite of most sweet wines, which are harvested late and often made with grapes affected by noble rot). They may be picked on different days for the different varieties, and usually pickers place the bunches directly into the boxes for drying, which must then be transported very carefully to the winery. Picking early ensures good acidity levels needed for balance.

The bunches are then left to dry and shrivel for at least six weeks, and sometimes up to three or four months. Traditionally they were suspended from the rafters and this is still practised by a few estates, including Domaine Blondeau in Menétru-le-Vignoble, and some other vignerons such as Domaine Pignier will suspend a few

Grapes for Vin de Paille must be hand-picked. Frédéric Lornet's team place grapes carefully into wooden boxes in the vineyards and then transfer them to dry in metal crates, stacked high. A few producers, such as Domaine Blondeau, still suspend the bunches from the rafters (bottom).

81

Rogue 'Vin de Paille'

Certain producers have either accidentally or deliberately made sweet wines in the Vin de Paille style which do not reach the obligatory 14% alcohol, either because the harvested grapes started with good ripeness and were left to dry for longer than usual, leading to very high sugar levels at pressing, and/or because fermentation simply stopped too early. Either way, the wines end up much sweeter than normal Vins de Paille and may be as low as 8% or 9% alcohol, though more usually 11–13%. All these wines must be sold as Vin de France (table wine), usually including the lengthy statement 'Moût de raisins partiellement fermenté issu de raisins passerillés' ('Partially fermented grape must from dried grapes').

As far as I know it was Stéphane Tissot who started this trend in the late 1990s, but several others have followed with different styles and colours. Often these are some of the most delicious sweet wines from the region, with intense flavours, very high sweetness but with the freshness from high acidity and low alcohol to balance. Usually the wines are given 'fantasy names' and many producers have tried wordplays on the word *'paille'*, but the local Repression des Fraudes (the fraud squad, which controls labelling) always seems to arrive at the door, insisting that the wines' names be changed. It seems unfair that these gorgeous wines and their makers are treated like criminals.

The grapes for Stéphane Tissot's 2009 Spirale were dried for five months in boxes on straw. The back label states: 'The wine achieved its balance at 8% alc, depriving it of its appellation but allowing it to express power, finesse and freshness.'

bunches. Otherwise grapes were dried in boxes with straw. Today very few producers do this due to the difficulties of obtaining good straw and many also believe that the grapes do not dry as well on straw. Most producers place the bunches, well separated, into small wooden or plastic boxes. The boxes are stacked up in a warm (but not heated), well-ventilated loft area. Fans may be used, as they help to limit the risk of rot. Regular inspections are made to remove any grapes affected by grey rot. The grapes will gradually shrivel, losing up to half their volume and becoming a dark colour, sometimes with beneficial noble rot appearing on the surface.

The grape sugar increases up to a potential of 19–22% alcohol and the grapes are pressed, usually in December or January but sometimes as late as April. Pressing is usually a very slow process, taking a day or more; at the most 20 litres of juice are extracted from 100kg of grapes. Fermentation of the sugary grape juice is usually in tank or *foudre* and is incredibly slow, taking up to 18 months. This is followed by ageing in the normal barrels or in smaller ones, particularly *feuillettes* of around 110 litres. Some traditional Jura producers age the wines in oak without topping up so that they gain a slightly oxidative character (though no *voile* forms), while others make a fresher style.

The taste of Vin de Paille

There is no one taste profile for Vin de Paille, as the wines vary greatly in sweetness, balance and flavours. First it's worth revelling in the colours, which vary from mid-yellow through gold and orangey/ amber to mahogany in those that have red grapes in the mix. The bouquet may include notes of honey, *pain d'épice* (spiced bread or gingerbread) or fruit cake; raisins, figs or other dried fruits or a slight nutty character if oxidative. Despite the high alcohol, this does not usually show through on the bouquet, but can be marked on the palate, especially when the wine exceeds 15%.

Residual sugar levels vary widely from as little as 60g/l up to about 130g/l and these wines taste medium sweet to sweet, rarely lusciously sweet. Ideally there should be good acidity to balance the sugar and this, together with the alcohol, ensures extremely long ageing potential. Wines from the 19th century are occasionally sold at the annual auction of old bottles at the Percée du Vin Jaune.

These are wines to drink with cheese, or with a fruit tart, rather than a sweeter dessert, or simply to drink on their own – *vino di meditazione*, as the Italians so nicely refer to their own Vin Santo from grapes dried in lofts.

Vin de Paille bottles

All producers sell Vin de Paille in half-bottles (37.5cl), which vary from a standard Burgundy-style half-bottle to a half of the classic Jura bottle (left), or a modern, square-shouldered clear glass bottle (middle). Based on an old bottle design and in dark green glass, there is also a delightfully shaped designated Vin de Paille bottle (right), which was introduced in 2004 but not made obligatory. Sadly, few producers use it. There are complaints about the dark glass and difficulties in stacking it for storage.

Macvin du Jura
and other spirited wines

We are in a realm beyond wine here. Macvin is part of the family known as Vins de Liqueur or *mistelles*, fortified wines made from a blend of grape juice and grape spirit. In Macvin, made only in the Jura, grape juice from any of the five permitted Jura varieties must be blended with Marc du Jura, which is distilled from the grape solids (skins, pips, etc.) that come from the press. Even though the name Macvin is a contraction of *marc* and *vin*, there is no wine involved in the process at all – it's all about the grapes. Usually about 17% alcohol, there are white, red and rosé Macvins, moderately dry, with heady, sometimes spirity characters, but the best are dominated by a spicy grape character.

The *marc* must come from the producer's own grapes. In most of France the *distillerie ambulante* (mobile distillery) has disappeared, but thanks to the success of Macvin one thrives in the Jura. It is operated by the Brulerie du Revermont, which has a distillery in Nevy-sur-Seille. It can be seen outside the cellars of larger producers during the autumn and winter, steaming and bubbling like a Heath Robinson contraption. Smaller producers take their *marc* to the distillery and oversee the distillation there and a few larger producers have their own in-house distillery. This spirit must be a minimum of 52% alcohol and is usually 60%. It is aged in oak barrels for at least 14 months before it can be blended with grape juice – consequently the *marc* in a Macvin will be from the harvest of at least two years previous to the vintage of the grape juice. From 2014 the *marc* has to be made under AOC rules but not aged for as long as a Marc du Jura spirit sold in its own right (see p. 320).

A special Macvin bottle was released in 2001. Made from dark green glass, it has square shoulders, classic for many aperitifs such as vermouths, and has a distinct seal on the neck on which Macvin is marked.

White Macvin, the most common, is very easy to make. After pressing grapes at good ripeness levels (no chaptalization is allowed), many producers allow the juice to start fermentation, but only to 1% alcohol at most. This start of fermentation allows for a better mix with the *marc* than just using juice, and in the case of red or rosé Macvin it helps to extract the colour. The juice or must is mixed with the *marc* in the proportion of two-thirds to one-third; some producers will add one to the other little by little in layers to ensure the most efficient integration of the two. After blending, the mix is immediately put into old barrels and aged for at least ten months before being released for sale. Some will age for 18 months or more, though this is often dependent on stock levels. *Marc* and Macvin barrels are usually stored in the most humid section of the producer's cellar to avoid too much evaporation.

The taste of Macvin and its friends

Even within the rules of Macvin AOC, every producer has his or her own recipe.

Chardonnay is inevitably the most widely used grape variety, but Savagnin is sometimes used on its own or in a blend. For reds, the commonest variety is Pinot Noir, though any of the three red grapes may be used. Whether white, red or rosé, the colour of Macvin is usually highly attractive, influenced by the barrels, with golden-amber hints in the whites and mahogany tinges even in the rosés, and especially in the reds.

When smelling a Macvin, usually the first thing that hits is the spirit character, but, as they age, this evolves into more of a spicy and sometimes dried fruit character. The taste varies from off-dry to fairly sweet and in the best the *marc* will have integrated well into the juice so there will not be a particularly spirity taste, despite the 16–22% alcohol level, but rather one of spices and dried or candied fruits.

Vins de Liqueur made outside the Macvin regime are often sweeter and made with *marc* of insufficient age or Fine (distilled from wine) and with even greater taste variations.

The age of the Galant Jurassiens

The name 'Galant' was given to Macvin's historic predecessor by Margaret of Flanders, wife of Philip the Bold, one of the dukes of Burgundy. She was said to be very partial to the drink, and to share it with her lady friends. In those days, and right up until the AOC in 1991, many of these Vins de Liqueur were made from grape juice that had been cooked in a copper cauldron, sometimes with spices added.

Every producer had a secret recipe and there are several references to Savagnin having been used. The tradition is continued by several producers, with two paying homage to the name: Domaine Jacques Tissot with its Galant and Caves de Bourdy with its Galant des Abbesses. The latter is made according to the recipe written down by the Château-Chalon abbesses in the 16th century.

HISTORY

THE STORY OF THE WINE REGION

LE JURA

53 — Polig

Published in 1926, British wine writer P
Morton Shand devoted six pages of his
Book of wine to the Jura. An equivalent
contemporary wine book might have
one page at most. In it Shand refers to
the region's glorious past, citing French
kings, foreign royalty, writers and great
chefs who extolled its virtues. He also
mentions that the Jura's most famous
'son', Louis Pasteur, conducted many of
his wine experiments in the region and
goes on to describe the wines, including
'vins jaunes' or 'vins de garde du Jura' and
Château-Chalon, citing their longevity. But
our author from three generations ago
also noticed the decline of the region:

> The wines of the French Jura . . . have
> as great a fame and as honourable
> history as any great wines in Europe,
> though they have latterly fallen sadly
> out of fashion, especially since the
> baneful Phylloxera diminished the area
> under vines by nearly half.

Much of the history of the Jura wine
region, both in terms of the sequence
of events and the region's social history,
is shared with the rest of France, even
of Europe. But in this tiny idiosyncratic
region there are quirks and specifics, and

the Jura people always like to do things their way. Drawn from numerous sources, what follows is my own short history of how the Jura wine region arrived where it is today.

Early vines and wines

When Julius Caesar arrived in Gaul, today's Franche-Comté region and part of Burgundy were inhabited by the Sequani in a region of the same name. The Sequani were divided from the Helvetii (Swiss) people by the Jura Mountains, which were under the control of the Sequani. The Sequani called Caesar in to help repel an invasion of the Germanic people, while at the same time the Aedui in Burgundy were under threat from the Helvetii. Caesar repelled both threats but decided to remain, gaining victory in 51 BC and gradually bringing Roman civilization to the whole of Gaul.

As elsewhere in the Roman Empire, vines were brought in and planted by the Romans, although there is some evidence that wine was being made by the Sequani and indeed possibly long before, with some texts citing archaeological evidence that wine was made around 5000 BC, but references are conflicting. Pliny the Elder's (Plinus Secundus, also known as Pliny the Naturalist) book *Natural history* mentions a wine from Sequani with a taste of pine

A portion of the map of 'Gallia' from The atlas of ancient and classical geography *by Samuel Butler and Ernest Rhys (1907) shows the Sequani and the Helvetii either side of the 'Jura Mons'.*

resin. He believed that it came from the grape, but it was more likely a residue from the amphorae used for transport. Many contemporary Jura texts misquote this as being written by Pliny the Younger, and draw over-optimistic conclusions that he referred to Savagnin. Gallo-Roman remains in Pupillin found at the end of the 19th century included amphorae, believed to be what Pliny was referring to, but it is not certain whether the wine they contained was local or imported. Remains of a Roman cellar were also found in Proby, near Arlay, where the Emperor Probus had his official residence. Around 280 AD Probus gave the Sequani authorization to replant vines that a former emperor had ordered to be pulled up.

From the 5th century the 'Burgundians', Germanic peoples from around the Baltic coast, migrated to settle and farm in the Saône Valley basin of Sequani; some created settlements by the banks of the Cuisance river not far from Arbois and planted vines. The Franks seized the Burgundian kingdom in 534 AD, but three centuries later the kingdom detached itself and finally, in the 11th century, it was divided in two, with the areas close to the Jura Mountains becoming the Comté and the areas by the Saône Valley becoming the Duché, part of what then became known as the Duchy of Burgundy.

As in many places, the wealth of the Church and other rich landowners played an important part in the history of wine in the Jura in medieval times. However, the development of important salt mines dating back to at least the 6th century undoubtedly benefited the wealth of the region, including the emerging wine industry.

Salt – the Jura region's white gold

The geology of the Jura Mountains not only provided good vineyard land, but, after the slippage following the formation of the Alps, seams of salt were formed, providing the region with a major resource. Salt mines were established at the foot of the Premier Plateau of the Jura Mountains, close to forests that could provide wood for fuel used in the manufacturing process. The two largest salt mines were at Lons-le-Saunier and Salins-les-Bains. The latter became one of the most important salt works in Europe until its wood supply ran out, when a new centre was developed, the Saline Royale at Arc-et-Senans (see 'Visiting the region', p. 329). The towns derive their names from the industry – salin is the word for 'salty', une saline means 'salt works' ('les Bains' was added later, when it became a spa town); un saunier means 'a salt worker' or 'salt merchant'.

Salt was such a precious and vital commodity for food preservation that it attracted wealthy landowners, including the Church, which contributed to the development of the wine industry. It was highly taxed too. The salt tax (gabelle), levied in France from the 13th century, was thought to have been a factor in the French Revolution. The salt industry in the Jura declined in the 19th century, and the towns reinvented themselves as spa towns, with some success. There is still salt extraction today. The Belgian company Solvay has an important factory near Dole and a site close to Poligny that extracts salt by hydrolysis and electrolysis.

The Church, the Duchy of Burgundy and the emergence of Franche-Comté

Religious groups arrived in the Jura from the 7th century and established abbeys in Salins, Montigny, St-Lothain and Baume-les-Moines (later Baume-les-Messieurs). In Château-Chalon the Benedictines established an abbey in the 9th century with a fortress to protect it, but some texts attribute an abbey to the Burgundian Norbert and his wife Eusébia as early as the 7th century. Over the centuries that followed Cluniacs, Augustinians, Carthusians and most particularly Cistercians all established centres here. Wine being essential both for the sacrament and for drinking by their own people and travellers they sheltered, the monks and nuns arranged to clear the slopes of vegetation to plant vines. Documents of this period show the importance of vineyards in what is now Franche-Comté.

The village and important Benedictine abbey of Baume-les-Messieurs at the foot of the reculée. Until quite recently vineyards were cultivated on the nearby slopes.

Although leadership of the Kingdom of Burgundy was regularly disputed, political connections remained between what we now know as Burgundy and Franche-Comté, lying on either side of the Saône. Jean I de Chalon (1190–1267), one of the counts of Burgundy, was the most important landowner in the region during the 13th century. His many assets included the important town of Salins, wealthy due to its salt mines, and Arlay, with its strategic hill. There had already been a fort on the top of this hill, with vineyards below, but Chalon rebuilt it and the ruins remain today.

Chalon saw to it that vineyards were established for him at Arlay and around Arbois, Poligny, Domblans and L'Etoile, roughly equating to today's vineyard region. His descendants had close connections with the Royal Court in Paris through marriage, and it is likely that it was the Chalon family's own wine from Arbois that was first offered to the future King Philippe V, enabling the fame of Jura wine to reach royal circles in Paris and beyond. By the 12th century vineyards were also widespread in the area to the north of the Jura in the Doubs, due to the importance of the Church in Besançon.

First recognition of quality Jura wines

In 1366 the name of Franche-Comté appeared in official documents for the first time; by 1384 the region was part of Burgundy, with Philippe the Bold being the first of the dynasty of Burgundy dukes. As well as Jura wines appearing in the Royal Courts, in 1331 wines were purchased by

Vincent or Vernier?

Saint Vincent is recognized across Europe as the principal Catholic patron saint of vines, wines and vignerons and in the Jura a church was dedicated to him in the village of Arlay in the year 650 AD. The village pays homage with an annual festival recently linked to the Pressée du Vin de Paille (see 'Visiting the region', p. 337). But the Jurassiens like to be different and it is the lesser-known Saint Vernier who is most revered in this region, as he is in two even more obscure winegrowing regions, the Auvergne (as St-Verny) and the Coteaux de l'Auxois in Burgundy.

Saint Vernier, a young German called Werner von Oberwesel, was born in 1271 in the Rhineland. He is said to have been either the son of a vigneron or a vineyard worker and was murdered aged 16. There are rather murky circumstances around why he was considered a Christian martyr and subsequently canonized in the 15th century. Around 100 years later a relic (his finger) was brought to a church in the vigneron quarter of Besançon. Ever since, he has been venerated as the Jurassien vignerons' saint of choice (though I wonder how many know he was German), to be revered when things go right and blamed when they don't. He is no longer on any official list of Catholic saints, but his saint's day is celebrated on 19 April and a minor festival is held in Château-Chalon on the nearest Sunday, as well as in various other villages.

This painting in the church at Lavigny depicts Saint Vernier.

Pope Jean XXII for delivery to his palace in Avignon. The importance of wine as a trading commodity was being recognized and facilitated by taxation being eased.

After being ruled by a series of Burgundian dukes, the period between 1477 and 1678 saw Franche-Comté become a pawn between the various rulers of Europe. It was briefly ruled by the French crown together with the Duchy of Burgundy, and then came under the rule of the Habsburgs through the marriage of Mary of Burgundy to Maximilian of Austria. Their son, Philip the Handsome, became the first Habsburg king of Spain. When he died his son, Charles, was too young to rule, so his sister Margaret of Austria ruled at first, bringing a period of stability and prosperity to Franche-Comté. Charles eventually united the various territories, becoming

Henri IV

Reflet de Roi

aimait ce "fin nectar" qui se distille au Bon Pays.
Henri IV, qui savait être un galant homme, ne refusait
rien aux gentes compagnes de la cour, à qui il
écrivait : "Je vous baille, en témoignage d'estime
et d'amitié, quatre bouteilles de mon vin
d'Arbois". Au dire de son ministre Sully,
l'Arbois était "propre à émoustiller fortement
les dames de Paris". Comment s'étonner que
l'auteur des "Économies royales" dépêche
tous les ans un courrier pour lui acheter sur
place le vin "qui égaie les amours" ? !

DOMAINE
DANIEL DUGOIS
PROPRIÉTAIRE-RÉCOLTANT

ARBOIS
APPELLATION ARBOIS CONTROLÉE

TROUSSEAU
Grevillière

Domaine Dugois labels honour Henri IV, who used the wine of Arbois freely to seduce Parisian ladies and to keep government ministers on his side.

Charles V, Holy Roman Emperor and King Charles I of Spain. There followed a period of Spanish rule often evoked in the wine region to explain why making wines aged *sous voile* came to be known in the Jura, but real evidence is scant.

At this time the Jura's wines were sold to people living in the mountain areas and the plains, where vineyards could not flourish, and they were also exported over the mountains to Switzerland. An old map from this period shows the Chemin Vinetier, a designated route over the mountains from Arbois via Salins. The wines were enjoyed by the courts of Europe and Maximilian I and Charles V allowed wines to travel freely within their vast territories. Unfortunately this was short-lived, as under Philip II of Spain a law was enacted in 1567 that vines should not be planted where the land was suitable for grain. Stubborn as ever, the Jurassien vignerons tricked the authorities into believing that their vineyard land was entirely unsuitable for grain. One of their – to this day, much-vaunted – admirers during this time was Henri IV of France, a lover and supporter of both wine and the arts, who managed to enjoy some Arbois wines between battles with the Spanish. Jura wines had become so popular through both the Church and the Royal Courts that by the 17th century fraudulent copies began to appear, inspiring Arbois and Poligny to forbid any non-local wines from the towns.

Much of the 17th century saw turmoil as the French crown battled to gain control of Franche-Comté, much valued for its woodlands and salt mines, and France eventually succeeded for good in 1678 under the reign of Louis XIV. In the meantime, in 1627 the first wine fraternity was formed in Arbois in the style of a medieval trade group, and named in honour of Saint Vernier. As well as organizing religious processions and services, the Confrérie de Saint Vernier acted as the first association of many here to battle for the rights of vignerons. The middle of the century saw an influx of both Swiss and Savoyards into the Jura, who brought with them their own expertise in viticulture as well as new vine varieties.

The big expansion: 1750–1850

Once political stability had returned to the region, a huge expansion of the vineyards began, and in the late 17th and early 18th centuries one begins to see references to good and bad grape varieties, with various orders to eradicate certain of the latter. It was the perennial battle of quantity versus quality. Savagnin was already valued as the best variety, but Chardonnay was more productive and deemed good for sparkling wines, and eventually became an accepted

The Vin Jaune mysteries – Arbois or the Abbesses?

Was Château-Chalon where the first Vin Jaune was made? Or was it Arbois? No one really knows and, although it seems certain from wine descriptions that Vin Jaune-style wines were made in the 17th century or possibly earlier, the term 'Vin Jaune' has been in use only since the early 19th century and, until more recently, mainly in connection with Arbois wines. Earlier, especially in Château-Chalon, such wine was known as either *vin de garde* ('wine for keeping') or *vin de gelée* ('wine from the frost'), indicating that grapes were picked after the first frosts.

The term 'Vin de Garde' was much more widely used than Vin Jaune until the 20th century. As AOC Château-Chalon is by definition a Vin Jaune, Domaine Macle marks Vin de Garde instead.

The history of Château-Chalon and its community of abbesses is inextricably linked with this mystery story. The earliest written mention of the abbey in Château-Chalon dates from 869 AD, when it was conceded by King Lothaire II to the Besançon Church. The abbey seems always to have been devoted to women, and 'les dames' ('the ladies') of the abbey

developed a fine reputation for their wines from early on. Novices were accepted only if they could prove 16 'quarters of nobility', meaning that they had noble connections for at least four generations. Many of the abbesses had royal lineage or were connected to the House of Burgundy, giving them excellent connections through which to sell the abbey's wine production.

The fact that at one time the Château-Chalon abbey was the richest and most powerful landowner in the Jura vineyard area makes it most likely that a wine of Vin Jaune type originated here, aged for many years in barrel. The history is linked with that of the Savagnin grape, but how the understanding of encouraging the *voile* to form in barrel came to arrive here is subject to much speculation. Were barrels simply left behind when at one point the abbesses had to escape into hiding due to persecution? Was it simply a happy accident and the wine found to be special? Or was there some connection due to the region's historical links with Jerez in Spain (Sherry) or Tokaj in Hungary? The latter theory seems most unlikely, but no one knows for sure.

As for Arbois, we only know that in the 18th century they made *vin de garde*, as witnessed by the Vercel collection of 1774 wines. Even by Pasteur's time these wines were still known as *vins de garde*, though they were held in the highest esteem, but the 'Vin Jaune' term seems to have crept in earlier here than in Château-Chalon.

variety, having once been banned, as it was considered as a 'bad' grape. As gastronomy developed and with it wine appreciation, quality wines (*vins fins*) were identified and the Jura became well known for its *vins de garde* (the forerunner of Vins Jaunes), Vins de Paille, Arbois reds and sparkling wines.

This period must be seen particularly in the context of the whole of France – a time of population expansion, but also just before the transport revolution of the railways allowed wine to be sent across the country. The vineyards extended south to St-Amour and north to the important city of Dole, and there were further vineyards in the Doubs and the upper Saône Valley around Besançon. By 1788 there were more than 15,000ha of vineyards and three generations later, in 1866, the area planted reached its peak of around 20,000ha. More than 80% of the grapes grown were red for everyday drinking wine – *vins communs*. Vintages varied hugely in terms of quantity and quality – some years no wine was made at all, and Vin Jaune was made only in very good vintages and by very few families.

The church of St-Pierre in the middle of the historic village of Château-Chalon above the vineyards.

This period also saw the first detailed studies of the best methods of viticulture. In 1774 a government inspector from Besançon issued a list of bad grape varieties, but Chardonnay was spared this time. Winemaking was studied too, in particular to avoid problems of the wine 'going off' when it travelled. Many of these studies were government sponsored. In 1801 came an important treatise and subsequent book, *L'art de faire, gouverner et perfectionner les vins* (*The art of making, managing and perfecting wines*), written by chemist and politician Jean-Antoine Chaptal on orders from Napoleon Bonaparte (Chaptal gave his name to the process of chaptalization, which was introduced in this era). This became a bible for all winemaking families.

Interlude: a view from afar in the 1850s

Dipping into British wine literature at the beginning of this period, we see how the

Jura was viewed from afar. Cyrus Redding (1785–1870) was a journalist who worked for a spell in Paris before turning to book writing on a range of subjects. His 1833 wine classic, *A history and description of modern wines*, was a highly regarded wine reference for years and in 1860 he published *French wines and vineyards; and the way to find them*. This includes three dense pages on the wines of Franche-Comté. Rating Jura wines far higher than those of Doubs or Haute-Saône, he noted that the Jura exported wine all over France. Redding gives precise figures of hectares planted (which tie in with the French literature),

production levels and prices for vintages in the early 1850s. He notes that quantities are down due to oidium, a foretaste of disasters to come.

Writing about the Lons-le-Saunier area, he observed:

> The best white wines *de garde* are made at Château Chalons [*sic*], the best *mousseux* at Etoile [*sic*] and Quintigny. The best reds are at Château Chalons, Menétru, Frontenay and Blandans. The straw wines are considered excellent and stomachic [assisting digestion], somewhat resembling Spanish wines. The reds are

La Vieille Loye and the *clavelin*

One of the reasons for Jura wines' success from the 18th century was the availability of glass relatively close to home, enabling the best wines to be bottled and aged. The forest of Chaux, east of the city of Dole, is one of the largest in France. Between the 13th and 19th centuries the forest became home to hundreds of woodcutters, and industries developed that relied on wood for heating. This included several glassworks, including La Vieille Loye, one of the largest and most famous in France, which was founded in 1506 on the instructions of Margaret of Austria. It continued production until 1931.

La Vieille Loye provided bottles mainly for Champagne and Burgundy, and Jura producers had to make do with lesser-quality rejects. The bottles were still very expensive, so only the best wines would have been bottled. The famous Vercel Arbois 1774 wines are in bottles of about 80cl made by La Vieille Loye, and many old

clavelin-style bottles made by the company for *vin de garde* still exist.

As early as the 18th century certain Château-Chalon families asked the glassworks to create a special bottle for their *vins de garde*, with the name of Château-Chalon moulded on to the bottle, and these appear to be the first *clavelins*, but it is not certain that the name was used. However, in 1914 Abbot Clavelin of Nevy-sur-Seille, the village at the foot of the vineyard hill of Château-Chalon, ordered 30 of this type of bottle with his name also moulded on to them. The origins of the size and shape are even less certain. Records of La Vieille Loye state that Clavelin ordered a bottle '*dite anglaise*' ('English type'), with a volume of 65cl. 'English type' probably refers to the way of making the bottle rather than the size, which relates to no English bottle size.

generous and heady. The nature of the season as to abundance or scarcity, little affects the straw wines or those *de garde*, as they are only drunk very old.

Moving on to wine around Arbois, Redding rates the red wines of Arsures, Salins, Vadans and Molamboz, mentioning Arsures (including Montigny, I presume) as 'in most esteem, having more strength and colour' and dismisses the reds of Poligny as 'common'. His descriptions from over 150 years ago of making wines *de garde* and straw wine are very close to how Vin Jaune and Vin de Paille are made today, the major difference being that the wines were aged in barrel for longer – according to Redding, 10–12 years for *vin de garde* and five to six years for Vin de Paille.

The end of the tax strike in Arbois in 1906. The banner reads: 'Long live freedom, wine and the still,' referring to the vignerons' right to distil their wines.

A century of battles: 1850–1950

How many disasters can one industry and one region bear? The series of vine diseases, wine adulteration problems, economic meltdowns and major wars that took place from the middle of the 19th century until after the Second World War affected all areas of Europe. However, despite their best efforts to combat them, the effects on the Jura wine region were more dramatic, as can be seen both by the much greater vineyard decline and by the slower rate of recovery.

Here is a list of the disasters in a short and brutal manner:

- 1850: increased competition from southern French wines due to railways, and from beer – a brewery is established in Poligny
- 1852: powdery mildew (the oidium fungus) attacks the vineyards
- 1870s: economic hardship sets in after the Franco-Prussian War
- 1879: phylloxera louse arrives in the south of the Jura at Beaufort
- 1884: downy mildew (the peronospera fungus) attacks the vineyards
- 1886: black rot, another fungal disease, appears
- 1892: the whole region is affected by phylloxera
- early 1900s: adulteration problems increase; sales and profits slump
- 1906: tax strike in Arbois to protest against new laws prohibiting distillation of own *marc*
- 1914–18: First World War – lives lost and vineyards neglected
- 1920–39: further economic hardship
- 1939–45: Second World War – yet more lives lost and neglected vineyards

An approximate comparison of areas planted for each grape variety between the 1850s and today

1850s

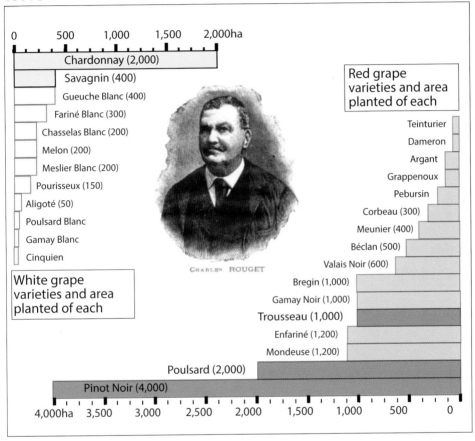

0   500   1,000   1,500   2,000ha

Chardonnay (2,000)
Savagnin (400)
Gueuche Blanc (400)
Fariné Blanc (300)
Chasselas Blanc (200)
Melon (200)
Meslier Blanc (200)
Pourisseux (150)
Aligoté (50)
Poulsard Blanc
Gamay Blanc
Cinquien

White grape
varieties and area
planted of each

CHARLES ROUGET

Red grape
varieties and area
planted of each

Teinturier
Dameron
Argant
Grappenoux
Pebursin
Corbeau (300)
Meunier (400)
Béclan (500)
Valais Noir (600)
Bregin (1,000)
Gamay Noir (1,000)
Trousseau (1,000)
Enfariné (1,200)
Mondeuse (1,200)
Poulsard (2,000)
Pinot Noir (4,000)

4,000ha   3,500   3,000   2,500   2,000   1,500   1,000   500   0

Today

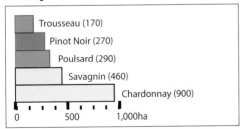

Trousseau (170)
Pinot Noir (270)
Poulsard (290)
Savagnin (460)
Chardonnay (900)

0   500   1,000ha

The figures in the top chart are an estimate of plantings at their peak in the mid-19th century, during the life of Charles Rouget, author of Les vignobles du Jura et de la Franche-Comté, *published in 1897. They indicate that much more red was grown than white, the reverse of today's plantings (see chart below). The top chart also indicates the preponderance of both Chardonnay and Pinot Noir over local varieties.*

During the phylloxera crisis, from the peak of plantations in 1873 to 1900 the vineyard area reduced in the Jura by 62%, compared to 27% on average for France as a whole. Although problems with vine diseases were universal throughout Europe, phylloxera always makes the headlines and takes the blame for the huge decline in vineyard plantings in the Jura and other minor wine regions, yet it was far from the sole reason. Explanation for the difference is complicated, because by the time phylloxera arrived in the Jura sales and production were already declining fast. Both mildew attacks hit hard because, unlike phylloxera, which kills individual vines slowly, mildew has an immediate effect, causing complete harvests to be lost. Another important factor was

that wines from southern France could now be transported long distances and customers found them stronger, more reliable and cheaper.

Many Jura vignerons simply gave up, packed up their families and homes, and left for the cities to find other work – population statistics for Arbois, for example, show nearly 7,000 people living there in 1850, while by 1900 this was down to 4,200; most Jura wine villages show a drop of 20–30% in the same period and this decline continued. Most vignerons owned less than 1ha of vines, which was no longer enough to live on, so many simply replanted only enough vines to make wine for their families, especially if they could find other work – most notably for the expanding railway network. Some became mixed farmers, practising polyculture, taking on dairy cows and planting cereal crops as well as vines. This trend continued throughout this century of crisis and beyond.

Certificate awarded to the Arbois Fruitière at the annual Société de Viticulture du Jura's competition in 1907, one year after the creation of the cooperative.

The period up to 1900 could easily have been the end of the Jura wine region, yet it was to be sorely tested for a further 50 years. However, this was in one sense survival of the fittest, as only the best vignerons stayed and Arbois in particular had stalwarts who fought both for Jura wine's honour and to give much-needed support to the vignerons. Born in Arbois, Auguste Napoléon Parandier (1804–1901) was one – a noted railway engineer, he also became a geologist, studying first the local mountains and next how water systems affected both industry and agriculture. In 1858 he founded the Société de Viticulture et d'Horticulture d'Arbois and was president until 1896. Its activities ranged from discussions on grape varieties, viticulture (including battling the prevalent diseases) and quality winemaking to finding ways of combating falling sales and increases in government restrictions and taxes. The Society was particularly active from 1877 until 1914, and its quarterly bulletins reveal discussions on many current preoccupations, such as submitting wines to national competitions, fighting anti-alcohol lobbies and, above all, trying to encourage vignerons to aim for quality rather than quantity to achieve better prices for their wines.

In terms of wine quality, the biggest problem was that much replanting after phylloxera was done with American vines (direct producers) or American vine hybrids, which are unsuitable for fine wines. As discussed in the 'Grape varieties' chapter, there had been over 40 grape varieties in Franche-Comté, documented by Charles Rouget, a vigneron from Salins, in his extraordinarily useful and comprehensive book of 1897, but many were never replanted. The big five varieties in today's AOC had already been established as the grapes that could produce high-quality wines, but convincing vignerons to plant these often fickle varieties

was another matter. Although some government subsidies were available for replanting, it was recommended that the new grafted vines should be planted in rows using wires – a much more labour-intensive method than earlier, when vines were planted *en foule* (literally 'in a crowd'), each supported by a single stake. Steeper and higher slopes were completely abandoned, yet there was one positive outcome – the phylloxera crisis improved viticultural techniques at a stroke. Vignerons learned to select the best vines for grafting, used improved machinery for ploughing, treated vines to prevent disease and even shared equipment and expertise.

Another cloud across France was that the period of phylloxera opened the door to fraudsters who made 'wine' by adding sugar and water to *marc* to referment. By the early 1900s there was a glut of poor-quality wines, both real and fraudulent, with prices plummeting. To add insult to injury, the government imposed more taxes, introduced regulations restricting the movement of wine, and withdrew the rights of vignerons to distil their own *marc*. This all became too much and in 1906 Arbois vignerons became probably the first in France to stage a *grève des impôts*, a tax protest against all government authorities – this was a year before a much bigger and more violent group protested in the Languedoc region. The strike in Arbois lasted almost two months and a petition garnered great support beyond the boundaries of the town, with 600 signatories. Although some vignerons lost heart, especially when local authorities decided to seize their furniture in lieu of tax and auction it off, incredibly, they won. Just before the furniture auction was to take place, the national government backed down on several measures, including giving back their rights to distillation.

Throughout this time the top wines of

Street mural in Arbois depicting the annual procession of the vignerons carrying Le Biou (a giant bunch of grapes) to be blessed in the church.

Arbois were being presented at important competitions in Paris, winning medals and respect. The traditional festival and procession of Le Biou (see 'Visiting the region', p. 337), in which four vignerons carry a massive 'bunch' of grapes to be blessed in church before the harvest, was re-created for the Paris Exhibition of 1900. Alexis Arpin (1867–1946), a vigneron and secretary of the Arbois association, was behind many of these actions, including the tax strike. To combat the incidence of fraudulent wines being sold under the Arbois name, he achieved protection on a national basis for the name Vin d'Arbois in 1907, which was an early precursor of AOCs.

The wine region as a whole was becoming more organized. The Société de Viticulture du Jura (SVJ), which plays a vital role to this day, was created around 1905 and links were forged with regional chambers of agriculture and with national wine organizations, such as the Syndicat National de la Viticulture, to help combat fraud. At the close of the 19th century the Crédit Agricole bank was established and a laboratory was set up by the Jura department. Meantime, once again it was the Arbois vignerons who were the first to create a cooperative, choosing the name Fruitière, as used for centuries by their Jura neighbours producing Comté cheese.

The meaning of 'fruitière' is debated, but one explanation is that each member brings in the 'fruit' of his or her labour. The Fruitière Vinicole d'Arbois was born in 1906 with an initial membership of 31 vignerons. With support from the town's mayor, their shared equipment was established in the cellars of Château Pécauld (today home to the Jura wine museum and the CIVJ, among other organizations). Not long afterwards a second cooperative, with different political persuasions, was set up just to sell wine, but it did not last long. Soon more wine cooperatives were set up in Montigny-les-Arsures, Pupillin, Poligny, Lavigny and L'Etoile. Of these, only Pupillin survives, though there are two more recent ones at Voiteur and Le Vernois. All these initiatives were actions of the strongest and most determined vignerons, who battled with the many crises facing the wine world to ensure the future of Jura wine. In the years leading up to 1914 they had to deal with a string of poor vintages, with frost, hail and serious mildew problems.

The First World War did untold damage here as elsewhere. When vignerons went to war their vines were kept alive by women, old people and children. Those who survived returned changed, and for many the hard work on the land was too much for them and they left. The tenacious held on, most notably Joseph Girard (1878–1955), who was president of the Arbois Société de Viticulture and subsequently a member of the Institut National des Appellations d'Origine (INAO). Thanks to his hard work, just under 30 years after protecting the name Vin d'Arbois, in 1936 Arbois became one of the first six AOCs in France, with Château-Chalon, L'Etoile and Côtes du Jura following soon after. Then the Second World War intervened, with more lives lost and German occupation from June

1940. There were serious difficulties for the vignerons during the war. Georges Tournier, director of Château d'Arlay's vineyards and president of the SVJ for many years, had to fight to procure copper sulphate to spray against mildew.

By the end of the Second World War there were less than 4,000ha of vineyards left (one-fifth of the mid-19th-century peak and less than half that of 1905). What was worse was that only around 1,000ha were of the five varieties eligible to make AOC wines, despite this being a requisite of members of the Arbois Fruitière since 1928. The bitter 1956 frost and subsequent tiny harvest drove away yet more vignerons. Planted vineyard area in the Jura plummeted to less than 2,000ha by 1960, with less than 800ha eligible for AOC.

Slow and steady recovery: 1960 onwards

The influence of Henri Maire's successful wine ventures in the Jura is undeniable in the recovery of the Jura wine region. He showed what could be done by introducing mechanization and, more importantly, proved that there was a demand for Jura wines. Yet there were other factors. At the end of the 1940s the Marshall Plan, funded by the Americans, was helping aspects of French agriculture, including providing lower-priced tractors, for the mechanization that was badly needed to make Jura viticulture viable. Even so, according to the de Brisis brothers in *Vins, vignes et vignobles du Jura*, only 70 out of 6,500 vine farmers owned a tractor in 1970, partly because the average holding remained tiny.

The French war with Algeria in its fight for independence between 1954 and 1962 meant that the sons of Jura's vignerons fought alongside young vignerons from more successful wine regions. This had a significant effect in changing attitudes, as had, to a lesser extent, the two world wars. Men returned from these wars changed, and were no longer willing to help their fathers with a farm that had perhaps a handful of cows, a small area of cereal crops and less than a hectare of vines. Partly inspired by Henri Maire, they could see a better future specializing in vineyards and, for the most adventurous, creating a wine domaine: growing vines and making and selling their own Jura wine. It doesn't sound very daring today, but back then it was a courageous move and a minor revolution in this sleepy backwater that had gone through so much in the preceding 100 years.

Around 1970 the Jura department took significant steps to help the wine industry, resulting in extensive plantings. This aid took several forms, the idea being to help young vignerons (usually defined as under 35) to obtain land for planting, at the same time ensuring that the wine region became more quality orientated, producing wines eligible for the AOC. The most important initiative

The view from the top of the vineyard slope in Le Vernois shows the distinct pattern of roadways built in the remembrement, *or restructuring, that took place in 1968.*

was that the region made compulsory land purchases in order to offer them at special prices to young vignerons. As was happening in agricultural areas across Europe, aid was offered to vineyard villages for *remembrement*. Under the scheme vineyard parcels were reconstructed, drainage and roads were added and larger, contiguous vineyards were established, replacing the small scattered parcels that had come about through generations of inheritance and marriage. Wine students may recognize this process as similar to the German *Flürbereinigung*, which extensively reshaped German wine regions.

The first vineyard village in France that undertook a *remembrement* was in the Jura – Le Vernois in 1968. Other Jura villages followed, including Château-Chalon, but on a smaller scale in 1977, and much later Pupillin in the 1990s. In Arbois Henri Maire and (on a smaller scale) the Rolet family and Roger Martin of Domaine de la Pinte carried out private *remembrements* from the 1940s to the 1970s, purchasing vineyards from neighbours and building up the infrastructure to improve their estates.

Another important influence in this period was better education, as vocational courses in viticulture and oenology began to be widely available. Many Jura winegrowers were able to take short or long viticulture and oenology courses at the *lycée* (college or high school) in Beaune or further afield. From 1970 the Jura established its own wine courses at the *lycée* in Montmorot, just outside Lons-le-Saunier, and vineyards were obtained for students to work on. In the meantime the departmental laboratory at Poligny also had a big influence in helping vignerons to improve the quality of their wines. The agricultural sector of the laboratory became permanent and was led by an exceptionally hard-working

and skilled man, André Blum, from 1946 until his death in 1974, when he was succeeded by his assistant Jacques Levaux, now retired, but still much respected. As well as analysis, the lab offered an advisory service to vignerons along with classes. In conjunction with the SVJ and other regional and national wine bodies, the lab conducted studies on anything from clonal selection of grape varieties to the mysteries of how the Vin Jaune yeasts work or where best to dry the grapes for Vin de Paille.

Three discoveries by the departmental laboratory in connection with Vin Jaune, and hence affecting all oxidative wines, have had a very important influence on the course of the history of Jura wines. First, André Blum and his laboratory analyzed Savagnin wines in barrel and discovered that, when the barrels were developing in the right direction for Vin Jaune, the level of acetaldehyde (ethanal) would rise, while the volatile acidity would fall. These two measures proved invaluable, and became the basis for the laboratory to offer the routine six-monthly testing procedure on all barrels aged oxidatively. Second, they identified that barrels stored in dry cellars were far more likely to establish a good veil of yeast than humid cellars. Third, in the 1960s the laboratory successfully isolated and tested the use of a cultured yeast to promote growth of the *voile* – the process of *ensemencement*. These developments paved the way for many producers to make Vin Jaune routinely each vintage.

Evolution of wine styles since the 1960s

In 1988 the region created the Comité Interprofessionnel des Vins du Jura (CIVJ) to bring together the producers of all sectors under one banner and to market the region as a whole. With a small permanent staff, the president alternates between a vigneron and someone working for a négociant. It is difficult to measure how much they have influenced the styles of wine marketed by the region, but they do at least gather some market statistics. The CIVJ also organizes export missions.

Styles of wines within the various Jura AOC rules have changed with the times, according to fashions in the broader wine world to an extent, but certain Jura producers have chosen to develop or reinvent different styles. From the 1970s the Arbois Fruitière, with its Cuvée Béthanie, followed by Henri Maire and others, promoted oxidative wines in particular, popularizing the Chardonnay/Savagnin blend. Often known as 'Tradition', it is a style that is not at all a traditional Jura wine, but is seen as a good entry into understanding the taste of Vin Jaune and it

has been highly successful on the regional market. As I write in 2013, more than 20 years after the first ones were made, a heated debate continues – is Savagnin *ouillé* (topped up) a mere fad or is it here to stay? Wine styles continue to evolve in many directions, such as adopting Burgundy methods for fermentation and ageing of Chardonnay, or using full or semi-carbonic maceration for reds.

The biggest recent successes in sales have undoubtedly been the rise of Macvin and Crémant, which have done particularly well since being awarded their AOCs in 1991 and 1995 respectively. And on a much smaller scale younger Jura producers, particularly the organic group, are increasingly finding a following for their Pétillant Naturel sparkling wines and non-Macvin-designated liqueur wines with no AOC. More fads or here to stay?

Sadly, both Vin de Paille and Vin Jaune (including Château-Chalon) do not achieve the sales or price levels they deserve, despite the huge publicity surrounding the Percée du Vin Jaune festival. Although everyone loves to taste these wines, sales remain difficult for many producers.

Despite some ongoing problems, the Jura wine region is in good health compared to other French wine regions, especially considering the poor state it was in only two generations ago. At last, at the start of the 21st century, it seems to be recovering the status it once had of intriguing and impressing palates around the world, just as it did in the 17th to 19th centuries (see 'The future for Jura producers', p. 308).

DOMAINE
DU
PÉLICAN

ARBOIS

SAVAGNIN OUILLÉ

2012

MARQUIS D'ANGERVILLE
PROPRIÉTAIRE-RÉCOLTANT À ARBOIS, JURA, FRANCE

A label from one of the newest Jura estates, which is focused on exports. Although the pelican is the old heraldic symbol of the town of Arbois, the label design is modern and the use of the word 'ouillé' is indicative of the growing appreciation of this white wine style.

THE PEOPLE WHO MADE A DIFFERENCE

In relatively recent history there have been a few strong, innovative characters in the Jura who have helped this tiny, diverse and intriguing wine region survive adversity, thrive while remaining authentic, and be noticed. Some of these key people were mentioned in the previous chapter, such as the founders of the various winegrowers' societies, the founders of the cooperatives, André Blum of the Poligny laboratory, Charles Rouget, who recorded the grape varieties, and Joseph Girard, who did so much to obtain the AOCs for the region.

Louis Pasteur and Henri Maire were also mentioned in passing, but they deserve more. This chapter tells the story of their influence and that of a few other people who have had a significant effect on the wine region as it is today. In the Pasteur profile I have included an often-forgotten Jurassien named Alexis Millardet, who helped to save the vineyards from pests. There is a profile about the Vercel family and their precious old wines, and a

section on the Bourdys. The Jeunets, Michelin-star chefs, have given invaluable support to the wine producers of the region and have helped Arbois to become a gastronomic centre. It was one bold vigneron, Bernard Badoz, who had the idea for the hugely successful Percée du Vin Jaune festival, and a whole group of vignerons for the more recent success story Le Nez dans le Vert. The most modest of them all is Pierre Overnoy, admired by many for his single-minded natural approach to winemaking, and of the same generation Jean Macle, who worked so tirelessly to maintain the high standards of Château-Chalon.

All these people are linked together by their profound love of the region and respect for the traditions of its wines, and within each profile you will find that there are links to at least one of the others – it seems almost as if everyone in the Jura is part of one big family. I feel confident too that there are successors to these important figures, who in generations to come will take over the mantle of those profiled here. Somehow the Jura invokes both intense passion and great determination in the people who live and work there – it is indeed a special place, shaped not only by its natural surroundings, but also by its people.

Photographed aged 89, Xavier Grandvaux, born in 1905, was a well-known grape-grower in Le Vernois and one of the founders of the Caveau des Byards wine cooperative. He had ten children and was the grandfather of Denis Grandvaux of Caveau des Byards and of Marie-Florence, Jean-Etienne and Antoine Pignier.

Louis Pasteur – scientist *1822–95*

Every wine region in the world has reason to be grateful for the studies and discoveries of Pasteur, but the Jura wine region is not only grateful, it is immensely proud to honour him as one of their own. Experiments in both the vineyard he owned and in the cellars of Arbois examining how micro-organisms functioned have had lasting significance not only for the world of wine and other alcoholic drinks, but for the medical world and our own health.

Louis Pasteur was born in Dole, the son of a tanner. In 1830 the family moved to Arbois, where his father had purchased a small tannery by the bridge over the River Cuisance. As a schoolboy in Arbois his studies were unremarkable, apart from his eye for detail, which manifested itself in his drawings of his family. However, he was encouraged to continue his studies, and left home for Besançon to pursue a Baccalauréat in Literature and Mathematics. Fortunately for us he continued with the sciences, and after two attempts was accepted into the elite Ecole Normale Supérieure, a first-rate university in Paris, obtaining a degree and subsequently a doctorate in sciences in 1847. He conducted his first researches into crystallography while a teaching professor at

the University of Strasbourg, where he also married. Moving on to the University of Lille for three years, he eventually returned to the Ecole Normale in Paris as director of scientific studies in 1856.

Each summer Pasteur would return to the family home in Arbois for the two-month summer holiday, taking his family and his microscopes on the ten-hour train journey from Paris. He created a laboratory in the house and pursued his experiments there as well as in the local wine cellars and vineyards. In 1858 he was examining a spoilt wine under the microscope and recognized a filament that was similar to lactic bacteria that he had identified the previous year in fermentation experiments on other alcoholic beverages. At the time the scientific thinking was that fermentation was spontaneous, but Pasteur wanted to prove that the process was caused by bacteria in the presence of air.

At this point he began to develop his germ theory – that an outside living organism was responsible for disease, thus proving how diseases could be contagious. Later he was motivated on a personal level in this work by the fact that two of his daughters died of typhoid fever. As the study of microbiology progressed, it was becoming better understood that drinking water could be dangerous; Pasteur often said that wine was the healthiest and most hygienic liquid to drink.

Pasteur's studies on wine

In the meantime the wine industry in France had a problem. By the mid-19th century it was a massive producer of wine, but there were many problems, with wines showing faults such as turning to vinegar,

One of Pasteur's sayings featured on a book of stamps: 'Wine is the most healthful and hygienic of all beverages.'

CARNET de 20 TIMBRES-POSTE à 0ʳ 50 | 10ᶜ|

Le vin est la plus saine et la plus hygiénique des boissons.

PASTEUR

Association de Propagande pour le vin. Béziers.

CARLOS COURMONT Concessionnaire

Jacques Tissot's barrel cellar under the arcades in the centre of Arbois is said to be one of the cellars in which Pasteur conducted his experiments.

being hazy or refermenting, meaning that exporting the wine was increasingly difficult. Put simply, most wines didn't travel well. Pasteur devised a plan: to prove his theory of different micro-organisms present in the atmosphere and potentially causing disease, rather than experiment on an animal or a person, he would experiment on wine ferments during harvest, thus helping the wine industry as well.

In 1862 Pasteur was elected to the illustrious Académie des Sciences (an occasion celebrated with the renowned Arbois 1774 made by Anatoile Vercel). He requested support from President Napoleon III for a research team to conduct experiments in Arbois during September and October 1863, and again in 1864. He rented a house with an abandoned café on the ground floor that he turned into a makeshift laboratory, something the locals who peered in apparently found incredible. 'Like something out of Nostradamus', wrote

Duclaux, one of Pasteur's assistants and later a great scientist in his own right. Here the team conducted a range of experiments on grapes purchased from local vignerons, pressing them and analysing the sugars and acidities of the juice.

While his team were in the laboratory, Pasteur would go on field studies, going from cellar to cellar, asking a multitude of questions about methods of making, storing and bottling the wines and trying to understand the problems the vignerons were having with faulty wines. Once Pasteur was back in Paris he asked his old neighbour and family friend Jules Vercel to conduct various tests on his wines.

Through this research he discovered the positive role oxygen could play during fermentation (oxygen was already known as an enemy to wine) as well as the action of various microbes. By 1865 he was recommending killing the microbes by raising the temperature of the wine to 55–65°C in cask or bottle and taking the heat away the moment it reached the desired temperature.

Pasteur and Vin Jaune

During his studies in the 1860s Pasteur identified that what he referred to as *Mycoderma vini* – known as the *fleur* ('flower') by the vignerons, now known as the micro-organisms that create the *voile* or layer of yeast that settles on the surface of wine in barrels – was different from what was known as *Mycoderma aceti* or acetic (vinegar) bacteria. He even showed that you could seed the surface of the wine with *Mycoderma vini* to create the right bouquet – anticipating the use of the *ensemencement* process by almost a century.

Pasteur's writings show that he already understood the importance of well-ripened grapes, leaving air space in barrels, dry storage areas and, importantly, that it was the *voile* of yeast together with the role of oxygen that gave the specificity of taste to Vin Jaune. Jacques Levaux, the retired director of the Jura wine laboratory, noted in a 2010 paper that, apart from the rigorous analytical testing, little had changed either in the making or the understanding of Vin Jaune since the time of Pasteur in the mid-19th century. He said that, although we know more about the nature of Vin Jaune yeasts, we still have not found any way of controlling how they act on the wine.

In a report he asserted that this method would prevent all types of problems from bitterness to yeast contamination to volatility and, what's more, that by using this method all sorts of cellar processes such as racking and topping up would become unnecessary. This was the birth of what later became known as pasteurization. However, Duclaux recorded that this was the start of the industrialization of wine: 'In the USA a winemaker from California wrote to a New York journal that to winemakers in California, Pasteur had become as popular as the President of the USA.'

Pasteur published his research on wine in *Etudes sur le vin* (*Studies on wine*) published in 1866 and revised in 1873. He would have preferred to continue his research, but was called away to study a disease affecting the important silk-worm industry, and other events took over. He did, however, buy a small vineyard, Clos de Rosières, just north of Arbois, near Montigny-les-Arsures. Here he was able to conduct an important experiment before the harvest of 1878 to refute a deceased eminent colleague who did not believe in Pasteur's theory that living yeasts were present in the atmosphere. He created a greenhouse for some of the vines and

Above: The reconstructed laboratory in the museum at Pasteur's house in Arbois features wine bottles. Right: The statue honouring him in Arbois, erected in 1901.

A
PASTEUR
La Ville d'Arbois
—
Monument élevé
par souscription publique
29 Septembre 1901

At the celebrations held in Arbois to mark 100 years since Pasteur's birth, pompiers (firemen) and traditionally dressed gardes-fruits (guards appointed in the 18th and 19th centuries to protect the vineyards from thieves near harvest time).

wrapped each bunch of grapes in sterilized cotton gauze. Sealed from the atmosphere without oxygen, the yeast was unable to settle on the berries, so the pressed grape juice did not ferment, proving his case.

Roger Gibey, Arbois historian and retired scientist, concludes his account of Pasteur's studies on wine by conjecturing that the failure of pasteurization to be accepted in winemaking was due to the success of Pasteur's vital research into micro-organisms and the realization of the importance of hygiene at every stage of the winemaking process. Pasteur's subsequent work on infectious diseases and their prevention through vaccines (such as that against rabies) were of course his greatest achievements, but the research he did on wine in Arbois was part of the journey.

Louis Pasteur was a great ambassador in France for Jura wines, including Vin Jaune, which he would have his vigneron friends send him when he was away. It was harvest time in Arbois when Pasteur died on 28 September 1895, and the vignerons of Arbois sent a huge wreath made of grapes to his funeral in Paris. A hundred years later the vignerons grouped together to make a special cuvée of wine in his honour as the 'most famous amongst us'.

Alexis Millardet – the unsung Jura wine botanist

Eminent botanist Pierre-Marie Alexis Millardet was born north of Dole in 1838 and was educated in Dole and Besançon. Continuing his studies first in medicine in Paris, he became interested in plants and, after teaching botany at the universities of Strasbourg and Nancy, he went west to Bordeaux in 1876. With the wine world in the grip of the phylloxera crisis, he became part of the team that invented the technique of grafting *Vitis vinifera* vines on to American rootstocks, preventing the phylloxera louse from attacking the vine.

Millardet's greatest achievement, however, was his invention of the fungicide we now know as Bordeaux mixture – lime mixed with copper sulphate. Introduced to prevent attacks of the downy mildew fungus, another plague on the vineyards of Europe, it is used today more than ever, with the move away from chemical sprays. If only it had been called after its inventor's birthplace instead of his place of work – it might have been Jura mixture.

The Vercel family – saviours of history

In 2011 the highlight of the auction of old bottles at the Percée du Vin Jaune festival in Arbois was a bottle of Arbois 1774, said to be of Vin Jaune style and made by Anatoile Vercel. It was sold for the staggering sum of €57,000, one of the highest prices ever paid for a bottle of unfortified wine, and it is one of the oldest unfortified wines in the world believed to be still drinkable.

At the end of the 18th century, if not wealthy, Arbois was nevertheless a thriving wine town. The 1774 wine produced by Anatoile Vercel (1725–86) survived with other bottles from the same lot, passed down through the family and stored in three different locations in Arbois. The Vercel family must have been relatively wealthy, in that they had a decent-sized house and chose to bottle this particular wine, something that was uncommon at the time, when most wines were drawn directly from the barrel or sold in barrel for transport.

A portrait of Altin Vercel painted by his friend and neighbour Louis Pasteur.

Jean-Claude (1767–1848), Anatoile's son, was a Jura Deputé (member of parliament), and when he died the wine collection was divided between his two youngest sons, Jules and Altin, with the latter setting up in a new house in Arbois, in which he created a wine cellar. Both brothers seem to have valued the now century-old 1774 wine highly. In 1867 the Arbois Viticultural Society submitted wines for judging at the Exposition Universel in Paris. The oldest wine was the 1774, for which Jules Vercel received a silver medal. When one of Altin's twin daughters, Elia (1852–1936), married Emile Grand in 1883, the menu for the wedding dinner included Arbois Jaune from 1811 (the famous 'comet year') and the now century-old 1774. The couple remained in Altin Vercel's home and had one son, Georges Grand (1886–1974), and it is from this line of the family that the most famous wine collection, including the 1774 wines, came.

Georges Grand, known as 'Commandant Grand' for his service in the First World War, became a historian in later life. Arguably he is the most important person in this family story, in part because there are people in Arbois today who remember him. He was fastidious in his care of the Vercel family wine collection, keeping the best bottles in a locked cupboard that he referred to as the 'tabernacle'. Georges Grand did not marry, but ensured the future of his precious wine

Arbois 1774: collaborative tasting note from 1994

Appearance: Superb deep colour of an amber-tinted old gold. Bright and clear, though some floaters.

Nose: Very intense, rich nose, both refined and delicate and typical of a Vin Jaune. The aromas come in waves with initially plenty of walnuts, spices such as curry [in French this usually means ginger, cumin and fenugreek rather than chilli], cinnamon and vanilla, plus dried apricots, figs and raisins, and some beeswax and wood. It then develops roasted coffee notes, with caramel, honey and gingerbread. The empty glass retained a smell of old *eau-de-vie*.

Palate: Structured and powerful, the marked acidity and alcohol were matched by a touch of not unpleasant bitterness and astringency. However, the flavours of nuts and curry were obvious too with some notes of oranges and roasted coffee.

Finish: The aftertaste was fine and surprising in length, even though slightly maderized.

The 1774 bottle sold for €57,000 at auction in 2011.

Plaque in Arbois near Maison Vercel stating that Pasteur used to meet his childhood friends Jules and Altin in the vigneron's house of the Vercel family.

collection by willing it to his god-daughter, Marie-José Dejean de St-Marcel (d. 1987), the daughter of a local winegrowing family (and the only Arbois wine producer recommended by Morton Shand in his 1926 book). Once again, the fine Vercel collection was in good hands, and was moved to the cellar of Marie-José and her husband, a local doctor, Pierre Millet (1914–2005).

Dr Pierre Millet was as fastidious as Commandant Grand, and it was thanks to him that we know so much about the 1774 bottles and about Vin Jaune in general. After his wife died in 1987 he devoted himself to research into Vin Jaune. In 1992 he gathered some friends together to open and taste a bottle. Among them was biochemist and historian Roger Gibey. At the end of the tasting Gibey retained some dregs of the wine to take back to his laboratory for analysis.

Dr Millet was so inspired by the experience of sharing the wine – now over two centuries old – that he founded a study group, the Groupe d'Etude des Vins Jaunes (GEVJ), sadly no longer active. Millet decided to donate a second bottle for a more formal and scientific tasting in the tasting room of the official Jura wine bodies at Château Pécauld. He stipulated that the wine should also be analyzed fully in comparison with other Vins Jaunes through the ages.

The tasters in 1994 alongside Dr Millet included two local vignerons, Pierre Overnoy and Lucien Aviet (Caveau de Bacchus); Jacques Levaux of the local wine laboratory; other wine officials; and experienced local tasters, including Roger Gibey. Their impressions were meticulously recorded and a collaborative tasting note was published. According to Gibey, emotions were high, with even the most erudite and serious of tasters lapsing into emotional descriptors. The two winegrowers were the most affected: Aviet said that the wine gave him goose bumps; Overnoy recalls that they tried hard to imagine the primitive working conditions of 220 years earlier. Jacques Levaux, perhaps one of the most dispassionate who attended the 1994 tasting, recalled that the aroma of the wine was so extraordinary that the palate was somewhat disappointing afterwards. He did say, however, that if he had tasted the wine blind, he might have suggested that it was around 50 years old.

At the time of writing the buyers of the

Pierre Millet selects a bottle from the precious cache of bottles in Commandant Grand's 'tabernacle'.

1774 in February 2011 have not yet drunk the bottle. A second from the collection, which may include up to 15 more bottles split between the three daughters of Pierre Millet, was sold through Christie's in 2012 at a lower price, and is for sale in Hedonism Wines in London. It is believed that the two bottles sold were those in best condition, with wine levels in the bottles relatively high and no noticeable flaws in the glass.

Through the sagacity of Commandant Grand and subsequently Pierre Millet, with the 1774 Arbois the descendants of the Vercel family preserved liquid history. These are wines made from grapes grown on vines planted, *en foule* (literally 'in a crowd') and ungrafted, quite possibly during the reign of Louis XIV (1643–1715). They were pruned in the year of the death of Louis XV (1774) and the grapes were harvested in the reign of Louis XVI. When the wine was bottled is not known, but almost certainly it would have been at least 10–20 years later, most likely during the time of the First Republic after the French Revolution.

The Bourdy family – two centuries of inventory

Now in its 15th generation, the Bourdy family of Arlay has been holding back substantial stocks of its wines on a systematic basis since the end of the 19th century and it owns many earlier bottles as well. In addition to making its own wines, this traditional vigneron family has run a négociant business for many years. Although some other vignerons, especially in and around Château-Chalon, preserve a number of bottles back to the late 19th century and offer them for sale occasionally, no other family has the quantities owned by the Bourdys, around 30,000 bottles of old stocks.

The wines, including Vin Jaune, Château-Chalon, Vin de Paille, Macvin, red and white, are stored in the 16th-century cellar below the family home. Current owners, brothers Jean-François and Jean-Philippe Bourdy, say that each bottle is checked with corks being changed on a systematic basis every 40 or 50 years, and topped up if needed with the very same wine. They note, however, that the storage conditions mean they rarely need topping up.

The bottles that go back to the 18th century are offered for sale at the tasting room, on export markets (where occasional tastings are staged), and at the annual auction of old bottles at the Percée. A spectacular vertical tasting of 120 old reds, whites and Vins Jaunes back to 1888 was staged in 2006 by the Bourdys with sommelier Christophe Menozzi for top French sommeliers, journalists and collectors.

A few Bourdy treasures. From the left: red Arlay 1932, Vin de Paille 1919, Vin Jaune 1928.

Henri Maire – visionary *1917–2003*

A few weeks before he died, Henri Maire was asked what might have happened to the Jura wine region if he had not been there to pull it up by its bootstraps. He answered modestly that if it had not been him, there would have been someone else. Henri Maire was a man who seized the opportunities of his age, and it is hard to visualize what would have become of the Jura wine region without his vision during the post-Second World War period.

Henri Maire was born in Paris and died in Arbois aged 86. There had been vines in the Maire family since the 17th century, and wines made in the Arbois family home in Rue Faramand, the old vigneron quarter, since 1632. His grandfather Henri farmed his various parcels of vines almost until he died, aged 95, in 1938, and the young Henri Maire would visit and spend time with him in his school holidays.

Henri Maire's parents had left Arbois to seek work in Paris in the big decline post-phylloxera around 1900. In the smart 16th *arrondissement* they ran an *épicerie*, a grocer's shop, also supplying the high society of Paris with wine and cheese. Henri's father Léon, who had fought in the First World War, died in 1934 when Henri was only 17, so it was Henri who would later inherit his grandfather's vines. In the meantime, seeking a career, his mother had sent him to Arbois and suggested he plant potatoes as a cash crop. Of course, inspired by his grandfather and uncles who had vines, he also started making wine on the side.

Called up at the start of the Second World War, he was demobbed in 1940 and back in Arbois. Somehow in 1941 he managed to obtain a licence to open a wine merchant premises at the house in Rue Faramand, which eventually became home, office and wine cellar combined. Still growing potatoes, it is said that in his early days during wartime he would swap potatoes for hard-to-obtain empty wine bottles in order to sell his bottled wine both to local restaurants and to private individuals, something no one else did in Arbois. Acquiring vineyards here and there, in 1942 he even obtained permission from Louis Pasteur's grandson to replant Pasteur's vineyard, Clos de Rosières, and replanted it with all five grape varieties permitted under AOC rules. This was definitely an entrepreneur in the making.

Henri Maire raises a toast in the Clos de Rosières vineyard, where Pasteur conducted his experiments and which was replanted by Henri Maire.

Vin Fou – an explosive idea

There is no one true place of origin for the term 'Vin Fou', or 'Mad Wine': the term simply evolved. The story of wine 'coming to life' when the weather warms up in spring is an old one – presumably some wines sparkled more than others, hence the madness. Sparkling wines have a long tradition in the Jura, and it was during the 1950s that Henri Maire came up with the brilliant concept of branding an innocuous fizz as 'Vin Fou'.

Henri Maire made Vin Fou into a huge sparkling wine brand known around the world. The idea came to him in 1950 from a conversation with French government minister Charles Brun, originally from the Jura, who thought it would be good to have an easy-drinking wine from the Jura to help publicize the region. Henri Maire delved into the history books, discovered the Vin Fou tradition, and put this together with the fact that sparkling wines had always been an important product in the Jura. All he needed was a good publicist and an artist and boom – Vin Fou exploded on to the scene.

His subsequent street-side advertising campaign has gone down in wine history as one of the best wine marketing campaigns ever seen. As well as colourful posters, there were publicity films, radio advertisements, lavish parties for dignitaries at Domaine de Grange Grillard and stunts, all making Vin Fou and Henri Maire famous. In 1955 it was even served to delegates at the Geneva summit, attended by US President Dwight D Eisenhower, British Prime Minister Anthony Eden, USSR First Secretary Nikita Khrushchev, and Henri Maire's good friend, the Prime Minister of France, Edgar Faure. It became so successful that the base wines had to be sourced outside the Jura.

One of many Vin Fou posters designed for Henri Maire by Paul Grimault. This example dates from 1955.

Creating the Henri Maire empire

Once war was over, still in his twenties, Henri's energy and ambition were unstoppable. This was a man who not only had the confidence in his region to produce great wines at a time when the Jura was in the doldrums, he wanted to prove it on a grand scale.

The Henri Maire wine firm was officially established in 1945. Advised by a French specialist and another from the University of California at Davis, he created his first estate – the Domaine de Monfort – in 1947 by piecing together plots from around 300 owners to make up 45ha of vineyards. This was followed in 1953 by the Domaine de Grange Grillard and in 1963 by the beautiful Domaine de Sorbief, a historically important manor house in need of complete renovation. Located on the hillside below Pupillin, it had some excellent marl-endowed vineyard soils.

In the meantime Henri was not only planting, he was plotting to put the Jura firmly on the map with his sales and marketing extravaganzas. At the time Jura wines were sold only in the local region and he planned to reverse the trend. He had the notion, earlier than anyone else in France, possibly even in Europe, that the way forward was to sell wine direct to the consumer with a network of direct sales representatives selling door-to-door and at fairs and exhibitions.

Marketing, marketing, marketing . . .

Perhaps it was his upbringing in Paris that meant Henri Maire was at ease rubbing shoulders with politicians. He was a good friend of the Radical French politician, writer and one-time French Prime Minister Edgar Faure, who was an important politician in the Jura and Franche-Comté for many years. Henri Maire enjoyed meeting politicians at the restaurants they frequented, such as the Tour d'Argent. At the same time as promoting Vin Fou (see 'Vin Fou'), Henri Maire believed in Vin Jaune as the Jura's flagship quality wine and wanted to promote it and produce greater quantities than ever before. In 1952 he persuaded the Tour d'Argent to embed a cask and some bottles of Vin Jaune into the walls of the restaurant to be enjoyed by future generations.

His PR stunts were conducted on a scale only previously done by Champenois such as Charles Heidsieck or Eugène Mercier in the previous century. He sent a barrel of Arbois rosé to Mauritius and back in an imitation of how Madeira journeyed. To celebrate its return, the wine, known as 'Retour des Isles' or 'Return from the Islands', was to be the focus of a dinner held simultaneously in Paris and London, the latter organized by Gerald Asher, his British importer. Asher gives a rather hilarious account of the proceedings at Prunier in London in his memoirs, *A carafe of red*. Another stunt was sending hundreds of bottles of Arbois wine to the Soviet cosmonauts to be drunk while photographing the moon; apparently all the bottles were drunk back at base.

Henri Maire married Marie-Thérèse Salles, a classics teacher from Salins-les-Bains, in 1947. When she went to teach in the Overseas French Department of Réunion in the Indian Ocean, Henri Maire pursued her to bring her back and marry him. They had two children, Henri-Michel (1948) and Marie-Christine (1951), but Marie-Thérèse died in 1968. According to Marie-Christine, Marie-Thérèse was a big influence on the aesthetics of the marketing side of the business and they were very much a partnership, something that was confirmed when I spoke to Gerald Asher shortly after Henri Maire's death.

The couple opened the restaurant La Finette in 1961, with its sobriquet 'Taverne d'Arbois'. It's hard to imagine today what a revolution this was in a small wine town – a large casual restaurant that was neither village café nor gourmet table, where all were encouraged to come – local farmers, top politicians, summer tourists. Decorated in mountain style, the idea was to showcase Jura wines, in particular those from Henri Maire, to accompany the most typical regional food. In 2012 the restaurant, no longer connected with the Henri Maire firm, but still run in the same way, celebrated receiving its 100,000th wheel of Comté cheese.

In 1955, on the return of the wine dubbed 'Retour des Isles', Henri Maire tastes the wine with friends, including renowned sailor Alain Bombard and chef Raymond Oliver of Paris restaurant Le Grand Véfour.

Building up the business

In the decades after Vin Fou was launched Henri Maire travelled the world, most particularly to the USA, bringing back not only marketing ideas but the latest in vineyard and wine technology. He remained the classic 'boy' who enjoyed his toys – in his eighties he was still seen at agricultural shows admiring the latest machinery. When he expanded his vineyards in the 1950s, he created rows that were up to a kilometre long with 3m spacing between each row to enable mechanization. Quality viticulture was not his strongest point; he was seduced by what the Gallos and others were doing in California.

In 1954 he moved the business from the cramped quarters in Arbois to a modern office and winery he built in the middle of the vineyards, grandly named Château de Boichailles, conveniently next to the railway line. Soon after his official retirement in

1987 the company was listed on the Lyon stock exchange; in 1997 its statutes were altered and Henri Maire, aged 80, stepped down. That same year he was awarded the French Légion d'Honneur.

Ask any tourist who travelled through France by car in the 1960s and 1970s and they are sure to remember the distinctive roadside publicity posters for Vin Fou and Prestige de l'Arbois. Ask anyone from Arbois over the age of 50 and they are sure to give you an opinion or even a story about Henri Maire. That story might come with a grimace, or perhaps a wry grin, or indeed a huge laugh, but even that grimace will be tinged with an expression of respect when you ask about the man.

Henri Maire built up his wine estate to 300ha, one of the largest in France (now the company has less, see profile p. 179), but he is remembered more for the support he offered all who grew grapes in the region. As a négociant he purchased grapes, never demanding exclusivity and paying quickly. The vast majority of vignerons, who were not attached to a *fruitière* (cooperative), would sell part or all of their crop to Henri Maire until the 1980s. And vigneron Lucien Aviet, who set up in the late 1960s, describes him as a catalyst for the region.

Henri Maire was an energetic, assertive businessman with a passion for his region. As restaurateur Jean-Paul Jeunet says: 'Who else could be said to have got things moving in the Jura?'

Henri Maire's children

How does anyone follow in the steps of such a hugely charismatic, energetic, dynamic and innovative father? Henri Maire's son Henri-Michel, born in 1948, worked in the business throughout his career until he retired. His profile was low: he was a businessman, possibly overshadowed by the past.

Born three years later, daughter Marie-Christine pursued her own career in the banking sector until she joined the family firm in 1991, taking charge of marketing and exports. Later she became an energetic president of the Comité Interprofessionnel des Vins du Jura (CIVJ) for three stints and, like her father, has been a tireless supporter of her region.

Marie-Christine recalls her father as a man with crazy ideas and enormous energy, who never stopped working, his whole life revolving around wine. In the late 1960s he took the two children, aged 18 and 15, to California, but of course the holiday meant visiting vineyards and wineries. They travelled in a chauffeured car and met Ernest and Julio Gallo, among others. As Henri Maire, despite regular visits to the USA, did not speak English, Marie-Christine acted as interpreter. It's a memory that stayed with her – their only family holiday.

She also recalls her father's attitude to wine as a beverage to take great pleasure in – but he also believed in exercising restraint. Marie-Christine thinks that it is this that propelled her into being one of the founding members and past president of the French wine industry pressure group, Vin et Société.

The Jeunets – chefs

André Jeunet: 1924–2001 and Jean-Paul Jeunet: b. 1954

Imagine the scenario. You are a young and ambitious French chef with your own restaurant, already boasting a Michelin star, building yourself a fine reputation. Having twice failed to win the top chefs' competition, you decide instead to enter the top sommeliers' competition in the country. You're a chef and you win . . . This is what happened in 1966 to André Jeunet, father of Jean-Paul Jeunet (at the time of writing the only two-star Michelin chef in the Jura and Franche-Comté).

In a familiar story for most French-born chefs, André Jeunet, who came from Arbois, was inspired by his mother, who taught him about the flavours of local food and drink. Like most Jura country folk, they had some vines, made wine and used the travelling still to make home-grown fruit spirits and liqueurs – and all turned up in the cooking pot. After catering studies and work in restaurants and teaching, André married Raymonde Bonjour, the daughter of a hotelier in Port-Lesney (once the Hotel Bonjour, today the delightful Hotel l'Edgar). In 1951 the couple took on the task of renovating the Hotel de Paris in Arbois, then on the main road between Paris and Geneva before the bypass was built. Their aim was to turn it into a busy Routier restaurant.

At that time Arbois already had two Michelin-rated restaurants (La Balance and the Hotel des Messageries) and the story goes that the local Michelin inspector, who had heard about the Hotel de Paris, encouraged them to take down their Routier sign so that they could be eligible for a star the next year. Losing the Routier customers was a risk, but they took it and won a star in 1959.

In the meantime André Jeunet supplemented his income by teaching at the girls' catering college in nearby Poligny.

André Jeunet decanting an old wine.

Along with cookery courses he included wine-tasting courses, and would take the young ladies off to visit vineyards around the country. He was hooked on wine and learning fast. After losing France's top chefs' competition in 1962 and 1964 to no less than the great chefs Paul Bocuse and Jean Troisgros he gave up, but then tried for the Meilleur Sommelier de France instead. He won the award in 1966 and with that in hand he was able to indulge his passion as well as pay particular attention to the wines of his own region. It is said that whenever he travelled out of the region to another restaurant, he always took a *clavelin* of Vin Jaune with him to help it become known among his colleagues.

This era coincided exactly with the time that a few small vignerons in the Jura were turning away from polyculture to set up wine estates, inspired partly by the fact that Henri Maire was succeeding in making Jura wines known around the world. According to Jean-Paul, his father André had respect for Henri Maire, whose estate wines in particular were very good at the time, but he wanted to help and encourage these younger vignerons. He would taste wines with Jacques Puffeney, Lucien Aviet (Caveau de Bacchus) or Roger Lornet

Arbois – a small town with a gourmet history

From the 18th century Arbois had a reputation as a good place to stop en route between Besançon and Lyon, with a dynasty of fine restaurateurs and hotels that the Jeunets have continued.

There was a difficult period when, apart from *chez* Jean-Paul Jeunet, Arbois suffered from having no restaurant with food worth talking about. And nowhere a visitor could go out to enjoy the good local wines either. When Thierry Moyne revived La Balance restaurant in 1998 he was helped financially by several local vignerons, and the restaurant has gone from strength to strength. Now there are other more casual choices where locals and visitors can enjoy drinking Jura wine and eating wholesome food. The famous chocolatier Hirsinger draws foodie visitors too. The winegrowers of the Jura today once again have a fine gastronomic centre in Arbois that does them proud.

La Balance restaurant offers the classic local dish: chicken with morels in Vin Jaune.

Every year Jean-Paul Jeunet, his wife Nadine and the whole hotel/restaurant team wait outside for the procession of Le Biou to pass.

(father of Frédéric) and suggest ways that they could make their wines better, and of course he sold their wines in his restaurant.

This being the era of fast improvements in cellar technologies, André encouraged the vignerons to be cautious with these new technologies, to value their land and to remain artisanal. He was an admirer of the philosophy of the Beaujolais wine merchant and natural wine advocate Jules Chauvet, who was a great influence on Pierre Overnoy.

Jean-Paul Jeunet spent a lot of time as a child with his grandmother – his parents being busy establishing their hotel and restaurant – and credits her with being as big an influence on his understanding of flavours as she had been for his father. He followed his father into the business after studying in Nice and worked in the kitchens of several grand restaurants. When his father became unwell in 1986, Jean-Paul and his wife Nadine took over the business. He had previously tried to work in the kitchen beside his father, but there was friction. When Jean-Paul received his second Michelin star in 1996, he finally believed he had done something good for himself, and eventually changed the name from Hotel de

Paris to Hotel Restaurant Jean-Paul Jeunet.

Naturally his father had taught him about the local wines, but Jean-Paul credits Stéphane Planche, who worked as the restaurant's head sommelier from 1998 to 2009, with helping him create a strategy for the restaurant's wine purchases and stocks, so that between 25% and 35% of all purchases are put aside to age. Stéphane says that the restaurant was already really driven by its excellent wine selection before his arrival, and both André (with whom he was able to spend time) and Jean-Paul taught him much about the Jura and its vignerons. Stéphane and Jean-Paul share an appreciation of wines that are simple and represent the land and their vignerons; they remain good friends and Jean-Paul helped Stéphane set up his Arbois wine shop and bar, Les Jardins de St-Vincent.

Jean-Paul believes that Jura wines have made great progress in the past 20 years or so, and he is a supporter of vignerons working with organic and biodynamic methods in particular. He believes in minimal intervention and seems to love the new fruity styles of reds that give pleasure without tannin and encourage one to drink a second glass. However, he fears that the real extremists may lose the Jura some clientele, and doesn't enjoy some of the really 'crazy' wines. Restraint in purchases should be assured by the sommelier since 2010, Alain Guillou, who was awarded Sommelier of the Year by the publisher Gault et Millau in 2013. Currently their list has 640 wines, including over 350 from the Jura.

On matching Jura wines with food, Jean-Paul starts with the comment that God must have been from the Jura to create such a divine marriage as Comté cheese with Vin Jaune. He also believes that the matches of basic local products like Morteau sausage with Poulsard or pike with Savagnin are essential, but he goes further: 'Give me a wine and I will give you a dish to match,' he says, and rates lobster with Savagnin a splendid marriage, though he refuses to be drawn into discussions about whether to choose *ouillé* or an oxidative version, believing each wine should be treated on its own merits without going too far into how it was made. For Jean-Paul the terroir (in which he includes the grape varieties) counts for 51% of the character of a wine, and the know-how and work of the vigneron for 49%. What's more, if you do not understand the fundamentals of that terroir, you can't begin to make a good wine, he claims.

Today the restaurant's cuisine is influenced by the greenness of the Jura and its soil, using many root vegetables – simple wines of the earth go well with these dishes, Jean-Paul says. According to Jean-Paul, both he and his father transmitted into their cuisine their own history and traditions, and these match the originality and history of the grape varieties and terroirs of Jura wines. Both men of strong personality, Jean-Paul believes that their individual and highly flavoured cuisine can bring out the best in Jura wines because their flavours are so powerful.

Jean-Paul Jeunet is regularly seen at wine events, and sometimes agrees to be one of the chefs for grand PR occasions as well as contributing recipes to the CIVJ's publications. He continues to be a great supporter of local vignerons, both established and new, and to be

excited by their wines. Very approachable, he puts a smile on younger growers' faces when he – always in conjunction with his sommelier – agrees to list one of their wines, often discovered by himself at a tasting.

The Jeunet dynasty has been important for Jura wines, providing a focal point for lovers of gastronomy. And for those who have loved the wines from a distance and visit Arbois for the first time, the Restaurant Jean-Paul Jeunet has become a place of pilgrimage. Fortunately the prices, relative to its status, have been held in check both for the food and the wines, as befits this region.

Sommelier Alain Guillou offers a tasting of Vins Jaunes to Jean-Paul Jeunet in the restaurant. Behind is an old photo of André Jeunet demonstrating the making of the sauce for poulet au Vin Jaune *to Jean-Paul.*

Bernard Badoz – festival impresario

b. 1943

By the 1990s Jura wines had a growing problem in Bernard Badoz' view. The postwar recovery had gone well but there was still confusion among consumers, and little was being done by the region to address it. He even came across wine drinkers who confused Vin Jaune with Vin de Paille. *Quelle horreur!* And, despite the existence by then of the Jura wine promotional office (CIVJ), there was little cohesion among growers. The idea for a celebratory festival took seed in the mid-1990s and in 1997 Bernard presided over the first Percée du Vin Jaune festival in his home town of Poligny. Held on the first weekend of February in a different Jura town or village each year, it has been the best-attended wine festival in France for several years.

Bernard Badoz took over his family's wine business in Poligny in 1970, the ninth generation of his family to make wine. Twenty-five years later he began reflecting on his mother's reaction near the start of every year when his father Pierre would deem it the right time to pierce the seal of the barrel of Vin Jaune to see whether it was fit for bottling, six or more years after harvest. In those days, before the local laboratory offered systematic testing, making Vin Jaune was a hit and miss affair and each barrel represented a significant investment – his mother was always nervous that it might be vinegar. But, if the Vin Jaune was deemed good for bottling, Madame Badoz would declare that the family would get by for the coming year – they could even buy some new clothes. It was a kind of celebration.

To honour this important time in the work of the Jura vigneron, the idea was born to stage a festival based around a religious service followed by the symbolic *percée* or 'piercing' of the latest vintage of Vin Jaune. Bernard was helped by his friend Jean-Louis Lemarchal, then director of the local *Le Progrès* newspaper, which became a partner in the event and, most importantly, provided media support. The timing was set around the earliest date that Jura growers are allowed to release the latest Vin Jaune vintage, at the start of the year seven years following the vintage (or as folklore will have it, after six years and three months in cask). Bernard's vineyard records showed that the first weekend of February, close to Candlemas (the Christian celebration on 2 February, 40 days after Christmas) was usually fine weather. This has held true on all but five occasions out of 18, depending on what you call 'fine'. Another plus was that it would not clash with Burgundy's successful Fête de la St-Vincent, held on the weekend nearest to 22 January.

There are similarities with Burgundy's St-Vincent Tournante, such as rotating between villages, but important differences. Bernard claims to have taken the best from the St-Vincent and eliminated the worst. Inevitably there was scepticism; at the time the Burgundy festival attracted 20,000 people over the weekend and Bernard thought it would take ten years to reach that figure in the Jura. He was wrong: the first event in Poligny went well and the follow-up in Arbois in 1998 saw 22,000 people attending over two days.

The skill Bernard Badoz had was in motivating the right people: vignerons such as Pierre Rolet, Alain Baud and Alain de Laguiche; others in the region who helped to manage the event; and locals as volunteers. He realized that the Jura wine region lacked a fraternity, so he created one to provide some pomp. He named the original organizers and supporters of the event the Ambassadeurs des Vins Jaunes. They dress in yellow robes and have to swear to spread the word about the region's wine and Vin Jaune in particular. New members are 'intronized' each year.

Bernard managed to bring together a significant proportion of producers of all sizes from across the region to offer their wines for tasting, and at the same time attracted volunteers both for the lengthy preparations and over the weekend itself. In recent years the Percée has attracted 35,000–50,000 visitors; 70–80 producers, each with a *caveau* (tasting station) and sales centre in cellars lent by local residents; and 700–800 volunteers taking care of tasks as various as decoration, car parking and security.

Security is a major issue and arose early on, with the festival becoming a victim of its own success. Highway police were naturally worried about the logistics of such large numbers of people driving to a remote location and about the drink-drive issues. Burgundy's St-Vincent festival had been through a difficult stage with issues of drunkenness and Bernard and the Ambassadeurs are determined to avoid this. 'On ne picole pas, on ne fait que de déguster . . .' ('No one gets drunk, they taste...'), he says. Visitors are issued with limited tasting tickets on entry and there are plenty of food stalls around. Drivers are encouraged to leave their keys at the entrance to the festival and do a breath test on exit.

The Ambassadeurs encouraged local food associations to get involved at an early stage, so there are representatives of the Comté cheese association and producers of the local Morteau and Mortadeau sausages and Bresse chickens in the Sunday morning ceremonial procession to church and at the main event, alongside representatives

Bernard Badoz in one of the tasting rooms of Domaine Badoz, in his cellar in Poligny.

of each Jura AOC. There is plenty apart from the wine itself to keep visitors busy. The Saturday wine auction of old bottles, originally suggested by Alain de Laguiche of Château d'Arlay and supported by his neighbour Jean-François Bourdy, attracts much interest and press coverage. There is also a cooking competition with a trophy named for chef André Jeunet, a range of local arts and crafts, and the usual French folk singers, dancers and clowns.

Bernard learned fast about the importance of the media, and a star guest of honour attracts people to come to the stage for the main ceremony on Sunday morning. A master of ceremonies builds up the crowd, waiting expectantly for a taste from the symbolic barrel after it has been 'pierced' or tapped, giving them a serious educational talk on how Vin Jaune is made and also making them wait for the obligatory singsong (yes, there is a Vin Jaune song . . .). Put simply this is not just a party, it is a reverent but enjoyable celebration that epitomizes what the Jura is all about.

Bernard's early vision was for a celebration of Vin Jaune that would bring together the producers of the region and help educate the public about their flagship product. In encouraging visitors to taste the whole range of wines available, it has become Jura wines' annual showcase and even market (much is sold there), and in more recent years it has also been seen as a hugely popular countryside festival, the largest in the Jura. Extensive press coverage has attracted visitors from outside Franche-Comté (now at a level of 50%, up from 10% at the start) and has developed into the biggest publicity machine for the Jura wine region since Henri Maire. February 2016 will see the 20th edition of the festival take place in Lons-le-Saunier. There is talk of taking a break after to hold the festival only every other year.

Dressed in the robes of an Ambassadeur des Vins Jaunes, Bernard Badoz addresses the audience of vignerons and people connected with Jura wines at a dinner held the evening before the Percée du Vin Jaune.

Le Nez dans le Vert – a green success

Though never intended to be competition for the Percée, Le Nez dans le Vert organic wine-tasting event (the name is a pun, sounding like 'The Nose in the Glass' but actually translated as 'The Nose in the Green') held each year in March since 2011 has given huge publicity for the organic wine movement in the Jura, especially for newly established growers. In an all-embracing modern or perhaps slightly hippy way, there is no one person to credit with creating this event, though it has to be said that Bruno Ciofi, director of Domaine de la Pinte in Arbois, has done his fair share of managing it, and La Pinte was the venue in 2011, 2013 and 2015. Château de Gevingey in the Sud Revermont was the location in 2012 and 2014.

Held over two days – Sunday for consumers and Monday morning for professionals – this is an event as full of joy as the Percée but totally devoted to the wines (and a good lunch too). The producers (around 30 exhibit) must be certified Ecocert (including those 'in conversion') and they are each allowed to present just six wines placed on an upturned barrel, creating a wonderful feeling of equality. At a busy event you find organic stars like Pierre Overnoy, Emmanuel Houillon, Jean-François Ganevat and Stéphane Tissot rubbing shoulders with newcomers like Patrice Hughes-Béguet, Céline Gormally and Renaud Bruyère. The most established organic producer, Claude Buchot, is there, as are newly

More than 1,000 visitors attend the consumer day on Sunday and over 300 professionals attend on Monday.

converted-to-organics stalwart producers like Jean-Michel Petit of Domaine de la Renardière and Jean Berthet-Bondet.

In a short time this event has become really significant for these organic producers, as they have found new customers not only among consumers, but retailers, wine bars and importers coming from as far away as Scandinavia and the USA for the event. It has also reinforced a sense of community and self-help among the producers, who don't hesitate to support a colleague in difficulty or recommend each other if they have sold out of wine.

Pierre Overnoy – naturally inspiring
b. 1937

The wines of Pierre Overnoy, retired vigneron, are revered from Japan to the USA and most points between, but for those who have met him they are perhaps not as revered as the man himself. The combination of his modesty, humour and his willingness to share what he has learned over five decades of making wine his own way in the small village of Pupillin is irresistible. Even more admirable is that he has inspired many younger Jura growers to go their own way too.

Any conversation with Pierre becomes a revelation, interspersed with his own philosophy and his perpetual desire to question everything. Every sentence delves deep into over seven decades of immersion in the people, vineyards and wines of his home village and region. It is this that inspired three long-term friends, retired local geologist Michel Campy, historian Roger Gibey, lawyer Michel Converset and Bernard Amiens, the mayor of Arbois, to record a

series of interviews with Pierre. At Pierre's insistence they also involved vigneron Emmanuel Houillon, who has taken over Pierre's estate. The book they published as a result of these interviews – *La parole de Pierre* (hard to translate but 'The gospel of Pierre' is close) – provides an extraordinary insight into his life and work. The following is but a glimpse into the man, of whom much has been written elsewhere, but it aims to highlight how he has been invaluable for the Jura wine region.

The youngest of five, Pierre was born into a winegrowing and farming family in Pupillin, and helped with the harvest and the cows from a very early age. He hated school with a vengeance, skipping it whenever he could to go hunting with his friends or generally cause mischief. After returning from military service in Algeria Pierre joined the

Harvest 1976 in Pupillin. Pierre Overnoy (second from left on the cart) helps other growers in the village, mostly members of the Pupillin Fruitière.

An unusual collection of jars

Every year on 2 July Pierre Overnoy goes out into the Pupillin vineyards and cuts off a few bunches of baby grapes and conserves them in alcohol in a jar. Usually this is just after flowering has finished, when the berries start to grow, but every jar shows something different. He has been doing this since 1990, when – in his words – climate change had already started and he wishes he had started earlier. From these bunches you can begin to predict the harvest date and even the quality, and this serves as a wonderful visual record of each vintage (see selection below).

family farm and eventually the land was divided within the family, with Pierre dedicating himself to wine production, starting with a very small area of vines.

In the vineyards Pierre was one of several vignerons who were suspicious of the chemical herbicides that were offered in the 1960s. He relates that customers would ask him whether he used them and were happy when he said no. He decided that, although they might make his life easier, herbicides were just too good to be true. Through all the years Pierre kept his vineyards organic: vines must be in balance, he maintains. But

it is his winemaking approach that makes him most unusual.

The only formal wine training Pierre had was a relatively short course in Beaune; he returned to make wine in 1968 with renewed confidence, only to find that it did not taste as good as his father's or brother's wine. He was a young man still, but it got him thinking, and Pierre has never stopped reviewing his actions. It was above all a chance meeting and subsequent friendship with Jacques Néauport, peripatetic sommelier, oenologist and all-round wine lover that led him to making wines without SO_2 or any other intervention. Néauport taught him the natural winemaking methods of Beaujolais-based négociant and consultant Jules Chauvet and introduced him to a circle of winemakers working in this way. He also found him potential customers, such as the famous Lyon restaurateur Alain Chapel, who sought out this type of wine.

From an age when, especially in the traditional European countryside, everyone married and had children by the age of 30 (unless war intervened), Pierre remained unmarried. He always says that it was having no dependants that enabled him to pursue his single-minded but risky strategy of farming organically and making wine the natural way, in particular with no added sulphur. Pierre holds Monsieur Chauvet, as he always calls him, in the utmost respect, quoting his teachings regularly.

Pierre is deeply religious, a practising Catholic with a nephew who is the Archbishop of Besançon, and he regularly attends mass in nearby Poligny with the Poor Clares (an order of nuns). Yet he is everything that I wish all deeply religious people would be – open, frank, questioning, respectful of everyone else's opinion although confident of his own, and above all generous with himself. In the often controversial world of natural wine, Pierre only ever explains what has worked for him.

Until the turn of this century, Pierre Overnoy was probably the only Jura vigneron making wines with zero SO_2. He has remained friends with vignerons who work otherwise, enjoys their wines and has always remained fully involved in local wine events. Quietly he has managed to inspire people, especially those from a generation younger than him, who were intrigued by this bachelor, who worked in a different way and who never held back when explaining things – how one should taste wine, for example, always sniffing the wine first (for 0.8 seconds, he told me once) before swirling, preferably tasting in the open air.

For those vignerons interested, Pierre has always been happy to share his methods, explain and encourage. Pascal Clairet of Domaine de la Tournelle in Arbois was much influenced by him; Philippe Bornard was encouraged by Pierre to leave the Pupillin Fruitière to go his own way. Stéphane Tissot

consulted him before making no-sulphur Poulsard. Even outside the Jura wine region Pierre is considered to be a founding father of the natural wine movement, and the very existence of this legend is of massive help to the Jura and its growing group of organic and natural wine producers. And all this is not to mention Manu Houillon ...

The parents of Emmanuel (or Manu – see producer profile, p. 207) were customers of Pierre, and Manu came to help Pierre in the vineyards when he was 14. Effectively he never left, and after his studies were complete he became a full-time employee, taking over from Pierre in 2001. The joy about meeting Manu is hearing him speak, not so much like an echo of Pierre, rather a reflection of him. Manu has learned at Pierre's side, but he has his own ideas too, which Pierre respects and even admires – just as the pair's attitude to the vineyards, it's all about balance. There is a closeness between Pierre

Pierre Overnoy with his wood-fired bread oven at Chaux d'eau.

and his adopted family (for now Manu has a wife, Anne, and four children) that is the envy of many a 'real' family.

Long retired, Pierre continues to spend a lot of time working in the vines or at Manu's side, tasting wines in the making or with friends and customers. But his life also revolves around another fermented product – bread. Having rebuilt an old barn on family land, Chaux d'eau, just outside the village, he takes huge pleasure in the ritual of bread-making in a wood-fired bread oven. Friends bring food, wine is shared, the dog gets underfoot, there is an air of delightful chaos. All is well with the world and Pierre remains a simple, wise man of the Jura, yet a man the world has adopted, with the hugest of hearts and a teasing grin.

Jean Macle – a *grand cru* vigneron?

Another Jura vigneron who deserves recognition for preserving a particular type of wine culture for future generations is Jean Macle of Château-Chalon, just a couple of years older than Pierre Overnoy. Not only as a wine producer but as mayor of the village for over two decades, Jean was active in preserving the cultural heritage of the village and its wine. He was keen to see the expansion of the vineyards of Château-Chalon while at the same time trying to ensure the wine quality was worthy of its old *vin de garde* designation, in all but name a *grand cru* of France.

Jean Macle is an entirely different character to Pierre Overnoy, but shares with him a never-ending quest for knowledge and a

---

Jean Macle photographed in his cellar in 2003.

generosity in sharing it. Jean studied the science of wine and is fascinated by how the *voile* works and how the *goût du jaune* is formed. He is one of the few vignerons in the Jura I know who has studied how Sherry is made. He also encouraged and helped disseminate research studies into the sotolon compound and its influence on Vin Jaune in the region.

Both vignerons share a huge respect for the land and Jean Macle has never used chemical fertilizers on his vineyards, only changing from a 100% organic approach a few years after establishing the estate in 1966, when he resorted to using a small amount of contact herbicide on his steepest vineyards. In the cellar he has questioned everything too, trying *ensemencement* and then giving it up.

Retired for several years, Jean has a worthy successor in his son Laurent (see producer profile, p. 255), but in his day he mentored Jean Berthet-Bondet who worked for him before setting up on his own, and also Jean-Pierre Salvadori. Jean-Pierre told me how, when working for Jean Macle, he was encouraged to set up on his own, and together the two men created the terraced vineyards on the incredibly steep Puits St-Pierre slopes below the hilltop village.

PLACES AND PEOPLE – THE WINE PRODUCERS

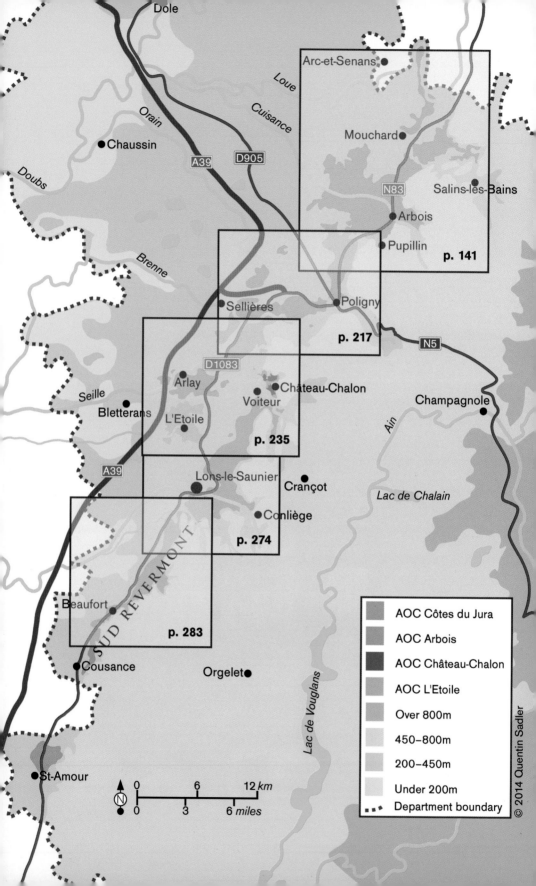

Dole

Loue

Arc-et-Senans

Cuisance

Orain

Chaussin

A39   D905

Mouchard

Doubs

N83   Salins-les-Bains

Brenne

Arbois

Pupillin

p. 141

Sellières

Poligny

p. 217

N5

D1083

Arlay

Château-Chalon

Voiteur

Seille

L'Etoile

Champagnole

Bletterans

p. 235

Ain

A39

Lons-le-Saunier

Crançot

Lac de Chalain

Conliège

p. 274

SUD REVERMONT

Beaufort

p. 283

Cousance

Orgelet

Lac de Vouglans

St-Amour

0   6   *12 km*

0   3   6 *miles*

N

	AOC Côtes du Jura
	AOC Arbois
	AOC Château-Chalon
	AOC L'Etoile
	Over 800m
	450–800m
	200–450m
	Under 200m
	Department boundary

© 2014 Quentin Sadler

Jura's Wine Producers

At first glance one might think that the Jura wine region's richness lies with its rugged yet beautiful landscape, the diversity of its wine styles and its unique terroir. Delve a little deeper and you discover that what gives the region soul is, of course, the people who produce the wine. Some of them are shy, many are outspoken, the vast majority of them are dedicated and yes, that over-used word, passionate, but each one is every bit as fascinating as his or her wines. Half of this book is dedicated to the stories of the producers and their wines.

Producers are listed in the sector of the Jura where they are based. Each town and village has its own character, shown not only through its terroir but also its buildings and cellars, as well as the styles of wines made. In the map opposite I have divided the region into five sectors and each has its own chapter. There follows a short chapter on Franche-Comté wines and producers outside Jura AOCs, particularly those in the Doubs and Haute-Saône.

Previous page: The village of L'Etoile in summer.
Left: The Jura wine region divides into logical sections north to south. Page numbers refer to the maps that begin each subsequent chapter, indicating the villages in each area and the location of the producers profiled.

The producer profiles include most of those who export, plus others who are significant in the region, either for their large size, quality reputation or historical importance. These profiles aim to give you the essence of each producer, small or large, to help understand what lies behind the taste of their wines.

The remainder of this chapter explains the types of producer in the region, how they operate and how the market is divided between them. It also details how the subsequent chapters and producer profiles are organized.

What of the future? The last chapter of this part of the book delves into the dilemmas and opportunities facing producers today.

Producers and markets

Fruitières: The four wine cooperatives – known as *fruitières* in the Jura – accounted for 24.7% of sales in 2012–13 and are dominated by the Fruitière Vinicole d'Arbois, founded in 1906 and one of the two largest producers in the region. Between the four they have around 215 members with a total of 450ha of vineyards (about 23% of the region's AOC vineyards). They are hugely important in providing stability and support to the wine region.

Négociants: The Jura is unusual in that most of its négociants have always purchased grapes rather than wine. As everywhere else, the négociants create their own house style for each type of wine and appellation, using grapes bought in from different growers.

Official regional statistics show that négociants' sales of Jura wine accounted for 33.9% in 2012–13, but these statistics are misleading. Until the turn of the century Henri Maire was the most important négociant, but between the mid-1990s and 2010 the company reduced its purchases to almost zero, though it owns more than 250ha of vineyards. Yet Henri Maire is still included in the négociant figures. Conversely, the domaine figures include Domaine Badoz, Caves de Bourdy and others who operate small négociant businesses. The largest négociant, La Maison du Vigneron (with the Arbois Fruitière one of the two largest producers), makes wine from around 280ha, including 40ha of its own vineyards. There are several smaller négociants, but only one is worthy of profiling, Cellier des Tiercelines.

Domaines: A vigneron is defined as a vineyard owner who bottles wine from at least some of his or her grapes. There are roughly 200 vignerons and in the text I refer to vignerons or to their businesses as either estates or domaines. They represented 41.3% of Jura wine sales in 2012–13 (not including Henri Maire). Most are very small, with 6ha or less. Although the figure is growing, fewer than 40 estates have more than 10ha. Vineyards are often leased, not owned, so holdings tend to fluctuate. The vast majority of these domaines are family owned and run, often with part-time or temporary staff. Using agency staff also avoids the endless paperwork involved in employing people in France.

Some producers share vineyard machinery (tractors, harvesters, etc.) and/or winery equipment (presses, filters, etc.) with others. Many will use an outside service provider for bottling, distillation of *marc* to make Macvin, and for some of the processes for making Crémant du Jura. Many vignerons sell some of their grapes to a négociant to help with cash-flow or with vat space in a large vintage.

Own labels: Large retailers select wines from any of the above to be labelled under their own name. In addition there is at least one company (Caves de la Muyre) that buys significant amounts of wine to sell under its own label in supermarkets and elsewhere. As it is not a producer in its own right it is not profiled here.

Where Jura wines are sold

The Jura has an unusually high level of direct-to-consumer sales. Pioneered by Henri Maire, producers of all sizes sell directly to the public from their tasting rooms or shops and at the many consumer wine shows held around France. It is estimated that around 60% of Jura wine is sold in this way, a much higher proportion than the rest of France. Other sales within France are through the usual channels. Although declining slowly, more than half is sold within the local Franche-Comté region.

Exports from the Jura have risen slowly and steadily this century from a minuscule base to reach around 10%, though they have been somewhat hampered by two small vintages in 2012 and 2013. No figures are available for exports to individual countries, but the principal markets are Belgium, Denmark, Sweden, Canada and the USA.

The producer chapters

Dividing up the region

The following five chapters focus on a geographical sector of the Jura, running roughly from north to south, some coinciding with village appellations. Within most chapters there is a further division by town and/or village, with some grouped together – these also run north to south. Each area is described in terms of its key points of interest, in particular its wine history and the terroir. Producers are listed alphabetically under village/town headings. Each sector includes a map that shows the location of the producers.

Producer profiles

Very few of the producers profiled have good, up-to-date websites and few are in English. I have attempted to plug the information gap, which means that inevitably there is repetition when I describe how each one works the vineyards or makes the wine. Instead of describing every wine a producer makes I have provided an overview of the range, with a few personal highlights.

Over the past ten years I have met with and tasted wines from all the producers profiled and visited almost all of them with the owner, winemaker or manager at least once, usually seeing their cellars and sometimes their vineyards. My aim has been to try to understand the essence of each vigneron and to grasp the differences in each sector of the region.

I have tasted Jura wines extensively for over a decade at the producers, at press events around the Percée festival and at wine fairs, in particular recently at Le Nez dans le Vert organic fair. Some producers have given me samples to taste at home.

Producer information boxes

Contact details are provided for the producer's main winery, including email and website when available. The date of establishment usually refers to the year the current producer name began to be used or when the family first grew vines or made wine.

Vineyard size is given as it is a more useful guide than annual bottle production, though some may sell part of their crop to négociants. The grape variety split is provided when known. Ecocert is the overall organic certifying body in France and certification is stated. Demeter (the biodynamic certification body) is also listed. If nothing is mentioned it means the producer has no certification, even if he or she is working organically or biodynamically.

Visits: To visit most producers it is essential to call or email ahead for an appointment (some are more receptive than others). When they have a tasting room this is mentioned, and it means tasting facilities (glasses, warmth and a toilet) are usually better. If there is no tasting room you may taste in the cellar or the producer's home. When a producer has a dedicated tasting room or a shop in the nearby town (mostly Arbois) this is mentioned. If nothing is stated it will usually be open Monday–Saturday but closed at lunchtime.

AROUND ARBOIS

The northern section of the Jura wine region is by far the most densely planted, with AOC Arbois itself having around 800ha (not including vineyards used for Crémant and Macvin). This chapter also covers those vineyards to the north of AOC Arbois towards the Loue river and Salins-les-Bains, which are classified as AOC Côtes du Jura, and a few IGP vineyards just over the departmental border in the Doubs. This whole area was historically the most important of the Jura wine region, partly due to the proximity to Salins and its salt mines attracting wealthy landowners. The wines that brought it fame were not, as you might expect, Vin Jaune, but its red and sparkling wines. Both are mentioned much more in old texts than *vins de garde* or white wines. Today, due to the warmer

soils and protected vineyard slopes, this part of the region remains the most planted with red grapes, in particular Trousseau around Montigny-les-Arsures and Ploussard (Poulsard) around Pupillin. All the producers of Pupillin use the name 'Ploussard', as do many others in AOC Arbois.

Vineyards are scattered in a patchwork of farmland, forests and houses in most villages, but, if coming from the north, once at Montigny-les-Arsures the vineyards dominate the landscape, continuing in a

Above: The Hermitage chapel above Arbois. Beyond the town lie some of the best-known vineyard sites. In a semi-circle from left to right these sites include La Mailloche, Curoulet, Les Bruyères, Les Corvées and Le Curon. The vineyards of Montigny-les-Arsures are in the distance.

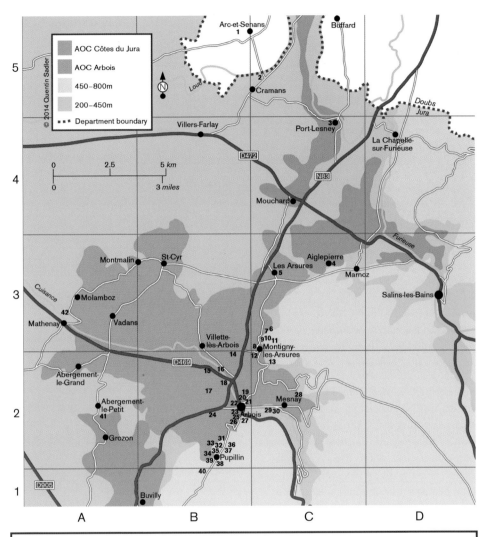

Producers by commune

Arc-et-Senans
1 Domaine Ratapoil

Cramans
2 Domaine des Cavarodes

Port-Lesney
3 Domaine de la Loue

Aiglepierre
4 Domaine Les Sarmentelles

Les Arsures
5 Domaine Daniel Dugois

Montigny-les-Arsures
6 Frédéric Lornet
7 Caveau de Bacchus
8 Domaine André et Mireille Tissot
9 Domaine du Pélican
10 Domaine Fumey-Chatelain
11 Jacques Puffeney

12 Michel Gahier
13 Domaine Jean-Louis Tissot

Arbois
14 Cellier des Tiercelines
15 Domaine Rolet Père et Fils
16 Domaine de la Touraize
17 Domaines Henri Maire
18 Domaine des Bodines
19 Domaine de l'Octavin
20 Camille Loye
21 Fruitière Vinicole d'Arbois
22 Domaine Jacques Tissot
23 Domaine de la Tournelle
24 Domaine de la Pinte
25 Domaine Gérard Villet
26 Domaine Ligier Père et Fils
27 Pierre et Georges Bouilleret

Mesnay
28 Domaine de la Cibellyne

29 Domaine Martin-Faudot
30 Domaine Hughes-Béguet

Pupillin
31 Renaud Bruyère
32 Domaine de la Renardière
33 Cellier Saint Benoit
34 Domaine de la Borde
35 Paul Benoit et Fils
36 Maison Pierre Overnoy/
     Emmanuel Houillon
37 Philippe Bornard
38 Fruitière Vinicole de Pupillin
39 Domaine Overnoy-Crinquand
40 Domaine Désiré Petit

Abergement-le-Petit
41 Les Bottes Rouges

Mathenay
42 Domaine de Saint-Pierre

Les Sites pittoresques
de Franche-Comté – C. L., F.
9 - SALINS-les-BAINS (Jura
L'Eglise Saint-Anatolle
et le Fort Saint-André
altitude 598m)

This postcard from the early 1900s shows the vineyards around Salins-les-Bains covering the entire hill below the cliffs. The building on top of the cliffs is Fort St-André, at 598m.

swathe below the forests to Arbois and beyond to the village of Pupillin, with its own appellation, Arbois-Pupillin.

The largest domaines of the Jura, including Domaines Henri Maire, are based in AOC Arbois, as well as the largest cooperative, although they all own some vineyards in other appellations of the Jura wine region. This part of the region also has more innovative producers than elsewhere, with more willingness to experiment. With the exception of the most southerly area of the Jura, the Sud Revermont, the Arbois area has the highest proportion of vineyards that have converted to organic or biodynamic viticulture, as well as more producers working in the natural way. Somehow the whole atmosphere of this area is more dynamic than the areas around Château-Chalon and L'Etoile.

Salins-les-Bains

Today it is hard to imagine the importance of the vineyards of the once prosperous salt-

mining town Salins-les-Bains and its surrounding villages, which covered around 800ha at their peak in the 19th century. Numerous old photos show the vineyards covering every slope below the imposing hills, both adorned with forts, on either side of the town. This was considered a prized red wine area, known in particular for its Trousseau, yet the vine disappeared here faster than elsewhere.

The most famous Salinois vigneron was Charles Rouget, author of *Les vignobles du Jura et de la Franche-Comté* (1897), which has been cited elsewhere in connection with his extraordinary documentation of the Jura's grape varieties. His descendants kept on his vines and these are farmed today by Montigny-based Frédéric Lornet, whose 4ha represent about half the vines in the Salins area. The vineyards here, including most notably the south-facing Chamoz vineyard west of the town, are classified as AOC Côtes du Jura, and I believe that more will be revived in the future. Salins' viticultural past was honoured when it was host to the Percée du Vin Jaune in 2007. A somewhat grey spa town, complete with casino, it nevertheless attracts tourists in summer and has glorious walking nearby, especially on the slopes of the imposing Mont Poupet.

Domaine Les Sarmentelles

Established by Patrick and Elizabeth Grandmaison in 1992, this small estate is one of the few with vineyards very close to Salins-les-Bains. Having worked at the

Société de Viticulture du Jura (SVJ) for several years, Adrien Robbe joined the estate in 2011 following the departure of Elizabeth Grandmaison and became a full partner with Patrick Grandmaison in 2013. They hope to expand the current vineyard holdings, in particular to plant more whites in Salins-les-Bains on old vineyard lands.

Currently the estate has some vines in AOC Arbois in Les Arsures, with the majority in AOC Côtes du Jura, near the estate's winery in Aiglepierre, plus a few in Salins on the lower slopes of Mont Poupet, in the historic vineyard of Chamoz. The vineyards are managed in *lutte raisonnée*, grassing down the rows, working every other one, and eschewing use of anti-botrytis sprays. Machine picking is used except for Crémant. Winemaking is fairly traditional, using only indigenous yeast and using old oak of various sizes for maturation of both reds and whites.

The mineral, spicy and dark fruit-flavoured Arbois Trousseau is the highlight of the reds, aged in large old *foudres*, with the fruit from three stony, warm parcels in Les Arsures, always reputed for this variety. A very Jurassien, minerally Côtes du Jura Chardonnay is released young – it is vinified in tank but aged in old *fûts* and, although there is no *voile*, it is not topped up to give, as Adrien puts it, 'a touch of the Jura'. Most Chardonnay is used for their soft and sweetish Crémant, made with a relatively high *dosage*. They have no wish to make a Savagnin *ouillé*, saying it is too 'Alsace in style', and the only traditional Savagnin I tasted was rather volatile. The Vin Jaune, however, aged in an underground cellar that is more of an old-style humid one, is very elegant, lemony and eminently drinkable on release. Sales are mainly directly to consumers at many tasting shows and local markets in and around Franche-Comté or via Pascal

Colin's wine shop in Salins-les-Bains. It is good to see this producer from the historic region of Salins find a ready market.

Domaine Les Sarmentelles
33 Rue des Orcières, 39110 Aiglepierre

Tel: 03 84 73 26 16

Email: robbe.adrien@orange.fr; patrick.grandmaison@wanadoo.fr

Web: vinsgrandmaison.fr

Contacts: Patrick Grandmaison and Adrien Robbe

Map ref: p. 141, C3

Established: 1992

Vineyards: 5.5ha (1.3ha Chardonnay, 1ha Savagnin, 2ha Trousseau, 0.6ha Pinot Noir, 0.6ha Poulsard)

Visits: No tasting room, but visits welcomed by appointment

Outside the **caveau** *(tasting room)* of Domaine Les Sarmentelles.

Arc-et-Senans to Villette-lès-Arbois

AOC Arbois stretches in a northwest arc from the town of Arbois as far as Molamboz, taking in first Villette-lès-Arbois, then Vadans and St-Cyr-Montmalin (two interlinked hamlets). On the road from Arbois towards Dole, the extensive vineyards on the left stop, giving way to pasture. On the right, across the River Cuisance, the hills rise gently towards woodlands interspersed with the few remaining vineyards. These vineyard slopes facing south and southeast were, unlike those of Salins, still widely planted and producing good enough wines to be included in the original 1936 Arbois AOC regulations.

Beyond, heading north towards the Loue river, Mouchard, Cramans and the peaceful village of Port-Lesney, which straddles the river, now have only very scattered vineyards between the forests. These are classified as AOC Côtes du Jura. Where the Loue river flows just north of Cramans marks the division between the Jura and Doubs departments and just on the other side is the small town of Arc-et-Senans, home to the magnificent heritage site of the Saline Royale (Royal Saltworks – see 'Visiting the region', p. 329). Producer Raphaël Monnier, who is based at Arc-et-Senans, along with Etienne Thiébaud in Cramans and Domaine des Bodines in Arbois, all profiled in this chapter, have reclaimed some of the almost abandoned vineyards, classified as IGP, on the edge of the vast Chaux forest.

Jean-Marc Brignot

After learning about wine with natural winemakers in Beaujolais and working for a short time with Domaine Pierre Overnoy followed by a spell at an organic Champagne producer, Jean-Marc Brignot, originally from Normandy, bought 4.5ha of the excellent Grand Curoulet vineyards from retired Arbois grower Robert Aviet in 2004. He set up his winery in an almost ruined house in Molamboz. The vineyards were farmed with a hands-off approach and the wines were made similarly, with no added SO_2. He made 17 different red, white and sparkling cuvées in 2004 and 15 in 2005, soon acquiring customers among natural wine fans around the world.

Jean-Marc's Jura wines had crazy names, were often cloudy, showed odd flavours depending on when they were tasted, yet in some there was incredible purity and liveliness on the palate, fully expressing both terroir and variety. After several vintages his vineyards produced so little that he gave up on them and instead made wines from grapes purchased in other regions of France under a négociant label. Eventually in 2012 he left the region to live in Japan. Domaine du Pélican bought the vineyards.

Domaine des Cavarodes

Etienne Thiébaud is a gentle soul whose hippy looks are in perfect harmony with his approach to farming the vines organically and making his wines the natural way. Behind the small stone house on the main road through Cramans is a traditional semi-underground winemaker's cellar, full of barrels and *foudres* of all sizes, carefully chalk-marked with the name of the cuvée. An amphora lurks in the corner, obtained for him by his Belgian importer.

Etienne worked for Pascal Clairet before completing formal wine studies and setting up on his own, still in his early twenties. He took over several very old small vineyard plots outside the AOC region just on the other side of the Loue river, with vines between 60 and 120 years old. These vines include several extremely rare varieties on the point of extinction that have caught the interest of Gaël Delorme of the SVJ and even the French national vine nursery in Montpellier. It was logical for Etienne to farm these organically from the start. He also converted the vineyard plots he gradually assembled in AOC Arbois, in Les Messagelins near Pasteur's vineyard and Chemenot near La Pinte, and in AOC Côtes du Jura, in Mouchard, to organics. New plantings have used mass selections, including Savagnin Jaune and Trousseau à la Dame.

Etienne Thiébaud of Domaine des Cavarodes outside his cellar.

Etienne's non-interventionist approach means no SO_2 addition to his reds. Some SO_2 is added to the whites before fermentation because he does not have a decent cooling system. Reds are hand-destemmed on a *crible* and fermentation is semi-carbonic maceration. He has exported to the USA and Japan since the early days and initially added some SO_2 before bottling for shipment, but stopped, as he found that it made no difference.

There are many different cuvées for this small holding of vineyards, some named after their vineyard and some after the soil type or fossils. An interesting curiosity is the rustic IGP Franche-Comté red field blend from one-third Trousseau, one-third Pinot Noir plus ten rare varieties. There is also a Chardonnay-based white IGP with some Savagnin, Savagnin Rose and the obscure-to-Jura Sauvignonasse. There are wonderfully pure fruit flavours in his single-variety AOC wines, which include Chardonnay Guille-Buiton and Trousseau Messagelin. His Savagnin *ouillé* wines, including Côtes du Jura Ostrea Virgula, are particularly expressive and, due to the reductive form of winemaking and some residual CO_2, these benefit from decanting. This thoughtful young vigneron wears the mantle of a natural winemaker very well.

Domaine des Cavarodes
28 Grande Rue, 39600 Cramans

Tel: 06 22 74 96 70

Email: etiennethiebaud@hotmail.fr

Web: domainedescavarodes.com

Contact: Etienne Thiébaud

Map ref: p. 141, C5

Established: 2007

Vineyards: 4.5ha (all varieties, plus rarities)

Certification: Ecocert

Visits: No tasting room, but visits welcomed by appointment

Domaine de la Loue

It is not that unusual to find someone from Paris who has made the lifestyle move to a small village in the Jura, but the leap from working as a successful film producer to becoming a one-woman-band tiny wine producer is something else entirely. Having worked as line producer on the wine documentary *Mondovino*, which was released in 2003, Catherine Hannoun later worked on a documentary in the region of Franche-Comté, during which she spent several weeks in Port-Lesney. She liked the area and decided to stay and make wine

It is no surprise that ex-film producer Catherine Hannoun chooses to illustrate her labels with modern art.

small-scale modern equipment, something she deems essential for working with no or very low SO_2 levels. In the short time she has been established she has made the whole range of Jura wine styles, but not every year – there will be a Vin Jaune in 2016 from the excellent 2009 vintage. For me, Savagnin is definitely her forte. The Pupillin Sous Roche vineyard was planted in 2005 and she took it over and converted it in 2009 to organics and the most recent Savagnin *ouillé* wines from here have been excellent. Catherine equates each stage of the wine production process to the film production sequence, with the harvest period equating to the actual filming. There is a fascinating storyboard evolving from this tiny producer.

Domaine de la Loue
5 Route de Lorette, 39600 Port-Lesney
Tel: 09 51 32 81 27; 06 14 70 19 53
Email: channoun@free.fr
Web: www.domainedelaloue.com
Contact: Catherine Hannoun
Map ref: p. 141, C4
Established: 2008
Vineyards: 1.5ha (Savagnin, Chardonnay, Trousseau)
Certification: Ecocert
Visits: No tasting room, but visits welcomed by appointment

in her own way, on her own, methodically working out what she wanted to achieve in the bottle, just like making a film.

First Catherine worked with Manu Houillon of Maison Pierre Overnoy. Then she set about buying and leasing some vineyards, immediately converting them to organics, and soon introduced biodynamic methods. Originally she had plots in Villette-lès-Arbois, Pupillin and Buffard, in the Doubs, from where she made her Trousseau Rouge de Colère or 'Angry Red'. A small interruption in the form of her baby daughter Raphaëlle arriving in 2011 meant that she had to let go the Villette and Buffard plots and part of the Pupillin plot. But since then she has replanted some at Pupillin and taken over a Trousseau plot in Marnoz, near Salins, bringing her estate back up to a mighty 1.5ha. Ideally Catherine would like a total of 2.5ha, a size she believes she can manage on her own.

Catherine equipped her winery with

Domaine Ratapoil

This tiny estate was officially established in 2009 by part-time history teacher Raphaël Monnier and his wife Estelle, but Raphaël had already made wine for himself for nearly a decade, originally in a small project with Jean-Baptiste Ménigoz. Raphaël had the foresight to register as his domaine name *ratapoil*, a local Arbois word meaning

Raphaël Monnier of Domaine Ratapoil has chosen a fresh style for his wine labels.

foudres for reds but for now, apart from some Pinot in *demi-muids*, they remain in tank. In the generous 2011 vintage they managed to make 90 hecto-litres (about 12,000 bottles), but production in the small 2012 and 2013 vintages together amounts to less than this. Exports are a staggering 70% of sales, with the rest going to restaurants and wine shops in France. This is one of the rare Jura vignerons who sells little directly to consumers, simply because he is off the beaten track and does few tasting shows.

either a newcomer to the wine world (with no family connections) or a hobby winemaker, something that has remained more prevalent in the Jura than elsewhere in France. This *ratapoil* is now producing serious wines, well worth seeking out.

Raphaël and Estelle have lived in an old farm in the forest just outside Arc-et-Senans since 2000. They farm 2ha of vineyards organically, using some biodynamic methods as well, mainly in the Arbois AOC, but also with one mixed parcel near Buffard of 60+-year-old vines, with several rare varieties. This creates a red field blend they name simply Le Ratapoil, which, as with all their reds, is fruit-forward and made with no SO₂ addition. Their Arbois Poulsard and Trousseau come from several parcels in Les Corvées and En Paradis, both prime sites. The whites are mainly from vineyards in Vadans, where Raphaël also planted more Chardonnay in 2012.

The garage winery is just through the kitchen door, with wines starting life in small stainless steel tanks. The whites are then put into oak. One day Raphaël hopes to use

A couple of Savagnin barrels were put aside in 2010 and 2011 for potential Vin Jaune. Both topped-up Chardonnay and Savagnin sing with a lovely balance and elegance, showing a great deal of mineral character and complexity. In the reds, the Trousseau Les Corvées appeals to me, with a structure behind an almost inevitable reduction, prevalent even more on the Poulsard and the IGP blend. A Pinot, L'Ingénu, made first in 2012 from vineyards in En Paradis, is tasting good.

This outsider has thought through carefully how to make his wines to get the best out of his interesting vineyard sites, which has brought him a strong following among natural wine supporters. With lovely innovative labels that could only have come from the mind of an outsider to the world of wine, I hope to see this little estate go from strength to strength.

Domaine Ratapoil
9 Rue du Deffois, 25610 Arc-et-Senans

Tel: 03 81 57 56 12

Email: monnierraphael@orange.fr

Contact: Raphaël Monnier

Map ref: p. 141, B5

Established: 2009

Vineyards: 2.4ha (all five varieties)

Certification: Ecocert

Visits: No tasting room, visits by appointment

Domaine de Saint-Pierre

The village of Vadans has a history of important vineyard holdings connected to one of the aristocratic families of the region going back 500 years. In the late 1980s successful lawyer Philippe Moyne, born in Paris but with Jura heritage on his father's side and practising in Dole, decided to replant a few hectares of vines above his house and the 13th-century chapel in the hamlet of St-Pierre-sous-Vadans. Arbois-born Fabrice Dodane joined the estate as manager in

1989 after wine studies at Beaune and several years' work at the Pupillin Fruitière and he took over the estate a year after Philippe Moyne's untimely death in 2011.

In 2002 Fabrice began conversion of the vineyards to organic viticulture with official 'in conversion' certification from 2008. At this time he also introduced some biodynamic methods and found that, increasingly, the nature of the terroir came out in the wines, proving to him that this was definitely the right method to work with. Half of the vines are between St-Pierre and Vadans, where the soil is extremely rocky with more limestone than clay, ideal for Chardonnay, and other plots are in nearby Molamboz, on more marl-based soils, as well as in Arbois and Pupillin. The purpose-built winery and tasting room are at the mill below St-Pierre on the edge of Mathenay.

In the flexible winery with small stainless steel tanks Fabrice enjoys working with several different cuvées to reflect the soil types and is working towards a natural winemaking approach. Until recently the oak has been a little too new, but no more new barrels are being purchased. He uses some SO_2 at the start of fermentation for whites, but none for reds, where he uses whole berries and mostly semi-carbonic maceration. The Chardonnay Les Brûlées, vinified with 25% new oak, has earned a good reputation and is reminiscent of a slightly old-fashioned village Burgundy. More interesting is a Melon à Queue Rouge from three

The church at St-Pierre-sous-Vadans below one of Domaine de Saint-Pierre's vineyards.

small plots of old vines and a delicious Savagnin *ouillé* named La Voivre, but this is not made every year. Château Renard with 85% Chardonnay and 15% Savagnin *ouillé* has an intense character and great balance. Savagnin is also matured *sous voile* for Vin Jaune or oxidative Savagnin in dry cellars up at the Moyne family house. The signature red is a 50/50 Pinot/Ploussard Les Corvées from a co-planted vineyard and there is also a Petit Curoulet blend from 50/50 Trousseau and Pinot. Two pure Pinots are made too. These reds are modern and fruit-forward in style. A non-Macvin-designated liqueur wine is also made from Pinot.

The late Philippe Moyne put his heart and soul into this project and Fabrice is keen to take the estate forward using the natural way.

Domaine de Saint-Pierre
6 Rue du Moulin, 39600 Mathenay

Tel: 06 79 63 00 27

Email: domainedesaintpierre2@wanadoo.fr

Contact: Fabrice Dodane

Map ref: p. 141, A3

Established: 1989

Vineyards: 5.8ha (3.4ha Chardonnay and Savagnin, 2.4ha Ploussard (Poulsard) and Pinot Noir)

Certification: Ecocert

Visits: Tasting room, visits possible by appointment, shop in summer at Place de la Liberté, Arbois

---

Rémi Treuvey

A young vigneron full of promise, Rémi Treuvey took over his family's small vineyards (his family also grew crops) from the 2003 vintage after studies in Beaune and winemaking stints in Spain and Chile. He improved the winery in Villette-lès-Arbois

and had ambitions to convert his vineyards to biodynamic farming for the simple reason, he told me, that the best wines he had ever tasted were biodynamic. His range was promising, in particular the Trousseau. Unfortunately, for personal reasons, things did not go the way he wanted them to and the last vintage he made was in 2010; after that he sold his grapes. In 2013 Rémi took on a full-time job managing the vineyards and cellars of the biodynamic Domaine du Pélican.

Montigny-les-Arsures and Les Arsures

With over 10% of the total Jura vineyards, stretching from the main N83 road up to the forest above the village, Montigny-les-Arsures has the largest area of vineyards of any village in the Jura (only the town of Arbois has more). The name Montigny comes from Mont Ignis – the mountain of fire. 'Arsures' also signifies 'burnt' and it is thought that extensive forests were burnt here in the 13th century, creating fertile land ideal for vineyards. It had a population of over 1,000 at the start of the 19th century, but half that number by the end of the century, and only around 270 today. During the first half of the 20th century almost all the grape growers of the village would have been in polyculture, delivering their grapes to the short-lived Montigny cooperative (1913–18) or to the Arbois Fruitière. Only from the 1960s did several Montigny growers decide to bottle and market their own wine, and yet today this is a village with an unusual number of top vignerons.

I have been told that all the children

The Tissot family of Montigny and Arbois

There are three domaines in this area with the name Tissot, all related, but these should not be confused with the Tissots of Nevy-sur-Seille (see Domaine De Lahaye, p. 254), who are no relation.

Maurice Tissot was a mixed farmer in Montigny-les-Arsures who planted a small vineyard at Les Rosières near La Vigne de Pasteur, with specific areas for each of his four sons, in 1957. He had six children, five of whom remained connected with wine:

- Bernadette, the eldest, married Albert Fumey. One of their sons is Raphaël Fumey who runs Domaine Fumey-Chatelain with his partner Adeline Chatelain. Another son, Christophe Fumey is a Champagne vigneron in the Aube.

- Jacques married Michelle and they created Domaine Jacques Tissot. Their children, who work in the domaine, are Nathalie and Philippe.

- André married Mireille and they created Domaine André et Mireille Tissot, which has been run for many years by their son Stéphane Tissot with his wife Bénédicte.

- Jean-Louis married Françoise and they created Domaine Jean-Louis Tissot, which is now run by their children Valérie and Jean-Christophe.

- Daniel, the youngest, after a short partnership with André, left the Jura and created Domaine du Pech in Buzet. He died young and the domaine is run by his daughter Magali Tissot with her partner Ludovic Bonnelle.

attending the Montigny village school (which closed in 1992) in the 1940s and early 1950s, whose parents owned and farmed their land, were presumed by the teacher to have no future except on the land and were not encouraged to aspire to education beyond the age of 14. Yet somehow, when one learns about the vignerons who emerged from this period, the teacher seems to have imbued them a zeal for achieving excellence with their meagre inheritance and education. Many of the stone houses surrounding the 12th-century church in the centre of the village have traditional

In the centre of the village of Montigny-les-Arsures the stone drinking fountain sports a plaque stating 'Drinking water – to be consumed with moderation' and 'Capitale de Trousseau'.

semi-underground cellars and signposts can be seen pointing the way to some of the most famous names in Jura wine, located in the different quarters of this spread-out village. There is a large privately owned château, hidden by trees, where Domaine Rolet ages some of its wines.

In the history books Les Arsures, a separate village a couple of kilometres north towards Salins-les-Bains, was most famous for Trousseau, but that mantle has been taken over by Montigny-les-Arsures, the unofficial capital of Trousseau. As much as half of the Trousseau grown in the Jura is probably grown in these two villages, on the warm *graviers gras* – stony limestone on Liassic marl – or on other warm, dark-coloured marls. The vineyards are sheltered too, with sites suitable for all the grapes of the Jura. The village limits include the Vigne de Pasteur at Les Rosières. Montigny will host the Percée festival in 2015.

Caveau de Bacchus

For his son Vincent, now in charge of the estate, Lucien Aviet, nicknamed Bacchus, is a tough act to follow. Much liked and respected locally, Bacchus seems like one of those dyed-in-the-wool traditionalists who believes there's only one way to do things, yet he presents his opinions almost as a challenge, always accompanied by a mischievous twinkle in his blue eyes. And there is nothing Lucien enjoys more than pouring his wines and sharing laughter and banter around the stove in their old cellars, full of *foudres* adorned with cartoons and *bons mots*. Lucien is retired now, but very much still in evidence, although at last he is allowing Vincent, who has worked with his father since 1993, to express his own quiet opinions, not usually so different from his father's.

Lucien comes from a local farming family who took their grapes to the cooperative. Soon after he returned from the Algerian war in 1960 he moved from mixed farming to making wines full-time, becoming one of the first in Montigny to bottle his own wine. The vineyards are in a dozen plots in or close to Montigny. They have always worked the soil and Vincent does not like to grass down the soils much, preferring to limit the nitrogen input for the vines. He uses herbicide under the vines and has worked in *lutte raisonnée* since early this century. Picking has always been by hand, with the same group of people each year, who practise strict selection at the vine. All the bunches are destemmed. The cellars are immaculately clean but as traditional as can be, with reds and Chardonnay fermented at controlled temperatures in large, well-maintained old Alsace *foudres*. Indigenous yeasts are used. Later the whites are moved to *fûts* or *demi-muids* for maturation. Bottling is done in small lots, by terroir as and when the wines are deemed ready, and the bottles have always been sealed with wax.

Nearly all the wine is sold direct from the tasting room to a regular clientele from far and wide, built up through word of mouth over the years. About 35 high-quality restaurants take the wines, including some in Switzerland and Italy. If you are not a habitué of the estate, the big challenge is what wine you are going to get, depending on when you turn up, since no differentiation is made on the label between the different terroirs and cuvées. Both Ploussard, (including a young-vine cuvée and an old-vine cuvée) and Chardonnay (some of which is an old-vine mass selection of Melon à Queue Rouge) are labelled Cuvée des Docteurs in homage to the medical students from Besançon who came to lend a hand with harvest in the early days. The Trousseau, from four different vineyards,

Vincent and his father Lucien Aviet of Caveau de Bacchus raise a glass of Trousseau in the cellar full of foudres where they welcome visitors.

yellow fruit character in these wines. Vincent says that it is always better to sell a great Savagnin than a mediocre Vin Jaune, but the Savagnin cuvée varies hugely. The Arbois Vin Jaune is always sublime, aged in various cellars, mainly at ground level, with only a little in a loft space. It is also bottled in several lots and never sold until six months later to allow the barrels to 'marry'. This Vin Jaune from Caveau de Bacchus is a truly authentic, rich, nutty and long-lived wine. Lucien Aviet has done much over the decades to preserve his interpretation of the authenticity of the Jura wine region and Vincent continues in the same vein.

two with old-vine selections, is named Cuvée des Géologues after the geologists who helped Lucien select the best terroirs. In addition there is the Savagnin Réserve du Caveau, which varies enormously from year to year, a Vin Jaune and a Macvin.

For reds Vincent does not look for too much tannin, but waits until the wine is integrated before bottling; Poulsard has less maceration time than in his father's day. The estate is justly renowned for its long-lived Trousseau, but you might get the lighter-structured Les Bruyères or the stony Nonceau; or will it be the richer En Poussot on red marl, or perhaps the one that Vincent asserts ages the best, the spicy, cherry-flavoured Rosières? Good question. In general, give these wines a couple of years' age and it is worth the risk whichever cuvée you buy – this is rustic, earthy but delicious Trousseau to linger with over a meal.

The Melon or Chardonnay, whichever you end up with, is bottled relatively young soon after malolactic fermentation finishes, but that could be in the spring following the harvest, or maybe the year after. I have always appreciated the minerality and

Caveau de Bacchus
Rue Boutière, 39600 Montigny-les-Arsures

Tel: 03 84 66 11 62; 03 84 66 20 54

Email: caveaubacchus@orange.fr

Contact: Vincent Aviet

Map ref: p. 141, C3

Established: 1960

Vineyards: 6ha (2ha Savagnin, 1ha Chardonnay, 2ha Trousseau, 1ha Ploussard (Poulsard))

Visits: No tasting room, but visits welcomed by appointment

Domaine Daniel Dugois

Dedicated hard workers for their estate and their region, the Dugois family has always combined tradition with technology and marketing in just the right measure. For many years Daniel Dugois was the only producer based in Les Arsures. In 1973, aged only 23, he bought his house, cellars and 2.7ha of vines from a vigneron whose main wine was the once fashionable Rosé du Jura, a field blend of red and white varieties. Daniel likes to remind people that during his first harvest in 1974 they had to pick in the snow. It was an awful vintage. For the first few years he sold his grapes to Henri Maire, but from 1983 began making his own wine, using an image of Henri IV taken from a history book about Arbois on the labels (see 'History', p. 94). Following studies in Beaune and harvests in South Africa and Australia, son Philippe has been in charge since 2013, having worked for several years alongside his parents, Daniel and Monique. Philippe seems set to follow the same pattern of making small changes to the estate, not for change's sake, but always for good reasons.

True to the traditions of Les Arsures, although it may not sound much, with over 4ha this estate has quite possibly the highest proportion of Trousseau of any domaine, 40% of its holdings. Their Trousseau vineyards include La Grevillière, with almost a hectare of wonderful old vines planted in 1950 on a south-facing slope of limestone covered in red marl and warm stones. The same plot covers 5ha in total, with some Trousseau à la Dame, along with Chardonnay, Savagnin and a little Ploussard. Nearby, on the edge of Montigny, is another plot of around 3ha named Chagnon, on dark marl with some dolomitic limestone, particularly good for Chardonnay, also with Ploussard and Trousseau that give less structured fruit, best for Crémant rosé. They have a small plot in Arbois and one more in Les Arsures of just under 1ha called Le Mouchet, partly on Kimmeridgian limestone, where they grow Chardonnay, and partly on red marl, which is planted with Trousseau. Soils are worked in all the vineyards, with some grassed down and mechanical weeding employed. Although they are not organic, the way they practise *lutte raisonnée* means treating every plot differently with very little chemical intervention.

All is hand-picked and Daniel was one of the earliest in the region to have a sorting table in the vineyards, which was used from the 2000 vintage. There is modern equipment in the winery, where they use cold maceration and only indigenous yeast. Everything except the base wine for the Crémant (18% of total production) is oak

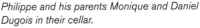

Philippe and his parents Monique and Daniel Dugois in their cellar.

matured, and this is another estate with old *foudres* used for reds and Chardonnay, aged for anything from one to four years. Some 600-litre *demi-muids* have been introduced more recently. Vin Jaune, often one of the best Arbois *jaunes*, aged half in an old stable with a relatively constant temperature and half in the loft of an old barn with big temperature differences, is ready to drink a year or two after release but able to last. The Dugois family has always supported the Percée du Vin Jaune in a big way and Monique Dugois was president of the Percée festival in Cramans in 2004.

The Chardonnays here are a lesson in how ageing in old *foudres* and rigorous topping up can give incredible depth and balance. Several cuvées are made, depending on the year, all of them showing varying degrees of minerality according to their terroir. Among them Cuvée Aigrefeu from dolomitic limestone has at least three years in *foudres* and, as well as being the richest, this is the most Jurassien in style, whereas Le Mouchet on the Kimmeridgian limestone is aged in a mixture of *demi-muids* and *fûts* and is more steely and stony. Since 2007 they have also made a citrussy Savagnin *ouillé* named Auréoline and there is also a white Trousseau Grevillière, both aged for almost a year in *foudres*. These are simply lovely, eminently drinkable wines. Fruity Ploussard has been made for some years, but the stars are the Trousseau cuvées, including Le Mouchet in some years, a deliciously fruity version from Trousseau à la Dame, called La Damelière, and the wonderful Grevillière, one of the best examples of this variety, aged in *foudres* for two or three years and a wine that really develops in bottle.

On a visit here or at a tasting at one of the many shows they participate in it is often possible to taste two vintages side by side of several cuvées, which is a real

bonus and proof – if needed – that every vintage varies greatly in the Jura. Exemplary Crémant, Vin de Paille and Macvin complete the range. Daniel and Monique have retired but lend a hand and Philippe seems happy and confident to be at the helm of this fine estate.

Domaine Daniel Dugois
4 Rue de la Mirode, 39600 Les Arsures

Tel: 03 84 66 03 41

Email: daniel.dugois@wanadoo.fr

Web: vins-danieldugois.com

Contact: Philippe Dugois

Map ref: p. 141, C3

Established: 1974

Vineyards: 10.2ha (3.1ha Chardonnay, 2.4ha Savagnin, 4.1ha Trousseau, 0.6ha Ploussard (Poulsard))

Visits: Tasting room, visits welcomed by appointment

Domaine Fumey-Chatelain

This is a Montigny estate that one hears little about, yet any visitor to Jacques Puffeney further up the road must be curious, passing the attractive cellar door, decked with flowers in summer. Raphaël Fumey's parents (his mother was a Tissot and he is a cousin

Entrance to the welcoming tasting room of Domaine Fumey-Chatelain.

of Frédéric Lornet) once ran the Château de Chavanes farm, selling the grapes from the 6ha of vines. However, the family was forced to leave and lease vines elsewhere when François de Chavanes returned to the estate. Raphaël followed his father's profession without any training, selling the grapes until 1991, when he began bottling part of the crop. Having been brought up at Chavanes, he always thought of it as his home, and in 1999, with his partner Adeline Chatelain from Salins, he bought a small house and old stables from the estate to create his home and winery.

The vineyards are in several different plots in Arbois and Montigny and are worked conventionally. Some of the soils are ploughed and harvesting is mostly by machine. As with making the wines, the very shy Raphaël follows few rules, working each year as he thinks most apt. Some grapes are sold and the rest form the domaine's good-value range. He is assisted by one full-time employee and his more outgoing partner Adeline, who handles sales.

The winery has a mixture of stainless steel and fibre tanks along with *foudres* and *fûts* and only indigenous yeasts are used. Raphaël practises very hands-off winemaking, with most wines seeing some oak, but occasionally he does something different, such as a small lot of Savagnin *ouillé* or an unoaked, unfiltered Trousseau. In general the domaine makes a range of highly drinkable reds, never released very early, combining fruit with spice and structure, reflecting their vintage. A particularly juicy and straightforward Ploussard is made with no oak ageing, and the Trousseau rightly provides a touch more serious and age-worthy style. Pinot is a little hit and miss. A classic stony but fruity Arbois Chardonnay comes from a blend of terroirs and is aged partly in *foudres* with its lees.

For Savagnin, aged *sous voile* in a loft space with big temperature differences, they are strict about selection. Only the best goes for Vin Jaune, which accounts for just 3% of production. Vintage-dated Savagnin is sold only in certain years, usually after five years *sous voile*, and the rest goes into a non-vintage Savagnin and a blend with Chardonnay. The Vin Jaune is nutty, weighty and rather alcoholic, but good. Nearly all sales are in Franche-Comté, some through restaurants and shops, and around 40% at their tasting room, looked after by the welcoming Adeline.

Domaine Fumey-Chatelain
Quartier St-Laurent, 39600 Montigny-les-Arsures

Tel: 03 84 66 27 84

Email: contact@fumey-chatelain.fr

Contact: Adeline Chatelain

Map ref: p. 141, C3

Established: 1991

Vineyards: 14ha (4ha Chardonnay, 3ha Savagnin, 2.5ha Ploussard (Poulsard), 2.5ha Trousseau, 2ha Pinot Noir)

Visits: Tasting room

Michel Gahier

Unless you visit this cellar in what was once the old forge opposite the Montigny church, the most likely places you are going to find a glass of Michel Gahier wine are in New York or at the homely Bistrot des Claquets in Arbois. From nowhere just a few years ago Michel Gahier now sells about a third of his production to the USA; bottles also find their way to Australia, Canada and the UK, among other export markets. All of this has been achieved through word of mouth, since Michel is rarely seen at any tasting, his wines are not certified organic, nor does he

Michel Gahier with one of his old Trousseau vines in his Grands Vergers vineyard.

In the old winery below the house everything is as simple as it can be, with all wines vinified using natural yeast in *foudres*. For temperature control Michel remarks that the best brand for a winery refrigeration system is a *crayère* ('chalk cellar'). SO$_2$ use is mainly avoided, with very low amounts occasionally added. For many years the Trousseau Grands Vergers and Chardonnay de la Fauquette have been the reference wines from this domaine, but little by little Michel has expanded his range. Along with a simple Arbois there are usually three named Chardonnay cuvées, which become progressively more intense: Les Follasses, from more calcareous soil, which has a lovely Arboisien yellow fruit and mineral character, enhanced by time in *foudres*; Les Crêts is aged for longer, partly in smaller oak and generally shows great purity and precision; and, finally, De La Fauquette. This last wine is made from Melon à Queue Rouge vines more than 60 years old. It is initially topped up in *foudres* and then transferred to spend around three years in barrel, not topped up, allowing a *voile* to form naturally. The result is not for everyone, as the oxidative character is extreme, with nuts, spice and curry, along with some volatile acidity when young. The texture on the palate is particularly good and it works well with food – this cuvée definitely needs time and ages very well.

belong to any natural wine grouping, even though he farms his vineyards organically and makes wines in the natural way.

Michel comes from a family of farmers and his parents ended up with 2ha of vineyards, selling most of the grapes to Henri Maire. Michel had no formal wine training but worked alongside his father from the age of 18 before setting up on his own. For the wine he made for family use Michel's father did not like using SO$_2$, maintaining that wines aged better without it – the family were friends with Pierre Overnoy and his family. Michel believes that, although clay-limestone soils, and marl in particular, are ideal for making natural wines due to the grapes' high acidity, it is meticulous vineyard work that makes it possible to make wines in this way. His several parcels of vines are scattered around Montigny, including the notable southwest-facing slope of old Trousseau vines behind the family house, named Les Grands Vergers. He has worked the soils for many years and uses classic Bordeaux mixture and sulphur sprays along with a few biodynamic preparations to reduce copper and sulphur. Each parcel is handled separately with yields kept low – around 36hl/ha for whites and 30hl/ha for reds in a normal year.

Michel makes only around 2,000 bottles of a Ploussard, but much more Trousseau with several cuvées. The Trousseaus are destemmed and spend around a month on their skins with very few punch-downs or pumpovers. They are aged in large oval-shaped *foudres* and it is the shape, Michel says, that means the solids settle easily, so that he does not need to filter. Once again the three named Trousseau cuvées become progressively more intense, structured and mineral. Le Clousot from younger vines on a southwesterly slope has a simple red fruit character; La Vigne de Louis is from a vineyard only 500m away but facing northwest and requires both time and food; finally, the excellent Grands Vergers, sourced from vines 55 to more than 80 years old, gives the most complexity and needs longest to open up.

Aged for now in the same underground aerated cellar below the house where he ages all his wines, it should be no surprise that Michel Gahier's Vin Jaune is excellent – the grand master of Arbois Vin Jaune, his neighbour Jacques Puffeney, was another influence on him. Again there is wonderful texture as well as complexity of flavour. Michel plans to build a new storage area behind the house in 2014 and will experiment with ageing some Savagnin *sous voile* in a higher loft space. Michel takes some getting to know, as do his wines, but, with his fine terroirs and confident approach to both viticulture and winemaking in a natural but measured way, he deserves the success that has come to him.

Michel Gahier
Place de l'Eglise, 39600 Montigny-les-Arsures

Tel: 03 84 66 17 63

Email: michel.gahier@free.fr

Map ref: p. 141, C2

Established: 1990

Vineyards: 6.5ha (2.4ha Chardonnay, 0.7ha Savagnin, 3ha Trousseau, 0.4ha Ploussard (Poulsard))

Visits: No tasting room, but visits welcomed by appointment

Frédéric Lornet

One of the very first wines I really fell for in the Jura, and was able to convince my peers about too, was Frédéric Lornet's Arbois Naturé 1999, a lemony, mineral-laden Savagnin *ouillé*, which showed how wonderfully the Savagnin grape expresses itself in a non-traditional Jura wine. Frédéric Lornet has long been convinced that, apart from Vin Jaune, the best white wines from the Jura should show no trace of oxidation. Railing against the 1980s fashion for oxidative wines that imitated the famous *goût du Jaune* ('taste of Vin Jaune') is just one aspect

Frédéric Lornet with some of the foudres *that date back to his father's time as a cooper.*

of Jura's 'modern' traditions that Frédéric challenges. He has always gone his own way, including forging new markets, being one of the first to sell in the USA from 1994, and in China from 2008. This is obviously a family trait, as his father Roger was one of the first in Montigny to bottle his own wines, starting from the early 1950s, selling wines later to restaurateur André Jeunet, who encouraged him, along with Lucien Aviet and Jacques Puffeney.

Fred's grandfather was a cooper in Montigny and his father Roger continued the business until the mid-1950s, making his own wine as well during the last few years. Roger passed on his 3ha of vineyards to Fred, who made his first wines in 1976, studying at the same time, having already worked with his father when young, helping with the cooperage and the winemaking. From 1981 Fred extended the vineyards and in 1989 he bought the magnificent Cistercian Abbaye de Genne, to live and to make his wine in, just as the monks had done back in the 13th century. He painstakingly restored the nave of the abbey chapel, complete with Gothic arches and renewed stained glass windows, to form his tasting room.

The vineyards are mostly around Montigny and Arbois, with 0.5ha of Savagnin in Côtes du Jura near Buvilly and a rare holding of 4ha in Salins-les-Bains on lands formerly owned by the Rouget family with some interesting old vine selections. He has some prized Arbois and Montigny plots that face southeast or south, warmer than the conventional west-facing vineyards. A thoughtful vigneron, Fred has worked the soils for some years and uses herbicide only directly below the vines; he also selects the most recently developed sprays that limit environmental impact. Fred has long been a staunch defender of machine harvesting and owns his own machine, saying that it enables him to harvest at exactly the right moment. In the cellar a mixture of tanks and *fûts* serve as fermentation vessels, with *foudres* – many repaired by Fred himself – used for ageing most of the wines. Ever questioning, he uses indigenous yeast for reds and Savagnin and cultured yeast for certain Chardonnays if he believes they will help promote a long slow fermentation or give a better base for Crémant. He is meticulous in avoiding any oxidation in all his wines, except for Savagnin *sous voile* of course.

Consistently over the years that I've tasted at this estate, of the range of 15 wines the Crémants have always been enjoyable, as have the Chardonnays and the Trousseaus. There is a particularly good Chardonnay Les Messagelins, made from vines grown on stony soils, partly old glacial moraine. The wine is usually fermented in barrel with just a touch of new oak. An elegant, deeply fruity old-vine Trousseau des Dames, from a selection that Roger and Fred Lornet made together of Trousseau à la Dame, is aged for less than a year in *foudres*. The stars are the Savagnins, both the Naturé, aged according to the vintage sometimes only in tank and sometimes in barrel, and the consistently fine Vin Jaune. This is aged not in the loft as is often done in this village, but in a semi-underground cellar. Fred is always rigorous in making sure the *voile* is thin and grey, never white. A lovely Vin de Paille is made with good sweetness and a spicy Macvin completes the range, both showing the good balance that runs through all Fred's wines.

Frédéric Lornet is very proud of his family history and the work his grandfather and father did as coopers and vignerons to help the Arbois wine region become re-established in the 20th century. He has always wanted to continue this tradition in the way that he thinks works best, flying the flag for his region around the world. However, this is a vigneron who does not always do things as others would like him to and I believe that his well-intentioned ambassadorial work is too rarely recognized. His wines remain eminently drinkable and enjoyable representatives of Arbois.

Frédéric Lornet
Cellier de Genne, L'Abbaye, 39600 Montigny-les-Arsures

Tel: 03 84 37 45 10

Email: frederic.lornet@orange.fr

Map ref: p. 141, C3

Established: 1981

Vineyards: 19ha (6ha Savagnin, 5ha Chardonnay, 5ha Trousseau, 2ha Ploussard (Poulsard), 1ha Pinot Noir)

Visits: Tasting room

Domaine du Pélican

With the creation in 2012 of the most significant new estate in Arbois for some years, it seems apt that its name and label feature a pelican. It is said that a pelican was brought to Arbois by Maximilian I of Habsburg in the 15th century as it was a favourite creature of his wife, Mary of Burgundy. Unfortunately the bird died, but as a recognized Christian symbol of the time the town of Arbois took it on as its town crest. The image shows the pelican nourishing its young from its heart. It seems amazing that no wine estate had ever used the pelican name and that it has taken an outsider – it was the domaine's co-owner François Duvivier's idea – to rectify this.

When Guillaume d'Angerville, proprietor of Domaine Marquis d'Angerville in Volnay, Burgundy, dines with his wife Pauline at the famous Taillevent restaurant in Paris, the sommelier knows he should surprise them with a wine from outside Burgundy to taste blind. However, back in 2007 the couple thought the sommelier had broken the rules when they tasted Stéphane Tissot's Chardonnay Les Bruyères 2005. They were so impressed that they set off to find out more about the Jura and, as others before them, fell for its landscape, its people and the potential of its vineyard land, available at a fraction of the price of the Burgundy equivalent. After discussion with François Duvivier, who had been managing

François Duvivier and Guillaume d'Angerville of Domaine du Pélican in their small barrel cellar.

the Volnay estate along biodynamic lines since 2005, they decided, with him joining as a partner, to invest when they could find the right land.

The partners are fastidious about the terroir they are looking for and hired Yves Hérody, a locally based consultant in pedogeology who works worldwide and has a special interest in biodynamic methods. After rejecting numerous sites as being too windy, too wet or too high, in 2012 they found that the 5ha of biodynamically farmed vineyards belonging to Château de Chavanes in Montigny were available, along with the bijou modern winery. The Chavanes estate was started by François de Chavanes, a film producer originally from the Jura, as a retirement project in 1999. He restored the grand family house (now run as a bed-and-breakfast) and planted the plot of land adjacent, named Le Clos, and four further small plots in prime Montigny sites, one with old vines. The others he planted (Barbi being the largest). The vines were farmed biodynamically from the start and the wines were made in a Burgundian style, but the family never marketed them properly and François de Chavanes began to lose interest. The vineyards were in very good shape and the only downside for d'Angerville is that the red grapes are predominantly Pinot Noir. Not surprisingly, as a Volnay producer he wants to focus more on white in the Jura.

Just as this sale was concluding, another opportunity arose to buy a further 5ha of vineyards in a prime AOC Arbois site, Grand Curoulet – the vines of natural wine legend Jean-Marc Brignot (see p. 144). The good news was that these fitted the criteria not only of having a fine terroir but also of land that had been treated with few chemicals. Unfortunately Brignot had neglected his vineyards for several years and the

Pélican team have uprooted half the vines, replacing them with rye and other crops to restructure the soil. It will be replanted in 2015 with 1.5ha of Savagnin and 1.5ha of Chardonnay. The remaining half, planted with 2ha of Savagnin and 0.4ha of Poulsard, is being strengthened by not allowing the vines to produce grapes until the 2015 vintage. They have found another 1ha of whites to lease from 2014.

The 2012 harvest from the Chavanes vineyards was picked just two months after purchase, and as they hadn't farmed the vines themselves, initially Guillaume d'Angerville was non-committal about whether he would bottle the wine himself, but, by the time the malolactic fermentations were finished in February, he was smiling. With no experience in making traditional Jura wines, they stuck to Burgundian methods, apart from the oak being somewhat older than they would use in Burgundy, and made three wines. The Chardonnay, matured mainly in 350-litre barrels with one new and the rest 1–5 years old, is resolutely Burgundian, but with more minerality emerging on the finish. Savagnin Ouillé, made in older 500-litre barrels, is a very exciting wine, both refined and vibrant. The tasty red is 60% Pinot, 35% Trousseau and 5% Poulsard and is very Burgundian on the nose, but the funky Jura character emerges on the palate. It was aged in older *fûts*. The wines are, no surprise, priced highly, especially for the first vintage, but the Marquis d'Angerville crest and name adorn the label alongside the pelican.

François Duvivier is in overall charge of the vineyards and winery and already had some vigneron friends in the region, notably Julien Mareschal and Jean-Michel Petit of Pupillin, with whom he is currently sharing a dynamizer (for preparing biodynamic sprays). As François is not based on site, in April 2013 he took on an experienced on-site manager, Rémi Treuvey (see p. 149). The search continues for more vineyards nearby in the Arbois AOC as the partners would like an estate of around 15ha, with 75% white and 25% red grapes, with a maximum of half the reds being Pinot Noir. They are also seeking to buy a larger permanent home for the Pélican winery. [Revised 2015: At the end of 2014 Domaine du Pélican leased 4.25ha of Jacques Puffeney's vineyards with a view to purchase.]

The arrival of this prestigious Burgundy domaine in the Jura is exciting indeed and I hope they will integrate well into the region and learn from it too. Once they have enough Savagnin, they are likely to put aside a barrel or two to make Vin Jaune. All their pelicans are not quite in a row yet, but Guillaume and François have prepared the ground well to create a wonderful estate.

Domaine du Pélican
39600 Montigny-les-Arsures

Email: fd@domainedupelican.fr

Contact: François Duvivier

Map ref: p. 141, C3

Established: 2012

Vineyards: 11ha (5ha in production 2013: 1.45ha Chardonnay, 1.15ha Savagnin, 1.6ha Pinot Noir, 0.7ha Trousseau, 0.1ha Poulsard)

Certification: Ecocert, Demeter

Visits: No tasting room, visits only occasionally possible by appointment

Jacques Puffeney

He is known affectionately as 'Le Puff' by some French wine lovers, or with more respect as 'Le Pape d'Arbois' ('the Pope of Arbois'), and worldwide Jacques Puffeney is probably the most recognizable bearded

winemaker from the Jura, even if he rarely travels to sell his wines. With no successors to hand over his wine estate to, in 2012 he made his 50th vintage, having made his first aged 17. Jacques Puffeney's father was a vineyard worker for Joseph Girard (the instigator of the Arbois AOC) and he also owned three cows and 0.5ha of vines, making wine for the family. The young Jacques turned and salted Comté cheese in a local cheese *fruitière* and did military service in Algeria before deciding that making wine was what he wanted to pursue.

During the many short visits and tastings I've experienced with Jacques, at each one he begins reticently, but then opens up to reveal a thoughtful, well-read man, where every action he takes to produce his wines is measured. Without looking anything up, Jacques regularly recites vintage conditions

An oval foudre *topped by two* fûts *in the ageing cellar where Jacques Puffeney receives visitors.*

going back decades. After the notorious heatwave year of 2003 he checked in an old book to verify that 1822 was the last vintage when the harvest had been so early. He always refers back to find similar conditions before deciding when to harvest. Jacques is one of the very few Jura vignerons who has travelled in search of knowledge to understand his own wines better – he has visited both Jerez and Tokaj, the other great homes of wines aged under a *voile*-type yeast.

Jacques Puffeney built up his vineyards through buying and leasing several different plots in Montigny, Arbois and Villette-lès-Arbois, reaching 8ha at one point with a little more white than red. When he reached 60 he decided to cut back the area by a third, but retained the half a hectare of old vines his father planted with Savagnin and Melon à Queue Rouge in 1945 and 1947. Apart from this, most of the other vineyards were planted in the 1970s and 1980s, and it is these that suffer more from Esca than the much older vines. The vineyard soils are worked every other row and in recent years the weeds have been cut down with a ride-on strimmer. Only in the difficult-to-work vineyard that his father planted does herbicide have to be used. Jacques does not work the vineyards organically, believing the use of certain modern chemical anti-fungal treatments to be more efficient and possibly less damaging than organic solutions. He uses low yields of 30–40hl/ha and generally picks late.

In his winery Jacques Puffeney works in a relatively natural way. Here is yet another Montigny cellar where the *foudre* rules and over the years Jacques has not hesitated to invest in new *foudres* or *fûts* when needed, and has used *demi-muids* recently as well. The *futaille* (a word that encompasses all the sizes of barrels) here is impeccable. Only indigenous yeast is used, but Jacques will not hesitate to chaptalize if needed and in 2003 acidified some of his musts; SO_2

Jacques Puffeney, one of the most revered vignerons of the Jura.

use is kept to a reasonable minimum. He makes no Crémant and all wines, except occasionally a barrel-fermented Chardonnay, are fermented in *foudres*, staying until at least after malolactic fermentation, often longer.

Since the mid-2000s Jacques has experimented with a Savagnin *ouillé*, aged in *foudres*, which he has released only a couple of times. Tangy and vinous, it is called Naturé. Jacques has reduced the Chardonnay vineyard holdings most, though he still makes a little of the gorgeously yellow fruit and minerally Melon Queue Rouge [*sic*] and also makes a small amount of Sacha, his blend with 20–35% Savagnin, an excellent introduction to oxidative whites. The Savagnin for potential Vin Jaune spends a year in *foudres* first, fully topped up, and is then moved to *fûts* for the statutory five years of ageing *sous voile*, mainly in a *cave à Vin Jaune* with big temperature changes where alcohol levels may increase by 1% alc. The barrels that stay the course – as little as a quarter in some years – spend another year in *foudres* after blending at cool cellar temperatures before bottling, and it is this that gives the Vin Jaune richness, Jacques maintains. In some years he retains a barrel or two *sous voile* for much longer, up to ten years or more, and these wines have extraordinary intensity. As far as his regular Vin Jaune goes, it is consistently wonderful, somehow combining typical Arbois power with elegance more associated with Château-Chalon, very expressive initially for up to a year after bottling, then closing up for a few years before evolving into something even more complex. Jacques Puffeney's Savagnin is hardly a baby *jaune*, more an interesting wine in its own right, very good value, usually having spent just two years *sous voile*.

The sheer quality of Puffeney's lightly filtered reds are a testament to the fine sites (classic *graviers gras*, warm south-facing stony gravel on red marl vineyards for the Trousseau, grey marl for the Poulsard), his meticulous work in the vineyard and cellar, and the quality of his *foudres*. For red wine vinification the grapes are destemmed but not crushed and pumpovers are just once a day in the *foudres*. Most years two Poulsards are made. The 'M' from Montigny usually shows some reduction at first, giving way to a lovely redcurrant jelly aroma, but this is no glugging Poulsard. Usually with obvious tannin, it cries out for charcuterie. Les Berangères Trousseau, from the eponymous vineyard site, shows fabulous minerality with earthy characters and deep red fruits. Jacques Puffeney loves to hunt small birds and game, and one senses that the wine is almost made to drink with his catch. Sadly, his leased co-planted red vineyard is no longer part of the estate, but he still has some Pinot Noir, which is given newer oak input and is simply outstanding in good vintages.

Jacques Puffeney's wines were the first Jura wines to make waves in the USA, thanks to importer Neal Rosenthal's wide distribution network – fine examples to kick off the trend there. With their waxed tops (specifically for certain export markets – in France these days usually only the Vin Jaune has a wax top), the wines seduced markets looking for new tastes. For a traditional estate there is somehow an honesty and meticulousness here that no one else offers – each cuvée bottled at one time, consistency of quality, and total respect for vintage conditions. The one question that remains unanswered is what will happen to this exemplary wine estate once Jacques feels he cannot continue working – he will be 70 in 2015. [Revised 2015: Jacques' last vintage was 2014 and he then leased 4.25ha of vineyards to Domaine du Pélican.]

This bearded gentleman has offered a great service to the Jura wine region in making his fine long-lived wines year after year, not afraid to experiment, improve and adapt. It is worth laying in stocks to remember him by.

Jacques Puffeney
Quartier de St-Laurent, 39600 Montigny-les-Arsures

Tel: 03 84 55 10 89

Email: jacques.puffeney@orange.fr

Map ref: p. 141, C3

Established: 1962

Vineyards: 5.6ha (2.05 Savagnin, 0.85ha Chardonnay, 1.4ha Poulsard, 1ha Trousseau, 0.3ha Pinot Noir)

Visits: No tasting room, but visits welcomed by appointment

Domaine André et Mireille Tissot

Stéphane Tissot, whose wines are the most widely distributed Jura wines worldwide today, was born into winemaking. At six years old he insisted on helping his father André in the winery as soon as he returned from school. Since André created the domaine in 1962, they have relentlessly expanded to reach 50 hectares and Stéphane has promised his wife he will stop there. Their daughter, aged nine at the time of writing, the youngest of three children, has always said she will be a vigneron; the two older boys are not so sure, although Aymeric at 16 already helps at tastings. Although there are 17 full-time employees, this is a family business, made successful through extremely hard work and some risk-taking on the part of both André, now retired, and Stéphane, supported by their wives Mireille and Bénédicte.

André Tissot was the most entrepreneurial of his brothers. When he returned from the Algerian war in 1962, he decided that alongside farming dairy cows he would make the wine from his 0.38ha of vines rather than join the cooperative as his father and elder brother Jacques had. The following year, in association with his younger brother Daniel, André leased some vines and planted 1ha at En Muzard. By 1968 Daniel had left and with 4.5ha of vines André decided to give up polyculture to make wine full-time.

In the 1970s the winery – at what was originally Mireille's family home – was expanded into the barn, still in use. André also planted more vineyards and some of the names live on in Stéphane's terroir cuvées, such as La Vasée (2ha), and in 1982 he took over 3ha of old vines at the famous Les Bruyères site. In the early years this was in a system of *métayage* where part of the harvest was given back to the owner, the famous vigneron Pierre-Emile Michel. A few years later André and his brother Jacques purchased 15ha in En Barberon in Bréry in AOC Côtes du Jura (split between them in 1989). By the time Stéphane returned in 1989 after five years of wine studies in Beaune and commercial studies in Annecy, the estate amounted to around 30ha. In a rare move at the time his mother, Mireille, had been added to the name on the label from 1983 in order to differentiate the estate from the other Tissots. Mireille was very much involved, not only in bringing up the three children (the other two chose different careers) but in the administration and above all the sales of the wines. With a relatively large estate, by the 1980s André and Mireille were offering their wines for sale far outside the region and exhibiting at tasting fairs in Paris. Thus they became known on export

Stéphane and Bénédicte Tissot in the cellar with their clay amphorae.

markets too – I remember seeing their Vin Jaune in London in the 1980s.

Stéphane took over winemaking from 1990 and from the start wanted to change everything and it is to André's credit that he allowed the then radical introduction of small barrels for Chardonnay fermentation and Pinot Noir ageing. In the early 1990s Stéphane also worked for five months in Australia with Brown Brothers and for three months with the Bergkelder in South Africa. In the meantime he met Bénédicte, who worked on the commercial side of the estate from 1993 after wine studies locally. Once Stéphane began winning the estate a plethora of wine medals, André and Mireille accepted his new methods. After a few years Stéphane realized that for what he wanted to do with the wines the vineyards needed to be worked in a more reasoned manner and he started working the soils and reducing herbicide use. As yields became uncomfortably low, André was not happy when Stéphane stated he wanted to convert the estate fully to organics. In the end, as

André has told me, Stéphane gave him an ultimatum, saying either we convert or I leave. André backed off, and while always supporting him, at a relatively young age he and Mireille handed the reins of the estate over to their son, who converted the whole estate to organics with Ecocert certification from 1999. Stéphane retains his parents' name on the label, even though his name appears too with Bénédicte.

Since the early 1990s there has been a gradual increase in plantings, notably in En Spois (Stéphane's first major planting of 4.3ha), La Mailloche (3ha of old vines), La Tour de Curon (see later) and 1.7ha in Lyas, Domblans (partly in AOC Château-Chalon). Stéphane was inspired to convert to biodynamics, no mean feat on such a large scale, and received Demeter certification from 2005. He believes that the heavy clay and marl soils, while hard to work, are ideal for biodynamics as long as one is prepared to put in hours of work and to take low yields – he aims for half the average yield in the region, helped by having either old vines or using mass selections for new plantings.

Whenever you meet or talk with him, Stéphane will always assure you that 'La vie est belle,' 'Life is beautiful' – never so much as when he is explaining a new winemaking project. And there are many. Starting in the mid-1990s Stéphane has moved the range from the solid Jura mix made by his parents to one of innovation. In some projects, like the single-terroir Chardonnays that he first made his name with, Savagnin *ouillé* (named Traminer in a nod to the ampelographic connection) and Poulsard made with no added sulphur, he was by no means the first. Others, like his sweet wines, Spirale, PMG and Audace, all non-Vins de Paille, first produced in the late 1990s, his Savagnin fermented on skins in amphorae, his Crémant Indigène made with a *liqueur de tirage* (to promote the second fermentation) with sugar and yeast from fermenting Vin de Paille, and his distinctly different terroir-specific Vins Jaunes (from the 2003 vintage) are styles that Stéphane has pioneered in the Jura. These winemaking projects have been done in an ever-questioning and evolving manner more often encountered among New World winemakers.

Stéphane is most proud of his project to rehabilitate the vineyards high above Arbois, around the Tour de Curon, a tower surrounded by a once renowned vineyard, Le Clos on land that had been abandoned. He purchased the land partly from the Henri Maire company and family and partly

Stéphane Tissot in his original Clos de la Tour de Curon vineyard above Arbois. The Chardonnay vines are close-planted, each grown on a single stake.

from the Millet family in 2001. (It was once owned by the Dejean de St-Marcel family: see 'History', p. 114.) It took over three months to clear the land (just over a hectare) for planting. With the terraced land facing southwest on steep stony limestone soil, more typical of Burgundy than the Jura, and partly a south-facing plateau area, Stéphane decided to plant Chardonnay in the old way, each vine on a single stake, at a density of 14,500 vines per hectare, worked initially only by horse. With additional plantings over the next few years, Stéphane now has 9ha in the vineyards close to La Tour de Curon that incorporate Le Curon and Les Corvées sous Curon – all prime Arbois sites.

The first vintage of Chardonnay La Tour de Curon, 2004, was released in 2006 and Stéphane set a price that was considerably higher than that of his Vin Jaune, unheard of at the time. Yet another gamble, but Stéphane was convinced that it was the equal of *grand cru* white Burgundy, and he has never had a problem selling the wine. Along with his other Chardonnays, notably La Mailloche, on its rock-hard clay, the wine demands opening early and decanting. All Stéphane's Chardonnays are made very reductively – the range starts with the good-value Empreinte ('Imprint'), made from a blend of different terroirs. These Chardonnays offer a gamut of stony, mineral and earthy flavours, each one different but with great balance and intensity, developing extremely well over time.

Reds include a delicious juicy Poulsard, an intense Trousseau Singulier from old, low-yielding vines, and thoughtfully made, slightly oaky Pinot. The Crémants are delightful. I love the BBF – standing for 'Blanc de Blancs *élevé en fûts*' – which is made from an oak-aged base wine. The luscious, low-alcohol Spirale and all his other non-Vins de Paille are excellent and worthy of ageing. The range is extensive but very good. For me the Traminer is the least successful, and not surprisingly his amphorae experiments, macerating for months on the skins – now with Trousseau as well as Savagnin – are some of his most intriguing wines. The range of Vins Jaunes is fascinating. However, due to being aged in dry conditions with much temperature variation, I find them sometimes over-alcoholic. The En Spois is for drinking first, La Vasée for keeping a while and Les Bruyères by far the most intense Jurassic style. There is one aged in a whisky cask from the Isle of Jura and Château-Chalon is the latest release.

From 1997 Bénédicte and Stéphane started the négociant business Caves de la Reine Jeanne, now evolved into the Cellier des Tiercelines with a partner (see p. 190). In 2002 they opened a stylish tasting room in Arbois, run by Bénédicte. Through this and direct requests to the winery they sell over 25% directly to consumers and an equal amount is sold through shops and restaurants in France. Half is exported, built up from a very small base over ten years,

going to the USA, Canada, Japan and many countries in Europe and beyond. Crémant, which accounts for nearly 30% of production, provides a great introduction to the estate.

Envied by some, respected by many others, Stéphane, like his father before him, supports his region and participates in regional events, even if he doesn't always toe the regional line with his wines. I believe that Stéphane Tissot has done more good for the region than any vigneron since Henri Maire. His wines are of the highest quality and reflect him – full of energy and good will, they and he are among the region's finest ambassadors. My hope is that now he will consolidate, although never stop questioning.

Domaine André et Mireille Tissot
Quartier Bernand, 39600 Montigny-les-Arsures

Tel: 03 84 66 08 27

Email: stephane.tissot.arbois@wanadoo.fr

Web: stephane-tissot.com

Contacts: Stéphane and Bénédicte Tissot

Map ref: p. 141, C3

Established: 1962

Vineyards: 50ha (19ha Chardonnay, 9ha Savagnin, 9.5ha Pinot Noir, 7ha Trousseau, 5.5ha Poulsard)

Certification: Ecocert, Demeter

Visits: Tasting room and shop at Place de la Liberté, Arbois. Visits to the winery by appointment

Domaine Jean-Louis Tissot

Sister and brother, bubbly Valérie and shy Jean-Christophe Tissot run this estate, but their retired parents Françoise and Jean-Louis lend them a willing hand, Françoise helping out with tastings and Jean-Louis in the vineyard – for them, retirement is theoretical. Françoise Masson from the hamlet of Vauxelles, between Arbois and Montigny, married Jean-Louis Tissot from Montigny (2km away) in 1965; she had two grandparents closely connected with the wine business. On her father's side, Albert Masson ran a service making sparkling wines for vignerons, important even back in the early 20th century. On her mother's side, Albert Pirouet was one of the founders of the Arbois Fruitière and among those who worked hard for Arbois to obtain the AOC in 1936. Françoise's father also joined the cooperative and she inherited his vines to pool with the 1.6ha that Jean-Louis inherited from his father Maurice Tissot. In the early years Jean-Louis was part of the Fruitière too, but after planting 8ha of vines in 1990 they decided to start producing their own wines.

Valérie studied wine production at Mâcon-Davayé and Jean-Christophe at Beaune. Today Valérie runs the commercial side of the business and Jean-Christophe makes the wine and is in charge of the vineyards together with their father Jean-Louis. They own various parcels around Montigny, including a few hectares in Les Bruyères with its heavy marl ideal for Poulsard and Savagnin. The vines are grassed down every other row, using herbicide only under the vine rows, and managed on *lutte raisonnée*

Sister and brother Valérie and Jean-Christophe Tissot in their cave à Vin Jaune *in a loft area.*

lines with one full-time employee and three seasonal workers. Harvest is partly by hand and partly by machine and a small quantity of grapes is sold to the Cellier des Tiercelines négociant. Originally the wine was made and matured in Vauxelles, but in the early 2000s they bought a large house in Les Arsures, where Jean-Louis and Françoise moved together with Jean-Christophe. They installed a winery in the outbuildings with a ventilated loft area to dry Vin de Paille grapes and to age barrels for Vin Jaune, although most of the wine ageing remains in Vauxelles.

Winemaking is simple and traditional. Reds are vinified in cement tank and, in the case of Trousseau and the Rouge Tradition (one-third each of Poulsard, Trousseau and Pinot Noir), aged in *foudres*. These reds in good years can be juicy and sappy, traditionally structured with those earthy tannins that are unexpected after the very pale colour of the wines. The Trousseau ages particularly well. There are two Chardonnays. The main cuvée is aged in tank and *foudres*, providing an excellent example of simple appley, mineral Arbois Chardonnay, needing a little time to emerge, and the Cuvée Jean-Christophe is partly aged in oak barrels; this is less successful. All Savagnin is aged for potential Vin Jaune and some withdrawn for a Reserve blend of 40% together with the classic Chardonnay, and some for a Savagnin. These are both decent examples, but the Vin Jaune shines as a very oxidative, nutty Arbois style with a touch of elegance.

This branch of the Tissot family may be less visible than the others, but this will surely change as Valérie Tissot becomes president of the Percée festival to be held in Montigny in 2015. The domaine is well worth seeking out for good-value, true-to-type wines produced by a family of real ambassadors for Arbois and its wines. So far they have not exported, selling directly to consumers and through wholesalers in France.

Domaine Jean-Louis Tissot
Vauxelles, 39600 Montigny-les-Arsures

Tel: 03 84 66 13 08

Email: valerie.tissot@wanadoo.fr

Web: domaine-jeanlouis-tissot.com

Contact: Valérie Tissot

Map ref: p. 141, C2

Established: 1976 (vineyards 1965)

Vineyards: 17ha (6ha Chardonnay, 4ha Savagnin, 4.5ha Poulsard, 2ha Trousseau, 0.5ha Pinot Noir)

Visits: Tasting room, visits welcomed by appointment here or at Rue de la Mirode, Les Arsures

Château Pécauld houses the CIVJ as well as the wine museum, which incorporates the demonstration vineyard seen outside.

Arbois and Mesnay

Arbois, the symbolic capital of the wine region, used to have a slogan on posters and labels that in our more politically correct times would certainly not be allowed in France: 'Le vin d'Arbois: plus on en boit, plus on va droit,' meaning 'Arbois wine: the more you drink, the straighter you go.' The wines have been cited by Henri IV and more recently by French singer Jacques Brel in his song 'My last supper'. In the history part of this book Arbois features more than any other town, and not only because of its fame as the town where Pasteur grew up. The heart of the town beats to the rhythm of wine, with several producer shops in the centre, vines next to the Eglise St-Just with its wonderful golden-coloured stone, and festivals in summer, such as the music festival, Festicaves, or the historical Fête du Biou (see 'Visiting the region', p. 337), all

inspired by wine. The town is home to the region's main wine museum as well as to the CIVJ, both housed in Château Pécauld. There are more good restaurants and good food shops here than any other town in the Jura wine region.

As well as the producer shops in Arbois, many producers have their cellars within the town limits. Indeed there are several hundred hectares of vines within its limits, including some of the most famous vineyards that appear on terroir selections: Mailloche, Curoulet, Curon, Les Corvées, En Paradis ... all with different aspects and variations of marl and limestone soils. The best way to view the vast bowl of vineyards with the town in the middle is from the viewpoint at the Hermitage chapel, off the road to the Cirque du Fer à Cheval.

The village of Mesnay is almost an extension of Arbois to the east and sits above the Reculée des Planches, also known as the Reculée d'Arbois. The Nouvelles vineyards form a long west-facing slope that extends into Mesnay and a few producers are preserving and reviving vineyards in the village. Les Planches itself down in the *reculée* used to have vineyards and it is well worth a visit to see the village and experience the view looking down on to the *reculée* from the viewpoints above.

Domaine des Bodines

Not everyone wants to live where they work, but in the wine world it is normal practice, although you usually have to jump into a van to reach the vineyards. In this sense Emilie and Alexis Porteret are the luckiest of all the young vignerons I know in the Jura – they can walk out of their front door and reach their 3ha of vines in less than a hundred paces. Yet, when this young couple bottled their first batch of wine in 2011 and looked at the 8,000 bottles in front of them, they cried – they were so worried about selling them, never envisaging that some would end up on sale in California.

Alexis and Emilie are both from the Doubs department – Alexis from Buffard, where his grandfather had a few rows of vines, the only small connection with wine they had. However, Alexis decided to swap a career in industry for one in the Jura vineyards, and Emilie, a trained childcare assistant, was happy to join him. Before the decision was taken Alexis worked for a couple of summer seasons with Pascal Clairet of Domaine de la Tournelle and studied for a

Emilie Porteret, who owns Domaine des Bodines with her husband Alexis.

wine diploma in order to benefit from state finance for young vignerons.

Their 3ha vineyard on a gentle west-facing slope on the edge of Arbois was sold to them by Jean-Paul Crinquand, a prominent member of the Arbois Fruitière. Although Crinquand had used herbicide under the vines, all but one part of the vineyard, with Trousseau, had been regularly ploughed, which meant that an immediate conversion to organics wasn't too hard, with yields remaining sensible. Alexis works half-time at the biodynamically run Domaine de la Pinte and would like one day to convert his vineyards fully to biodynamics, but for now he restricts himself to using some plant preparations. The main vineyard has little Savagnin, so they have managed to take over 0.5ha of Savagnin vines close to La Pinte in Pupillin, previously farmed organically by Catherine Hannoun. They also make an IGP Franche-Comté wine from grandfather's old Chardonnay vineyard, which had been organic for some ten years.

The winery is full of second-hand equipment with an array of *foudres* and barrels from Burgundy, though all the wines start in tank. The wines are made resolutely in the natural way, and after checking to see whether they could withstand it, in the 2012 vintage both reds and whites had no SO_2 added at any stage. Emilie manages to fit in helping in the winery and the vineyard between childcare services for others along with their own two toddlers and she also looks after sales and administration. Keen to learn, she hopes to take the organic viticulture and winemaking diploma in Lons. Other help through the year comes from their parents and from a group of friends for harvesting over a couple of weekends. Alexis credits both Bruno Ciofi of La Pinte and Pascal Clairet for helping him to learn the ropes.

The wines appeal to those looking for natural fruit flavours, whether in their Poulsard Pétillant Naturel, Red Bulle, or in the juicy Poulsard and Trousseau reds, both to drink early. The Arbois Chardonnay is also fruit-forward, though with some good minerality; Savagnin *ouillé* sells out quickly and they hope for Vin Jaune from the 2011 vintage. Non-AOC-approved Vin de Paille is made from older vines and likewise there is a Macvin-style Vin de Liqueur.

Total annual production has been about 12,000 bottles a year, with sales initially to family and friends, wine shops with an interest in natural wines and through tasting shows. They have quickly snowballed. This couple, now in their early thirties, have ideas and confidence and are already enjoying success, with half their sales going to export markets. Quite rightly they are taking their project slowly, step by step.

Domaine des Bodines
Route de Dole, 39600 Arbois

Tel: 03 84 66 05 23; 06 86 48 68 38

Email: domainedesbodines@gmail.com

Contacts: Emilie and Alexis Porteret

Map ref: p. 141, B2

Established: 2010

Vineyards: 3.7ha (1.3ha white, 2.4ha red)

Certification: Ecocert

Visits: No tasting room, but visits welcomed by appointment

Les Bottes Rouges

From the town of Pontarlier in the high Jura Mountains (in the Doubs department), Jean-Baptiste Ménigoz is another who never imagined he might one day be a vigneron. His passion was cross-country skiing, in which he competed when young, and he subsequently trained to be a teacher.

He and his friend Raphaël Monnier, also from Pontarlier, moved to the Jura to take up teaching positions. The pair loved wine and decided to take on a small vineyard for fun back in 2000 and make some wine, learning as they went. They went their separate ways and Raphaël established Domaine Ratapoil.

Meantime, Jean-Baptiste got the wine bug and took a viticulture and oenology distance course at Beaune, doing his practical experience with Stéphane Tissot in Montigny. Whenever he was working in the cellars and visitors came around, Stéphane would introduce Jean-Baptiste as a future Arbois vigneron. For Jean-Baptiste this belief in him was really quite incredible, so far removed from his roots, so, at 40 years old, he took on some vineyards and established his own wine estate, naming it Les Bottes Rouges (red boots) after a rock song he liked.

His vineyards are mainly relatively mature vines in the Arbois AOC that he leased in 2011 and started conversion to organic methods. He has also leased a fine 0.3ha southwest-facing slope with a mixed vineyard on grey marl in Grozon, just outside Arbois in Côtes du Jura. Close to here he and his partner have purchased land and converted a building into a small winery. They plan to build a home there and

---

Jean-Baptiste Ménigoz of Les Bottes Rouges enjoying his new role as a vigneron.

to plant 0.3ha of Ploussard.

It is obvious that Jean-Baptiste is making wines he loves to share and drink in a resolutely natural way, and I have enjoyed both his light and appley Chardonnay and his juicy red blend, La Pépée (60% Pinot, 40% Ploussard). For now he still works as a teacher a couple of days a week in Poligny, working with students with learning difficulties. However, he is ready to move on and hopes to expand the vineyards and production sufficiently to become a full-time vigneron. He credits all his wine sales, mainly to shops and restaurants locally, in Paris and on export markets, to showing his wines in 2012 and 2013 at Le Nez dans le Vert organic wine fair, and he values hugely the help and support of his colleagues in the Jura organic wine world. He is indeed a friendly and intelligent addition to this informal group and should produce even better wines in future.

Les Bottes Rouges
10 Rue du Lavoir Limpide,
39800 Abergement-le-Petit

Tel: 06 08 07 46 61

Email: lesbottesrouges@free.fr

Contact: Jean-Baptiste Ménigoz

Map ref: p. 141, A2

Established: 2012

Vineyards: 4ha (1.4ha white, 2.6ha red)

Certification: Ecocert

Visits: No tasting room, but visits welcomed by appointment

Domaine de la Cibellyne

'Allez ma belle, marche, marche ...' ('Come on, walk on, my lovely ...'). The words that Benoît Royer says to encourage his Comtois mare Kigali while ploughing the vineyards (see photo, p. 52) seem to echo from

another age, when horses were routinely used to work the vineyards. Today Benoît and Kigali work his tiny, steep, densely planted old Poulsard vineyard in Mesnay as well as a couple of other vineyards, usually close-planted, including Claude Buchot's in Maynal. This is just one of several jobs that Benoît does, along with teaching biology and viticulture on the organic wine production course at the Lons college and running his very small wine estate.

Benoît originally wanted to be a veterinary surgeon, but ended up studying oenology at Dijon. From Arbois, his parents were not involved in wine, although his uncles had vineyards. After work experience in Burgundy Benoît worked for five years at Domaine de la Pinte before setting up on his own. He took on old vineyards in

Kigali the Comtois mare with Benoît Royer of Domaine de la Cibellyne.

Mesnay and Molamboz in AOC Arbois and a younger one in Buvilly, classified AOC Côtes du Jura, starting conversion to organics right away, and later took on a parcel in Poligny to plant.

Over the few years he has made wine in the small cellar under his house yields have fluctuated wildly, often being too low to be economic, partly because some vineyards, mostly those with younger vines, previously chemically managed, did not convert easily to organics. Benoît has now relinquished the Buvilly vineyards so that he can manage the estate better on his own.

Most of his wines are blends and in recent years there have been various cuvées from different blends and plots. He is a skilful and thoughtful winemaker and results are deliciously simple and elegant in style. Reds are usually made using punch-downs in stainless steel, some small oak ageing, and judicious amounts of SO$_2$. The whites start off in tank and then move into oak, mostly topped up, though he has dabbled with *sous voile* when he has enough volume and in 2005 he made a Vin Jaune. He makes both white Macvin and red Macvin (the latter not every year) and stresses the importance of ageing longer than the minimum time in oak as well as using juice from good ripe fruit. With his wines on some of the best restaurant wine lists in Scandinavia, Benoît's estate epitomizes the 'small is beautiful' approach, and now, with an even smaller domaine, life should get easier for him.

Domaine de la Cibellyne
1 Rue Bernarde, 39600 Mesnay

Tel: 03 84 66 29 71

Email: ben.royer@wanadoo.fr

Contact: Benoît Royer

Map ref: p. 141, C2

Established: 2004

Vineyards: 2ha (1.2ha white, 0.8ha red)

Certification: Ecocert

Visits: No tasting room, but visits welcomed by appointment

Fruitière Vinicole d'Arbois

Established for over 100 years, one of the earliest wine cooperatives established in France, the Arbois Fruitière has played a significant role in the history and development of the modern Jura wine region. In the early days its members fought hard to protect the name of Arbois, leading to the AOC in 1936 (see 'The story of the wine region') and today it remains influential in how the wine region is managed. With around 100 members owning nearly one-third of AOC Arbois vineyards, in terms of sales it shares the top spot with the négociant La Maison du Vigneron in Crançot. One-third of its output is distributed through supermarkets and 37% is sold directly to consumers, mainly through its tasting rooms in Arbois and elsewhere in the Jura. With a reasoned approach in the vast majority of its vineyards combined with modern cellars, the wines from this cooperative have been extremely reliable representatives of Jura wines for many years.

The fundamental rules of the cooperative have remained the same over the years – one member, one vote – each member must bring 100% of his or her grapes to the cooperative, and profits are shared out at the end of each year. The development over the years illustrates the changing economics of growing vines in the region. The 31 founding members in 1906 owned just 31.15ha of vines. In 1958 135 members owned only 119ha, less than 1ha on average. By 2013, while the average holding is nearly 3ha, there is one member (an association of growers) with 40ha and half a dozen members with more than 15ha each. For some years around three-quarters of the grapes have been delivered by just a quarter of the members. Around 20 members are full-time vine growers who own by far the majority of the vineyard area and another ten are farmers who farm vines as well as crops

Bottling by hand at the Fruitière Vinicole d'Arbois in the days when everyone lent a hand.

and cattle. The remaining members with small holdings either have full-time jobs, working their vines only during weekends and evenings, or are retired.

Vineyards are primarily in the main communes of AOC Arbois – Arbois itself, Montigny-les-Arsures and Villette-lès-Arbois (Pupillin has its own Fruitière). A few are farmed organically without certification, such as those belonging to Claire Subtil, known also for offering a service to organic producers with her horse trained to work in the vineyards. The vast majority are farmed in *lutte raisonnée*, with reduced herbicide. These include the vineyards of Joël Morin, one of the larger growers, who has been president of the cooperative since 2001. Growers have to provide proof of how they work, and the Fruitière has had ISO 9001 certification for several years, having also been the earliest in the region to install a plant to deal with effluent.

The small Caveau du Jacobin cooperative in Poligny was incorporated into the Arbois Fruitière in 2005, with 13 members joining with vineyards in AOC Côtes du Jura. Apart from allowing the Arbois Fruitière to extend its range, it meant that it had an extra public tasting facility in the form of

the historic L'Eglise des Jacobins in the middle of Poligny (see p. 218). The Caveau du Jacobin name is used on the cooperative's Côtes du Jura wines.

From its beginnings making wine in Château Pécauld, the Fruitière added premises for storage in different parts of the town, eventually purchasing the grand Château Béthanie and its grounds in 1962. A modern purpose-built winery was constructed and equipped in several stages, with the château itself being used for administration. In the early 1990s a large, ventilated *cave à Vin Jaune* was constructed in a nearby house that was already being used for storage by the cooperative – today around 3,000 barrels of Savagnin *sous voile* age there at any one time. The cooperative is an important Vin Jaune producer, accounting for 8% of its production, about double the average in the Jura, and it is consistently good, though rarely thrilling. Cuvée Béthanie, first made in the late 1960s, was a pioneer of this style, made from 40% Savagnin *sous voile* and 60% Chardonnay aged in large *foudres*, so itself slightly oxidative although not aged *sous voile*. Béthanie has a classic walnut, cream and lemon character, good weight and zingy acidity, and the wine has served as a very good introduction to the oxidative style over the years. A decent Savagnin is made too, usually sold at around five or six years old.

There is a remarkable cellar of well-maintained old *foudres* and most of the red range is aged in *foudres*, as are the Chardonnays, in typical Arbois manner. The reds suffer somewhat from an old-fashioned, slightly hard character, but this is what customers seek. The basic Chardonnay reflects each vintage well, softened usually by the *foudres*, and the single-terroir En Sauvagny shows more minerality and length.

Sparkling wine has always been important for the Arbois Fruitière. In 1982 it was one of the earliest producers in France to invest in a bank of gyropalettes, even before the Crémant du Jura AOC. Crémant is now made in a separate warehouse in Poligny and accounts for 15% of production. The range shows consistent good quality, especially the top-of-the-range Cuvée Montboisie, which has a large proportion of Pinot Noir in the blend. A recent addition is Cuvée Béthanie Crémant, with some Savagnin aged *sous voile* blended in with the Chardonnay. Other Jura specialities are made, all very true to style.

Exports are small, but the consistently decent range represents the region well. The health of this cooperative is vital for Arbois, for the Jura wine region, and most of all for its members. The cooperative is cherished by older producers, who remember the history of members helping each other survive through crises, whether economic or otherwise, which is what the cooperative movement should be all about. Younger members continue to join and, although the sense of self-help is ever present, they need to ensure that the cooperative keeps up with the times in every sense.

Fruitière Vinicole d'Arbois
Château Béthanie, 2 Rue des Fossés, 39600 Arbois

Tel: 03 84 66 11 67

Email: contact@chateau-bethanie.com

Web: chateau-bethanie.com

Contacts: Sylvie Cambray and Christophe Botté

Map ref: p. 141, B2

Established: 1906

Vineyards: 270ha (101ha Chardonnay, 63ha Savagnin, 47ha Poulsard, 44ha Pinot Noir, 15ha Trousseau)

Visits: Tasting room and shop at 43 Place de la Liberté and at 40 Rue Jean Jaurès

Domaine Hughes-Béguet

It is hard to believe that British woman Caroline Hughes, while studying at a French university, could have ever imagined ending up as a vigneron's wife in deepest Jura when she met Patrice Béguet, a maths student and computer nerd. However, after a few years of city life in Paris the couple became disillusioned and Patrice decided to give up his well-paid work as an IT consultant to find something to do in the countryside. As he was already a wine lover, he chose to take a wine diploma in Beaune followed by an oenology degree in Montpellier. Although not from the wine area, Patrice was born in the Jura and it was here that the couple decided to settle, having first found a suitable house with a cellar big enough to act as a winery. Patrice then found various plots of vines, all on excellent terroirs, but mostly those that no one else wanted to work because the land was steep or vines were missing. As they had mostly been neglected, they were not too hard to convert to organic growing.

Patrice is adamant that he wants to keep

the estate small so that he can continue to do most of the work on his own, with assistance from a part-time trainee, from Caroline and other members of his family. Among their small holdings are a couple of plots in their own village, Mesnay, including the northwest-facing Champ Fort on classic grey and white marl, and some holdings in Pupillin, including one on the superb Côte de Feule slope, plus nearly 0.5ha in Les Corvées in Arbois. In the short time since starting in 2009 they have become certified organic and in 2012 converted officially to biodynamics with Demeter certification, a rare thing among smaller growers. Patrice has equipped a small winery and storage area in the semi-underground cellar of the house. He is happy to work hard at marketing and sales too and has won the custom of Arbois restaurateur Jean-Paul Jeunet and a few mentions in guides and reviews. It's hard work but Patrice obviously relishes most of it, if ruing the toll the vineyard work takes on his back. He believes strongly in environmental issues and keeping things small and local, believing this is the most sustainable approach for a vigneron in the

Jura. And life in Mesnay obviously suits Caroline too, who juggles a part-time job in human resources with freelance translations, work on their vineyard and the inevitable paperwork, along with caring for their two young children.

Each year the range is somewhat different and the winemaking is good, although almost deliberately work in progress as Patrice learns what works best with each harvest. The couple have fun with dreaming up names for their cuvées – often with Anglo-French humour involved. Patrice enjoys most working with Ploussard, making various cuvées of rosé (including the barrel-fermented Pulp Fraction with 25% Trousseau), several reds and even a rosé Macvin-type Vin de Liqueur named Coup de Plouss. He makes two single-vineyard red Ploussards, naming only the vineyard, not the grape (how Burgundian!) from Champ Fort and Côte de Feule. The latter is the most successful so far, made deliberately to age, with punch-downs and oak maturation, far from the currently fashionable easy-drinking Poulsards, and it works. So True is very good Trousseau, from grapes grown in Les Corvées and Côte de Feule, made with part carbonic maceration and relatively new oak.

Patrice Hughes-Béguet takes a sample of Ploussard from a **demi-muid** *in his bijou wine cellar.*

There is potential Vin Jaune, and some *sous voile* Savagnin in the meantime, but the star white for me is the delightfully named Très OrDinaire, a delicate and fresh Savagnin *ouillé*, and some years there is a good topped-up Chardonnay/ Savagnin blend too. Crémant, a Pétillant Naturel from a blend of grapes named Plouss Mousse and a Vin de Paille-type red called Straw Berry complete the range for now. Yes, Patrice, like everyone here, loves to play with both his children and his wines, and the games are starting to give some serious results.

Domaine Hughes-Béguet
1 Rue Bardenet, 39600 Mesnay

Tel: 03 84 66 26 39

Email: patrice@hughesbeguet.com

Web: hughesbeguet.com

Contacts: Patrice and Caroline Hughes-Béguet

Map ref: p. 141, C2

Established: 2009

Vineyards: 4.3ha (1.7ha Savagnin, 0.8ha Chardonnay, 1.4ha Ploussard (Poulsard), 0.4ha Trousseau)

Certification: Ecocert, Demeter

Visits: No tasting room, but visits welcomed by appointment

Domaine Ligier Père et Fils

As in many Arbois families, vines were in the blood of the Ligier family, and Jean-Pierre Ligier's father owned 0.7ha of vines, selling the grapes to Henri Maire. In 1986, knowing that his sons Hervé and Stéphane were interested in working in the business too, Jean-Pierre gave up his job in a local bank to take on and expand the vineyards and create a wine estate. First making wine at the family home in Mont-sous-Vaudrey in the northwest of the region, from 2002 they inaugurated a purpose-built, temperature-controlled vinification and ageing cellar on the edge of Arbois. Stéphane is in charge of the vineyards and Hervé manages the cellars; both help with commercialization. Jean-Pierre is still involved.

The vineyards include 2ha in Buvilly in AOC Côtes du Jura and the rest are in Villette-lès-Arbois and in Arbois itself. Having originally taken over vines planted primarily in the 1970s, recently they have been replanting little by little. They always like to leave at least two years fallow before replanting. The vineyards have been managed in *lutte raisonnée* for several years and the estate is at the forefront of those aiming to join the Terra Vitis group in 2014. The vineyards are grassed down every other row and in 2013 they purchased an *intercep* tractor attachment to eliminate herbicide use. They have also created a specific place to wash the tractor after spraying to recover and dispose of the chemicals. Harvesting is by hand.

The winery is flexible and practical, equipped with small tanks mainly of stainless steel, and ageing is in a mixture of *fûts* and *demi-muids*, with Vin Jaune matured partly in the aerated upper level of the winery under the roof. Direct consumer sales dominate both from their own tasting room and at the Vignerons Indépendants and other tasting shows, with 20% exports mainly to Belgium and Japan. I have always enjoyed their Crémant du Jura Chardonnay, which spends at least 24 months on lees before disgorging and is very good value. Of the reds the Trousseaus are pleasant, with an interesting comparison between the Côtes du Jura Trousseau with more limestone in the soil at Buvilly and the more structured Arbois Trousseau on grey marl and from slightly older vines. The Arbois Vieilles Vignes Chardonnay from 70-year-old vines works well with ageing in small barrels, with a very small proportion of new oak. Over the years that I have known the Savagnin *ouillé* Arbois Cuvée des Poètes it has changed in style a little, depending on whether they use oak, which varies with the vintage, but it always has good weight and a lemon character.

The Ligier *sous voile* wines are quite markedly oxidative, starting with a blend of two-thirds Savagnin *sous voile* with basic Chardonnay and I think their non-oxidative wines are more successful. This is a reliable estate, but one that never sets off fireworks, apart from perhaps with its Crémant.

Domaine Ligier Père et Fils
56 Route de Pupillin, 39600 Arbois

Tel: 03 84 66 28 06

Email: gaec.ligier@wanadoo.fr

Web: domaine-ligier.com

Contact: Hervé Ligier

Map ref: p. 141, B2

Established: 1986

Vineyards: 10.25ha (3.65ha Savagnin, 3ha Chardonnay, 1.8ha Trousseau, 1ha Poulsard, 0.8ha Pinot Noir)

Visits: Tasting room and shop

Camille Loye

Camille Loye, who is in his nineties, and his wife Paulette, a decade his junior, are still happy to welcome customers by appointment to come to their immaculate bottle cellars. From a family of vignerons who used to be prominent members of the Arbois Fruitière, Camille Loye started making wine for himself from 1958, building up an estate to 6ha of Trousseau, Poulsard and Chardonnay, mainly in the vineyards of Curon and St-Paul. He never made any Savagnin. Known for his meticulous vineyard work, he always worked the soils and limited yields, using green harvest, leaf plucking and strict selection at harvest. He

used principally natural methods to make his wines too, with no filtration and low sulphur levels, all aged for several years in old wood. His last vintage was 1990.

Until recently his two Chardonnay cuvées were still available to purchase and on my limited tastings of these 20+-year-old wines, they showed extraordinary intensity, redolent of old-vine spicy yellow fruit character. The red Cuvée Saint-Paul was predominantly Trousseau, though in some years with a touch of Poulsard. On a visit in 2013 the 1988 and the 1989 were tasting wonderful. 'Still too young,' commented Camille, aged 93, about the 1989, and 'Solid' of the 1988. He jokes that he is an 'antiquaire des vins' – an antique wine dealer.

Camille Loye
1 Rue du Petit Changin, 39600 Arbois

Tel: 03 84 66 04 93

Map ref: p. 141, B2

A sign in Arbois points the way to the legendary retired vigneron Camille Loye.

Domaines Henri Maire

It is a tribute to the vision of Henri Maire (see 'History', p. 117) and to all who worked with him over the first few decades of the company that the name remains synonymous with the Jura wine region for many wine consumers in Europe. From the 1940s to the

The restored abbey building of Domaine de Grange Grillard, owned by Domaines Henri Maire and used for important events and entertaining since the days of Henri Maire himself. His vigneron family can be traced back to 1632.

1960s Henri Maire replanted large areas of vineyards in AOC Arbois and beyond. Until the 1990s the company bought large quantities of grapes from as many as 250 growers from all over the region and has always been considered locally as more of a négociant than a grower. However, since the turn of the century the quantities of grapes purchased dwindled steadily, causing consternation among grape growers from whom the company had purchased year after year. Since 2010 Henri Maire has no longer purchased any grapes from the Jura, though it does not preclude doing so in future if it needs to supplement the grapes from its vast Jura vineyard holdings. Its négociant activities, although based in Arbois, are now confined to buying grapes or base wine from outside the region to make Vin Fou sparkling wine (see p. 118) and other non-Jura wines. Henri Maire remains the largest single owner of vineyard land in the region by far, with over a quarter of the vineyards in AOC Arbois. For many years the largest, Henri Maire is now the third-largest producer in the region.

Having replanted four estates and built the large winery and offices called Boichailles at the centre of its vineyards,

the company was doing very well by the 1970s through its policy of direct consumer sales and innovative marketing campaigns. Henri Maire's son Henri-Michel joined the company in 1973, but by the mid-1980s the company was in trouble and raised finance by going public. This boost allowed further vineyard acquisitions in Château-Chalon and L'Etoile, bringing the domaine's holdings up to 300ha. Marie-Christine Tarby, Henri's daughter, joined in an export and marketing capacity in 1991 and in 1997 Henri Maire retired, leaving the company in the hands of managing director Pierre Menez with Henri-Michel Maire and Marie-Christine Tarby as directors. More troubled times followed and several small areas of historic vineyards were sold off. In 2010 a Luxembourg finance company, Verdoso Industries, a newcomer to the wine industry, acquired the majority holding. Only Marie-Christine Tarby stayed on; she had a consultancy role until 2013. Verdoso is conducting a programme of investments in the vineyards and the winery, as well as in

Château Boichailles, the large winery and office complex built by Henri Maire in the 1950s, is located in the middle of fields and vineyards. The sign pointing in the other direction is to La Finette, the restaurant founded by Henri Maire in 1961.

the French direct sales force, to turn around recent losses. Exports remain very small, less than 3% of production, and in 2013 purchases of Burgundy wine companies Dufouleur, Labouré-Roi and Nicolas Potel were made partly to help the company expand its export reach.

One of the most important changes made by Verdoso was to install an experienced oenologist, who joined just before the 2011 harvest. Emmanuel Laurent, who had previously worked for Antonin Rodet in Burgundy, was put in charge of the winery and the vineyards. The vineyards have not been in good shape. Although the notorious – at the time innovative – widely spaced vineyards installed by Henri Maire for ease of mechanization had all been changed some years ago to higher density, they were giving uneconomic yields. The mix of grape varieties was also wrong for today's market, being top-heavy in reds, especially Pinot Noir. Much replanting is under way, with the aim of having 50/50 red and white on around 270ha. Herbicide use is being reduced and more cover crops are being planted instead of grass between the rows to reduce fuel consumption – they now require mowing just once a year. A weather

station allows a more reasonable use of fungal treatments. For many years Henri Maire has had a token organic estate of 4ha, Domaine Brégand, planted with Pinot Noir. Another 7ha site has been prepared for organic farming, to be planted in 2014 with Chardonnay and Savagnin.

Apart from the small Domaine Brégand, the other estates in Arbois are Croix d'Argis (of which Brégand is technically part), Grange Grillard, Monfort and Sorbief. The latter, with about 60ha of all five varieties, is partly in AOC Arbois-Pupillin and is the finest site, protected by hills behind from north winds and with the steepest land, facing south-southwest. They also own 4.6ha in L'Etoile, 2.7ha in Château-Chalon and 2.2ha in Côtes du Jura in Ménétru-le-Vignoble. Henri Maire has always farmed the small Vigne de Pasteur, owned by the Académie des Sciences, and makes a field blend from the grapes planted in the 1940s. A joint project with the Académie is in place to document the vines and replant as an experimental vineyard.

Since Emmanuel Laurent's arrival he has been able to invest in a smaller press, a sorting table for red grapes, smaller tanks, manual punch-down equipment, a micro-oxygenation system to test on Poulsard, and better barrels. He made some changes to the base for Crémant, adding some Pinot Noir to the Chardonnay blend and is also focussing on the top-level Domaine de Sorbief wines. Vins Jaunes have always been aged in the extensive cellars below the old Maire family house in the vigneron quarter of Rue Faramand, usually left *sous voile* for ten years. Atmospheric though these cellars are, they have been neglected and from 2011 Vin Jaune is being aged at Boichailles and in future may be aged for a shorter time.

The Jura wines produced by Henri Maire are sold under a large number of labels, including those of the individual domaines. Henri Maire himself understood early the concept of branding for different markets and created the brand name Auguste Pirou, still used today for wines sold in supermarkets. All too often the Auguste Pirou wines are sold at a price that is an insult to the Jura wine region for a quality that is usually, as the French put it so nicely, 'correct' (i.e. far from brilliant, but not appalling either). There is a plethora of other brands and my tastings of the wines in the past decade have been very hit and miss. Recent releases of the top estate wines from Domaine de Sorbief are good, resoundingly Jura if a little overladen with oak. Domaine de Brégand Pinot is good too.

For many years the question of the future of Henri Maire has been a hot topic of conversation in Arbois, since it is a large local employer and among older people a level of respect is given quite rightly to the great man himself, who, after all, died only in 2003. Too many questions remain. At present the visitor to Arbois sees constant sales discounts plastered across the windows of the legendary, atmospheric but dated tasting room and shop, Les Deux Tonneaux, in the middle of the town, although the company plans to update it. It would be wonderful for this region if Domaines Henri Maire would emerge once again as a producer of some really reliable and representative wines of the Jura. [Revised 2015: In early 2015 Henri Maire was purchased by the giant Boisset Group of Burgundy.]

Domaines Henri Maire
Château Boichailles, 39600 Arbois

Tel: 03 84 66 12 34

Email: info@henri-maire.fr

Web: www.henri-maire.fr

Contact: François-Xavier Henry

Map ref: p. 141, B2

Established: 1945 (vineyards 1939)

Vineyards: 236ha in production in 2013 (62ha Chardonnay, 32ha Savagnin, 83ha Pinot Noir, 36ha Poulsard, 23ha Trousseau)

Visits: Tasting room and shop at Place de la Liberté, Arbois

Domaine Martin-Faudot

If you attend any of the tasting shows that buzz around France, in particular those of the Vignerons Indépendants, you will almost certainly find this estate, for they exhibit at no less than 40 shows a year, in addition to having a prime site shop under the arcades near Arbois' main square. The Faudots are an old Jura vigneron family and Michel Faudot's grandfather Louis Faudot bottled his own wines and was at the forefront of experimentation in grafting vines after phylloxera. Michel's father sold his grapes, but when Michel started in 1984 he decided to establish his own estate and bottle his own wine. In 1998 he was joined by Jean-Pierre Martin, who took over the commercial side of the business, enabling them to expand their vineyards. Michel's son Joris Faudot has joined the estate after studies in Beaune and work experience with a large Australian winery. Currently they sell mainly in Franche-Comté, but want to open up more to exports, so far selling Crémant to Norway.

The vineyards are in several different sites, including some old vines in Mesnay and Buvilly, especially of Poulsard and Savagnin. The vineyards are farmed conventionally, though recently they have started grassing down every other row. The winery in Mesnay has a mixture of tanks, with *foudres* used for reds and Chardonnay, and a Naturé *ouillé* Savagnin aged in *fûts*.

The range covers all styles, and is somewhat unexciting, with all cuvées bottled as and when needed – I sense that an enthusiastic new broom could make this estate's wine so much better. The reds are more successful than the whites. In particular there is a juicy Trousseau from vineyards in Mesnay and Arbois Les Corvées and a traditional blend of the three red varieties called Cuvée des Chasseurs. Vin Jaune is a mid-weight, fairly oxidative style to drink as soon as bottled, and a Vin de Paille is also on the oxidative side. Their *marc*, a very decent Chardonnay Macvin and Vin de Paille are aged in a dedicated humid cellar in Mesnay. One wine that I have not been able to taste, but is well regarded in France, is a late-harvest Savagnin, Cuvée de la Sainte-Cécile.

Charles Dagand and Alice Bouvot of Domaine de l'Octavin serving wine after the Fête du Biou in Arbois.

Domaine Martin-Faudot
1 Rue Bardenet, 39600 Mesnay

Tel: 03 84 66 29 97

Email: info@domaine-martin.fr

Web: domaine-martin.fr

Contacts: Jean-Pierre Martin and Michel Faudot

Map ref: p. 141, C2

Established: 1984

Vineyards: 12ha (50% white, 50% red)

Visits: Shop at 24 Grande Rue, Arbois, cellar visits in Mesnay by appointment

Domaine de l'Octavin

'I have always believed that opera is a planet where the muses work together, join hands and celebrate all the arts.' So spoke film and opera director Franco Zeffirelli many years ago, yet I venture this might also describe the way Alice Bouvot and Charles Dagand work in harmony to make their most natural of wines – Dorabella, Zerlinga, Pamina, Don Giovanni . . . A couple in their thirties with two young sons, single-minded

and hard-working, Alice and Charles have come a long way since they founded their estate in 2005. Certified by Demeter since 2010, their wines are exported to several countries and they rarely have wine left to sell. Recently they seem to have more *joie de vivre* and greater confidence than in the years when they were struggling to make this dream work.

There is no way around this: it is Alice Bouvot who wears the trousers here, even if they are usually short ones, while working in the sunshine of her beloved vineyards. Alice came from Besançon and studied wine first in Bordeaux followed by an oenology degree in Dijon, and then she set off around the world, working for three years with some pretty snazzy wineries in California, Chile and New Zealand. She returned to France with one idea in mind, to work in the vineyards of the Jura. Originally from Perpignan, Charles' father, an agronomist, was the grape buyer for the Henri Maire company. As for Charles, he studied wine production in Beaune, returning to work for the Arbois Fruitière, but soon after met Alice, who was managing a 20-hectare wine estate in the Côtes du Jura. She immediately hired him to manage the winery. After a short time they left to set up on their own from a rather ramshackle house with a cellar in the middle of Arbois.

Their plots include a hectare of vines in La Mailloche, which was previously farmed organically by Domaine Villet, and vineyards in prime sites at Curon, Les Corvées, En Poussot and Les Nouvelles, all of which they converted to organics. Some vineyards had very old vines, some of which had to be replaced, and the early years were not easy. Their first tiny vintage was 2005 and from the start they aimed to bring out the fruit in their wines, waiting to pick the grapes till as late as possible. The wines were made initially using methods learned at wine school and Alice's travels, though always with plenty of CO_2 to protect the fruit character and limit the SO_2 additions.

The couple are opera lovers, so named their enterprise Opus Vinum and baptized many of their wines with the names of characters from Mozart operas. Despite Alice's travels she never expected the letter from Opus One in the Napa Valley, the Mondavi–Rothschild venture, owned by the giant Constellation group, which demanded that they cease using the name Opus Vinum. Amazed and angry, they realized that it was pointless to fight and changed the name to Domaine de l'Octavin.

Meanwhile this young couple had been given much local support from other vignerons, especially from Stéphane Tissot, who encouraged them to move to biodynamic methods in the vineyards and adapt their winemaking methods to use solely indigenous yeasts. This wasn't enough for the couple, who decided to go all the way and make wines completely in the natural way, including shunning the use of SO_2. They have a small winery in what is almost a garage, away from the house, and more wines are made in tank rather than oak, especially the reds, and, again aided and abetted by Stéphane, they have invested in an amphora, which they will use for Trousseau. More amphorae to be used for maturation are, as I write, being shipped from natural wine producer Frank Cornelissen, who makes wine in Etna, Sicily.

Among the best-known wines are the chewy red fruit, gulpable Dorabella Ploussard, and Zerlinga, a more structured 50/50 Pinot/Trousseau blend, not forgetting the pure Don Giovanni Pinot and very ripe Commendatore Trousseau Les Corvées. Occasionally they make a Ploussard as a white wine called (not for Mozart this time) Cul Rond à la Cuisse Rose, which I'm not translating . . . Their most serious white, from old vines in La Mailloche, is the Chardonnay Pamina, a mineral reductive wine as always from this clay-rich terroir, needing time to open up after around 18 months in cask. They have very little Savagnin but make an interesting blend named Reine de la Nuit from La Mailloche Chardonnay and 40% Savagnin, picked and vinified together, put into barrel after a year and aged for a short time *sous voile*, and tiny quantities of a fruit-forward Savagnin *ouillé* called Comtesse A . . . Throw into the mix a range of specialities (the first Vin Jaune Cherubin was released in 2013) and the popular Pétillant Naturel, and it's easy to see that quantities of each wine are very limited.

Every year the couple make more cuvées – it's fun and the more you make, the more you want to make, Alice says. Charles keeps working and smiling, liking nothing better than lifting their two sons on to the tractor, though he also participates in presenting the wines at tastings around the world. At the end of 2013 they declared that, following many rejections of their (and other vignerons') natural wines by the tasters who have to approve the AOC label (through the *agrément* process), they were leaving the AOC system. It is a risky strategy, but as long as there continue to be customers for the wines that Alice and Charles enjoy making and sharing, their hard work in the vineyards allied with humour on the labels should carry them onwards.

Domaine de l'Octavin

1 Rue de la Faïencerie, 39600 Arbois

Tel: 03 84 66 27 39

Email: contact@octavin.fr

Web: octavin.fr

Contacts: Alice Bouvot and Charles Dagand

Map ref: p. 141, B2

Established: 2005

Vineyards: 4.5ha (2ha Chardonnay and Savagnin, 2.5ha Ploussard (Poulsard), Trousseau and Pinot Noir)

Certification: Ecocert, Demeter

Visits: No tasting room, but visits welcomed by appointment

Domaine de la Pinte

Over 60 years La Pinte has developed into an emblematic Arbois winery through the vision and good sense of the hands-off owners, the Martin family, fourth-generation owners of a company that builds motorways and massive concrete projects; once Jura-based, it now operates from Dijon. The estate was started by Roger Martin in 1952, inspired by his love for Arbois' heritage and specifically for Vin

Jaune. Originally he was in partnership with Marcel Poux, then mayor of Arbois and a well-known vigneron and négociant, but he died soon after the project began. The pair purchased a superb large plot below Pupillin on the edge of Arbois with the name of La Pinte à la Capitaine, where there had once been vineyards. Based on an ideal grey marl soil, they planted nearly 20ha initially with an unusually high proportion of Savagnin, aiming to revive the popularity of Vin Jaune. A massive winery was constructed, which took three years to build, using traditional stone building methods and design, with three long, wide, arched cellars below. The first vintage was 1959 and Roger chose to name his wine estate La Pinte, giving it the motto: 'Plante beau, cueille bon, et pinte bien,' which means something like: 'Plant prettily, pick good stuff and knock it back well.' It definitely sounds better in French.

From the 1980s Roger Martin's son Pierre and his sisters took over ownership and in the early 1990s, after further expansion, Philippe Chatillon arrived as director. More care was taken in the vineyards, grassing down the vines and ploughing soon giving way to organic conversion by 1999, including early use of silica and plant sprays. In 2009 Bruno Ciofi, who had been vineyard manager for over a decade at biodynamic producer Pierre Frick in Alsace, started full conversion of the vineyards to biodynamic methods, removing some of the grass in order to plough the heavy marl soils. They make and dynamize their own compost and preparations. Bruno replaced Philippe as director the following year and with winemaker Emmanuelle Perraut instigated changes in the cellar and the approach to winemaking.

Most of the vineyards are on the La Pinte estate itself, the top part of the slope (mainly whites) in AOC Arbois-Pupillin, and the reds lower down in AOC Arbois. It is very exposed to wind, which helps keep disease pressure down, but it means late ripening. Replanting in recent years has been done with mass selection – they are particularly proud of a 1.5ha plot of Melon à Queue Rouge. As well as a small plot of vines in Villette-lès-Arbois and 0.2ha in Château-Chalon, they own a particularly interesting small, steep vineyard in Port-Lesney (AOC Côtes du Jura), which is co-planted with old Savagnin, Chardonnay and a few red grapes. These vines are replaced as needed with white varieties.

The fermentation area at ground level is newly insulated, and has mainly epoxy-lined concrete tanks. One of the vaulted cellars is reserved for red and white oak maturation with a mixture of *foudres* and *demi-muids*, many of 800 litres, plus a few *fûts*; the second cellar is for Savagnin ageing *sous voile* and can be ventilated as required; the third for bottle storage. It is a very impressive setup. Philippe Chatillon favoured picking very ripe and avoiding chaptalization, but he did like extraction for reds and introduced new oak for some cuvées of Savagnin and Pinot Noir. Some very interesting wines were made, but they were of their era. The new regime has changed the way reds are made in particular, using shorter maceration and oak ageing periods. SO_2 levels have been reduced as well.

The Arbois-Pupillin Melon à Queue Rouge is consistently delicious, with an exotic character in some years, and the Côtes du Jura white field blend from Port-Lesney is expensive but a really intense, delicious wine. Whites have historically been much better than reds here, but the reds have taken a big leap forward. Arbois Poulsard de l'Ami Karl is very juicy and there is a good, more traditionally structured, oak-aged blend named after the vineyard 'A la Capitaine', with two-thirds Pinot and one-third Poulsard with a touch of Trousseau. The stars are the range of Savagnins, including that labelled simply 'Savagnin', which is aged for around five years in *foudres*, regularly topped up but tasting slightly oxidative, and really excellent though expensive Vin Jaune, with more curry and spice character than walnuts, and usually aged for a year longer than required. Even Macvin is made with Savagnin. Crémant is consistently good, with around 20% Savagnin in the blend, aged for at least 30 months on yeast pre-disgorgement. A lovely non-Vin de Paille blend is named Paradoxe. With 17ha La Pinte owns possibly the largest single plot of Savagnin in the world and makes fine wines from it, but this estate is making better and better wines across the range.

Pierre Martin in the spectacular barrel cellar of Domaine de la Pinte.

The vineyards and large buildings of Domaine de la Pinte, an estate below Pupillin created in the 1950s.

In his day Philippe Chatillon was a fine ambassador for La Pinte, for Arbois and for the Jura, and Bruno Ciofi continues this tradition very well indeed, including supporting the organic group of growers in particular through Le Nez dans le Vert. The Martins have always taken a back seat as owners of La Pinte, leaving the estate personnel to get on with it and take the credit where it's due. However, the Martin family has the last word in allowing their director's vision to become real – long may this continue, as the Jura needs estates of this size working so conscientiously.

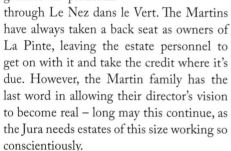

Domaine de la Pinte

Route de Lyon, 39600 Arbois

Tel: 03 84 66 06 47

Email: contact@lapinte.fr

Web: lapinte.fr

Contact: Bruno Ciofi

Map ref: p. 141, B2

Established: 1952

Vineyards: 34ha (17ha Savagnin, 6ha Chardonnay, 7ha Poulsard, 2ha Pinot Noir, 2ha Trousseau)

Certification: Ecocert, Demeter

Visits: Tasting room and a shop in the centre of Arbois

Maison Rijckaert

This unusual estate owns vineyards with white grapes only in AOC Arbois and AOC Côtes du Jura, with the wines made in a small winery in Les Planches, but bottled and commercialized in the Mâconnais in Burgundy. Founder Jean Rijckaert is a talented Belgian winemaker who was originally in partnership with Jean-Marie Guffens at Domaine Verget in southern Burgundy before branching out to start his own estate and small négociant business in the Mâconnais in the late 1990s. At the same time, attracted by the potential quality, the old vines and the low price of land, he purchased several plots of old vines in the Jura. The wines themselves are rarely seen in the Jura region and Jean has never participated in Jura regional activities, instead selling the wines to restaurants and exporting the majority (today 80% of production) to great acclaim. In September 2013, with a view to retirement, Jean concluded an agreement to sell the estate to Florent Rouve in conjunction with the négociant house of Collovray et Terroirs, although he will remain as a consultant winemaker for at least two years.

In the mid-1990s Florent Rouve, originally from Montpellier, caught the wine bug while studying in the Jura and worked for a short while with wine producer Jean-Luc Mouillard and for the CIVJ. Agricultural, wine and teaching studies, partly at Dijon, led him in 2007 to a post at the Lycée in Mâcon-Davayé managing the college wine estate. There he became friends with his contemporary Julien Collovray and also met Jean Rijckaert. He was always impressed with the instinctive way that Jean made his wines and this is something he hopes to be able to continue. Florent will be in charge of the technical and commercial sides of the business, with the Collovray company providing administrative support. Although the Mâconnais winery has moved, the existing setup for the Jura estate has remained the same.

The vineyards are farmed by Michel Boivin of Arbois, who is from a long line of vineyard workers and proprietors. The two Arbois vineyards are in En Paradis above the St-Just church cemetery and En Chantemerle close to Villette; the two Côtes du Jura vineyards, Les Sarres and Les Voises, are just south of Arbois between Buvilly and Grozon. Chardonnay vines are more than 40 years old and the Savagnin vines more than 60 years old. They do not claim to be in *lutte raisonnée* but low levels of herbicide are used, with every other vine row worked.

Florent hopes to acquire more vineyards in the future and to branch out into producing red Jura wine.

Yields are kept low and harvest – the most crucial time according to both Jean and Florent – is by hand into small boxes. Although Florent maintains quite rightly that 80% of the quality is made in the vineyard, the key to Jean Rijckaert's Jura wines has always been his very skilful winemaking – a long, slow and gentle pressing, indigenous yeasts, chaptalization when needed, vinification 100% in barrels that have already held at least three wines. Wines stay a long time on the lees, but with little stirring as they are not looking for a buttery character. Clarification is earth filtration and wines are transported to the Mâconnais only for bottling, which, depending on the wine, may not take place until two or three years after harvest.

Jean Rijckaert never wanted to make anything other than *ouillé* wines, but a little more than a decade after starting the Jura venture he is experimenting with the 2010 vintage and trying to make a Vin Jaune. Apart from a blended Arbois Chardonnay, the other wines are bottled with their vineyard names. Over the years I have tasted

Jean Rijckaert, founder of Maison Rijckaert, with Florent Rouve, who has taken over the business.

them, these wines have shown great quality and consistency, in the early years a touch too oaky, but this and the lees stirring have been toned down. The wines show the mineral character of the Jura well and have great finesse. Of all of them perhaps the Arbois En Chantemerle is the most Jurassien – the site is the more clay-dominated one. Jean has always made deliciously tangy lemony, stony and mineral Savagnin *ouillé* – these days the principal cuvée is Les Sarres. It ages well, as do the Chardonnays. These are fine expressions of Jura wines and I hope that with the enthusiastic Florent learning from the master, the future for the domaine is assured.

Maison Rijckaert

En Cuette, 71960 Davayé

Tel: 03 85 35 15 09

Email: florentrouve@hotmail.com

Contact: Florent Rouve

Established: 1998

Vineyards: 5ha (4ha Chardonnay, 1ha Savagnin)

Visits: No tasting room, visits possible only occasionally by appointment, usually in the Mâconnais

Domaine Rolet Père et Fils

The Rolet family conducts business quietly, considering that for many years this has been the largest family-owned estate in the Jura. The four hard-working siblings – Pierre the front man, his sister Eliane, who shares responsibility for sales with Pierre, and their brothers Bernard and Guy who run, respectively, the vineyards and winery – are all at an age at which most French people have long since retired. None of their children want to take the business over, so they simply continue what they have been doing well for several decades, waiting for someone to make them an offer they can't refuse – it is no secret that the domaine is for sale. Meanwhile, Pierre and Eliane travel France and occasionally beyond, waving the flag for the estate's own exemplary, if unadventurous, range of Jura wines, as well as for the region they have worked so hard for.

From a village close to Salins-les-Bains, the family had been mixed farmers owning some vineyards up to phylloxera. Their father Désiré Rolet first planted vineyards in Montigny in 1941 while working in a factory. Once the vines were productive he took the grapes to the Arbois Fruitière and became a full-time grower in 1951. The estate had grown to 5ha by the time Pierre joined his father in 1958, so they left the cooperative to sell their own grapes and make wine. As Pierre's siblings joined the company, they expanded the vineyards from 1965 first in several locations in Montigny and Arbois and later in AOC Côtes du Jura in the Grandvaux vineyards of Passenans for

In the vineyards: Pierre Rolet, one of the four siblings who own Domaine Rolet.

reds and on the borders of Le Vernois and Voiteur for whites. They now have 22.5ha in AOC Côtes du Jura and 39ha in AOC Arbois, as well as 3.4ha of vineyards in a single plot in Plainoiseau in AOC L'Etoile. The plantings used many mass selections of vines that they grafted themselves, having for some years run a small vine nursery business – at the time they looked for vines that would ripen easily with good sugar levels. The vineyards are farmed in *lutte raisonnée* with a policy to limit erosion, especially on steeper slopes, by using big tractors as little as possible. A wider track is grassed down every five rows for the tractor to go up and down and cover crops are grown between the rows with herbicide below the vines. With nine full-time employees along with seasonal part-timers specifically for the vineyards, they conduct a lot of the work, such as trimming the vines, by hand, and harvest is also entirely by hand with 80 harvesters.

The cellars were originally in Montigny, but a large – at the time, modern – winery was constructed on the edge of Arbois in 1978, equipped with stainless steel tanks, *foudres* and ageing cellars, and expanded in 1993. The cellar equipment remains relatively modern by Jura standards and is meticulously maintained by Guy. Chardonnays are fermented in *fûts* and some may then be transferred to *foudres* and topped up regularly. Domaine Rolet offers the rare chance to taste, side by side, the same vintage of Chardonnay produced from AOCs Arbois, Côtes du Jura and L'Etoile, all made in exactly the same way. The L'Etoile is consistently interesting, with a chalky and citrus character; Arbois seems best in the less ripe years when the tangy fruit emerges; and the Côtes du Jura reflects perhaps best the heavy marl terroir, seeming the most oxidative even though technically it is not.

Eliane Rolet serving wine at the Fête du Biou in Arbois.

Harmonie is an Arbois Chardonnay aged in newer oak, which appeals to some markets, but not to me.

There is a range of single-varietal Arbois reds and up to three red blends – Arbois Mémorial from mainly Trousseau and Pinot Noir, Côtes du Jura Les Grandvaux from Poulsard and Pinot, and Arbois Tradition from all three varieties. All the reds are vinified in stainless steel and aged in *foudres*; they can be a touch hard in the old-fashioned Jura style, but the Mémorial shows consistently best, with dark sweet fruits melding with minerals and earthy characters. Large stocks are held of red magnums, but I've not had the chance to taste many older vintages.

Naturé *ouillé* Savagnin is made in tank with a touch of oak and Savagnin for the oxidative wines and Vin Jaune is aged partly at the large cellars of the Château de Montigny and partly at the main winery. The oxidative range is very classic with a couple of blends and an excellent baby Vin Jaune-like Savagnin. Often two vintages of

Arbois Vin Jaune can be tasted side by side and they are consistently good, rich, curried and spicy styles. A honeyed Vin de Paille is usually delicious.

For me, the stars at Domaine Rolet have always been the range of Crémants, including the main cuvée, released after at least three years *sur lattes*, from a base wine blend of Chardonnay with up to 30% Savagnin and red grapes. Consistently good and finer too is their Coeur du Chardonnay, from the free-run juice of Chardonnay. Crémants represent 29% of the Rolets' production and perhaps this and their quality reflects the fact that Pierre Rolet was the producer president of the CIVJ during the time when the region was applying for the AOC Crémant designation.

There is always a warm welcome at their large Arbois tasting room and shop, next door to Restaurant Jean-Paul Jeunet. Much of their distinctively packaged wine is sold here and at Vignerons Indépendents tasting fairs. Domaine Rolet is also a member of the prestigious Vignobles et Signatures group of family-owned wineries. Exports remain relatively small, though they are present in the USA, UK, the Far East and many countries in Europe. There is some anxiety in the region as to the future of this family-owned domaine, which has been so carefully built up over the years. No one can envisage who, apart from a large négociant, could be interested in buying it and the family does not want to split up the vine holdings, which is what the younger local vignerons would like to see happen. For a buyer with patience, dedication and deep pockets, this could make a wonderful investment.

Email: rolet@wanadoo.fr

Web: www.rolet-arbois.com

Contacts: Pierre and Eliane Rolet

Map ref: p. 141, B2

Established: 1941

Vineyards: 65ha (24.3ha Chardonnay, 18ha Savagnin, 10.3ha Poulsard, 6.6ha Pinot Noir, 5.8ha Trousseau)

Visits: Tasting room and shop at Rue de l'Hôtel de Ville, Arbois

Cellier des Tiercelines

This small Arbois négociant started by Stéphane and Bénédicte Tissot in 1997 is better known in France under the name of Cave de la Reine Jeanne, a label found in supermarkets and sold directly to consumers. The name comes from the beautiful cellars in the middle of Arbois, which were leased by Stéphane and continue to be used by the Cellier des Tiercelines to age their wines in barrel and occasionally conduct tastings. For many years Stéphane Tissot made the wines in Montigny at his own cellars and sold the wines alongside the wines for Domaine André et Mireille Tissot. However, in 2009 Benoît Mulin purchased 50% of the business and took over all the

The magnificent historic cellars of La Cave de la Reine Jeanne in Arbois, leased by Cellier des Tiercelines.

Domaine Rolet Père et Fils

Route de Dole, 39600 Arbois

Tel: 03 84 66 00 05

commercial aspects, and from the 2011 vintage converted a building in one of the small Arbois industrial estates to create a separate winery. Jérôme Arnoux took over as winery manager, having worked for many years with Stéphane and later at Château de Chavanes. Today there are two further brand names – the Jérôme Arnoux label for small cuvées made for wine shops and restaurants and the Benoît Mulin label for exports. Recently the Tissots have reduced their share further and Stéphane acts only as a winemaking consultant for the business.

Grapes are purchased from about 30 grape farmers, mainly in AOC Arbois. Most of the very small farmers previously sold these grapes to Henri Maire and it is almost an act of mercy that Cellier des Tiercelines now takes them, as the owners (not being part of the cooperative) would not know what to do with them otherwise. There are some larger growers, such as André-Jean Morin of Domaine de la Touraize. Most of the grapes are from vineyards farmed conventionally or *raisonnée* with grassed-down rows; they do buy some organic Chardonnay, but none of the grapes grown by Stéphane Tissot's estate are used for the négociant. They make the whole range of Jura wines (all sold under the Reine Jeanne label, only some under other labels) and the practical brick-built winery is equipped to make everything from Crémant (apart from disgorgement) to Vin Jaune, which is aged partly there and partly in an older building. Indigenous yeasts are used with relatively low levels of SO_2.

Depending on the vintage, Crémant du Jura forms 20–30% of annual production of around 150,000–180,000 bottles and the basic one sold under either the Reine Jeanne or Benoît Mulin labels is a blend of 50% Chardonnay with 50% red grapes (Pinot Noir and Poulsard), spending almost two years on yeast lees. It offers a good vinous

and spiced apple style and is very good value indeed. An Extra Brut and a rosé Crémant are delicious too. Of the rest of the range, wines I have enjoyed include their basic Chardonnay, the Pinot Noir Les Rusards, a traditional Trousseau aged in *foudres* and a Pinot Noir-based red Macvin.

The general quality of the wines from Tiercelines is a big step up from other négociant wines in the Jura and exactly what the region needs. Exports are under way to the USA, Canada and Norway. The next project from 2014 is that the company is leasing a few hectares of vines in Arbois, which will be managed by Jérôme Arnoux (figures not included in the box), so these will quite possibly form another domaine label in the future.

Cellier des Tiercelines

23 Route de Villeneuve, 39600 Arbois

Tel: 03 84 37 36 09

Email: benoitmulin@cavereinejeanne.com

Web: cavereinejeanne.com

Contact: Benoît Mulin

Map ref: p. 141, B2

Established: 1997

Vineyards: 30ha (15ha Chardonnay, 4ha Savagnin, 5ha Pinot Noir, 4ha Trousseau, 2ha Poulsard)

Visits: No tasting room, but visits welcomed by appointment

Domaine Jacques Tissot

As I write, Jacques, the eldest of the Tissot brothers of Montigny, is the one who's holding on, refusing to let go of the reins of his estate even though his son and daughter Philippe and Nathalie have worked with him for some time. In his mid-seventies, this is a man who still wants to know every-thing and to be present everywhere: in the

Jacques and Philippe Tissot outside one of their Arbois shops.

mixture of stainless steel and enamelled tanks, although the tanks have had cooling systems only since 2008. Built on different levels, the ease of working here must be the envy of some of the neighbours, despite its looks. Large stocks of Savagnin barrels *sous voile* are aged here and at several wonderful old Vin Jaune cellars in the middle of Arbois, including one below the shop in Grande Rue where Pasteur is said to have conducted his experiments (see photo, p. 109).

The vineyards are predominantly in AOC Arbois, including sites at Les Bruyères, En Sauvagny, La Mailloche and Curon, with some in Pupillin too, and there are also a few hectares in the En Barberon vineyard in Bréry, near Voiteur in AOC Côtes du Jura (part of the plot originally purchased with André Tissot). The vineyards are partly grassed down and run along *lutte raisonnée* lines. Harvest is partly by machine. For winemaking expertise the estate has for many years had a self-taught winemaker, Pedro, working with Jacques and latterly Philippe, but has also relied heavily on local consultants and advisers, including the Poligny laboratory. The approach has always been to keep things as clean as possible and marry the traditional with the modern to create a large range of commercially attractive and medal-winning wines that are sold mainly in France, with only around 5% going to export markets.

The 30-odd wines cover every Jura style, evolved over the years to keep up with

vines, in the winery, tasting with customers at one of their central Arbois shops or at Vignerons Indépendents wine tasting fairs and even exploring new markets in the Far East. You will see him at the Percée, in the Biou procession and tasting at the regional wine competitions. Having started out sending his grapes to the Arbois Fruitière, Jacques has always given his all in terms of enthusiasm and dedication to his region and its wines, and to the estate he and his wife Michelle built up from just 2ha given to him by his father.

Whether you bump into the big man himself or not, if you visit Arbois you can't fail to miss Domaine Jacques Tissot – either you will see one of its two prominent town centre shops or, looking down on to the gorgeous Arbois vineyards from one of the viewpoints, you will see the pale green monster of a building where the domaine makes its wines. Next to the vineyards of Les Bruyères, by the side of the main N83 road, the spacious winery is something of a blot on the landscape. It was constructed in 1991 on a large scale to cope with the growing vineyard acquisitions and equipped with a fashions – previously old-vine cuvées and reserve wines were offered, more recently single-terroir selections are emerging. Although the region's typicity shows through well, in the past few years the wines have lacked some excitement and soul, especially the reds, which waver between a resolutely old-fashioned drying style and a somewhat cooked jammy fruit style. Whites are better. The Chardonnays usually show good minerality and balance, especially Les Corvées sous Curon, aged in relatively new oak, and I have always enjoyed the lemony freshness of the Naturé Savagnin *ouillé* that is matured in tank. Oxidative styles are always decent representations, but the best is rightly saved for the Arbois Vin Jaune, which shows good intensity, great length and ageing potential. The Crémant is an enjoyable fizz and Vin de Paille, one-third Poulsard, one-third Chardonnay and one-third Savagnin, is usually excellent after a year or two in bottle. As well as a classic Macvin, Jacques Tissot has for many years produced the liqueur wine Le Galant, based on an old recipe, mixing spices into grape juice and cooking it up in a copper cauldron to reduce volume before blending with *marc* or Fine (brandy).

Philippe Tissot is beginning to enjoy presenting the estate's wines to its loyal customers almost as much as his father, though the production challenges are not so easy for him. At present this estate lives and breathes the image that its founder – the strident and sometimes over-opinionated Jacques – has stamped on it, something that is not easy for the future generation to take on.

Domaine Jacques Tissot

39 Rue de Courcelles, 39600 Arbois

Tel: 03 84 66 24 54

Email: courrierjt@yahoo.fr

Web: domaine-jacques-tissot.fr

Contact: Philippe Tissot

Map ref: p. 141, B2

Established: 1962 (vineyards)

Vineyards: 30ha (8.7ha Savagnin, 8.4ha Chardonnay, 4.8ha Trousseau, 4.2ha Poulsard, 3.9ha Pinot Noir)

Visits: Tasting room and shop at this address and at 32 Grand Rue, Arbois

Domaine de la Touraize

Every year on the first Sunday of September in Arbois André-Jean Morin is a proud carrier of the Biou – the huge bunch of grapes that is taken in a procession from the Maison de Vercel to the Eglise St-Just for a blessing, as it has been for centuries. His father Michel carried it before him and his grandfather Marius before that. In his mid-forties, André-Jean, who had followed his father into wine farming as a member of the Arbois Fruitière, changed direction. A dramatic change for him, he left the cooperative

André-Jean Morin in the snow in his old Chardonnay vineyard Touraize, above Arbois.

to become, as he puts it, a 'grey-haired young vigneron'. His grandfather and several generations before him had made wine, but apart from making a tiny amount for home use with his father, he had no training or experience. He consulted with the local laboratory and the first vintage from his new estate was 2010 – just three years later in September 2013 he was the featured vigneron on the cover of French news magazine *Le Point*'s annual wine review.

André-Jean farms 12ha in various sites in AOC Arbois – Les Corvées for Trousseau, Petit Curoulet for Savagnin and Ploussard, and some old Chardonnay vines in several plots, including one known as Touraize above the cemetery in Arbois. Since he left the cooperative he has sold grapes beyond his own requirements to Cellier des Tiercelines, who appreciate his meticulous work in the vineyards, which he has managed with two full-time workers in *lutte raisonnée* for several years. He uses herbicide below the vine rows once a year. Harvest is by machine for the grapes he sells and for the hardy Savagnin variety, but by hand for the rest. He built a practical wooden winery in the town and has the capacity there to make wine from up to 4ha of grapes. From 2011 he has used natural yeast by making a starter culture from the first vinification of grapes for Crémant. Reds are handled particularly carefully with hand-destemming and whole grapes for Poulsard and a light crushing for Trousseau. He ages part of his red cuvées in *fûts* and *demi-muids* and whites are also part-fermented in oak.

Another partnership that gave André-Jean a boost was with friends Ans and Kees Baker, a Dutch couple who run a bed-and-breakfast, Le Moulin, in the nearby village of Ferté. The Bakers owned a small vineyard and made wine as a hobby. André-Jean had farmed their vineyards for several years, and when he wanted to start making his own

wines the Bakers offered him their winery equipment and the domaine name. In their honour he names a co-planted Chardonnay/Savagnin field blend Les Moulins. Fermented in oak and then aged in tank, fully topped up, it is an excellent weighty and lightly spiced wine, with the 50% Savagnin the dominant variety in taste.

The whole range I tasted from his early vintages has been excellent, including a redcurrant-flavoured Ploussard La Cabane and a nicely structured Trousseau Les Corvées, and in whites along with Les Moulins a delicious stony Savagnin *ouillé* Terres Bleues and minerally Chardonnay. He used *ensemencement* for his first Savagnin *sous voile* and the 2010 Savagnin was a light, decent style. The first Vin Jaune will be released in 2015. If all continues to go well he hopes to expand the winery and include a tasting room by 2015. His labels feature a fossil because as a child he always loved to collect fossils from the vineyards, running behind the tractor while his father ploughed. Explanatory back labels and a website detailing the wines show a keen eye for marketing the wines and André-Jean has made an excellent start in his new career as vigneron.

Domaine de la Touraize
7 Route de Villette, 39600 Arbois

Tel: 06 83 41 74 60

Email: aj.morin@wanadoo.fr

Web: domaine-touraize.fr

Contact: André-Jean Morin

Map ref: p. 141, B2

Established: 2010

Vineyards: 12ha (5.5ha Chardonnay, 2ha Savagnin, 2ha Trousseau, 1.5ha Pinot Noir, 1ha Poulsard)

Visits: No tasting room, but welcomed by appointment

Domaine de la Tournelle

Reflecting their own aspirations, Evelyne and Pascal Clairet created a little wine lovers' paradise in opening up their riverside garden in the middle of Arbois, turning it each summer into a delightful outdoor wine bar. Much of what this couple do to ensure their wines are fully enjoyed at their best is not only highly commendable but highly unusual for the Jura. Neither Pascal nor Evelyne had any family wine connections, but both ended up working in the world of wine, Pascal in Arbois at the CIVJ and Evelyne as a vineyard technician for AOC Côtes du Rhône. They met on a professional vineyard visit in Cahors.

Pascal was from St-Cyr-Montmalin and alongside his main job in the 1990s he ran a short-lived négociant business with Jean-Michel Petit and leased a small plot of vines. His first vintage was the disastrous 1991, when frost hit in late April – a learning experience, he says. Evelyne, one-quarter Corsican and three-quarters Asian, was born in Savoie, moving later to southern France. Both took oenology courses and Pascal expanded his vineyards little by little and became a full-time vigneron in 1995, buying an old house and cellar in Arbois. In 1999 Evelyne joined him and soon they became very much equal partners in bringing up their children and running the estate.

The couple have always been reluctant to be 'labelled' in terms of how they grow their vines and make their wines. They prefer to talk about a shared philosophy, but with exports at a third of production they have had little choice. From the beginning the vineyards were worked in *lutte raisonnée* and they favoured old vines when taking on vineyards; plantings were with old mass selections. By 2003 the vineyards were in full conversion to organics, though they did not seek certification until 2007, the year they also adopted biodynamic methods (but without certification). It was a tough year, as Pascal broke his leg badly before harvest, an injury that plagued him for some time. Early on Pascal had attended tastings with Pierre Overnoy in Pupillin and appreciated both Overnoy's approach in working without SO₂ and his *ouillé* wines. Making his first Savagnin *ouillé* in 1994 Pascal was convinced that, apart from for Vin Jaune, Arbois whites should be topped up, protected from oxygen. Another important influence was meeting growers from other French regions who were part of the burgeoning natural wine movement. Evelyne and Pascal liked the simplicity of making non-interventionist wines that were enjoyable to sit down and drink with family and friends.

Pascal and Evelyne Clairet in their garden next to the River Cuisance, where they set out tables for their summer Bistrot de la Tournelle.

The 12th-century Cistercian cellars restored by Domaine de la Tournelle.

Pascal does most of the vineyard work, with part-time help, though they took on a full-time employee in 2013. The vineyards are grassed down every other row, the soil worked in the other row and below the vines, and animal compost added every few years. Bordeaux mixture and biodynamic preparations are used for disease prevention. Green harvest is used if needed. The aim is to achieve balanced vines with a low yield, but not too low, not only for financial reasons but to keep freshness in the wines; they look for ripeness without super-concentration.

The process of harvesting and making the wines is very much a two-person operation. The harvesters are supervised by Pascal and the 20kg plastic perforated picking boxes are transported down the vine rows on little metal sledges to avoid contamination from the soil. Reds are hand-destemmed in the vineyard on a *crible*. Back at the winery at Pascal's parents' house in St-Cyr-Montmalin, Evelyne looks after the press in one of the barns. There is a small tank room close by and a large open working space – all is kept immaculately clean. Once the wines are ready to go into oak barrels, where the whites complete fermentation, they are transferred to the Arbois cellars, where they remain until bottling. A few years ago they extended the cellars, restoring a beautiful Cistercian vaulted cellar under the neighbours' house. Their natural way of winemaking means use of indigenous yeast first and foremost, with chaptalization used only if essential. From 2003 L'Uva Arbosiana Ploussard was made with no added SO_2. Initially it was made by 100% carbonic maceration but now maceration is semi-carbonic. SO_2 is rarely added, only sometimes for stability in the whites. This, together with their ultra-clean vinification methods, means that wines can taste very unforthcoming or reduced on first opening, needing several hours open or decanting to reveal themselves.

They have a modest family-sized holding of fine vineyards in Arbois, Vadans (for whites only), Montmalin and their latest acquisition in Mesnay. At the end of the *reculée* is a stony, clay-limestone warm site where they have planted Chardonnay and Trousseau. In whites the two Chardonnays, aged in old oak for 18–24 months, are Terre de Gryphées, a blend from two grey marl vineyards with the characteristic layer of limestone and fossils between heavy marl, and Les Corvées sous Curon, from the famous warm vineyard site of heavy clay with limestone outcrops above Arbois. Both offer differing nuances but are excellent, mineral-laden Chardonnays that express their vintage well. The *ouillé* Fleur de Savagnin has become leaner and more expressively mineral in recent years – after time open it evolves into an elegant and crystalline wine. Some years there is a rich late-harvest *ouillé* Savagnin, Solstice, intensely lemon in flavour, but the last made was in 2007. The oxidative Savagnin de Voile needs time open too and the Clairets have mastered this style and Vin Jaune well. The exuberant, cherry-fruited L'Uva Arbosiana 2003 remains focused on the fruit, tamed by just a few months in *foudres* – any reduction is swiftly disposed of in a decanter. Trousseau des Corvées is every bit as drinkable as the Ploussard, but with more complexity and depth, along with structure provided by longer ageing in *foudres*.

The Bistrot de la Tournelle is open from late June to early September, and closed if the weather is bad, but it is the perfect place to enjoy Evelyne and Pascal's wines, though today they can also be found in naturally orientated wine bars around the world. This couple have brought a different dimension to Arbois wines. Through their hard work, great attention to detail and a style evolved over two decades, they set a very good example to younger vignerons.

Domaine de la Tournelle

5 Petite Place, 39600 Arbois

Tel: 03 84 66 25 76

Email: domainedelatournelle@wanadoo.fr

Web: domainedelatournelle.com

Contacts: Evelyne and Pascal Clairet

Map ref: p. 141, B2

Established: 1991

Vineyards: 7.8ha (2.4ha Chardonnay, 2ha Savagnin, 1.9ha Ploussard (Poulsard), 1.5ha Trousseau)

Certification: Ecocert

Visits: Tasting room, visits welcomed by appointment

Domaine Gérard Villet

Gérard Villet is happy that so many vignerons have turned to organic viticulture in the Jura. Back in 1988 not one wine estate in Arbois was working this way (although

Pierre Overnoy was in nearby Pupillin) and there were only around 12ha of organic vineyards in the whole of the Jura. So when he took over the 3ha of vineyards in La Mailloche from his father-in-law and started conversion it was a brave move, perhaps ideally suited to someone who wasn't originally destined to be a vigneron, possibly too brave to be scared. For the first couple of vintages he sold most of the grapes to Henri Maire as his father-in-law had done, but he started making some wine in 1990 and two years later bottled and sold all of it. His wife Christine worked as a teacher, bringing in a stable salary, but she was born into a family who had been Arbois vignerons since the 1900s and the couple have always been very much part of vigneron life in Arbois. There was a tradition in the family of carrying the Biou, something Gérard continues to be involved in to this day.

The vineyard holdings have gone up and down in size over the years and are in several plots around Arbois, with the largest ones at La Mailloche, next to Domaine de l'Octavin and latterly at Les Bodines, next to Alexis Porteret, which they converted to organics in 2009. Today Gérard works the

Christine and Gérard Villet.

vines along biodynamic lines, in particular using plant sprays to reduce the amount of Bordeaux mixture used. Yields are kept low and the range made depends on what nature provides.

If you are driving from Arbois to Pupillin you can't miss the Villets' winery, house and tasting room near the middle of town with a prominent sign outside. Here the typical Arbois range of Jura wines is made simply, using very classic methods, with indigenous yeasts, including much maturation in old *foudres* and low doses of SO_2.

Since 2003 Christine Villet has worked with her husband, having retired from teaching. Much is sold directly at the tasting room or at small tasting fairs, and they export a little. While fruit from the Bodines vineyards is still in conversion to organics there are two ranges, but these will be merged soon. In the past there was some inconsistency in the wines, but they are improving and this is a lovely range of good-value wines with very decent balance and structure. Domaine Villet is both an underrated and understated Arbois producer.

Domaine Gérard Villet

16 Rue de Pupillin, 39600 Arbois

Tel: 03 84 37 40 98

Email: domaine.villet@orange.fr

Web: domaine-villet.fr

Contacts: Gérard and Christine Villet

Map ref: p. 141, B2

Established: 1988

Vineyards: 5.4ha (2.7ha Chardonnay, 1.1ha Savagnin, 0.9ha Poulsard, 0.4ha Pinot Noir, 0.3ha Trousseau)

Certification: Ecocert

Visits: Tasting room, visits welcomed by appointment

Pupillin

The centre of Pupillin lies at 460m altitude, above the vineyards, at the bottom edge of the Premier Plateau. When approached from Arbois, the entrance to the village always raises a smile with its painted barrel, tiny demonstration vineyard, floral decorations and, above all, its signs proclaiming the village to be the 'Capitale mondiale du Ploussard', the world capital of Ploussard. The term was coined in 1991 when the village hosted the first Fête de Ploussard, a wine festival that is held every other year in summer. The main street is named Rue du Ploussard; the village also has streets named Chardonnay and Savagnin as well as a Rue des Vendanges and a Chemin des Vignes – this is indeed a dedicated wine village. Pupillin is also the only wine village around Arbois to have a thriving restaurant, Le Grapiot, which offers wines from most of the village's producers.

The village dates back to Roman times. From the 11th century its vineyards were connected with the monasteries, including that at Vaux-sur-Poligny. In later times this became a village of modest farmers and winegrowers and in the heyday of the vineyards in 1806 the village reached a peak of population with 650 people, but this had fallen to 148 by 1975. Unlike Montigny, the

Ploussard has become inextricably linked with the village of Pupillin, its capital.

wine cooperative, created three years after that of Arbois, actually thrives to this day and in recent times the village has attracted newcomers, increasing the population to around 270. Its fame is due mainly to its star vignerons.

The vineyards stretch out in a wide bowl below the village, varying in altitude from 280m near the main road to nearly 450m, with expositions from northwest through to southeast and deep marl-based soils with stony limestone outcrops. The land is particularly steep in places and hard to cultivate, hence the attraction of having vineyards rather than crops; today only one family (the Crinquands) grows crops here. Much used to be made in the past of the rivalry in wine terms between Arbois and Pupillin – the saying about the wine 'à Arbois le renom, à Pupillin le bon', meaning roughly that the wine is 'famous in Arbois, good in Pupillin' came from a book about Franche-Comté villages, *Dictionnaire géographique, historique et statistique des communes de la Franche-Comté*, written in six volumes during the 1850s by Alphonse Rousset, a Jura notary. And yet, despite having only 25ha at the turn of the 20th century, Pupillin was keen to be recognized as part of the Arbois AOC. Eventually, in 1970 its terroir was considered sufficiently individual for it to have its own sub-appellation, AOC Arbois-Pupillin.

In the late 1990s a *remembrement* took place in the Pupillin vineyards and today there are almost 150ha of vineyards. Ploussard, especially that grown on Pupillin's most famous southwest-facing vineyards, Feule and Côte de Feule, is the renowned variety here, but there are excellent soils for both Savagnin and Chardonnay. Pinot is grown too, but for now there is little Trousseau, mainly because the warmest soils have been traditionally planted with Ploussard. The vineyards are contiguous with those of

Buvilly to the south; however, because this village is in the canton of Poligny (a minor political division) rather than Arbois it was excluded from AOC Arbois, so wines from Buvilly must be labelled AOC Côtes du Jura. Many Pupillin vignerons also own vineyards in Buvilly.

Paul Benoit et Fils

Father and son Paul and Christophe Benoit are rugby men through and through. Christophe played at a high level until recently and Paul continues to be actively involved in the Jura rugby federation. Their Crémant is called Troy de Meslay in homage to the rugby scrum (*meslay* is a maul in English). Somehow it is not surprising that this pair enjoy making wines with bold flavours, many of which are very successful. About 35% of the wines are sold from their beautiful village house in Pupillin and the

Rugby-loving father and son Paul and Christophe Benoit outside their tasting room.

large tasting room is full of rugby and wine memorabilia. They sell much through local shops and restaurants, and at a few wine shows in France and Belgium; a little is exported to Japan and Estonia.

Paul Benoit established the estate after a few years working at La Pinte, and following wine studies in Beaune, Christophe joined him in 2001. Technically Paul retired in December 2012, but is still very active on the domaine. The vineyards are in Pupillin and a few in neighbouring Buvilly (AOC Côtes du Jura), with some in Arbois. They were early to adopt the practice of grassing down the vines and today they work the soil every other row, using herbicide only directly under the vines. They conduct what they call 'reasonable' rather than officially *raisonné* viticulture and partly use machine harvesting. Winemaking is broadly speaking conventional, with some traditional practices in red such as hand-destemming, but also some experimentation with oak barrels from different countries.

Made usually only in stainless steel tanks, rigorously topped up, the basic Arbois-Pupillin Chardonnay is from vineyards where there are layers of *calcaire à gryphées* between the marl and it shows good freshness and minerality. Since the 2002 vintage they have made a Savagnin *ouillé* from La Loge, a steep south-facing Pupillin vineyard near La Feule. In early years I really enjoyed this wine with its intense lemony and rich character, but lately I find it a little over-oaked. Christophe likes to mature it in 100% new French oak.

There is an attractive, light Ploussard, aged only in tank, and an easy-going Trousseau from Arbois. Unusual for the region, Pinot Noir is a variety that Paul Benoit has always valued and he has planted a selection of Burgundian clones that ripen early on the Pupillin soils. The basic Pinot sees some

time in oak barrels, but the oak does not marry so well with the fruit. A special selection is bottled under the name La Grande Chenevière, with ageing in new oak barrels, the identity of which the Benoits like to keep secret. They used to use American oak, now I suspect it might be Russian or eastern European.

Savagnin barrels aged *sous voile* are stored in a dry, well-ventilated and insulated loft area and the Savagnin is usually bottled very late, so a real 'baby *jaune*', making it very good value for money – I prefer it to their Vin Jaune. The Crémant (about 15% of production) has included 40% Pinot in the blend since 2008, which adds some pleasant vinosity, though for now the *dosage* is relatively high, as clients demand this. Their white Macvin from Chardonnay shows less spirit than some – another secret 'recipe' that the Benoits won't reveal. A Vin de Paille with good sweetness completes the range. With his brother Michel, Paul Benoit also cultivates 5ha of various varieties of hazelnut trees on the edge of the village towards Buvilly.

Paul Benoit et Fils

Rue du Chardonnay, 39600 Pupillin

Tel: 03 84 37 43 72

Email: paul-benoit-et-fils@orange.fr

Web: paulbenoitetfils-pupillin.com

Contacts: Christophe and Paul Benoit

Map ref: p. 141, B2

Established: 1976

Vineyards: 12ha (4ha Chardonnay, 1.5ha Savagnin, 3ha Pinot Noir, 2ha Ploussard (Poulsard), 1.5ha Trousseau)

Visits: Tasting room

Domaine de la Borde

Julien Mareschal came to my notice in 2004. In the previous year no less than ten young vignerons set up in the Jura – at 23 years old Julien was one of the youngest and notable in being a complete outsider with no family wine connections. He was from a cereal-growing family and studied agriculture initially but followed up with a winemaking diploma in Dijon and work experience in Burgundy and Bordeaux. He also worked for short spells in the Jura with traditionalist Xavier Reverchon in Poligny and the more modern Pascal Clairet in Arbois. To Julien the appeal of wine was to take an agricultural product right through to a finished consumable. Having decided that he wanted to set himself up in the Jura, with the help of government subsidies he took over 3.5ha of well-tended, mainly 25-year-old vines in some of the best sites of Pupillin, along with leased space for a winery. In year two he took on another hectare, replanting half of it, and later added another hectare. For the first few years, alongside making wine Julien sold some of his grapes and supported himself giving music lessons. His interest in music continues and he organizes regular jazz, folk and wine evenings at his winery.

Unlike some others who set up at the same time, despite inevitable ups and downs Julien is still hanging on. Now with a wife and children, a house, a small purpose-built winery and a tasting room with a view, his wines go from strength to strength, reflecting hard work in the vineyards and careful winemaking. Having worked his vineyards in a reasoned approach from the start, in 2009 he converted half his parcels to either organic or biodynamic growing and has been officially 'in conversion' directly to biodynamic viticulture since 2012, helped by his friend and previous teacher in Beaune, François Duvivier of Domaines Marquis d'Angerville and Pélican.

Each of Julien's wines is given a name, either of a particular vineyard plot or something more esoteric. Proportionately, he has a substantial amount of Savagnin – nearly 50% of his holdings, all on grey marl, so it's no surprise that he uses this versatile variety for a characteristic range of wines. His Savagnin *ouillé* is called Foudre à Canon, fermented in *foudres* and bottled a little after a year, and Savagnin is aged *sous voile* for Vin Jaune and Savagnin Les Ecrins, made from various plots. Under a Vin de France label the Gelées de Novembre is made from Savagnin grown in a particularly windy plot that stays rot-free, enabling the bunches to be left on the vine until the first frost. Honeyed and medium sweet but with excellent acidity, it is a lighter style than

Julien Mareschal outside the cellars he built for Domaine de la Borde.

his Vin de Paille (40% Savagnin plus equal amounts of Chardonnay and Ploussard). Savagnin is also used for Macvin, which accounts for 10% of sales.

One of the best wines from Domaine de la Borde is Chardonnay Caillot, from a steep south-facing limestone-dominated plot, one of the highest-altitude vineyards in the Jura at nearly 450m. It is more nervy than his Sous la Roche Chardonnay, which is grown on marl. Reds include Ploussard from La Feule, which from 2012 Julien is making without SO$_2$, whereas his other wines receive a small dose. The most recent addition to the range is a Trousseau grown in Sous la Roche.

As many here, somehow Julien manages all the work from vineyards to winery to sales alone, with only part-time help. He sells mainly to private clients in France, but exports to North America and the Far East have reached a quarter of sales. It is a precarious existence, but tasting Julien's wine in his lovely little tasting room, you feel somehow that he has already become, after only a decade, a worthy part of the Jura wine's establishment.

Domaine de la Borde

Chemin des Vignes, 39600 Pupillin

Tel: 03 84 66 25 61

Email: mareschal.julien@gmail.com

Web: domaine-de-la-borde.fr

Contact: Julien Mareschal

Map ref: p. 141, B2

Established: 2003

Vineyards: 5ha (2.4ha Savagnin, 1ha Chardonnay, 0.8ha Ploussard (Poulsard), 0.5ha Pinot Noir, 0.3ha Trousseau)

Certification: Ecocert

Visits: Tasting room, visits welcomed by appointment

Philippe Bornard

He looks like a throwback to the 1970s and is most comfortable posing for photographs with a guitar in his hands, but since his unusual TV debut in 2012 Philippe Bornard has been far from camera shy. In his fifties and separated, Philippe, a busy vigneron, was looking for a girlfriend. His secretary suggested that he should apply to a French TV match-making reality show, *L'Amour est dans le Pré* ('Love is in the Pasture'), which features farmers searching for love. He was the first Jura farmer to appear and drew a horde of women competing for the attractions of this laid-back, dark-haired vigneron, who just happens to live in a large, modernized 17th-century house with a view of the countryside. With lovely footage of the vineyards and surrounding countryside, the programme provided great publicity, especially for Pupillin and the Jura.

Both Philippe's grandfathers made wine (one is part of the Désiré Petit family), but his father took his grapes to the Pupillin cooperative and this is where Philippe worked for a decade as a youngster, later taking over the farming of 12.5ha of vineyards. He always made a little wine on the side for family use and, encouraged by Pierre Overnoy, after 30 years he left the cooperative to go his own way. He sold and leased out some of his vineyard holdings and stopped use of any herbicides and machine harvesting on the remaining 7ha, but applied for official organic certification only in 2010. Since 2011 he has been working with biodynamics and shares a dynamizer with Manu Houillon.

The vineyards are in the bowl of Pupillin, including some in neighbouring Buvilly (AOC Côtes du Jura). Philippe values the heavier clay subsoils of Pupillin for his reds in particular and doesn't mind ploughing the heavy soils, though he also grasses down

Philippe Bornard with one of his fox sculptures, fashioned after his wine labels.

several vineyards. He also values his old vines and carefully preserves the Melon à Queue Rouge variety by getting the local nursery to propagate selections from it. He likes harvest to be as much like the old days as possible, manual of course, and he destems on the *crible* in the vineyard.

Winemaking remains inspired by Pierre Overnoy with use of CO_2 to protect the wines, but Philippe is not averse to using some SO_2 early in the winemaking process if needed, though never just before bottling. In a somewhat cluttered winery he has stainless steel and fibreglass fermenters and has invested in a concrete egg fermenter. Old oak *foudres* are still very much in use for maturation, along with increasingly varied sizes of old barrels in the atmospheric cellar beneath the house. The result is an incredibly expressive, wide range of wines, although it has to be said that there is sometimes bottle variation and a somewhat over-rustic character. When Philippe created his winery less than a decade ago he chose a particularly distinctive logo and fox sculptures and images are all over his house and cellar. Fox in French is 'renard' and the word resonates with Bornard – hence the inspiration. The wily but friendly fox, so reminiscent of the man himself, appears on the right of the label for the whites, and on the left for the reds.

A speciality that Philippe enjoys playing with is a range of low-alcohol, sweetish Pétillant Naturel wines sold under the Vin de France designation. This fizz is increasingly lapped up by clients around the world. It now accounts for more than 10% of his production and he even offers it in magnums. In 2006 he launched Tant Mieux ('So Much the Better') from Ploussard, in 2007 En Go-Guette (Chardonnay) and in 2008 Ca Va Bien (Savagnin) – even though I am not a fan of Pet Nats in general, I confess the tangy lemon sherbet flavours of Savagnin in fizz form are somewhat seductive. No wonder he served it to his prospective girlfriends on the TV show.

His Chardonnay Le Blanc de la Rouge is from the La Rouge vineyard on red marl soils and the much more interesting Melon Le Rouge-queue speaks for itself. I have enjoyed both his Côtes du Jura Savagnins, the *ouillé* Les Chassagnes and the *sous voile* Les Marnes, as well as another expression of this grape, L'Ivresse de Noé ('The Drunkenness of Noah'). This sweetish but fresh late-harvest wine is quite different from his luscious Vin de Pagaille, a non-Vin de Paille made in the classic method from Poulsard, Chardonnay and Savagnin, but with only around 13% alcohol.

Philippe is best known for his string of red cuvées, which are quite deliciously fruity when on form, and in some cases well structured – funky or weird are other descriptors. The name of one of his Ploussards sums him up best – Point Barre ('Full Stop' or 'End of Story'), as in 'If you don't like my wines, tough.'

Philippe's son Tony now works with him in all aspects of running the estate. Tony has also started his own small vineyard venture with 1.2ha for his own label and he also runs a small Internet sales company selling local wines and foods. And did Philippe find a mate on the reality show? Well, no, he had actually found one just before filming started, but kept this a little quiet. With son Tony at his side and the success of his wines growing around the world of natural wine fans, the colourful and smiling Philippe seems at ease with the world.

Philippe Bornard

Rue de la Croix Bagier, 39600 Pupillin

Tel: 03 84 66 13 51

Email: bornard.philippe@akeonet.com

Contacts: Philippe and Tony Bornard

Map ref: p. 141, B2

Established: 2005

Vineyards: 7ha (50% Chardonnay and Savagnin, 50% Ploussard (Poulsard) and Trousseau)

Certification: Ecocert

Visits: No tasting room, but visits welcomed by appointment

Pierre et Georges Bouilleret

Brothers Pierre and Georges were originally farmers and owned vines in some of the best plots of Pupillin, planted mainly with Ploussard and Savagnin. They were among the earliest vignerons in the village to bottle their wines. Pierre, who died a few years ago, was married to Madeleine, one of Pierre Overnoy's older sisters, and Pierre Overnoy was close to the Bouilleret family. When the brothers retired Pierre Overnoy and Emmanuel Houillon took over some of their vines and later, when Pierre and Madeleine moved to Arbois, Emmanuel and Anne Houillon took on their house and cellar in Pupillin.

Madeleine is in her mid-eighties at the time of writing and still offers the remaining stocks of Savagnin and Vin Jaune for sale – their last vintage of any quantity was 1990. I have had the chance to taste several vintages, which are extraordinarily alive and vibrant, authenticity assured. The 1989 Vin Jaune is especially splendid.

Pierre et Georges Bouilleret

8 Rue du Pupillin, 39600 Arbois

Tel: 03 84 66 14 81

Web: bouilleret.fr

Contact: Madeleine Bouilleret

Map ref: p. 141, B2

Renaud Bruyère

Renaud and his partner Adeline Houillon are the new kids on the block in Pupillin in terms of having their own domaine, but if I were doing pedigrees theirs would make an interesting one. Adeline is the sister of Manu Houillon and worked with him at Domaine Pierre Overnoy until 2011; Renaud is from Tain l'Hermitage and the couple met some years ago when they were both studying at the well-known hotel school there. Renaud worked as a chef for several years before coming to live in Pupillin with Adeline in 2004, alternating work in the vineyards with restaurant work. In 2007 he started work for

Stéphane Tissot, mainly in the vineyards, but lent a hand in the cellars over harvest and is currently one of Stéphane's vineyard managers.

In 2011 Stéphane encouraged Renaud to take on 0.7ha of vineyards in one of the highest plots in Arbois at around 400m. Les Tourillons was co-planted in the 1970s with Chardonnay, Savagnin and a little Trousseau, and farmed by several different owners over the years. Renaud immediately started conversion to organic methods. In that year he and Adeline made around 250 bottles of red and around 700 bottles of a promising white blend. In 2012 the couple rented an organically farmed plot in Pupillin that included Ploussard, bringing up production to around 3,500 bottles. In 2013 another 2ha were secured, some already organic and the rest now in conversion. They farm all their vineyards using the biodynamic methods that Renaud is totally convinced by. They have two children and Adeline works full-time in the vineyards and cellars.

The cellar below their house in Pupillin is tiny and they badly need space to expand. But in the meantime this is micro-vinification, barrel by barrel, and all with a completely non-interventionist approach, the natural way. Their belief is that to express the best combination of terroir, grape and the vintage, they should use no additives at all in the winery – SO$_2$ is used only in extremis, and then only at the start of fermentation. They do of course use oak, but at least five years old if possible. So far they are making topped-up wines but in future they will put a Savagnin aside to age *sous voile* if they believe the structure is right.

It is early days to discuss the wines, but there is a real purity of fruit shining through, especially on the Pupillin Ploussard and, despite launching at quite a high price, they have found a ready market among natural wine enthusiasts and have already exported a little. Adeline and Renaud show a love for the land and the wines it can produce and they seem to have a fine touch with winemaking.

Renaud Bruyère
24 Rue du Ploussard, 39600 Pupillin

Tel: 03 84 66 26 55

Email: renaud.bruyere22@orange.fr

Contacts: Adeline Houillon and Renaud Bruyère

Map ref: p. 141, B2

Established: 2011

Vineyards: 4ha from 2014
(70% white, 30% red)

Certification: Ecocert

Visits: No tasting room, but visits welcomed by appointment

Young vignerons Adeline Houillon and Renaud Bruyère in the tiny barrel cellar below their house.

Fruitière Vinicole de Pupillin

Even though Pupillin is only 3km from Arbois, the village has managed to keep its own wine cooperative through the ups and downs of the 20th century and today this continues to thrive, vinifying around 40% of the wines of AOC Arbois-Pupillin. It has 45 members, averaging a little more than 1.5ha of vineyards, mostly in Pupillin, Buvilly (AOC Côtes du Jura) and Arbois,

The centrally located tasting room and foudre *cellar of the Fruitière Vinicole de Pupillin.*

with around ten full-time growers farming 80% of the vineyards. The cooperative seems to have recovered well from being convicted of a major fraud and adulteration scandal at the turn of the century, with new management replacing the individuals implicated. Today it lives in harmony with the individual vignerons at the heart of this wine village.

When the *fruitière* was founded there were 33 farmers practising polyculture owning a total of 23ha of vines. They shared equipment in premises in the middle of the village, where the cooperative is still based today. After the First World War the cooperative continued, initially with only 10ha remaining, but the growers were determined to expand and become part of the new AOC Arbois. From 1946 the cooperative accepted only grapes from the five varieties permitted in the AOC. Once mechanization made the vineyards easier to work in the 1960s and 1970s and more farmers turned exclusively to vineyards, the cooperative expanded. In 1998 they built and equipped a modern winery, but the *foudres* have remained in

the original premises in the middle of the village. Being in Pupillin, Ploussard is a key wine (at least a quarter of its production) and the aim is to avoid reduction by ageing in *foudres* for at least a year. From 2009 they extended the modern winery to create a purpose-built, ventilated Vin Jaune cellar to store 1,200 barrels, with temperatures fluctuating between 3°C and 25°C through the year. Currently the Fruitière makes around 10,000 *clavelins* of Vin Jaune and the aim is to make more in the future. The first vintage of Vin Jaune to be aged here will be the 2008, for release in 2015.

My tasting opportunities here have been somewhat erratic with large gaps, but I did taste the range in 2013. In general they are of decent quality, though unexciting, with the whites more successful than the reds. The largest-volume wines seem to be the best here, including a pleasant stainless-steel-matured Chardonnay and their traditional *sous voile* blend, Margillat, which is 50/50 Chardonnay and Savagnin. Crémant accounts for about 20% of sales. The basic Papillette Crémant from 100% Chardonnay with 12–18 months on lees is a pretty, easy-drinking sparkler, as is the Papillette Crémant rosé from 70% Pinot and 30% Ploussard. However, I have been surprised to find the reds rather unyielding, even from the very ripe 2009 vintage, and suspect the harvest needs to be handled more carefully. Unusually, Pinot Noir was the best of those tasted, as it was in notes from years ago. Both Vin Jaune and Vin de Paille (from one-third each of Ploussard, Savagnin and Chardonnay) are decent representatives of the style. The Fruitière sells on export markets, together with the Fruitière Vinicole de Voiteur (see p. 261) under the name Juravinum.

Fruitière Vinicole de Pupillin
35 Rue du Ploussard, 39600 Pupillin

Tel: 03 84 66 12 88

Email: info@pupillin.com

Web: pupillin.com

Contact: Stéphane Curti

Map ref: p. 141, B2

Established: 1909

Vineyards: 70ha (24ha Chardonnay, 15ha Savagnin, 18ha Ploussard (Poulsard), 7ha Trousseau, 6ha Pinot Noir)

Visits: Tasting room and shop

Maison Pierre Overnoy/ Emmanuel Houillon

In 1990 Emmanuel Houillon (Manu), aged 14, worked his first vintage with Pierre Overnoy and he seems to have been destined to be a vigneron even if he is not from a family of vignerons. As discussed in the profile of Pierre Overnoy (see 'History', p. 130), Manu has learned by Pierre's side and has gradually taken over the running of the estate in a seamless continuation of the work, but without ever assuming Pierre's mantle, which would be impossible to do. This does not mean that everything remains exactly the same: on the contrary, each vintage brings a different nuance and it is hard to describe a typical Overnoy wine. However, what never changes and what sets this domaine apart is that SO_2 is never added to the wines at any stage of the process of winemaking, from harvesting the grapes to bottling the wines, and this has been the case without exception since the 1986 vintage.

Pierre Overnoy's family were mixed farmers in Pupillin and his father Louis Overnoy made wine from just under 2ha of vines. Pierre and his older brothers helped with everything from milking the cows to tending the vines, as their father had been handicapped after an accident in 1947. When Pierre started on his own, he received only 0.35ha of the family holdings and some cows (later relinquished), but he started planting 0.2ha at a time on bare land, building up his vineyard holdings to around 2.5ha. As related earlier, Pierre decided to farm his vines organically in the 1960s at a time when almost everyone else was turning to chemicals. Later, after making wines conventionally following brief wine studies in Beaune, Pierre was dissatisfied with the results, and was introduced to the consultant Jacques Néauport in the 1980s. Jacques helped Pierre

Pierre Overnoy and Emmanuel Houillon sharing lunch at Pierre's restored farm at Chaux d'eau.

An international team joins Anne and Emmanuel Houillon (second and third from left) and Pierre Overnoy (far right) for harvesting in their Pupillin vineyards.

for several vintages and introduced him to the teachings of Jules Chauvet, who made wine without SO_2. Pierre never met Jules Chauvet, but continues to quote Monsieur Chauvet to this day.

From Franche-Comté, Manu's parents were regular customers and brought Manu as a boy to visit, especially around harvest. In 1989 Manu spent three days with Pierre at harvest and, hating school, he decided that this was what he wanted to do. The following year Pierre took him on as an apprentice, working between studies at Beaune. As Pierre had no wife or family, Manu became like a son to him, and during the 1990s Pierre began to envisage that Manu would take on the estate. After his studies Manu worked for Pierre from 1995 to 2001 and purchased vineyards of his own. In 2001, with help from a support group of Pierre's friends, Manu took over the business officially. Anne, Manu's wife, joined shortly after and they purchased their house and cellars from Pierre's sister Madeleine Bouilleret. For several years Manu's sister Adeline and brother Aurélien worked with them, but the siblings parted on poor terms. Today Manu runs the estate together with Anne and they have recently changed their last name to Houillon-Overnoy. Pierre still participates fully in most of the estate's activities.

The vineyard holdings, all in Pupillin, reached 6ha, but since the split with Adeline and Aurélien they have dipped. Having only ever grown the three traditional grape varieties of Pupillin – Ploussard, Chardonnay and Savagnin – they are planting a first 0.2ha plot of Trousseau in 2014 on a warm site, La Sainterre, near the Côte de Feule. They prefer to plant only on land that has been left fallow for a few years and to use mass selections. The vineyards have been certified organic by Ecocert since 1997 and Manu has been using biodynamic preparations since 2007, believing that these methods are vital for the future. The vineyard work is meticulously thought out, as working without SO_2 requires perfectly healthy grapes, in particular for reds. Hand-destemming on the *crible* enables a second selection, the first being by the pickers at the vine.

In the book *La parole de Pierre*, lawyer Michel Converset says to Pierre: 'There are few vignerons who are as scrupulous as you and who have gone as deep in their analyses.

You try to understand. You experiment . . . Indeed there is an intelligent, structured and scientific chain of events.' Pierre brushes this off, saying, 'The fundamental thing is that the grapes should be ripe,' but later he stresses how hard it is to work without adding SO_2, something that is fundamental to their philosophy of winemaking. The essentials about the winemaking conditions at this domaine seem to me to be the use of good hygiene, temperature control, CO_2 to protect the wine at crucial moments, and bottling at the right time, often after several years of ageing. The main vinification cellar, along with an ageing cellar that is dry with wide temperature variations, remains at Pierre's house and the cellars of Manu's house are fully underground and damp with a constant temperature, giving a choice of ageing facilities. Manu says he works to no rules: some Chardonnay may be fermented in stainless steel, another part in *foudres* and some in *fûts* – it depends on space and the vintage. For Ploussard it's the same, and from 2012 Manu has been experimenting with an egg-shaped concrete tank, which he fills first with CO_2 before putting in the grapes, then adding more CO_2, followed by a maceration of up to ten weeks.

Pierre used to chaptalize regularly, but in recent years this has not been needed, although Manu would be prepared to do so if necessary. In the unusually hot year of 2003 they did not chaptalize or acidify and Pierre was very nervous about making sulphur-free wines, but Manu, long converted to the practice, insisted they try – and they succeeded. In 2013 he bottled the Savagnin 2003 after nine years in 600-litre oak barrels, topped up regularly. The wine is simply excellent, very dry, rich and more appley than lemony. Pierre was converted to making topped-up Savagnin by Jacques Néauport, making his first Savagnin *ouillé*

in 1985 and always ageing for several years before release. Chardonnay, which is aged for two or more years, has always been rigorously topped up. Savagnin matured *sous voile* for Vin Jaune is attempted only occasionally and aged for eight, ten or more years before bottling. The last release of Vin Jaune was the 1999 vintage and no clues are given as to the next. This estate makes a tiny range of wines by Jura standards – usually three wines – Chardonnay, Savagnin and Ploussard.

Free of SO_2, the deposits settle more easily, so wines are never fined or filtered. Once bottled, these wines require stable, low temperatures for storage and, when opened, are very reductive. This of course is most noticeable in Ploussard, yet when it opens up this is the most thrilling wine, with vibrant fruit. It has always shown the ability to age. With Manu's experimentation the fruit has become even more lifted, with a floral element emerging – lovely to drink young. There is always excellent length on these wines, which command a high price. The estate sells about a third of its small production on export markets, a third directly to consumers and a third to restaurants and wine shops in France. Demand outstrips supply by a long way.

Manu seems to have integrated into Pupillin almost as if he were born there. His wife Anne is one of the lady vignerons who carries the Biou at the small village festival on the third Sunday in September. Manu may be a very different character from Pierre, but he has learned well from him, most particularly to question everything and to be generous with his help to other vignerons – he takes part in the annual Le Nez dans le Vert tasting. It will be fascinating to watch how this estate develops over the next decade.

**Maison Pierre Overnoy/
Emmanuel Houillon**
14 Rue Abbé Guichard, 39600 Pupillin

Tel: 03 84 66 24 27

Email: emmanuel.houillon@wanadoo.fr

Contacts: Emmanuel and Anne Houillon

Map ref: p. 141, B2

Established: 1968 (2001 for Emmanuel
Houillon)

Vineyards: 4.8ha (1.8ha Chardonnay, 1.8ha
Savagnin, 1.2ha Ploussard (Poulsard))

Certification: Ecocert

Visits: No tasting room, but visits welcomed
by appointment

Domaine Overnoy-Crinquand

The Crinquand brothers Romaric and
Mickaël are mixed farmers in Pupillin,
with cereal crops, 25 dairy cows and the
vineyards that they took over from their
parents in 2004. Romaric is in charge of the
cows and Mickaël the vineyards, although
they lend each other a hand when needed.
All is farmed organically, the cows grazing
in pastures in Chaux d'eau, where Pierre
Overnoy (a cousin) has his smallholding,
and their milk is sent to a small organic
cheesemaker in Grange de Vaivre, near
Port-Lesney. Mickaël is a fourth-generation
vigneron through the Overnoy line. His
father, Daniel Overnoy-Crinquand, had
expanded the vineyards from 1.5ha to 4ha
and had always worked the soils. He farmed
organically from 1976 and sought Ecocert
certification in 1999.

Exclusively in Pupillin, the vineyards are
in two large blocks mainly in the southwest-
facing La Bidode, with small blocks nearby
in La Rouge and La Marcette. Mickaël has
expanded them little by little, most recently
planting some more Savagnin. Below the
house are wonderfully atmospheric old

barrel cellars, dating back to 1650, which
were used by the monks of Vaux-sur-
Poligny. Everything seems from another
age here. Until very recently Mickaël used
a manual wooden press, which he has now
replaced with an old pneumatic press. Everything is aged in wood, ranging from *fûts*
to 500–600-litre *demi-muids* and 1,200-litre
foudres. The only time SO₂ is added is at
harvest; to protect the wine, bottling is done
under CO_2 (perhaps the only concession to
modernity?).

The range of wines is small, with slightly
more red than white. The Ploussard is
destemmed and crushed before fermenting
in *foudres* for two weeks with regular punch-
downs. It needs time open to rid it of its
reductive character and to reveal its wonderfully delicate redcurrant characteristics.
Trousseau is made similarly and, like the
Ploussard, after time reveals its fruit, this
time more cherry-like with fuller flavours
and good tannins behind.

Whites are all made oxidatively to some
extent, though not necessarily courting a
veil of yeast for Chardonnay. It is fermented
in all sizes of old oak that are topped up
only after fermentation and then left for as
long as possible before bottling, which for
the basic Chardonnay takes place up to five
times for one vintage. A *voile* sometimes
forms, sometimes not, but there is a definite
smoky oxidative character, but with forward
mineral fruit flavours too. A Vieilles Vignes
version from 60-year-old vines is often
picked long after Savagnin and aged three
years in *fûts*, not topped up. Despite the late
picking it is very dry, but rich and aromatic,
balanced by the acidity. These are very original, old-style Jura wines.

Some years a Vin Jaune is made, others
not, especially when Mickaël deems the
wine too alcoholic to put aside for Vin
Jaune. The excellent Savagnin is aged *sous*

voile for just a couple of years. A Crémant and a Vin de Liqueur are also made. The wines are sold mainly locally and at organic tasting fairs, plus exports to the USA and Canada. With the family still being mixed farmers, it is perhaps the closest one might find to how a typical Jura vigneron made wine 50 years ago.

Domaine Overnoy-Crinquand
Chemin des Vignes, 39600 Pupillin

Tel: 03 84 66 01 45

Email:
domaine_overnoycrinquand@yahoo.fr

Contact: Mickaël Crinquand

Map ref: p. 141, B2

Established: 2004 (Mickaël)

Vineyards: 6ha (1.5ha Chardonnay, 1ha Savagnin, 2.5ha Ploussard (Poulsard), 1ha Trousseau)

Certification: Ecocert

Visits: No tasting room, but welcomed by appointment

Domaine Désiré Petit

A tradition here since 1995, for four days each year at the end of May, over the Ascension Day weekend, the Petit family opens the doors of its large cellars for a massive *portes ouvertes* ('open doors') tasting and celebration. Many other vignerons stage this type of open day or open weekend, encouraging their customers to taste the latest vintage and stock up their cellars, but the Petits do this on a really grand scale, engaging local artists, seamstresses and musicians, winning loyal customers in the process. This is the largest family-owned estate in Pupillin and when they constructed and equipped new cellars in 1989 they incorporated a large tasting room, started a small museum and have always been most welcoming to visitors.

Today sister and brother Anne-Laure

and Damien are in charge, but their father and mother Marcel and Michèle, as well as their uncle, Gérard Petit, are all still present on the estate. Gérard and Marcel's father Désiré founded the estate in 1932, although the family can trace their ancestry as vignerons back to 1657. When Gérard and Marcel took over in 1970 there were less than 1.5ha of vines, but they expanded the vineyards steadily, in particular over the next two decades. They mainly planted in Pupillin, but have just over 3ha in nearby Grozon (AOC Côtes du Jura). They also bought vineyards in Arbois and a small plot in AOC Château-Chalon. Today their vineyards are spread over 25 parcels, managed in *lutte raisonnée*, working some of the soils and grassing down others. They have managed to eliminate herbicide on 5ha so far. All harvesting is by hand.

The spacious, nicely kept cellars combine modern and old. There is a bank of stainless steel tanks and pneumatic presses, but they also continue to use oak barrels, kept back from each generation. Désiré used small *foudres* of 2,500–3,000 litres; Gérard and Marcel brought in larger *foudres* of 6,000 litres and Damien has gone small again, introducing 600-litre *demi-muids* for some wines, using one-third new barrels for their topped-up whites. Crémants are important, representing almost one-third of production. It is made in four styles, though I prefer their basic Brut. In an indication of how important direct sales are to them in gauging customer preference through the course of the year, they use a higher *dosage* in winter than in summer.

Reds have been somewhat old-fashioned and hard, but I sense that Damien is improving the wines and bringing out more fruit. He has introduced an enjoyable single-vineyard selection, Ploussard La Feule, in which, if possible, he uses

Third-generation Pupillin vignerons Damien and Anne-Laure Petit of Domaine Désiré Petit at the viewpoint looking over the vineyards of Pupillin.

each of Savagnin, Chardonnay and Ploussard and they aim for 350g/l sugar before pressing. The wine is put into barrel several months after pressing and remains in barrel for nearly four years. The result is the type of Paille I enjoy, with an attractive amber colour and a great balance of sweetness and acidity. The Petits have been great ambassadors for Jura wines and for their village Pupillin for decades – Anne-Laure is one of the four women who carry the Biou. They have a loyal customer following, with growing exports, now up to 20%, the principal markets being Canada, Belgium and the UK. I feel confident that the latest generation will develop the estate and improve the wines further.

no SO₂. In his first vintage in 2004, Damien launched a Savagnin *ouillé* called L'Essen'ciel, which spends six months in *demi-muids*. It is growing in popularity but, as with the other topped-up whites, for me it needs a little more zip and a touch less new oak input. The same applies to the Chardonnay Cuvée Jules selection. On the other hand, the oxidative Savagnin and the Vins Jaunes, including Château-Chalon, are classic, with great typicity. The Vin Jaune cellars are partly in the main cellars in a large loft area, but, as the area suffers from insufficient ventilation, part is still stored in one of the original family houses in the village.

By far the most successful wine for this estate for many years has been its Vin de Paille, a real speciality of the house, made in most years from around 1ha of their vines. Indeed it was Gérard Petit who researched, pioneered and encouraged the region to accept the attractive, dedicated Vin de Paille bottle. The usual grape mix is one-third

Domaine Désiré Petit
62 Rue du Ploussard, 39600 Pupillin

Tel: 03 84 66 01 20

Email: contact@desirepetit.com

Web: desirepetit.com

Contacts: Damien and Anne-Laure Petit

Map ref: p. 141, B1

Vineyards: 26ha (9ha Chardonnay, 5ha Savagnin, 4.5ha Ploussard (Poulsard), 4ha Trousseau, 3.5ha Pinot Noir)

Visits: Tasting room

Domaine de la Renardière

He might be running between commitments, but Jean-Michel Petit always offers a twinkly smile together with a straight answer to any question. More than anyone in Pupillin, Jean-Michel Petit has been as much involved in the 'mother appellation' Arbois as he has in his own village. AOC Arbois syndicate president for many years, I've seen him carrying the Biou in Arbois; he was president of the Percée festival in Arbois in 2011; and he always turns up to greet the media with a regional hat firmly on his head. Somehow, between supporting his village, region and even the young and up-and-coming producers in the appellation, he finds time to produce a consistently lively and eminently drinkable range of wines. Jean-Michel's stated aim in his brochure is to 'make music from the mosaic of soils below our feet', but the imprint on his labels is of a hand – his own, representing the importance of hand-harvesting, lending a hand and much more.

Quite rightly, the vineyards are the focus for Jean-Michel. Growing up in Pupillin (distantly related to the other Petit family in the village) with parents and grandparents who farmed vines and took their grapes to the cooperative, he returned after five years of wine studies and work experience around the world of wine to create his own estate with his wife Laurence. He took over his family's 2ha of vines and accumulated other vineyards little by little, in various parcels on the different terroirs within Pupillin. He has always believed in working the soil and using only organic fertilizer and, after years working in *lutte raisonnée*, he made the move to start organic certification in 2012, although he had been using biodynamic preparations 500 and 501 on some of his plots for a couple of years.

The small winery lies on both sides of

Jean-Michel Petit of Domaine de la Renardière poses by the mural depicting him in his cellar.

one of Pupillin's roads with an amusing and distinctive colourful mural depicting several generations of the family adorning one side. Jean-Michel's winemaking has always been thoughtful – vinifying the grapes from each plot apart, fermentation using indigenous yeast, and little use of other standard winery interventions. With the exception of Ploussard, he is not likely to go down the no sulphur route, yet he told me that, as with most producers, today he uses around a third of the amount of SO_2 than when he started making wine 20 years ago.

All styles of whites and reds are matured in wood of varying sizes. Reds, including Ploussard, are aged in large *foudres* – his is the example from this village that I have always found to be one of the most accessible. Yet it is his clear-cut topped-up whites that really sing, starting with the tangy and lemony Savagnin *ouillé* Les Terrasses, which comes from a steep south-facing terraced plot. From the mid-2000s Jean-Michel has made two Chardonnay cuvées that show the Jura terroir character well – Jurassique is from plots with more limestone and the more profound Les Vianderies is from older vines in a gravelly vineyard with marl below – the latter is aged in both 500-litre and 228-litre barrels.

In his quiet way Jean-Michel has experimented with his range without extending it dramatically as some wineries do, keeping to a modest (for the Jura) 14 different wines. A late-harvest white blend of two-thirds Chardonnay and one-third Savagnin was once called Vendange Oublié ('Forgotten Harvest' – as it literally was the first time it was made) and has morphed into Les Oubliées, as the labelling fraud squad did not like the original name. The wine is made only in good years and, though usually dry, can be rather over-rich for my taste, but with plenty of intensity of flavour. The usual range of specialities from Crémant through to Vin Jaune, Paille and Macvin are made but account for only a quarter of production, including the Pétillant Naturel called Le Pet de Léo. This was first made by son Léo at 14 years old from a Ploussard vineyard planted in 1993, the year of his birth. Léo has studied wine production at Mâcon and is continuing his education in wine marketing at Suze-la-Rousse, so this estate should be in safe hands in the future.

Domaine de la Renardière exports account for about a third of sales, but it is the combination of a well-deserved string of medals in French wine competitions and mentions in guides, with a very open and educational approach to welcoming customers at the estate, that keeps his regular French customers returning. For several years each Saturday in June Jean-Michel and Laurence have conducted vineyard tours, followed by a tasting and lunch, an innovative approach for the Jura and something that has helped build up their loyal following. I sincerely hope that they throw a big party to celebrate the quarter-century of their domaine, which is a huge credit to the Arbois-Pupillin appellation, a *valeur sûre* or safe bet, as they say in France.

Domaine de la Renardière
Rue du Chardonnay, 39600 Pupillin

Tel: 03 84 66 25 10

Email: renardiere@libertysurf.fr

Contact: Jean-Michel Petit

Map ref: p. 141, B2

Established: 1990

Certification: Ecocert

Vineyards: 6.8ha (2.4ha Chardonnay, 1.3ha Savagnin, 1.7ha Ploussard (Poulsard), 0.7ha Trousseau, 0.7ha Pinot Noir)

Visits: Tasting room, visits welcomed by appointment

Cellier Saint Benoit

The genial Denis Benoit has mapped out for me the development of his career and how he created his estate in stages. His father, a mixed farmer with 3ha of vines, was a member of the Pupillin Fruitière. After viticultural and winemaking studies Denis worked for seven years at Domaine Désiré Petit before starting to farm his own vineyards from 1989, later taking over from his father. Initially Denis too was part of the cooperative, but left in 2003, keen to make his own wines. Today he sells the grapes from two-thirds of his vineyards to La Maison du Vigneron, keeping the rest to bottle under the Cellier Saint Benoit name that he created to differentiate his domaine from that of his Benoit relative and neighbour. Around 90% of the 10,000 bottles he makes each year are sold directly to private customers from the tasting room or at wine tasting shows. Now he is looking forward to the next stage, when his son Benjamin, currently 18 and studying wine at Beaune, should join him. Then, Denis hopes, they will be able to develop sales sufficiently to bottle all their own wines.

The vineyards are all in Pupillin, including some very well-known sites, and Denis is a keen member of the group of Jura vignerons who hope to join Terra Vitis, the sustainable viticulture organization, in 2014. He has worked in *lutte raisonnée* since 1989, working his soils and reducing herbicide to just below the vine row. He uses only small machinery in the vines to limit soil damage and harvesting is done manually. Denis is obviously fascinated by the vineyards and takes the trouble – as Pierre Overnoy does (see photo, p. 131) – to collect and preserve bunches of baby Ploussard grapes each year on 1 July to keep a record of development through the years.

Over the years I have seen a steady improvement in all the wines and I am not sure whether this is a question of the vineyards being better or Denis gaining in winemaking expertise, perhaps a combination of both. The reds are more successful than the whites. Denis makes a lovely Côte de Feule Ploussard from vines grown on this famous south-facing slope, with around 5% of Trousseau co-planted. He plans to plant more Trousseau there. The Trousseau is pleasant and a red blend of the three varieties is more successful than his Pinot, which has somewhat unbalanced oak use.

In 2011 Denis experimented with Chardonnay, ageing some in tank and some in 600-litre barrels; the latter showed better balance, the oak bringing out the terroir character. Of the oxidative wines, the best is the Tradition, made from two-thirds Chardonnay with oxidative Savagnin. Other specialities are made, including a pale mahogany-coloured, honeyed and spicy Vin de Paille with an unusually high proportion of Ploussard – 50% blended with equal amounts of Chardonnay and Savagnin. This is a small estate to keep an eye on in the future.

Denis Benoit of Cellier Saint Benoit outside the tasting room.

Cellier Saint Benoit
36 Rue du Chardonnay, 39600 Pupillin

Tel: 03 84 66 06 07

Email: celliersaintbenoit@wanadoo.fr

Web: celliersaintbenoit.com

Contact: Denis Benoit

Map ref: p. 141, B2

Established: 2003 (vineyards 1989)

Vineyards: 6.3ha (3ha Chardonnay, 0.65ha Savagnin, 1.85ha Ploussard (Poulsard), 0.55ha Pinot Noir, 0.25ha Trousseau)

Visits: Tasting room, vineyard visits welcomed by appointment

AROUND POLIGNY

Unless it's for a quick stop for Comté cheese, many people coming to the Jura for wine tend to visit Arbois and Château-Chalon, zooming past Poligny on the N83 bypass. Yet Poligny was a fortified town steeped in history, with numerous religious connections. It was also an important centre for wine. Just as Arbois wines ended up in the Royal Courts in medieval times, so did Poligny's. The string of villages to the southwest, Toulouse-le-Château, St-Lothain and Passenans in particular, can also trace back a glorious history of growing vines for religious centres or noble landowners.

Above: A small parcel of old Chardonnay vines above the town of Poligny. The slopes would once have been covered with vineyards.

By the 18th century the vineyards of the town of Poligny were some of the most extensive in Franche-Comté. However, many of the Poligny winegrowers planted poor grape varieties in the 19th century and when a *fruitière* (wine cooperative) was set up in Poligny in 1907 (later becoming the Caveau des Jacobins), they initially chose quantity over quality. Once AOCs were established, there was no question of a specific village appellation for Poligny, so the vineyards are eligible only for the generic Côtes du Jura AOC.

However, Poligny is once again well worth exploring. From the 1960s growers began to focus on quality and a few producers began to make an important difference, notably the Badoz and Reverchon families in Poligny and the Grand family in Passenans. Vineyard plantings have now reached about 160ha, half of which are in Poligny itself. In this area vignerons are likely to be loners fighting their own battles to cope with the intricacies of the world of wine.

There are some wonderful vineyard sites with good exposures on excellent marl-rich soils for white grapes in particular; good warm soils for reds are harder to find.

Poligny

The town of Poligny lies at the opening of one of the smallest *reculées* (blind valleys) in the Jura, the Reculée de Poligny or Reculée

de Vaux (the village towards its source). The town lies at an important crossroads between Burgundy and the Alps and many French and British people travelled to Switzerland on the N5 main road through the town before motorways were built. In less than ten minutes you can drive out of town on to the broad Premier Plateau, where Montbéliarde cows graze in summer, and drop into one of the Comté cheese *fruitières*.

The best way to explore Poligny is by foot. Apart from numerous cheese shops – this is the capital of Comté, after all – there are two churches, a convent and the classic courtyard of the Clos des Ursulines to visit. Add to this interesting back streets with houses stretching back to the town

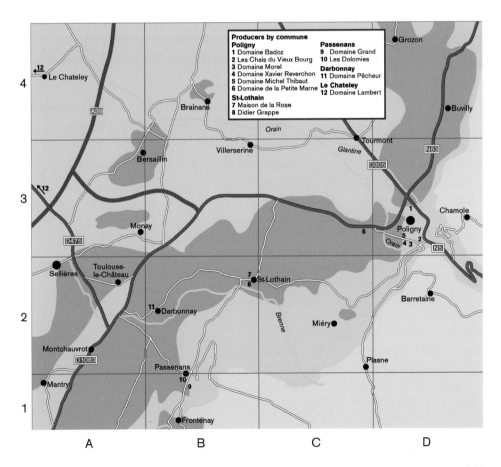

Producers by commune

Poligny
1 Domaine Badoz
2 Les Chais du Vieux Bourg
3 Domaine Morel
4 Domaine Xavier Reverchon
5 Domaine Michel Thibaut
6 Domaine de la Petite Marne

St-Lothain
7 Maison de la Rose
8 Didier Grappe

Passenans
9 Domaine Grand
10 Les Dolomies

Darbonnay
11 Domaine Pêcheur

Le Chateley
12 Domaine Lambert

ramparts, all sporting a distinctive cellar entrance, and it is well worth picking up a town map for a stroll (there are two marked walking routes).

The Caveau des Jacobins, the former Poligny wine cooperative, was absorbed into the Arbois Fruitière in 2005 because most of the larger members had pulled out or ceased activity. When the Poligny Fruitière was founded in 1907, the town allowed the cooperative to use the Eglise des Jacobins, a church unused since the Revolution, as its cellar. For many years the cooperative made wine in the church and eventually opened it for tastings and wine sales. Old *foudres* remain there and a much-needed renovation programme is under way. The exterior has been beautifully restored and work will be done on the interior over the next few years. The town wants the Arbois Fruitière to maintain the wine-tasting facility to ensure that the church is visited regularly.

As well as being home to the Comté Cheese Information Centre and to one of Jura's most important catering colleges, Poligny is also the site of the regional laboratory, consulting many of the vignerons and doing routine testing on most of the barrels ageing *sous voile*. Situated in the centre of the wine region, the town would make a wonderful base for a Maison du Vin or wine information centre showcasing the whole region's wines.

The vineyards of Poligny are on either side of the *reculée*, and by far the best way to see them is from the Croix du Dan, a huge cross erected in the 19th century on the cliffs of the southern side of the *reculée*. You can find the road by driving towards the village of Plasne and following the signs to Croix du Dan. From there you can peer down at the mainly west-facing vineyards of St-Savin and Boutasses; straight ahead, just above the church, is the sector of old

vineyards of Charcigny that have mostly disappeared; beyond that is the large area of Roussots and Grands Roussots, revived by the Badoz family; and, finally, there are Les Trouillots, the large south-facing vineyards across the valley, which were reconstructed in the 1970s.

Domaine Badoz

It's relatively rare to find CVs of winemakers in the Jura that include experience at so many internationally known estates, but Benoît Badoz' features Louis Carillon in Puligny-Montrachet, Pétrus in Pomerol, Dominus in the Napa Valley and Hardy's Tintara in South Australia. He is the tenth generation of a family that claims the longest known history as vignerons in Poligny, with records going back to 1659. Early in the 20th century grandfather Pierre developed the Roussots vineyard slope, but it was from the 1970s, when Bernard Badoz, Benoît's indomitable father, took over, that the estate became devoted to wine production with a small négociant business alongside.

Equally rare is to find a relatively small producer in the Jura with 10ha of vineyards in one block. The Roussots and Grands Roussots vineyards lie just north of the town with a view of the Côte d'Or. Sweeping around the hill underneath the limestone cliffs below the Premier Plateau, there are several expositions and a variety of soils, rocky at the top on the Bajocian limestone, more clay below, with marl from both the Liassic and Triassic periods, including the grey marl preferred for Savagnin. When he was expanding the vineyards Bernard Badoz was a great believer in the potential of both Vin Jaune as a style that was unique in the world (he was the founder of the Percée festival, after all – see 'History', p. 126), so it's no surprise that plantings include more than 50% of Savagnin.

The vineyards are not organic yet, but the Badoz family has not used chemical fertilizers or weed-killer for many years. They use only sulphur and copper sprays for mildew prevention, but do use one low dose of chemical anti-botrytis spray. Benoît says that the most important thing he seeks is balance in the vines and at the time of writing he is hesitating about whether to convert completely to organic viticulture.

When Benoît returned to the estate in the late 1990s (fully taking over the reins in 2003) he brought with him international experience of vinification methods and a desire to make different wines. The age-old method of making Vin Jaune and Vin de Paille has been little touched of course, and the family owns six splendid Vin Jaune cellars in the middle of town storing upwards of 450 barrels. However, a new vinification and ageing cellar was built and equipped in 2004. Picking for reds is by hand and the grapes go through a gentle destemmer with a sorting table attached. Some Savagnin is picked by machine, which Benoît maintains works particularly well for Savagnin *ouillé*, as the berries stay whole and undamaged.

The traditional Vin Jaune and Vin de Paille from the estate are exemplary, and other traditional styles have been joined by some simple fresh styles, including especially enjoyable Trousseau. A more expensive range uses newer oak barrels and includes the much admired Arrogance Chardonnay, which is technically excellent if too oaky for my taste; similarly the Pinot Noir Dédicace à Pierre (a homage to Benoît's grandfather) is also oaky, though with time this may tone down. Experiments with Savagnin *ouillé* include the very well-made, oaky Cuvée Victoria named after his daughter, and Benoît's latest trial with the 2011 vintage is a cuvée fermented and aged in barrels made from Jura oak from the Forêt de Chaux. He

Benoît Badoz checks his Savagnin ouillé *fermented and aged in a Jura oak barrel.*

thinks of it as 200% Jura wine, but it will be named Cuvée Edouard after the latest addition to the family – a first taste of it from barrel promised well.

Benoît says that his father put everything in place to make the handover of the estate easy for him; in his early 70s, Bernard is still working and hugely supportive of his son's work. Bernard always points out with a mixture of pride and amazement that his son has modernized things and introduced these new-fangled wine styles, but he is adamant that things need to change with the generations. Benoît, with support from his wife Virginie, who is often found in their main tasting room, is driving this estate forward at a careful pace and, with exports now up to 12%, he has already garnered admirers from Canada, the UK, Denmark and Hong Kong, with many points between.

Domaine Badoz
3 Avenue de la Gare, 39800 Poligny

Tel: 03 84 37 18 00

Email: contact@domaine-badoz.fr

Web: domaine-badoz.fr

Contact: Benoît Badoz

Map ref: p. 217, D3

Established: 1692 (or 1970, when Bernard Badoz revitalized the estate)

Vineyards: 10ha (5.5ha Savagnin, 1.5ha Chardonnay, 1.2ha Trousseau, 1ha Poulsard, 0.8ha Pinot Noir)

Visits: Tasting room and shop, also at Bernard Badoz' tasting room at 15 Rue Collège

Les Chais du Vieux Bourg

Ludwig Bindernagel must rate among the most unusual of the recently established Jura vignerons setting up since the turn of the 21st century. From Bavaria, Germany,

Ludwig practised as an architect for many years in Paris, where he met his partner Nathalie Eigenschenk. Both loved food and wine and dreamed of leaving Paris to settle in Burgundy, where Ludwig studied viticulture and oenology part-time. Finding vineyards too expensive there, they arrived in Arlay in 2003 and began acquiring parcels of old vines. Today, although they still have a cellar in Arlay, their base is in a huge rambling house, cellar and garden in the middle of Poligny, within 20 minutes' drive of their vineyards.

Ludwig farms more than five different plots, the largest being 1.6ha at Le Vernois that used to belong to the Chalandard family, who scaled down their holdings a decade ago. It is sited on a layer of *calcaire à gryphées*, the fossil-rich limestone that produces very mineral-laden Chardonnays. He has old vines at Quintigny in AOC L'Etoile, at Ruffey near Arlay, and in Poligny, and was recently able to acquire and plant a plot in the Château-Chalon AOC, as well as some land at L'Etoile above the church. The old vines include Melon à Queue Rouge and what is known as Savagnin Noir, a local Pinot Noir selection. Ludwig would like to farm 100% organically, but at Le Vernois he has had to use some contact herbicide in recent years, so there's no question of certification.

In 2003 Ludwig knew nothing about making wine in the Jura, but he was helped by Julien Labet, who taught him to forget everything he had learned at wine school in Beaune, and was a big influence on Ludwig choosing to make wine in a natural way. The old cellars house a mishmash of equipment and his aim is to let the wines make themselves: after traditional hand-harvesting and destemming red grapes have punch-downs three times a day and are left to macerate

Ludwig Bindernagel of Les Chais du Vieux Bourg in his vineyard directly above Poligny.

until the tannins are no longer dry, then put in barrel; whites are all fermented and aged in barrel and kept at very low temperatures. Using natural yeasts, most of the whites take at least a year to ferment, with malolactic fermentation happening as and when. SO_2 levels are kept low.

The range is typically Jurassien-wide, from Crémants through reds, topped-up whites to a Vin Jaune, a non-Vin de Paille (ingeniously named Le Papaille, i.e. 'Pas Paille', 'Not Paille') and two Macvins. Ludwig enjoys making the whole Jura range in his own way. He never imagined that the venture would take so much work (he has one part-time person to help) and he doesn't earn a living from it, but he seems to relish the challenge.

Nathalie is an accomplished chef and their bed-and-breakfast business provides a way for the couple to share their wines in situ, as they also offer dinner. In particular they can accommodate their customers from Germany, France, the USA, Canada and beyond, and all are called on to help with the harvest, which becomes one long party.

Le Chais du Vieux Bourg is named after the street in Arlay where they were first based, and both the cuvée names

and labels are carefully thought out and original. The wines remind me of good old-fashioned Burgundy in some ways. I'm not convinced of the quality of the reds (the Poulsard is delightfully named 'Ce n'est pas du rosé, c'est du Poulsard' – 'It's not rosé, it's Poulsard'), but the whites have certainly won me over. They are stony and mineral with a vibrant intensity. Currently the range includes Sous le Cerisier Chardonnay, plus two Chardonnay/Savagnin blends named BB1 (pronounced 'bébé', so his 'first baby') and my favourite, the QV d'Etoiles (pronounced 'Cuvée d'Etoiles', which is AOC L'Etoile). Ludwig is excited about having more vines in L'Etoile, which he considers a most underrated terroir. The Crémant Délire des Lyres (a reference to some unusual Lyre-trained vines in Le Vernois) is a zero *dosage* 2008 with four years' ageing on yeast, made up of 70% Chardonnay, 20% Savagnin and 10% Pinot Noir. There is a Vin Jaune from 2004 (with 2005 to come) and the only vintage of Papaille is also from 2004. I just hope that future vintages are as good as these, but wonder why there have been no follow-up vintages. This is an intriguing estate.

The cellar entrance in the courtyard of the old Poligny house restored by Ludwig Bindernagel and Nathalie Eigenschenk.

Les Chais du Vieux Bourg
30 Grand Rue, 39800 Poligny

Tel: 03 63 86 50 78

Email: lbindernagel@gmail.com

Web: bindernagel.fr

Contact: Ludwig Bindernagel

Map ref: p. 217, D3

Established: 2003

Vineyards: 3.1ha (1ha Chardonnay, 1ha Savagnin, 0.8ha Pinot Noir, 0.3ha Poulsard)

Visits: No tasting room, but visits possible by appointment

Domaine Morel
8 Rue Jacques Coittier, 39800 Poligny

Tel: 03 84 52 62 55

Email: domaine.morel@orange.fr

Web: domaine-morel.fr

Contact: Jean-Luc Morel

Map ref: p. 217, D3

Established: 2014 (vineyards and previous estate in 1989)

Vineyards: 4.5ha (50% white, 50% red)

Visits: Tasting room, visits by appointment

Domaine Morel

This new estate was created by Jean-Luc Morel with his sons Louis and Valentin in January 2014 following the division of the Domaine Morel-Thibaut estate after 24 years working with Michel Thibaut. The partners divided the vineyards and the remaining wine stocks, both in bottle and those still ageing, for sale under each of their new labels. The Morel family plans to convert their vineyards to organic cultivation and will retain the premises of Domaine Morel-Thibaut.

The profile of Domaine Morel-Thibaut below gives more details.

Jean-Luc Morel of Domaine Morel in his St-Savin vineyard.

Domaine Morel-Thibaut

This was a rare setup in the Jura: two friends from childhood becoming partners to form a wine estate. Jean-Luc Morel and Michel Thibaut worked together for nearly a quarter of a century. However, times move on and, as we were going to press in early 2014, the partners decided to split the domaine to work separately (see Domaine Morel above and Domaine Michel Thibaut, p. 225, for contact details). The rest of this profile concerns the vines and wines of the previous domaine and has been retained as a guide to the vineyards, wines and proprietors of the two new estates.

Most of the vineyards came from Jean-Luc, who, together with his father, belonged to the Caveau des Jacobins cooperative. At Morel-Thibaut Jean-Luc managed the vineyards and administration and Michel was in charge of winemaking in a winery they modernized extensively in 1995. Before returning to Poligny Michel had worked in wine estates across France, ending up as a winemaker in Provence.

Their vineyards are in three main plots: St-Savin was planted originally by Jean-Luc's father in the 1970s, a stony vineyard with marl underneath, below the cliff with the imposing Croix du Dan and one of the highest vineyards in the Jura at about 450m facing west/northwest, so late ripening. They grass down to help stabilize the steep slope. Their other plots, the clay-rich Boutasses just below and the south-facing Les Trouillots across the valley, are grassed down or ploughed every other row. Weed-killers were phased out from 2000, with none used since 2002.

The modern winery allows for temperature control and a simple hands-off approach was practised. A dry and ventilated Vin Jaune cellar below Jean-Luc's house in the oldest part of Poligny provides normal cellar temperature variations, but a lot of loss from evaporation and concentration. Vin de Paille barrels are also aged here – many are the small 110–115-litre *feuillettes* – and these are allowed some slight oxidation. Morel-Thibaut has been justly famous for its Vin de Paille, which accounted for an unusually high 10% of production. They used all four permitted grape varieties, with around 30% each of Poulsard, Savagnin and Chardonnay, and 10% Trousseau, preferring the Trousseau à la Dame selection, which is sweet and juicy. Pressing was usually at the end of December, although if needed they waited until January/February, aiming for an alcohol level of 15% and 100g/l minimum of residual sugar.

Of the rest of this competent range, the reds were very characteristic of their grape varieties, including a consistently good fruity Trousseau (no rustic animal flavours here – they considered this a fault). From an old Jura vine selection, Pinot was partly aged in old oak. A competent topped-up Chardonnay was also made; the rest of the whites were made oxidatively.

Both Michel and Jean-Luc are big supporters of local wine events, with Michel having been part of the original Ambassadeurs des Vins Jaunes, who organize the Percée festival, and president when it was held in Poligny in 2010.

Domaine de la Petite Marne

You can't miss their white winery, with its large black sign promoting both the domaine and the wines of Jura, by the main road immediately south of Poligny. It is here that the Noir brothers – Philippe and Jean-Yves – converted a large barn into a new winery in 2003. Behind it is an attractive old building housing their vaulted ageing cellars, half below ground, including a tasting room. They have a further classic dry, ventilated, underground Vin Jaune cellar in the centre of town. The brothers, who previously sold their grapes to the Caveau des Jacobins cooperative, have put a lot of thought into creating this domaine.

The Noirs have a mixed farm. In addition to vines they have a herd of Montbéliarde cows for Comté cheese, managed mainly by their uncle. Their father Jean first planted the

Philippe Noir, who runs Domaine de la Petite Marne with his brother Jean-Yves.

vines in 1973, but, when the brothers joined in 1991 (Jean-Yves) and 1997 (Philippe), the area was increased to its current size, with around 80% of the vines in Poligny, mostly on the south/southeast-facing sweep of vineyards, Les Trouillots, above the town, and the rest in nearby Grozon. Since leaving the cooperative they have sold about a third of their grapes to La Maison du Vigneron and the remaining crop is vinified for sale under their own label. Most of their vineyards are grassed down at least every other row and they have reduced systemic anti-fungal spray levels steadily over the years, practising *lutte raisonnée* since 1991. Harvests are by hand with selection at the vine.

The brothers, who studied viticulture and oenology at Beaune, have created an impressive modern winery, with 30hl stainless steel tanks, small enough to keep lots separately. They use cultured yeasts for the whole range, and *ensemencement* for the oxidative wines. The Poulsard, macerated for ten days but not put in oak, is marketed as rosé (*faux* or 'false' rosé), whereas Trousseau and Pinot spend 8–10 months in barrel. Topped-up whites are also made, aged in oak – four months for Chardonnay Flora, 14 months for Creux d'Enfer, a 50/50 blend of Savagnin and Chardonnay selected from a splendid parcel of the same name beyond Les Trouillots.

Everything is in place at this estate to make an excellent range of wines, and indeed they have won awards at various competitions and have been regularly selected in the French guides. However, I feel they could do much better: while really sound, the wines lack excitement. Perhaps the yields are a little high. However, their Vins Jaunes are good, the Trousseau light but pleasant, and I enjoy the Creux d'Enfer.

Domaine de la Petite Marne
RN83, 39800 Poligny

Tel: 06 83 33 88 74 (Philippe)

Email: contact@noir-freres.com

Web: noir-freres.com

Contacts: Philippe and Jean-Yves Noir

Map ref: p. 217, C3

Established: 1973 (vineyards); 2003 (winery)

Vineyards: 10.8ha (4ha Chardonnay, 3.5ha Savagnin, 1.4ha Pinot Noir, 1.1ha Poulsard, 0.8ha Trousseau)

Visits: Tasting room, visits welcomed by appointment

Domaine Xavier Reverchon

Were he younger – he is in his mid-fifties – Xavier Reverchon would convert his 6ha of vineyards in Poligny to organic farming. An outspoken and affable man, I sense that, although not a joiner by nature, he would fit right in with the mixed bunch of characters that make up the ever-growing band of Jura's organic producers. Xavier's great-grandfather Joseph founded the domaine in 1900, his grandfather Henri followed on, and in 1960 his father Joseph moved from polyculture to dedicated wine production with 3.5ha of vineyards. Xavier joined in 1978 after studies and work experience, notably with Jean-Marie Courbet of Nevy-sur-Seille, and he has built up the domaine gradually to its current size.

Apart from two half-time workers, Xavier is on his own – on the tractor, in the cellar and at the paperwork, as he says. His vineyards are on both sides of Poligny, the original family plantings being the west-facing Boutasses and St-Savin, and newer plantings are in a 2ha parcel on Les Trouillots facing south. He likes a clean-earth vineyard, not grassed down, but uses

Xavier Reverchon outside his tasting room.

no weed-killer, working the soil regularly with a specially adapted plough and a small tractor. To save on labour, he uses two or three systemic anti-fungal sprays at the start of the season before moving on to the classic sulphur and Bordeaux mixture sprays.

All his wines have markedly high acidity levels due, Xavier claims, to the combination of no potassium in the vineyard, as he has never used artificial fertilizer, and very gentle pressing, but there is ample fruit to balance the acidity. Since 2003 reds have been aged in tank only, with cold maceration at the start and only a light fining at the end. This results in a fresh, juicy fruit style, with light tannins in the Trousseau. Pinot is used in a red blend and for Crémant.

Accounting for around a quarter of his 30,000-bottle production, the excellent white Crémant is made from about 20% Pinot with Chardonnay and occasionally a drop of Savagnin. Xavier makes his own *liqueur de tirage* using 24g/l of sugar in the Champenois style, rather than the Jura norm of 20g/l. He also does his own hand-riddling, using a service only for bottling and disgorgement. The result is elegant, with a good mousse and a vinous character from the Pinot.

Xavier's whites are all traditional oxidative styles but with some differences. Les Trouillots is a Chardonnay aged in *demi-muids*, completely filled at the start but never topped up, hence a *voile* forms. Vin Jaune and Savagnin Réserve are good, but outstanding is Les Boutasses Savagnin aged in a single large oak *foudre* (4,100 litres) and not topped up so that it forms a *voile* – this is extremely risky as, if the *voile* did not take, it would be a huge amount to lose. The first was 2007, and as I write the cask contains 2011. Good Vin de Paille and Macvin complete the range.

A few years ago Xavier built a beautiful modern tasting room in his old house in the middle of Poligny which can receive groups. Much is sold here and through various wine shows. Xavier is hoping that his son, currently studying agriculture, may want to join him. I hope so, for this is an estate producing really enjoyable wines.

Domaine Xavier Reverchon
2 Rue du Clos, 39800 Poligny

Tel: 03 84 37 02 58

Email: reverchon.chantemerle@wanadoo.fr

Contact: Xavier Reverchon

Map ref: p. 217, D3

Established: 1900 (Xavier from 1978)

Vineyards: 6.15ha (2.3ha Chardonnay, 2ha Savagnin, 0.9ha Poulsard, 0.7ha Pinot Noir, 0.25ha Trousseau)

Visits: Tasting room, visits welcomed by appointment

Domaine Michel Thibaut

This new estate was created by Michel Thibaut with his wife Catherine in January 2014 following the division of the Domaine Morel-Thibaut estate after 24 years working with Jean-Luc Morel. The partners divided the vineyards and the remaining wine stocks, both in bottle and those still ageing, for sale under each of their new labels. Michel is currently establishing new premises in Poligny.

The profile of Domaine Morel-Thibaut gives more details (see p. 222).

Domaine Michel Thibaut
1 Rue des Perchées, 39800 Poligny

Tel: 03 84 37 07 41

Email: domaine.thibaut.michel@orange.fr

Contact: Michel Thibaut

Map ref: p. 217, D3

Established: 2014 (vineyards and previous estate in 1989)

Vineyards: 5.5ha (50% white, 50% red)

Visits: No tasting room, visits welcomed by appointment

St-Lothain

The village of St-Lothain, best reached from Poligny through the vineyards via Miéry, is dominated by a huge church, built over a crypt that dates back to the 10th century, the oldest Roman church in the Jura. Its location, protected from the *la bise* (north wind) by the forest above is close to the site of a large abbey and monastery that were founded after a religious hermit settled here around 600 AD. In the 17th century the abbey was linked with that of Château-Chalon, and St-Lothain's wines also earned a high reputation.

Some of what is forest today would once have been vineyards stretching above, around and below the village with around 250ha in 1900, declining to only 5ha by the 1990s. Today there are about 15ha in a few different locations, so one could class it as a mini-revival. The village has several

traditional stone fountains, wash-houses and vignerons' houses – it made a wonderful host village for the Percée festival in 2005.

Didier Grappe

Born in St-Lothain, Didier likes to emphasize his advantage in not being from a vigneron family without the associated pressure to take on the job. He chose to be a vigneron, studying in Beaune and returning to create his estate from nothing in 2001. His vineyards, farmed organically since 2007, are all around the village of St-Lothain, with some old vines and some planted by him. This thoughtful man also points out how much easier it is to rent suitable vineyard land in this part of Côtes du Jura rather than in AOC Arbois, which meant that he could test various plots until he was satisfied.

Didier's three vineyard plots have different expositions and soils suitable for different varieties. He credits Antoine Pignier as a big influence on his vineyard work, and although he is not planning to convert to biodynamic farming (he doesn't like the astrological aspects), he uses several plant-

Didier Grappe in his St-Lothain vineyards.

based sprays as well as goats' whey from a local farm to reduce the amount of copper he uses. Didier prefers natural green cover (weeds!) and ploughs every other row, even in the vineyard that has very heavy clays. The other row is mowed when needed, and he hoes around each vine in the old laborious way. Keeping things local is important to him and he is not afraid of low yields and taking his time to get the vineyards right.

Didier's parents are retired and based in the village, so his father helps with tractor work and his mother looks after the tasting room and some sales. Initially selling only locally, exports have taken off – much to Didier's surprise. Much of this came about through recommendations from other organic growers and Le Nez dans le Vert tastings. In his tiny winery, partly in an old cheese-making facility, he manages to make the whole range of Jura wine styles, working in a natural but measured way with small doses of SO_2 if necessary.

Didier makes a small volume of just one red called Insouciantes, meaning 'carefree' – a blend of the three red varieties, with Pinot dominating – but more is promised, as he has planted Trousseau à la Dame on a warm, south-facing site. His Chardonnay is a little hit and miss, but both *ouillé* and oxidative Savagnins are well made with great character. His first and only Vin Jaune from 2005 tastes very good and he made five barrels. There is much joyous spirit in this man and his wines.

Didier Grappe
81 Route du Revermont, 39230 St-Lothain

Tel: 03 84 37 19 21; 03 84 37 09 22

Email: didier.grappe@orange.fr

Web: vindujura.com

Map ref: p. 217, B2

Established: 2001

Vineyards: 3.8ha (Chardonnay, Savagnin, Pinot Noir, Poulsard, Trousseau, mainly white)

Certification: Ecocert

Visits: Tasting room

Maison de la Rose

I first met Dominique Grand a long time ago when he was president of the AOC Côtes du Jura syndicate – he didn't seem to fit the mould, yet he must have put his hand up and wanted to change things, just as his successor Henri Le Roy from Vincelles is trying to do. Dominique is the younger brother of Lothain of Domaine Grand in Passenans and originally worked in the family business. Dominique and his wife Elisabeth decided to set up on their own because they prefer to work in a very small and individualist way and are not keen on traditional oxidative wines.

The house, with large cellars below, was purchased by Dominique and Elisabeth, a science teacher, in 1987. It is a small 17th-century priory in the village's pretty Quartier des Roses (Rose Quarter). Elisabeth comes from a typical Jurassien farming family, which had milk cows and corn crops. In the 1960s her father decided to convert to organics and Elisabeth and her family were considered freaks for not accepting the modern way of using chemicals for an easier life. She claims to know nothing about wine, but from the start they used no chemicals in the vineyards and sought organic certification from 2009.

They make a little deliciously pure Pinot red, named Rubis, whites that are all topped up except for the occasional Vin Jaune; Crémant, Macvin and Vin de Paille are also made. Hidden treasures include a fresh, intense and stony Savagnin *ouillé*, named after its vineyard Novelin (there is also a lighter-styled more aromatic version named Traminer), and equally mineral, but also appley Saugeot Chardonnay. There is also an exotic and delicious late-harvest Savagnin that does not meet AOC rules named Ecole Buissonnière ('playing truant').

These are straightforward but original people making more than decent organic wines of integrity in their traditional, somewhat chaotic cellar. All three grown-up children are in some way involved in the wine business elsewhere. However, their youngest, Désiré, works part-time at the family estate, and he and Dominique want to brew some beer here too.

Maison de la Rose
8 Rue de l'Eglise, 39230 St-Lothain

Tel: 03 84 37 01 32

Contacts: Dominique and Elizabeth Grand

Map ref: p. 217, B2

Established: 2000

Vineyards: 3ha (Chardonnay, Savagnin, Poulsard, Pinot Noir, mainly whites)

Certification: Ecocert

Visits: No tasting room, but visits welcomed by appointment

Toulouse-le-Château

The village of Toulouse-le-Château lies to the west of the main road on a small hill, similar in geological structure to that of Arlay and L'Etoile to the south. The château was constructed as a look-out post to protect the salt route, but was destroyed in the 14th century and never rebuilt. The ruins still remain at the top of the hill, from where there is a wide view of the vineyards to the east from St-Lothain to Le Vernois, and to the south to Arlay. With classic Jura soils, including grey marl, it's no wonder that this was once a very important wine village and a testament to that are the lovely vignerons' houses in the village and its associated hamlets.

Today there are around 12ha of vines scattered around the Toulouse-le-Château hillside with different expositions – three farmed professionally, and several privately owned. I have included Domaine Lambert in this section because their winemaking facilities and most of their vineyards are here, but the tasting room and original winery are in Le Chateley a few kilometres up the road.

Domaine Frédéric Lambert

Proudly displaying the ruined tower of Toulouse-le-Château on their label, Frédéric and Marie-Anne Lambert are a hard-working couple who sell most of their wines through word of mouth, building up a clientele through the annual Percée festival. For ten years Frédéric worked for the vineyards section at the Société de Viticulture du Jura (SVJ), so he was very familiar with the region and the various choices of vineyard and winemaking practices before embarking on his own project in 2003, having already acquired vineyards from 1993. Bubbly Marie-Anne worked with her husband part-time at first, but in 2009 she joined him full-time, working mainly in the vineyards, something she clearly enjoys.

Most of the vineyards are in Toulouse-le-Château, with one plot of over 2ha on varied marl soils. There is also a recently purchased vineyard in Passenans and two plots in Château-Chalon. Herbicide is limited to use below the vines with vineyards either grassed down every other row or ploughed throughout; spray programmes are strictly controlled according to *lutte raisonnée* methods. Yields are kept low, especially for Trousseau, where a special selection that Frédéric was involved in developing at the SVJ is grown.

Until 2013 the winery was by the house in Le Chateley, but from 2013 only the ageing cellars remain there. The rest has moved to larger premises in an old honey factory (and yes, they have had the air checked to ensure that the honey smells don't penetrate the wines). Wine production is – as everything on this estate – carefully considered, with an excellent range that bridges the gap between traditional and modern.

Crémant du Jura, once 50% of production, is now 35% and a very good Crémant it is too, with 20% Pinot Noir adding some vinous character to the Chardonnay. This spends 24 months on yeast before disgorgement. Their value range includes two classic Jura reds and mainly *sous voile* whites, with one excellent exception of around 1,000 bottles a year of a stylish and mineral oak-aged Chardonnay, Les Gryphées, named after the incredible density of fossils found in the vineyards where the 40–50-year-old vines are grown. Côtes du Jura Vin Jaune, matured partly in a rather humid cellar and partly in a loft, is an intensely oxidative style. Their first Château-Chalon will be released in 2014, from the 2007 vintage. Both Vin de Paille and an unusual Savagnin-based Macvin add to this exemplary range. One of Frédéric and Marie-Anne's sons is expected to join the estate after his studies and the domaine should then expand further.

Domaine Frédéric Lambert
14 Pont du Bourg, 39230 Le Chateley

Tel: 03 84 25 97 83

Email: domainefredericlambert@orange.fr

Web: domaine-frederic-lambert.fr

Contacts: Frédéric and Marie-Anne Lambert

Map ref: p. 217, A4

Established: 2003 (vineyards 1993)

Vineyards: 6ha (3.15ha Chardonnay, 1.5ha Savagnin, 0.65 ha Trousseau, 0.5 ha Poulsard, 0.2ha Pinot Noir)

Darbonnay, Passenans and Frontenay

Between the main D1083 and the cliffs rising to the Premier Plateau it's worth trying to imagine these three villages 150 years ago, when vineyards would have covered every available space. The dramatic decline here happened after the First World War, when cows took precedence over vines. Today only Passenans has more than pocket-sized vineyards, with around 35ha mainly sited in one large bowl stretching north from the edge of the village near the large Hotel du Revermont and west towards the railway below. Very sheltered, this vineyard area is called Les Grandvaux and, as is often the case in this part of the Jura, it was re-created and planted mainly in the 1970s on a mixture of marl soils.

The lovely village of Passenans (another that hosted the Percée festival, combining with neighbour Frontenay in 2009) has a long history, with connections to the abbey at Château-Chalon. Darbonnay has one important vigneron but no vineyards, whereas Frontenay has a few vineyards but no vignerons. Frontenay's claim to fame is the château that dominates the hillside. It was built in the 12th century to guard the salt route and today's replacement dates from the 14th to the 18th centuries.

Côtes du Jura vineyards just north of the village of Passenans.

Les Dolomies

In 2008 Céline Gormally created her small organic estate in Passenans from nothing, but she has built it up in a wholly original way with the support of an unusually wide community. Husband Steve gives her a hand, but works full-time as an arts consultant. Sixty per cent of her production of less than 9,000 bottles a year is already on export markets in Denmark, USA, Belgium and beyond.

Céline, who worked for several Jura producers, including Domaine Badoz and Domaine St-Pierre, before setting up, chose to work organically from the start. The Dolomies vineyards are located in Passenans, Frontenay, St-Lothain and Château-Chalon (though the latter are Côtes du Jura AOC) and all are leased, but not in any conventional way. In 2008, having rented less than half a hectare of vines in Passenans, an opportunity arose to acquire a further hectare and Céline approached the organization Terre de Liens for assistance. Established in France in 2003, Terre de Liens is an ethical association and foundation that helps provide project support for farmers using organic methods. Terre de Liens' objectives include acquiring agricultural land to protect it from development and encouraging an ethical and environmental approach to farming. Céline

is the first woman farmer they have helped, and also one of only a handful of vignerons. Terre de Liens bought the land and leased it back to her, with a guarantee that they will not sell it. At the same time, for added cash-flow Céline established a scheme to lease individual vines on a three-year contract to around 60 families, who receive a certain amount of wine each year and can get involved in harvest and other activities. In 2010 she leased further plots, taking her up to 4ha of vines, a level that allows her to stop working for other people.

Initially Céline had to work hard to convert certain vineyards from conventional farming, introducing ploughing and use of organic compost, sometimes with a small tractor, at other times manually or with her horse. She also uses biodynamic methods, including silica and horn compost sprays and herbal teas, as well as mixing goats' whey into Bordeaux mixture. Quantities remain very small.

In winemaking Céline cites Julien Labet as an important influence. With a large proportion of whites, the three terroir selections of Chardonnay (Les Combes, Les Boutonniers and En Novelin) are fermented in barrel and topped up regularly, resting on lees, sometimes with stirring. One cuvée of Savagnin *ouillé* En Rolion is made similarly and some Savagnin has been set aside to mature *sous voile*. Pinot La Cabane and Trousseau En Rollion (with two 'l's, from a different vineyard to the Savagnin) are aged in barrel too. She has also made some Vin de Paille and a Macvin-type liqueur wine called Carmina, but, like all her cuvées, these are tiny amounts. Use of SO_2 is kept very low; it is added if needed after malolactic fermentation and pre-bottling – both reds and whites retain some slight fizz from the carbon dioxide that keeps them fresh. These are wines full of fruit and finesse but also, in the case of Chardonnay in particular, showing the minerality of the soil as one might expect. The name Les Dolomies was given in honour of the Dolomitic limestone found in the colourful marls in the vineyards.

Céline credits her success (or should that be survival?) so far to the help she is given by her neighbours in Passenans (vignerons and others), by the wider Jura community of organic producers who participate in Le Nez dans le Vert, and by the community of families who have invested in her. She shows what can be achieved in less than five years by a young grower in the Jura – particularly notable are her winery's listings, among other prestigious outlets, at a restaurant of the calibre of Noma in Denmark.

Céline Gormally in the cellar she created for her estate Les Dolomies.

Les Dolomies
40 Rue de l'Asile, 39230 Passenans

Tel: 03 84 44 98 25

Email: contact@les-dolomies.com

Web: les-dolomies.com

Contacts: Céline and Steve Gormally

Map ref: p. 217, B1

Established: 2008

Vineyards: 4ha (Chardonnay 2.4ha, Savagnin 0.75ha, Pinot Noir 0.75ha, Trousseau 0.1ha)

Certification: Ecocert

Visits: No tasting room and visits possible only occasionally by appointment

Domaine Grand

Whereas in Pupillin you find the little people (two vignerons named Petit or 'Small'), here in Passenans and nearby St-Lothain you find the big people (two vignerons – brothers – named Grand or 'Big/Tall'). And Lothain Grand has certainly thought big over the past 40 years, which is possibly why Dominique, his younger brother, preferred to set up his own estate, Maison de la Rose. You will see Domaine Grand popping up in many places, with wines appearing in medal lists and the 130,000-bottle production being sold through export markets (20%), in supermarkets in France, and at many wine shows. Lothain is technically retired now and his two sons, Sébastien and Emmanuel, have joined the business, Sébastien taking care of vineyards, Emmanuel the winemaking and administration. However, in 2013 the estate was put up for sale, as the brothers want to go their separate ways.

The family tree goes back to 1692, but it was not until Lothain took over his father's 2ha of vines in 1976 and subsequently planted land to bring the holdings up to 10ha that the business got going properly.

Lothain Grand in the Macvin cellar of Domaine Grand, which he founded in 1976.

After wine studies at Beaune, Lothain worked with Domaine Michelot in Meursault and then back in the Jura with Henri Maire and the laboratory at Poligny, so it is no surprise that he wanted to create an up-to-date winery and bring in modern vinification techniques, including topping up the Chardonnays. Today the sizeable vineyard holdings include 0.7ha in Château-Chalon. The largest vineyard is in Les Grandvaux (yes, 'grand' again) and the most recent plantings are on a warm, steep slope behind the winery with lighter, sandy soils, mainly for Chardonnay and Pinot Noir. All are grassed down one in two rows with the other worked, and herbicide used below the vines. Spray programmes follow the *lutte raisonnée* system. The modern, practical winery also includes an excellent purpose-built, ventilated Vin Jaune cellar, with a temperature range of 7–22°C. They age their spirits for Macvin and Fine just down the road in a beautiful old, damp cellar.

Always impressive and consistent is their Crémant from 100% Chardonnay, these days named Prestige. Unusually for Jura, Domaine Grand, as in Champagne, retains up to a third of reserve wine in large oak casks to blend in the following year. They bottle with the *liqueur de tirage* themselves, using the local sparkling service only for disgorging. Since 2004 they have also made an excellent Vintage in good years, which stays at least three years *sur lattes* before disgorgement. The 2008 has lovely intensity, yeastiness and superb length. A Trousseau Crémant rosé is less successful.

Reds are led in quality by Trousseau and are on the light side, typical for Côtes du Jura, with the Poulsard unhelpfully labelled rosé (not to be confused with their Rosé d'Eté – 'Summer Rosé'– mostly from young Trousseau vines). The sound Chardonnay is overshadowed for me by the newest addition to the range, a deliciously tangy and mineral Savagnin *ouillé* named Expression. Vin Jaune, Château-Chalon En Beaumont, Vin de Paille and Macvin are all very good quality and made in some quantity – in fact these 'specialities' together with the Crémants (40,000 bottles a year) make up over half the production. Domaine Grand is well respected and quality has improved in recent years. [Revised 2015: The domaine is off the market, as Emmanuel and his partner Nathalie have taken it over with a reduced vineyard area of 9.5ha. Sébastien has left to pursue other things.]

Domaine Grand
139 Rue du Savagnin, 39230 Passenans

Tel: 03 84 85 28 88

Email: domaine-grand@wanadoo.fr

Web: domaine-grand.com

Contacts: Emmanuel and Sébastien Grand

Map ref: p. 217, B1

Established: 1976

Vineyards: 24ha (11ha Chardonnay, 5ha Savagnin, 5ha Trousseau, 3ha Pinot Noir/Poulsard)

Visits: Tasting room

Domaine Pêcheur

It's hard not to smile when you visit the cramped tasting room in Darbonnay where someone from the friendly Pêcheur family is always there to greet you, even if only in French. That may change soon, as their teenage daughter enjoys speaking English and already helps her cheerful mother Patricia at wine shows or her grandmother in the tasting room. Justly proud of his small domaine, Christian Pêcheur is one of those salt-of-the-earth, traditional hard-working vignerons who deserves great respect for his work.

It was thanks to the restructuring of the Grandvaux vineyard in Passenans that Christian's parents established the domaine in 1976 and most of their vines are here. Christian joined the estate after wine studies in Beaune in 1992, by which time there were 2ha, and he has gradually expanded the estate to its present size, including 0.34ha in the Gaillardon vineyard in AOC Château-Chalon, acquired in 2006. His wife Patricia joined from the restaurant business to help with sales and Christian's mother also works part-time. The Passenans vineyards have varied soils, including red marl ideal for reds, and dolomitic limestone perfect for Chardonnay. Christian has worked with *lutte raisonnée* methods for several years, grassing down every other row and ploughing the soil except for the area of dolomite which is too hard to work. He still uses some herbicide beneath the vine rows but has now bought the *intercep* tractor attachment to work between the vines.

For a mainly local and French clientele, built up through presenting at 15 wine shows through the year, around 40,000 bottles are produced, with around a quarter in Crémant and the rest divided across the usual range, though no *ouillé* whites are made so far. Both Trousseau and Pinot Noir are delicious and true to their varieties, reflecting the fact that Christian uses strict selection at the vine, destems and ages for just a few months in old oak. The oxidative range of whites is exemplary, including the Cuvée Spéciale blend, and culminating in the elegant Vin Jaune. At present they have no space to move in their various cellars and hope to ease the pressure by expanding soon. Through this family's hard work a real joyousness emerges, which is reflected in their wines.

Domaine Pêcheur
Rue Philibert, 39230 Darbonnay

Tel: 03 84 85 50 19

Email: contact@domaine-pecheur.fr

Web: domaine-pecheur.fr

Contacts: Christian and Patricia Pêcheur

Map ref: p. 217, B2

Established: 1976

Vineyards: 7.7ha (3.2ha Chardonnay, 2.5ha Savagnin, 2ha reds)

Visits: Tasting room

Christian Pêcheur, whose Vins Jaunes are highly respected in the region.

CHÂTEAU-CHALON, THE UPPER SEILLE AND L'ETOILE

Château-Chalon, with its own appellation and historical fame, is the *grand cru* of the Jura in all but name. The village, together with other nearby wine villages, is part of the area known as the Upper Seille. Many Château-Chalon producers own vineyards in these other villages and vice versa. L'Etoile, also with its own appellation, lies just to the southwest. To get your bearings, the viewpoints in the village of Château-Chalon enable you to look up

the valley towards Nevy and Baume-les-Messieurs or down the valley to the old ruined château of Arlay, south to L'Etoile and then over the Bresse plain to the Côte de Beaune.

The village of Château-Chalon is on the Premier Plateau, with its vineyards below, and the Château-Chalon AOC includes the village of Menétru-le-Vignoble, also high up on the plateau, plus the villages of Domblans and Nevy-sur-Seille along the Seille river. Confusingly, some of the vineyards are designated AOC Côtes du

Above: The River Seille flows along the bottom of the Château-Chalon vineyards.

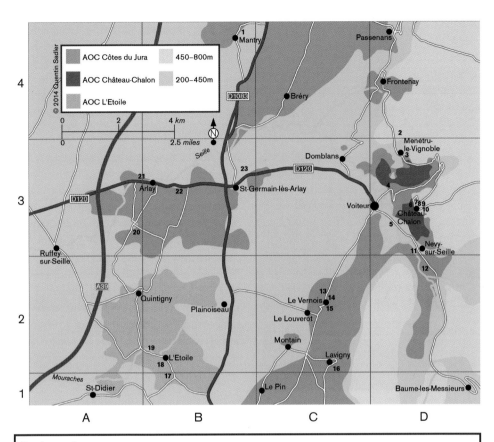

Producers by commune

Mantry
1 Domaine Jean-Luc Mouillard

Menétru-le-Vignoble
2 Domaine Chevassu-Fassenet
3 Domaine Blondeau

Voiteur
4 François Mossu
5 Fruitière Vinicole de Voiteur

Château-Chalon
6 Domaine Macle
7 Domaine Jean-Claude Crédoz
8 Domaine Salvadori

9 Domaine Berthet-Bondet
10 Domaine Geneletti

Nevy-sur-Seille
11 Domaine Courbet
12 Domaine De Lahaye

Le Vernois
13 Caveau des Byards
14 Domaine Baud Père et Fils
15 Domaine Hubert Clavelin et Fils

Lavigny
16 Philippe Butin

L'Etoile
17 Domaine Philippe Vandelle
18 Château de l'Etoile
19 Domaine de Montbourgeau

Arlay
20 Domaine Cartaux-Bougaud
21 Caves Jean Bourdy
22 Château d'Arlay

St-Germain-lès-Arlay
23 Domaine Luc et Sylvie Boilley

Jura, not AOC Château-Chalon, but there is no way of telling just by looking which plots are eligible for which AOC. Even some of those directly below the hilltop Château-Chalon village are not eligible for AOC Château-Chalon. These AOC boundaries are archaic and complicated. In theory those eligible for Château-

Chalon are the best exposed on grey marl, but in practice you need to be with a local vigneron to know which is which. The map on p. 245 gives an indication of the boundaries.

There are 180 properties of vines in AOC Château-Chalon (approximately 50ha)

A typical stone marker in the Château-Chalon vineyards shows those belonging to Domaine Chevassu-Fassenet.

and a tourist destination. The two main attractions have always been the historic villages of Château-Chalon and Baume-les-Messieurs. The de Laguiche family of Château d'Arlay has worked hard to attract tourists and the Haute Seille tourist office has also helped.

The AOC Côtes du Jura vineyards stretching south of Voiteur to Pannessières, just north of Lons-le-Saunier, saw the biggest vineyard revival when Le Vernois became the first village in France to instigate a *remembrement* (restructuring of the vineyards) in 1968. The area of Le Vernois south to Lavigny and Pannessières has the greatest concentration of vineyards in the southern part of the Jura, with more than 150ha, mainly white varieties. L'Etoile is also predominantly planted with white varieties, with just 67ha.

and many own tiny plots. Some make their own wines, others take their grapes to the Voiteur Fruitière, and a large number sell their grapes to La Maison du Vigneron. The latter accounts for about half the crop. The largest vineyard owners in the appellation are Domaine Berthet-Bondet and Domaine Macle, each with around 4ha. Many distinctive stone markers can be seen in the vineyards with the name of the appellation and the owner of the plot.

This whole area, including Château-Chalon, suffered far more reduction of vineyard area and deprivation after the Second World War than Arbois, and has taken a long time to recover its former glory both as a wine-producing region

Mantry and Arlay

Along with Toulouse-le-Château just to the north, the villages of Mantry and Arlay are built around the limestone hills that broke off from the Premier Plateau many millennia ago. In the mid-19th century the small village of Mantry had a population similar to nearby Passenans and L'Etoile, all making a living from the vineyards. Since the 1970s there has been a small revival, with several vineyards planted and two vignerons based there.

One of the most ancient settlements of the Jura wine region, the beautiful village of Arlay lies on the eastern edge of the Bresse plain. Its fine buildings straggle alongside the River Seille below the ruined fortified château and it made a perfect host village

for the Percée festival in 2003. The vineyards are mainly on the hillside below the fort and on the other side of the river, with varied soils.

Château d'Arlay: The courtyard formed by the elegant Pavillon de l'Horloge (left) and the 18th-century château itself.

Château d'Arlay

Below the ruins of the 13th-century fortified château the vineyards of Château d'Arlay boast the most aristocratic heritage of any in the Jura. These, possibly the oldest château vineyards in France, are thought to have been planted on the orders of John, Count of Chalon, known as Jean l'Antique or John the Old (1190–1267). His son, John I of Chalon-Arlay (1258–1315), did much to expand the renown of Jura wines, something that has continued with family owners right up to today's proprietor, Comte Alain de Laguiche.

In the 15th century the Chalon-Arlay dynasty was succeeded by the Orange-Nassau dynasty and the château passed through the hands of the Spanish, British and French royal families. Eventually it was given to a descendant of the Princes of Orange, the Countess of Lauraguais, who purchased a convent at the foot of the hill in 1770 and built the château we see today. The countess was guillotined during the French Revolution, but the château was restored by her grandson, the Prince of d'Arenberg.

Through marriage the château was inherited by Louis, Marquis de Vogüé (1868–1948), a banker and businessman, also credited as an important figure in democratizing the business of agriculture. The extended de Vogüé family has connections in the most aristocratic vineyards of France. He was responsible for replanting 5ha of grafted vines at Arlay after phylloxera and in 1911 installed a brilliant manager, Georges Tournier, who remained until the 1960s, also becoming president of the Société de Viticulture du Jura (SVJ). Louis' son, Comte Robert-Jean de Vogüé (1896–1976), who inherited Château d'Arlay, was managing director of Moët & Chandon for many years.

Until the 1950s the vineyards below the old fort were split between many owners, but gradually the family took them over and expanded their vineyards to around 10ha. Originally Pinot Noir dominated, but Georges Tournier planted other varieties in 1953 and began to make Vin Jaune, helping the estate to develop a fine reputation. Robert-Jean de Vogüé's daughter Annie had married a military man, Comte Renaud de Laguiche, and in 1960 de Vogüé agreed that his son-in-law should take over the château.

During the 1960s Robert-Jean de Vogüé almost sold the property to Henri Maire, but Annie was adamant that the château and its vineyards should remain in family hands. To help with the upkeep Renaud de Laguiche opened up the château to visitors. De Vogüé agreed to expand the wine estate by buying the next-door farm in Proby, a settlement that had vineyards even in Roman times. The winery was moved there and in the 1970s this farm was replanted with vines and the château vineyards were also expanded, bringing total holdings to 33ha. In 1975 Renaud and Annie de Laguiche inherited the château and their son, Comte Alain de Laguiche, and his wife Anne joined them in 1985.

In the intervening years the château has become an official French Historic Monument (see 'Visiting the region', p. 334). The wines have been exported around the world, but in recent years they have suffered from insufficient investment in the cellar and vineyards, and I have noticed a significant drop in quality.

Today the vineyard area has been reduced by more than a third, and just under 8ha remain below the ruins, mostly of old vines planted in the 1950s and 1960s. The remainder is at Proby, with vines planted between 1972 and 1991, but these are in bad shape, having been planted and nurtured according to methods prevalent at the time in Champagne, with close-spaced vines and household waste as fertilizer. Viticulture is now being converted to more environmentally friendly methods and the focus is turning to the vineyards below the ruins, which are in conversion to organic farming and are being replanted little by little. The estate is somewhat top-heavy in Pinot Noir, but, with plenty of grey marl soils, replantings below the ruins favour Poulsard. Valuable old Savagnin and Chardonnay vines remain, which are being nurtured and replaced only as needed.

The winery is badly in need of modernization. However, in 2012 a new vineyard and winery manager joined: Philippe Soulard, who has experience in Burgundy and at an organic estate in Provence. Philippe seems determined to help Alain de Laguiche improve the wine quality. He has acquired an *intercep* to work the soil and has installed a cooling system and modern winery equipment.

A great ambassador for the Jura wine region, Alain de Laguiche with a demonstration barrel of Vin Jaune in the cellar he opens up for visitors each summer.

The ageing cellars below the 18th-century château are full of old *foudres* and casks that need some loving care, but are typical for the Jura.

It is hard to speak of a flagship wine for this estate, as the Pinot Noir, Corail ('Coral', a pale red made from all five varieties), Vin Jaune and Vin de Paille all have the potential to be great wines in different ways. Blended from the five Jura varieties, Corail deserves to be loved for its originality, but is aged for too long in old wood; the Pinot Noir at its finest can be truly Burgundian, but recent releases have been somewhat harsh. However, the *ouillé* Chardonnay à la Reine shows well, with a Jurassic mineral edge and richness from the old vines. My early experiences of Château d'Arlay Vin Jaune were of a very fine *jaune*, reminiscent of Château-Chalon in elegance, but stronger in peaty character; recent vintages have been less convincing. Vin de Paille can be unctuous and spicy, with excellent ageing potential, and the spicy, intense Pinot Noir Macvin was one of the earliest red Macvins. The wines are packaged beautifully and hand-sold on export markets and French wine fairs by Alain and Anne de Laguiche themselves.

For over half a century first Comte Renaud de Laguiche and his wife Annie and then Alain and Anne de Laguiche have worked incessantly to keep this amazing piece of Jura wine history alive. It is nearly time for a new generation to take over – son Pierre Armand and his wife have already shown interest and the way is being prepared for them. Let us hope that the wines of Château d'Arlay can once again represent the Jura wine region as well as Alain de Laguiche himself has over the past three decades.

Château d'Arlay
Route de St-Germain, 39140 Arlay
Tel: 03 84 85 04 22
Email: chateau@arlay.com
Web: arlay.com
Contact: Alain de Laguiche
Map ref: p. 235, B3
Established: 13th century
Vineyards: 19ha (5.5ha Savagnin, 4ha Chardonnay, 7.8ha Pinot Noir, 1.2ha Trousseau, 0.5ha Poulsard)
Visits: Tasting room and shop

Domaine Luc et Sylvie Boilley

Luc Boilley was the son of a farmer and worked in the food-processing industry before establishing his wine estate with his wife Sylvie in his home village of Chissey-sur-Loue, northwest of Arbois. In addition to his father's small mixed vineyard in nearby Champagne-sur-Loue, they purchased land for vineyards on south-facing slopes in Arlay and Mantry, the latter with ideal terroir for Savagnin, and took on some mature plots in L'Etoile. With most of their vineyards around 40km from their winery and home, in 2000 the Boilleys built a new vinification and ageing cellar closer to the vineyards in St-Germain-lès-Arlay.

Luc has firm views on how the vineyards should be farmed. They have been grassed down for many years to avoid erosion, herbicide is used only below the vines, and he is adamantly against copper treatments. He likes to harvest late, looking for greater ripeness than most – they often have to be given a derogation by the INAO to allow an alcohol level of over 14% for Savagnin. Cultured yeasts are used to ensure complete dryness, which Luc says is vital for ageing Savagnin *sous voile*, especially as here a large part of the Vin Jaune production is aged for

With his wife Sylvie, Luc Boilley draws a sample of Savagnin from one of their newer barrels.

autumn). As well as Vin de Paille, in some years there is a sweet Savagnin de Gelée, picked after the first frosts.

The Boilleys were one of the earlier estates to export regularly within Europe and these clients no doubt appreciate the extra ripeness, lower acidities and greater oak character of their wines.

Domaine Luc et Sylvie Boilley
Route de Domblans,
39210 St-Germain-lès-Arlay

Tel: 03 84 44 97 33

Email: boilley.fremiot@wanadoo.fr

Web: monvindujura.com

Contacts: Luc and Sylvie Boilley

Map ref: p. 235, B3

Established: 1978

Vineyards: 15ha (7ha Savagnin, 4.5ha Chardonnay, 2ha Trousseau, 1ha Pinot Noir, 0.5ha Poulsard)

Visits: Tasting room, visits welcomed by appointment

---

ten years before bottling. Another difference from most Jura producers is the relatively high proportion of new oak barrels used for certain wines, although they were also early adopters of the larger *demi-muids*.

The flagship reds, made only in good years, are Trousseau Les Goulesses from old vines in Champagne-sur-Loue, sometimes with a touch of Poulsard, and Pinot Noir Chaze from Arlay. Both are well made but somewhat over-oaked – classic Jura lightness and minerality show better in their simple Trousseau bottling. The *ouillé* whites are vinified partly in new oak and are less interesting than their second Champagne-sur-Loue wine, a field blend of red and white grapes called Cuvée Flor vinified as a white wine. 'Flor' is a reference to Sherry's *flor* because the wine is aged for two years, partly *ouillé* and partly *sous voile*; the result is an intriguing mix of very ripe fruit and spices.

Domaine Boilley offers at least two vintages of Vin Jaune at any time – one with six years of ageing *sous voile* and the other with ten years. To me, they are almost overwhelmingly oxidative and somewhat flat in acidity, not for ageing. Making around 20,000 *clavelins* a year, accounting for 30% of production, it is no wonder that some of this Vin Jaune appears at a scandalously low price at the annual supermarket Foires aux Vins (wine promotional weeks held each

Caves Jean Bourdy

This is possibly the best-known Jura wine producer overseas thanks to Jean-François Bourdy spreading the gospel of the family's old wines around the world, following a great tradition of exports since the 1930s. Jean-François and his brother Jean-Philippe Bourdy have a cellar of old vintage wines like no other (see 'History', p. 116). However, as well as their fascinating museum, which traces the history of their family as vignerons in Arlay back 14 generations, they have a living museum in the form of their active, but very traditional, wine cellar.

Born in 1904, as a young man Jean Bourdy decided to revive the family wine business after the ravages of phylloxera. The beginning of their 'modern' development started with the extension of both vineyards and cellars and, one presumes, a consolidation of the extensive stocks accumulated by his father, François Bourdy, who from 1896 systematically kept back stocks of each wine. Despite the dedication of the current generation to their museum, the history of exactly how the commerce of wines was conducted at this time is somewhat hazy. How many of the very old bottles they sell today were actually made by the family from their own grapes is somewhat open to question, as they have always had a négociant's licence as well.

Jean's son Christian Bourdy, who died in 2014, took over and developed the business, becoming a great ambassador for the region, and passed the business on to his two sons in 1990. Jean-Philippe had completed wine studies at Beaune, while Jean-François studied commerce at the prestigious Parisian ISG business school, followed by an MBA qualification. Their vineyards are close to the winery in Arlay and nearby Ruffey-sur-Seille, with 0.5ha in Sous-Roche, Château-Chalon. From early 2006 Jean-Philippe, in charge of the vineyards and the winemaking, converted the vineyards to biodynamic methods and in 2010 received full Demeter certification.

Whereas big changes were needed to convert to biodynamics in the vineyards, there was nothing to change in the cellars, where both winemaking (including use of indigenous yeast) and the domaine's range of wine have remained virtually unchanged for more than a century. When Jean-Philippe took over, the only obvious change he made was to adopt the normal practice of inviting the regional laboratory to analyze each of the barrels *sous voile*. At this point they introduced a Côtes du Jura Savagnin, about the only wine that Jean-François dismisses

as not for ageing, as it is effectively a reject Vin Jaune. Actually, it's one of my favourites from their range. Old wooden casks of all sizes are to be found in every corner of these dark, rambling cellars, lined on one side with their massive stocks of old bottles. The policy is to hold back 200–300 bottles a year each of the Côtes du Jura red and white, the Vin Jaune and the Château-Chalon.

The white wine is 100% Chardonnay, aged for three to four years in casks of various sizes, topped up only in the first year. Because their cellars are cool and damp, there is little loss of volume and a *voile* does not form. The old-style red is from a third each of Poulsard, Trousseau and Pinot, harvested and vinified together, remaining with the skins for up to two weeks before pressing. It is aged for three to four years in old *foudres* and, as with the

Above: Brothers Jean-Philippe and Jean-François Bourdy, grandsons of Jean Bourdy. Below: Old barrels in the 16th-century cellars, with some of the extensive old bottle stocks behind.

white, given a light filtration and small dose of SO₂ before bottling.

Vin Jaune and Château-Chalon are made in the usual manner, matured in even older *fûts* than most producers have, favouring cool and damp cellars with aeration, very much as Vin Jaune cellars were many years ago. Vin de Paille, not made every year, is from a variable mix of varieties, unusually with Poulsard predominant joining mainly with Savagnin – another nod to tradition. The grapes are dried partly in boxes and partly suspended from the rafters. Although the Bourdys make a conventional Macvin, they are most proud of their Galant des Abbesses, a historic version of Macvin, made from a 16th-century recipe from the lady abbesses of Château-Chalon. A heady mix of grape must steeped with spices is heated in a copper cauldron and then blended with old *marc* or sometimes Fine (brandy).

An appley Chardonnay Crémant completes the range, but is a négociant wine made from bought-in grapes. This and the Savagnin apart, the Bourdys claim decades of ageing potential for the rest of their wines, yet always state that they are ready to drink immediately. This applies even to the Vin Jaune and Château-Chalon (between them 10% of production), both typically minerally and peaty examples of their terroir, with the Château-Chalon even more intense.

Having the opportunity to taste a range or even drink one of the Bourdys' decades-old wines is always a fine experience, though I do find the quality somewhat hit and miss. As for the younger wines, if purchased on release at their very reasonable prices, the red in particular is a lovely example of old-style Jura and recent vintages indicate more purity of fruit since they have converted their vineyards to biodynamics. However, the prices shoot up rather dramatically as soon as a wine is deemed old enough to put on their 'old

vintage wines' list. As this is often only three years after release it seems a touch excessive, but for now export markets, accounting for three-quarters of sales, love them.

Caves Jean Bourdy
41 Rue St-Vincent, 39140 Arlay

Tel: 03 84 85 03 70

Email: cavesjeanbourdy@wanadoo.fr

Web: www.cavesjeanbourdy.com

Contact: Jean-François Bourdy

Map ref: p. 235, B3

Established: around 1500, with bottling since the early 19th century

Vineyards: 10ha (approximately two-thirds white, one-third red)

Certification: Ecocert, Demeter

Visits: No tasting room, but visits welcomed

Domaine Cartaux-Bougaud

What began as a labour of love for the parents of Sébastien Cartaux-Bougaud, who planted their first small vineyard in the 1970s close to the Château de Quintigny, has ended up as one of the larger quality estates in this sector, extended mainly by Sébastien when he joined the estate after his studies in 1993. The château, in the middle of the village of Quintigny, with its chapel now forming part of the village, has foundations dating back to the 14th century, but was extensively restored in the 18th century. In 1983 the Cartaux-Bougauds bought the château and the outbuildings were purchased by Claude Jacquier, one of the large sparkling wine services in the Jura. Below the château, occupied only in summer, are the domaine's excellent cellars for Vins Jaunes and other *sous voile* wines. And almost outside the back door are some of their vineyards. With this venture the Cartaux-Bougaud family has revived an old

Sébastien Cartaux-Bougaud outside the cellar below his house.

tradition, since this village, between L'Etoile and Arlay, was once a very important vineyard village.

A little over half of the vineyards today are in AOC L'Etoile in the villages of Quintigny and L'Etoile itself. The rest are nearby in Ruffey-sur-Seille (particularly Trousseau and Poulsard in the warmer gravelly soils) and in Arlay (mainly Pinot). Sébastien currently grasses down every other row and uses herbicide underneath the vines, but he hopes to give up the herbicide soon. Harvesting is by machine apart from grapes for Crémant and a small amount of Vin de Paille. The wines were originally made at the château, but in 1999 Sébastien and his wife Sandrine bought an old farmhouse in Juhans, which lies half-way between Arlay and Quintigny. Behind this they constructed a practical winery. Barrel ageing is split between the cellars below their house and that of the château.

About a quarter of production is a very decent Crémant and the rest is a range of traditional Jura wines. All three single-varietal reds are extremely pleasant, easy-drinking styles, with only the Pinot Noir partly aged in oak. The whites are all *sous voile*, with a marked oxidative character that is very successful in the really complex

L'Etoile Cuvée de Paradis with 80% Chardonnay and 20% Savagnin, picked at the same time. L'Etoile Savagnin is also very good, as is the Vin Jaune. Sébastien notes that conditions for ageing *sous voile* at the château are very good indeed. From one-third each of Chardonnay, Savagnin and Poulsard, Sébastien has made Vin de Paille only since the 2008 vintage and achieves a really good balance of sweetness, alcohol and acidity, with lovely spiced honey character. There is a peachy white Macvin and a sweet, rich unoaked Pinot liqueur wine named Coeur du Pinot. For now this estate does not export, although it has loyal clients who visit from Switzerland and Belgium. Apart from sales to a few restaurants, most of this extremely decent range is sold direct to consumers at the domaine or at tasting shows, managed by Sandrine.

Domaine Cartaux-Bougaud
Rue des Vines, Juhans, 39140 Arlay

Tel: 03 84 48 11 51

Email: contact@vinscartaux.fr

Web: vinscartaux.fr

Map ref: p. 235, A3

Contacts: Sébastien and Sandrine Cartaux-Bougaud

Established: 1993

Vineyards: 16ha (9ha Chardonnay, 3.5ha Savagnin, 3.5ha reds)

Visits: No tasting room, but visits welcomed by appointment, also at Château de Quintigny July–August

Domaine Jean-Luc Mouillard

Born into a family of vignerons in Nevy-sur-Seille, Jean-Luc Mouillard set up his own estate after a year studying in Beaune, and in 1997 moved his winery to his home in Mantry. His grandfather had been one of the founders of the Voiteur Fruitière and his father took his grapes there too, before passing on his vineyards to Jean-Luc in 2006. Today Jean-Luc farms his vineyards in *lutte raisonnée* with some plots near Mantry, but mainly in and around L'Etoile and Nevy, including 0.7ha at Château-Chalon.

The house in Mantry is thought to be an old *relais diligence* (coaching inn) and, after installing a modern vinification cellar in 2005, Jean-Luc set about restoring the magnificent 16th-century vaulted cellar. His *sous voile* wines are matured here and in the loft above.

With over half the estate planted to Chardonnay, he sells some to La Maison du Vigneron and also makes a lot of Crémant du Jura Chardonnay with 10% Pinot. Up to 2013 the local service made the Crémant, but, apart from disgorgement, he is taking on this task himself and planning to make a fresher, dryer style. Reds get better all

the time, but his whites are the real stars, with a minerally Côtes du Jura Chardonnay from Nevy, topped up in oak barrels for 18 months, a classic *sous voile* L'Etoile Chardonnay and a Côtes du Jura Savagnin, which in some vintages ends up like a baby Vin Jaune. He makes no Côtes du Jura Vin Jaune but offers a very classy, consistently good Château-Chalon. The Vin de Paille is redolent of gingerbread and a golden apricotty Macvin is made from a Chardonnay/ Savagnin blend, aged for two years before release. Overall, the genial Jean-Luc makes a very decent range of wines, sold mainly to consumers at tasting shows.

Domaine Jean-Luc Mouillard
379 Rue de Parron, 39230 Mantry
Tel: 03 84 25 94 30
Email: domainemouillard@hotmail.fr
Web: domainemouillard.com
Contact: Jean-Luc Mouillard
Map ref: p. 235, B4
Established: 1991
Vineyards: 8ha (4.5ha Chardonnay, 2ha Savagnin, 1.5ha Poulsard, Trousseau and Pinot Noir)
Visits: Tasting room, visits welcomed by appointment

Jean-Luc Mouillard in his restored vaulted barrel cellar.

Voiteur and the villages of AOC Château-Chalon

The small town of Voiteur has a useful tourist office and a few shops and is home to several vignerons. The pretty River Seille runs through it, flowing from Nevy-sur-Seille along the base of the impressive Château-Chalon hill.

The two hilltop villages of Menétru and Château-Chalon could not be more different and there is a certain rivalry. Within the communal boundaries of Menétru are said to be the finest, best-exposed vineyards of the appellation, including En Beaumont and Vigne-aux-Dames. The distinctive vineyard cabin in the middle of the vineyards, Clos Bacchus, is owned by several vignerons. It seems a shame that more cannot be done to make the cabin into somewhere one could visit. In the vineyards, you can see the grey marl soil, which looks like heavy clay, as well as the star-like fossils more associated with L'Etoile. However, the village of Menétru is sleepy, without even a bar or restaurant.

This map, taken from the collaborative book Le Château-Chalon, *published by Méta-Jura in 2013, shows the areas designated AOC Château-Chalon and Côtes du Jura, and marks the names of the specific Château-Chalon vineyards.*

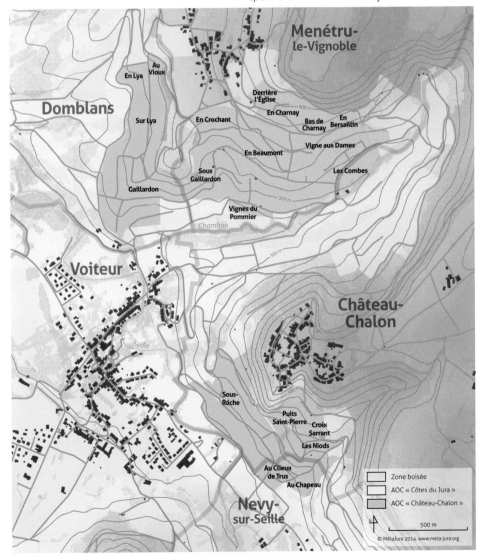

As you drive up to Château-Chalon the vineyards stop just before you arrive in this pretty, pleasantly touristy village. The Maison de la Haute Seille close to the church provides an excellent introduction to both the history of the village and the region (and indeed Vin Jaune). The vineyards can be accessed down a path near the church and you will first go past the vine conservatory (see p. 46). The two most spectacularly steep and highest vineyard areas are named Sous-Roche (meaning 'Underneath the Rock') and Puits St-Pierre. These can also be accessed from the valley on foot, but it is a steep climb.

The village of Domblans includes a fair proportion of the AOC Château-Chalon vineyards, contiguous with those of Menétru, the best known being Lya and Gaillardon. In the other direction, past the Fruitière of Voiteur, it is hard not to become distracted by the vineyards above you driving along this road towards the attractive village of Nevy-sur-Seille. Straddling the River Seille, Nevy marks more or less the end of the vineyards, though they once spread into the *reculée* of Baume-les-Messieurs. Baume is truly beautiful in a spectacular setting and is home to a famous Cluniac abbey – it is a good place to find lunch between tastings too.

Domaine Berthet-Bondet

Over a period of nearly 30 years in Château-Chalon Jean and Chantal Berthet-Bondet have contributed greatly and have encouraged people to visit and learn about the village and their wine estate. They have earned respect through their hard work and results, with a Château-Chalon wine eminently worthy of its prestigious label. Due to his quiet demeanour it takes some time to realize that Jean is truly a driven man.

The beautiful manor house, a former priory, owned by Jean and Chantal Berthet-Bondet.

Jean's parents were plastics manufacturers in the department of Ain, just southeast of the Jura, but Jean was attracted to a career in agriculture from an early age. He did a degree in agronomy and further studies at Montpellier University, where he met Chantal, who was also studying agronomy. After a spell of volunteer work in Nepal Jean returned to France to pursue a career in wine and worked for a year with Jean Macle. In 1984 Jean and Chantal decided to settle in Château-Chalon, having found 3ha of vines to farm and a fabulous old priory house.

The estate's vineyards are made up partly of old vines and partly those they planted between 1985 and 1990 – 4ha are in AOC Château-Chalon, in Sous-Roche, En Beaumont and Gaillardon, and the rest are in Côtes du Jura, in Voiteur, Lavigny and Pannessières. In 1993 Jean began to work the vineyards in *lutte raisonnée*, most particularly grassing down or ploughing every other row and using only organic fertilizer. Although he would have liked to have converted to organic farming earlier, he wanted to be financially stable before doing so, and made the move to conversion in 2010. The most difficult part was the elimination of chemical weed-killers on his steepest vineyard sites. There are three employees.

The Berthet-Bondets' beautiful house dates from the 16th century. Jean and Chantal built a modern winery in an adjoining barn in 1986 and restored the amazing vaulted semi-underground cellars into barrel storage for Vin Jaune. Jean was mayor of Château-Chalon for several years and has been more aware than many of the need to offer more tourism opportunities. Recently the couple converted a barn into a comfortable *gîte*. Jean was also very involved in the creation of the Maison de la Haute Seille.

Jean Berthet-Bondet.

With a relatively large holding of Savagnin in prime Château-Chalon sites, it is no wonder that a quarter of their production is of a sublimely elegant Château-Chalon, which shows a character of peat as well as curry spices, flavours that I associate strongly with this appellation. For several years Jean used *ensemencement* for the *voile* in some barrels, but, finding results no different, he stopped from the 2006 vintage. The fine character of this wine is certainly partly due to the excellent vineyard sites, but also the wonderful ageing conditions in the perfect Vin Jaune cellar, dry and well ventilated. The other traditional whites are exemplary too. Since 2007 they have made a delightfully fresh Savagnin *ouillé* called Naturé, aged in stainless steel, which gets better every vintage, as does the Crémant, made with a blend including around 10% Savagnin, which adds a touch of lemon to the Chardonnay. The blended red, Rubis, and the Vin de Paille are also worth looking out for. The entire range is on the up here.

Since 2012 Chantal has worked full-time on the administrative side. Their daughter Hélène, a linguist, started working with them in 2013 and is taking the organic viticulture and oenology course at the local Montmorot college. With a young family, it is too early to say whether Hélène will remain, but Jean and Chantal have built up a fine Château-Chalon estate that is worth preserving.

Domaine Berthet-Bondet
Rue de la Tour, 39210 Château-Chalon

Tel: 03 84 44 60 48

Email: berthet-bondet@orange.fr

Web: berthet-bondet.net

Contacts: Jean and Chantal Berthet-Bondet

Map ref: p. 235, D3

Established: 1985

Vineyards: 11ha (5ha Savagnin, 4.5ha Chardonnay, 1.5ha Poulsard, Trousseau and Pinot Noir)

Certification: Ecocert

Visits: Tasting room, visits welcomed by appointment

Domaine Blondeau

Yves Blondeau is a reserved but confident man, whose wines are all aged for longer than most estates. The large winery was built in 1991, six years after Yves joined his father Alain with the aim of creating a larger estate with Yves' brother, who subsequently left. The family had been farmers with a few vines, and Alain started with just 1ha, expanding gradually from 1975 to 1985, taking advantage of the *remembrement* in nearby Domblans.

The vineyards are located mainly on the south- and southwestern-facing slopes below Menétru-le-Vignoble and above Domblans, farmed in *lutte raisonnée*, with the soil worked by hand and most parts grassed down every other row. Grapes from around 2ha of Chardonnay for Crémant and 1ha of Savagnin for AOC Château-Chalon are sold to La Maison du Vigneron (for the Savagnin he receives double the price) and the rest Yves vinifies for sales of around 25,000 bottles a year, including 40% Crémant. Karine, Yves' wife, helps with bottling and sales, but otherwise he relies on part-time help. Grapes are harvested partly by machine.

The spacious, insulated winery is practical, with a mixture of concrete and stainless steel tanks, and Yves is equipped with everything he needs to make Crémant from start to finish, with a bank of mechanically operated gyropalettes. All the Crémant is kept for at least three years *sur lattes*, and the main cuvée, a fairly dry Chardonnay, is very pleasant. Whites are aged *sous voile* in a ventilated cellar at the back of the winery underneath the garden, with no need for *ensemencement*. Château-Chalon and the other oxidative whites on sale may be five to 15 years old and show maturity, but well-balanced acidity and the typical curry and smoky flavours of this terroir.

The top level of the winery is a huge loft space for drying Vin de Paille grapes. Unusually, most of the bunches are suspended on wires, which, according to Yves, gives less potential for rot and concentrates the sugars faster. This method is a family tradition; before the winery was built the grapes were suspended in the kitchen. Recently they had so much Vin de Paille stock that they had to stop production for a few years. Aged in wood for longer than the minimum, and slightly oxidative, from two-thirds

Chardonnay and one-third Poulsard, there is also a particularly intense version from old vines. The Chardonnay-based Macvin benefits from an extra two years in oak beyond the minimum required, giving well-integrated *marc* and orangey flavours. Some Château-Chalon has been exported to Japan, but sales from this interesting estate are mainly within France.

Domaine Blondeau
Rue Fontaine, 39120 Menétru-le-Vignoble

Tel: 03 84 85 21 02

Email: blondeau.yves@9business.fr

Contacts: Yves and Karine Blondeau

Map ref: p. 235, D3

Established: 1965

Vineyards: 10ha (6ha Chardonnay, 3ha Savagnin, 1ha Poulsard and Pinot Noir)

Visits: Tasting room

Domaine Chevassu-Fassenet

Les Granges-Bernard is a wonderful old Jurassien farm surrounded by pastures on the plateau behind Menétru, and it is here that Marie-Pierre Chevassu-Fassenet was brought up with her three sisters. Her mother Marie came from a family of vignerons and her father Denis farmed mainly cows. He took on some vineyards in the 1980s and, as all his daughters enjoyed helping, he expanded the business and started making and selling wine. Marie-Pierre chose a career in wine and after wine studies in Beaune and an oenology degree at Dijon she worked in New Zealand, Châteauneuf-du-Pape and Champagne before returning to work in the Jura for several years as an oenologist at Maison du Vigneron. She took over the wine estate in 2008, whilst one of her sisters runs the farm.

Marie-Pierre's husband, Cédric Fassenet, is a theatre director in Lons, but helps with tastings, and Marie-Pierre continues to receive help from her parents. However, she is very keen to keep the estate small, in particular so that she can take care of the vineyards personally, and everything is worked in a sustainable way. Marie-Pierre manually hoes 3ha of the vineyards but explains that, due to erosion of the steep slopes, there are some parcels in Château-Chalon where it is simply impossible to work without herbicide. She uses systemic treatments early and late in the season but is a keen member of the local group working in *lutte raisonnée* towards Terra Vitis certification. The atmospheric cellars at the farm are full of old wood from large *foudres* down to *fûts* and *feuillettes*.

The biggest change that Marie-Pierre has made since taking over has been with the two reds, which she makes in a resolutely

Marie-Pierre Chevassu-Fassenet outside the farmhouse she was brought up in, which also houses the estate's cellars.

modern Jura way, with careful sorting at harvest during the manual destemming and filling the tanks with carbon dioxide to avoid using SO₂ at harvest. There is no oak ageing. The resulting Pinot Noir (I have not tasted the Poulsard) is deliciously full of fruit, with a touch of CO₂ gas that disappears with some aeration. Whites are no less carefully thought out, but this time resolutely traditional, never topping up, yet for the excellent Chardonnay, aged in *foudres* or *demi-muids*, there is only a hint of the oxidative character: the process simply brings out the minerality of the marl soil.

The Savagnins, which come from En Beaumont, are aged in three locations: a small amount in a loft, another small part in a semi-underground cellar, and three-quarters underground, meaning, as is classic for Château-Chalon, less temperature variation during ageing, aiming at finesse and elegance. The Château-Chalons since 1999 have been blended and bottled by Marie-Pierre, but of course were vinified by her father Denis until 2008. There is, however, a Savagnin 2008 already released and I sense from this there will be changes, with Marie-Pierre bringing out even more elegance and finesse in these wines, which need plenty of time open to show their best. A delicious Vin de Paille made from Chardonnay, Savagnin and Poulsard and a Chardonnay Macvin are very good too. This is a fine estate in excellent hands.

Domaine Chevassu-Fassenet
Les Granges Bernard, 39210 Menétru-le-Vignoble

Tel: 03 84 48 17 50

Email: mpchevassu@yahoo.fr

Contact: Marie-Pierre Chevassu-Fassenet

Map ref: p. 235, D4

Established: 1980

Vineyards: 4.5ha (80% Chardonnay and Savagnin, 20% Poulsard and Pinot Noir)

Visits: No tasting room, but visits welcomed by appointment

Domaine Courbet

In this very traditional sector of the Jura wine region, young vigneron Damien Courbet is a man of projects, someone who really wants to move things forward while remaining true to tradition. Damien's father, Jean-Marie Courbet, studied classics but continued with oenology studies in Dijon before taking over and expanding the family vineyards in the 1970s. Jean-Marie has always been much involved in the politics and activities of the wine region, becoming president of the SVJ between 1995 and 2004. After his wine studies, Damien worked in South Africa and California (with Jim Clendenen), and in France with Nicolas Potel, Olivier Merlin and Olivier Zind Humbrecht. With that experience, it is hardly a surprise that Damien is gradually converting the estate to biodynamics. He is already convinced that the methods give wines with more substance and fruit.

Damien joined his father on the estate in 2003 and took charge fully on Jean-Marie's retirement in 2011. Jean-Marie still helps with certain vineyard and cellar activities and Damien's mother Brigitte works part-time in administration and sales. After following some of Pierre Masson's biodynamic courses Damien started conversion of their vineyards in Menétru-le-Vignoble in 2004 and 4ha have been converted. The rest of the vincyards, which are above Nevy-sur-Seille in Sous-Roche, are farmed with *lutte raisonnée* methods, including using herbicide directly below the vines, but he hopes to convert these to biodynamics within five years, even though he may have to sell some

Damien Courbet in the disused church in Nevy that his family took over for barrel storage.

of the steepest vineyards that are simply too difficult to work in this way without dramatic loss of quantity.

Damien is reducing the amount of Crémant he makes because it is too difficult to make according to biodynamic principles; also, the heavy marl soils in his vineyards are not ideal for a Crémant Chardonnay base. Instead he is increasing the whites, possibly moving towards making some *ouillé* wines from 2013. Although this is primarily a white wine estate, the reds have slowly increased in quality recently, especially Trousseau; one plot has low-yielding old vines from a mass selection. From these Damien makes one barrel (an old one, of course), for a wine named Trousseau Violette, full of raspberry and cherry creamy fruit and sold only from the estate tasting room.

The oxidative whites include a Tradition blend with up to 20–30% Savagnin, which has been aged less than two years *sous voile*, so is elegant and smoky with only a slight oxidative character, with pride of place going to the Château-Chalon. Maturation of the barrels is partly in an old stable, where relatively little volume is lost to give a very fine style, and this is blended with

barrels matured a little below the loft space, giving a more exuberant and alcoholic style. Working with low yields, they pick at a potential of around 13%, so the wine often ends up at 14.5–15.5% alc after evaporation and concentration during ageing. Despite this relatively high alcohol there is excellent acidity and concentration of flavour to balance. Damien bottles everything at the same time, 2,000–3,000 *clavelins* a year, and puts aside 120 to sell in future years. He plans to release a special cuvée of Château-Chalon starting with the 2006 vintage, selected from two barrels, unfiltered and in numbered *clavelins*. There are also small quantities of a very good Vin de Paille.

With local help the family restored a distinctive small vineyard cabin, known as 'Le Nid' or 'The Nest', much photographed from the roadside near Nevy. They also own a listed old church in the village, which is used for ageing certain wines, mainly Chardonnay, and for hosting tastings. Damien is concerned about the amount of grapes from AOC Château-Chalon that are sold to La Maison du Vigneron and would like to start his own small quality-focused négociant business. This bright young man could prove to be very good for this corner of the Jura.

Domaine Courbet
1130 Route de la Vallée, 39210 Nevy-sur-Seille

Tel: 03 84 85 28 70

Email: dcourbet@hotmail.com

Contact: Damien Courbet

Map ref: p. 235, D3

Established: 1873

Vineyards: 7.5ha (3ha Chardonnay, 3ha Savagnin, 1ha Trousseau, 0.4ha Poulsard, 0.1ha Pinot Noir)

Visits: Tasting room, visits welcomed by appointment

Domaine Jean-Claude Crédoz

An inviting and imposing house tempts Château-Chalon's many visitors into the tasting room, where Jean-Claude and Annie Crédoz sell 70% of their production of around 50,000 bottles a year. Yet Jean-Claude's family, who have owned vines back to 1859, is from the village of Menétru-le-Vignoble, a world apart from Château-Chalon, if one is to believe Jean-Claude's tales of the rivalries. In 1991 he and his two brothers established an estate they named for their grandfather Victor Crédoz, but 11 years later the partnership failed and Jean-Claude and his wife moved to Château-Chalon to start their own estate. Brother Daniel ran his own estate between 2002 and 2006, then sold his vineyards partly to Jean-Claude and partly to Stéphane Tissot.

The domaine has nearly 3ha in AOC Château-Chalon, built up over the years by Jean-Claude's father, Marcel Crédoz, one of the founders of the Voiteur cooperative, and his grandfather Victor. This includes plots in En Beaumont and Vigne-aux-Dames in Menétru, and Lya in Domblans. The AOC Côtes du Jura vineyards are here too and stretch into Voiteur. With help from one full-time employee the vineyards are managed in *lutte raisonnée* and Jean-Claude is a member of the group that hopes to be certified by Terra Vitis. Some of the Voiteur vineyards are terraced, where he uses a contact herbicide directly below the vines. In the other vineyards he grasses down between the rows where possible. The winery is at the house in Château-Chalon, with some Vin Jaune stored there, and some in Menétru. Jean-Claude works only with indigenous yeast and believes that to preserve the terroir taste SO_2 should be added at harvest and, if needed, after malolactic fermentation, but never before bottling. There are some 70–80-year-old partly

An old press outside the welcoming tasting room of Domaine Jean-Claude Crédoz in the middle of Château-Chalon.

ungrafted Melon à Queue Rouge vines among Jean-Claude's Chardonnay holdings, which he bottles separately sometimes, as in the deliciously mineral and rich 2011. Otherwise he blends it with his other Chardonnays, ageing for 18 months in *fûts* at least ten years old, topped up. His excellent Sélection blend is from topped-up young Chardonnay of the year stated blended with a maximum of 10% Savagnin *sous voile* from an earlier year. Both wines are tremendous value for money. The Savagnin is a real baby Château-Chalon, showing elegance and minerality, and the Château-Chalon is very fine indeed, with great complexity and length. As well as the usual laboratory testing, Jean-Claude believes in regularly tasting to check the development of each barrel, deciding whether it is good enough to stay the course for Château-Chalon.

Jean-Claude claims that Menétru was the original village for Vin de Paille and from a third each of Poulsard, Chardonnay and Savagnin he makes significant quantities in a slightly oxidative style with around

15% alc and not overly sweet. In his 100% Savagnin Macvin the juice is blended with a four-year-old *marc*. Alongside the interesting whites the star wine is undoubtedly the Château-Chalon, of which Jean-Claude makes upwards of 4,000 *clavelins* a year. They are a credit to his adopted village.

Domaine Jean-Claude Crédoz
Rue des Chèvres, 39210 Château-Chalon

Tel: 03 84 44 64 91

Email: domjccredoz@orange.fr

Contacts: Jean-Claude and Annie Crédoz

Map ref: p. 235, D3

Established: 2002

Vineyards: 9ha (90% Chardonnay and Savagnin, 10% Trousseau and Pinot Noir)

Visits: Tasting room

Domaine Durand-Perron/ Marius Perron

In 2011 this Voiteur estate was taken over by La Maison du Vigneron, with the name Domaine Durand-Perron continuing for the Château-Chalon made from grapes grown on the estate. It had been run since 1987 by Jacques Durand, the son-in-law of legendary producer Marius Perron. Jacques was a winemaker from Minervois and, although he became immersed in his adopted region, the wines never attained their former reputation. Marius Perron moved from mixed farming to full-time wine production in the 1950s and his Château-Chalons, especially from Vigne-aux-Dames below Menétru, were regarded as among the very best, and some still appear at auctions.

Domaine Geneletti

This estate has bases in the two smallest Jura appellations, L'Etoile and Château-Chalon. L'Etoile is the original family home, where Michel Geneletti built up his wine domaine in the mid-1970s, and where the winery is still based. Château-Chalon is where son David has his home, tasting room and very old cellars, purchased in 2000 from Henri Maire. David's great-grandfather emigrated from Piedmont in northwest Italy and found a bride in L'Etoile who inherited a small vineyard. Michel Geneletti inherited his grandmother's vineyard and expanded mainly in L'Etoile, with the focus on white wines. David joined his father in 1997, taking over fully from 2009 and today his estate is one of the few in the region to own vineyards in each of the four appellations.

In AOC Château-Chalon the domaine has 1.8ha in Menétru, in En Beaumont and Vigne-aux-Dames; most of the other vineyards are in L'Etoile itself and in nearby Plainoiseau for AOC Côtes du Jura. In 2005 David decided to take on 0.5ha in AOC Arbois near Villette-lès-Arbois, co-planted with old vines of all three red varieties. He

David Geneletti relaxes by the fireside in his restored Château-Chalon house.

is currently doing a trial of organic farming there; all the other vineyards have been farmed using *lutte raisonnée* for many years, grassing down every other row and working the soil in the other, except on the steepest slopes, where herbicide is used. Harvest is by hand.

The winery in L'Etoile is equipped with stainless steel and a range of barrel sizes. There is a range of very decent wines from this estate, true to their styles and appellations, without any radical approaches. The Arbois red field blend was matured in oak at first, but now David uses tank only, yet even so a lovely rustic and spicy flavour emerges together with red fruits. Another field blend, the traditional *sous voile* L'Etoile Vieilles Vignes, is made from a vineyard co-planted with Chardonnay and Savagnin in the 1960s. The oxidative character is not overly strong, giving an elegant wine with a mixture of spicy apples and cream. The L'Etoile Au Désaire is another appley Chardonnay but with more minerality, from a vineyard on deep marl. Aged in *fût* and topped up for two years, this is exactly the sort of Jura Chardonnay that you might mistake for being oxidative, but that is the terroir showing through.

David's Vins Jaunes sell well and rightly so, and he is making increasing amounts of both the L'Etoile and the very fine Château-Chalon. L'Etoile Vin de Paille is made from Chardonnay and Savagnin with a little Poulsard, aged in both *fûts* and the smaller *feuillettes*. Rigorously topped up and not overly sweet, it shows real intensity of flavour from a combination of raisins and spice with freshness to balance. Most of the wine is sold direct to loyal customers built up at the Vigneron Indépendent tastings around France, and also sales from the two tasting rooms.

Domaine Geneletti
Rue St-Jean, 39210 Château-Chalon

Tel: 03 84 47 46 25

Email: domaine.geneletti@free.fr

Web: domaine-geneletti.com

Contact: David Geneletti

Map ref: p. 235, D3

Established: 1976

Vineyards: 15ha (90% Chardonnay and Savagnin, 10% red)

Visits: Tasting room and a second one in Rue Bouillod, L'Etoile

Domaine De Lahaye

When Guillaume Tissot joined his father Jean-Pierre in 2003 they decided to change the Tissot name to De Lahaye, the name of Guillaume's maternal grandmother. The Tissots of Nevy-sur-Seille (no relation to the Tissots in Arbois and Montigny-les-Arsures) had been mixed farmers with vines since the 17th century and began to make wines in the 1930s. As well as making their own wine Jean-Pierre's father Michel and his sons ran a successful négociant business, which was bought by the Henri Maire company in 2005. In 1991 the family purchased the important Brulerie de Revermont, which distils *marc* for most of the vignerons in the Jura and this continues to be run by Jean-Pierre's brother Pascal Tissot and his children, together with a small négociant business named for Michel's mother Marie-Louise Tissot. The family vineyards were retained by Jean-Pierre and now form part of Domaine De Lahaye.

Guillaume studied both the technical and commercial sides of the drinks business at Beaune and did practical training in the Languedoc. He proved to be a very capable president of the 2013 Percée in Voiteur, no small task when the festival has a budget of €500,000. Father and son share the responsibilities of the estate. The vineyards are nearly all on marl soils in the immediate locality above Nevy, with a small area, mainly Poulsard, in Lavigny. Their steepest vineyard of 0.25ha can be accessed only by ladders, but everywhere it is possible the soils are worked and grassed down every other row, with herbicide used only below the vines.

A proportion of Chardonnay for Crémant and Savagnin for Château-Chalon is sold to La Maison du Vigneron, but the Tissots make and bottle the whole range of Jura wines, selling directly from their tasting room and at more than 20 tasting shows around France. Whites are much better than reds. The *ouillé* Côtes du Jura is 100% Chardonnay (not marked on the label), from grapes grown below the AOC Château-Chalon vineyards. The grey marl soils influence the distinctive Jurassien mineral taste and the blend is mainly matured in tank. The *sous voile* barrels are stocked in a warm, uninsulated ground-level cellar and the Tissots offer both a Château-Chalon and a Côtes du Jura Vin Jaune, with the latter from very gravelly and stony vineyards near the top of the hill. Both are good, the Château-Chalon

especially, showing distinctive smoky, peaty and mineral flavours. An unusual Vin de Paille is made from 100% Chardonnay and an excellent Macvin, which always includes a barrel from the previous year, is also made from Chardonnay; it has an attractive spicy and perfumed character.

In 1930 Guillaume's grandfather Michel Tissot built a cabin in their vineyards above Nevy to store vineyard implements. Visible from the Voiteur–Nevy road, the cabin always arouses curiosity as it has a large '?' hung from the roof. Michel was an aviator fan and the '?' was his tribute to the first successful east–west transatlantic flight by French aviators Dieudonné Costes and Maurice Bellonte. The Paris–New York flight was completed in September just before harvest, flown in a Breguet 19 Super Bidon plane named '?'. In the capable hands of Guillaume Tissot one hopes this estate has a more certain future.

Domaine De Lahaye
45 Impasse Jeanne d'Arc,
39210 Nevy-sur-Seille

Tel: 03 84 44 99 38

Email: domainedelahaye@yahoo.fr

Web: domaine-de-lahaye.fr

Contacts: Guillaume and Jean-Pierre Tissot

Map ref: p. 235, D2

Established: 2003 (vineyards from earlier)

Vineyards: 6ha (2.7ha Savagnin, 2.3ha Chardonnay, 0.6ha Pinot Noir, 0.3ha Poulsard, 0.1ha Trousseau)

Visits: Tasting room

President of the Percée du Vin Jaune in 2013, Guillaume Tissot of Domaine De Lahaye raises the first glass of Vin Jaune 2006 from the 'pierced' barrel.

Domaine Macle

Some tourists make the pilgrimage to Château-Chalon to see one of the most beautiful villages in France, but most wine lovers head there to find the pretty painted sign marked E & J Macle and access the hidden wine treasures behind. As the seventh generation to farm vineyards here, taking over from his father Jean, Laurent Macle has had big shoes to fill. However, without assuming his father's Pope-like status, he has quietly got on with the job of making the very best Château-Chalon wines that his vineyards will allow.

Following oenology studies at Dijon and the University of Suze-la-Rousse, Jean Macle (see 'History', p. 133) created the estate with his wife Eliane in 1966, taking on 2ha of vines, including 1ha in AOC Château-Chalon, from his father, who had been a mixed farmer. The family had immigrated from Italy in the 17th century, originally bearing the name Mascolino, and had farmed vines since 1850. It has only been in recent years that Laurent's name has appeared as the person running the estate, yet he has managed the vineyards since the early 1990s and took on the winemaking in 1995 under the watchful eye of his father. He still has ongoing sales help from his mother Eliane, who receives visitors in the tasting room.

Almost from the start, Jean Macle wanted to be 100% organic. After persisting for ten years, he resorted to using contact herbicide directly under the vine rows in the steepest vineyards and that remains Laurent's policy today; it is the only thing that stops the estate being classified as organic. Spray programmes are of copper and sulphur, and soils are worked as needed. The 4ha of Château-Chalon vines are split between Vigne-aux-Dames, En Beaumont (planted in 1970), Sous-Roche and terraced vineyards in Puits St-Pierre.

Facing south-southwest, the Puits St-Pierre vineyards are on very steep slopes (more than 20° or 40% incline) and Jean Macle built the terraces in 1987 as the only solution to huge erosion. There are around 3,000 vines at a density that is lower than normally required for the AOC, but a derogation is given for vines on terraces. Since 2003 Esca has attacked, requiring regular replacement of vines, and Laurent had to replant 250 vines just in this location in 2012. This is, however, one of the finest spots for Savagnin: it has the classic grey marl soil, it is high up for slower ripening and it benefits from regular air currents coming up the slope from the Seille Valley, meaning that the ripening grape bunches can be kept hanging for longer without risk of rotting. Jean Macle always looked for over-maturity but not noble rot, as this gives a tendency to maderization, he told me once. Yields are kept very low.

Chardonnay vines are also grown in the vineyards around Château-Chalon in those parts designated AOC Côtes du Jura. Laurent is phasing out production of Crémant du Jura, but some Chardonnay still goes to make Macvin. Most of the Chardonnay is used for the very respected

Enticed by the beautiful sign, visitors beat a path to the door of Domaine Macle, founded by Eliane and Jean Macle in 1966.

Laurent Macle with three vintages of his family's much-revered Château-Chalon.

Côtes du Jura, which is usually blended with 15% Savagnin. Domaine Macle has always done several bottlings under the same label, and Laurent continues to experiment with Chardonnay, sometimes ageing *sous voile* in *fûts*, sometimes in *demi-muids*, altering proportions of Savagnin and once making 100% Chardonnay. I prefer the blend with some Savagnin, which combines a little citrus character with the gorgeous walnut, lightly oxidative flavours and apple from the Chardonnay. This wine ages amazingly well and Laurent notes that 30-year-old Côtes du Jura wines will be less oxidized than white Burgundies of the same age.

The most radical move that Laurent has made since 2007 is to experiment with *ouillé* wines, much to the disapproval of his parents, but for now Laurent makes very little and it is not usually available for sale. Each year he experiments with Chardonnay from a different terroir, once even blending with Poulsard, vinified as white. Any red the estate grows is usually made into a wine for family and staff. In 2013 he made one barrel of Savagnin *ouillé*. Those I have tasted show Laurent's supreme care in making his wines and reflect the hallmark minerality of these vineyards. The barrels used are a few years old and have never contained *sous voile*

wines, but are aged among the *sous voile* barrels.

Laurent has a choice of locations to age the Château-Chalon, the true *raison d'être* of this estate, and he believes that terroir is not as important a factor in quality and style as the storage conditions. Exploring the cellars is one of the joys of a visit here, as one walks from one cellar to another below the 17th-century house. At ground level there is an insulated cellar, then a few steps down is a cellar semi-below ground, and below that a series of fully underground cellars, ventilated but without a wide temperature difference. It is this small temperature change that preserves delicacy and complexity and means the aromas are maintained, Laurent believes. Indeed his father Jean has always said that one should never open his Château-Chalon until at least ten years after bottling. Laurent smiles at this and is not so insistent, although he values their age-worthiness too. The Macles have a policy of keeping back around 100 bottles each of Côtes du Jura and Château-Chalon in case of problems, though one hopes to enjoy too – they are never for sale, but there is usually an older wine on offer to taste.

Château-Chalon is aged here *sous voile* for six to eight years and every barrel is tasted using the *guillette* tap twice a year. There are around 8,000 *clavelins* produced each vintage (about 15–20% of the estate's production), with up to three bottlings (marked on the bottles with a code L01, L02, L03), but I have not had the opportunity to taste the differences between them. Domaine Macle Château-Chalon is simply sublime, without doubt one of the pinnacles of tasting experiences from the Jura, even when tasting it young, especially if it has been open for a day or more. There is restraint in everything, with alcohol never exceeding 14%, and aromas more powerful than the taste, which exudes elegance and wonderful singing acidity. Peat is a hallmark in many years, and as it matures in some years there can be candied fruit, blending in with walnuts and a myriad of spices. The label proudly proclaims 'Vin de Garde' as of old, and there is every reason to believe that these wines will live up to their labels just as well with Laurent at the helm as with Jean.

Domaine Macle
Rue de la Roche, 39210 Château-Chalon

Tel: 03 84 85 21 85

Email: maclelaurent@orange.fr

Contact: Laurent Macle

Map ref: p. 235, D3

Established: 1966 (vineyards since 1860)

Vineyards: 12ha (7.6ha Chardonnay, 4ha Savagnin, 0.4ha red)

Visits: Tasting room, visits welcomed by appointment

François Mossu

If there is a mould of Jura vigneron, or even several different ones, somehow François Mossu does not fit any of them. For over 25 years this vigneron has always followed his own way, and both his exceptional wines and forthright manner are appreciated by a loyal group of private and restaurant clients, who beat a path to his door, almost the only place he sells his wines. He relishes fine wines and food, but he also loves to share his vision of the world, especially the world of food and wine.

François' vineyards are in the very spot, just above Voiteur in Domblans, that his maternal grandfather Jules Marguet planted vines in the early 20th century to make Vin de Paille. But when the AOC laws were being drawn up, according to Philippe Bétry's book *Le Vin de Paille du Jura*, Marguet wanted to continue stating on his labels 'Vin de Paille du Château-Chalon' and the law would not allow it. With the other problems of the age this was the final straw. In 1934 he pulled up the vines and planted fruit trees instead, mainly Mirabelle plums. François' father was born in Switzerland and the family moved to the Jura and took up farming. When his father married he took on his father-in-law's fruit-growing business and started selling fruit direct. By the early 1980s the fruit business was suffering and the *remembrement* in Château-Chalon's vineyards had made growing vines more interesting, so François, aged 18 but with an elderly father, decided to take over his grandfather's land to plant vines.

From the start François' interest was in making Vin de Paille alongside Château-Chalon and these two wines are still his main focus: he makes 1,000–1,500 *clavelins* of Château-Chalon and 2,000–3,000 half-bottles of Vin de Paille each year. With a focus on these two high-end products and only 3ha, François has supported his wife and family and preserved his inheritance. The vineyards have been fully grassed down since 2009 and are mowed when required;

before that he used weed-killer under the vines, working every other row. For disease management, in addition to Bordeaux mixture and sulphur, he chooses a systemic spray that will continue to act on the vines after rain. He says that organic growers need to spray too often and that this is no better for the vineyards. Although he shows real respect for Pierre Overnoy, as someone who 'has lived as an organic grower, not only worked as one', he shows disdain for others in the movement, believing it to be fashion and money motivated, two things he evidently hates.

François refuses to make *ouillé* wines, but makes a small amount of an intense Savagnin, a blend of several vintages matured in *demi-muids sous voile*. His Château-Chalon is redolent of the terroir. He vinifies the wine in tank and then transfers it to *foudres* to lose as much CO_2 as possible before putting in unwashed barrels in July or August. He has no trouble with the *voile* forming and considers that making a Vin Jaune is like playing a game without any rules. He ages in a combination of dry cellars with moderate temperature changes from 10°C to 20°C, and a loft that may vary from −10°C to 30°C.

François Mossu is known as the master of Vin de Paille, the 'Pope of Vin de Paille' as they like to say in the Jura. His original plantings of Chardonnay, Savagnin and Poulsard were selected deliberately to make Vin de Paille and he dedicates between 20% and 30% of his total production to this wine. The grapes are dried in large wooden crates with metal grids at the bottom and stacked in a loft space open to the south wind to keep the grapes free from rot. Rather than the requisite 19% potential sugar at pressing, he aims for at least 22%. After fermentation in tank he ages the wine in normal-sized *fûts* for a year or two and then racks it into

This old bottle of Vin de Paille made by François Mossu's grandfather shows Château-Chalon on the label as well, a designation no longer allowed.

tiny 'quarto' barrels (made in the 1920s and containing only 50–60 litres), where it stays for three or four years. He discovered this 'secret' recipe for making Vin de Paille in his grandfather's records, and was able to restore the old barrels. In summer 2013 he had just released his 2007 vintage, which mixed exotic herbs and spices on the nose with an unctuous but balanced palate with dried fruits on the finish. Flavours of dates or figs and a balance of sweetness and acidity are the crucial things that François is seeking in his Vin de Paille.

François says that he splits his time in three – one-third is devoted to caring for the vineyards in a reasonable way, one-third he works as a winemaker in his cellars and the last third he spends with his clients. He is a strong believer in his power to inspire visitors to learn not only about his wines but the Jura's wines in general, spending hours discussing how they are made and how they might match food. There is something very special about him and his wines that drives people back to visit and to recommend him to their friends.

François Mossu by the large wooden claies *(crates) he uses for drying grapes for his legendary Vin de Paille. Air circulation is vital to keep the grapes free from rot.*

François Mossu
Route de Menétru-le-Vignoble, 39210 Voiteur

Tel: 03 84 85 26 35

Email: francoismossu@orange.fr

Map ref: p. 235, D3

Established: 1986

Vineyards: 3ha (2.7ha white, 0.3ha red)

Visits: Tasting room, visits welcomed by appointment

Domaine Salvadori

It would take a hard soul not to be wowed by the tiny, authentic cellar Jean-Pierre Salvadori has restored in the middle of Château-Chalon where he welcomes groups by appointment to talk about his wines and adopted village. Although his family were originally from Trentino, Jean-Pierre was born not far away, down the valley in Bréry, where his father worked for a nearby wine estate, owned a few vines and let the young

Jean-Pierre lend a hand making the wines. After studies in Beaune, Jean-Pierre worked for Jean Macle for ten years and planted his own vineyards at the same time, partly on the steep terraces they created together in Puits St-Pierre – an illustration of these vineyards proudly adorns his labels.

In the early years Jean-Pierre sold grapes to Henri Maire while building up some stocks of Chateau-Chalon; as he points out, when planting from scratch it takes ten years to have a Château-Chalon to sell. Setting up on his own three decades ago, he has had a life of very hard work – it's all manual labour in the vineyards. He doesn't even own a tractor and sprays on foot with the atomizer on his back. With vineyards in all the prime sites – Gaillardon, En Beaumont, Sous-Roche and Puits St-Pierre – he allows the weeds to build up, cutting down as needed, and using herbicide below the vines only when necessary. In the 1990s he had 6ha of vineyards and rented a winery, but in 1998 moved to his current cellars and reduced the vineyard area.

Crémant du Jura is made in lesser years; otherwise Chardonnay is used for the Côtes du Jura blend of 60% Chardonnay in tank and 40% *sous voile* Savagnin. Over-mature Chardonnay grapes are also used for the Macvin, which is full of spicy dried fruit and nuts. One star here is the tangy, elegant, stony Savagnin, freely admitted by Jean-Pierre to be a baby Château-Chalon and called Marnes Bleues after the famous soil. The other is the Château-Chalon itself, stylish and delicate, needing time. He bottles by hand, one *fût* at a time, and wrestles with the dilemma of how much Savagnin to make and how much Château-Chalon, three to four years older and sold at twice the price. His wife Marie-Ange helps with sales in the tasting room and the administration. Sadly their three children

Jean-Pierre Salvadori with an old press in his tasting room.

are not interested in taking on the hard work of this authentic estate.

Domaine Salvadori
Rue des Chèvres, 39210 Château-Chalon

Tel: 03 84 44 62 86

Email: minifader@hotmail.com

Contacts: Jean-Pierre and Marie-Ange Salvadori

Map ref: p. 235, D3

Established: 1983

Vineyards: 3.5ha (Savagnin, Chardonnay, a little Poulsard)

Visits: Tasting room, visits welcomed by appointment

Fruitière Vinicole de Voiteur

Known as the Château-Chalon cooperative, I'm sure they've been tempted to change the name, but this *fruitière* does of course represent all the wines it produces from the grapes of its 55 members. If considered as one group, the Fruitière is the largest grower of Savagnin grapes in Château-Chalon, with access to 13ha, just over 25% of the AOC, ending up with a production of 20,000–25,000 *clavelins* a year. It does an excellent job of making a fine Château-Chalon, worthy of the name and not sold cheaply either. Any discounting is reserved for the Côtes du Jura Vin Jaune they make as well. Between them the two Vins Jaunes account for 15% of their production.

Of the 80ha, eight members own 60ha and 40ha of these are farmed using *lutte raisonnée* methods, likely to be part of the future Terra Vitis group. The cooperative is unusual in that it took a decision in 2007 to allow members to keep back up to 25% of their grapes to make their own wine for sale. This gives young vignerons an opportunity to set up slowly, but it also stops members from leaving and keeps things honest. Director of the cooperative Bertrand Delannay explains that, although most cooperatives insist that members deliver all their production exclusively to the cooperative in order to keep up the quality level, certain producers 'cheat', for example by setting up sales facilities under a spouse's name.

The cellars are well placed at the foot of the Château-Chalon vineyard hill, within easy reach of their members, the furthest away being in Lavigny and L'Etoile. The vinification and ageing facilities are relatively modern, with regular improvements put in place. At the time of writing they are hoping to build a new pressing area for more efficient working, but they already have two pneumatic presses used for grapes for Crémant; for Savagnin and Chardonnay aged *sous voile*, a Vaslin screw press is deemed better to extract a juice that is not too clear, which will form the yeast veil more easily. *Ensemencement* is not used here and the barrels are always kept full, and never washed between wines. There are several ageing cellars, including one that is underground but ventilated, which is used for Chardonnay that stays a maximum of 18 months *sous voile*; one newly built with air-conditioning for Vin Jaune; and one

The tasting room and cellars of the Fruitière Vinicole de Voiteur.

Fruitière Vinicole de Voiteur
60 Rue de Nevy, 39210 Voiteur

Tel: 03 84 85 21 29

Email: voiteur@fvv.fr

Web: www.fruitiere-vinicole-voiteur.fr

Contact: Bertrand Delannay

Map ref: p. 235, D3

Established: 1957

Vineyards: 80ha (45ha Chardonnay, 25ha Savagnin, 5ha Poulsard, 3ha Pinot Noir, 2ha Trousseau)

Visits: Tasting room and shop

that is almost a loft, although this is less in favour, producing more alcoholic and very oxidative wines with high levels of acetaldehyde, but blending means they can work with this too. They buy second-hand barrels from white wine areas of Burgundy such as Pouilly-Fuissé and replace any wooden hoops with metal ones to withstand the years of ageing.

Both bottling and Crémant production are done by a service facility that comes to the cooperative. Crémant represents around 25% of production with one sole cuvée, but a vintage cuvée is planned from the 2011 vintage with 18 months instead of 12 months *sur lattes*. The Crémant is decent, as is the rest of the range, including the consistently good Château-Chalon. In a break from tradition there is a small amount of Côtes du Jura Cuvée Premium, a really good Savagnin *ouillé*, aged only in tank. Around a quarter of production is sold directly from the tasting room. The rest is through distributors and supermarkets in France, with a small amount exported under the Juravinum label together with the Fruitière Vinicole de Pupillin (see p. 205).

Le Vernois, Lavigny and Pannessières

Le Vernois has always been one of the most important vineyard villages in this sector and several vignerons are based in the middle of the village, as is the Caveau des Byards cooperative, named after one of the vineyards here. The vineyards of Le Vernois stretch south to those of the pretty village of Lavigny, with its distinctive château and church, and then continue to Pannessières. From the vineyards, looking across a small valley (along which runs the D70 road) is a hillside with the privately owned Château Le Pin and the villages of Montain and Le Louverot. At one time this hillside would have been completely covered with vineyards, but few remain today.

The soils in this sector are varied forms of marl: where it is grey, Savagnin or Poulsard (sometimes) is grown; in the few warmer sites with coloured marls and gravels on top the other red varieties may be grown. Chardonnay dominates, however.

Montbéliarde cows next to a vineyard above Lavigny.

Domaine Baud Père et Fils

Descended from a long line of vignerons in Le Vernois, dating back to pre-Revolutionary times, the genial Alain Baud and his brother Jean-Michel took over from their father René in 1978, expanding the estate from 4ha initially to 10ha. Jean-Michel takes care of the vineyards, Alain the winery and sales. Alain is a past president of the Côtes du Jura AOC syndicate and went on to be the president of the SVJ for many years.

The vines today include 2.5ha in AOC Château-Chalon in the fine En Beaumont vineyards and 3ha in AOC L'Etoile in Quintigny; the remainder are mainly in Le Vernois, where the winery is, plus some in warmer gravelly soils for reds in nearby Frontenay and Domblans. The vineyards have been run along *lutte raisonnée* lines for many years, grassing down one in two rows, aiming for moderate yields and using some machine harvesting. The winery straddles traditional and modern with some stainless steel vats and some *foudres*. In Alain's time as president of the SVJ he was responsible for cajoling the vignerons to accept what was best for them, usually a compromise, when the rewriting of AOC legislation was

taking place. Given this background, it is unsurprising that the estate has always been a classic example of one that toes the line, staying in the quality middle ground in terms of how it has operated, neither particularly innovatory nor over-traditional, always producing wines that are true to type.

In a range that covers all the main traditional styles of the Jura, around a quarter of production is devoted to Crémant. The Brut Sauvage stands out in particular. A Chardonnay/Pinot blend (30% Pinot Noir), it stays 30–36 months *sur lattes* before disgorgement and is given a low *dosage*. Usually from one vintage, but not marked on the label, the base wine uses more free-run juice than for their other Crémants, giving delicious fruit character, and the long lees ageing gives a lovely spicy edge. Among the reds the Cuvée Ancestrale blend of 70% Trousseau and 30% Pinot is consistently the best; for the whites, among the *ouillé* Chardonnays, the Vieilles Vignes, from 50+-year-old vines and aged partly in *foudres*, is always a fine Jurassien in the best sense. One of the joys of a tasting with this estate is to be able to compare Côtes du Jura Vin Jaune with Château-Chalon En Beaumont, usually offered from the same vintage and both consistently good – 10% of production is Vin Jaune.

Alain and Jean-Michel are very well versed in explaining the Jura to newcomers

Alain Baud at a tasting show.

and sell much direct to consumers at the tasting room and at tasting shows in France and Belgium. There are successful exports of Crémant in particular to Canada and to the Ukraine. Alain, who speaks Russian, is involved with a local initiative to help a region in Siberia create an experimental vineyard. Through this the domaine, along with Vignobles Guillaume in Charcenne, Haute-Saône, receives wine students on an exchange programme. Both Alain and Jean-Michel have children who have worked part-time with them between their studies and are likely to join the estate soon.

Domaine Baud Père et Fils

Route de Voiteur, 39201 Le Vernois

Tel: 03 84 25 31 41

Email: info@domainebaud.fr

Web: domainebaud.fr

Contact: Alain Baud

Map ref: p. 235, C2

Established: 1742 (1950 in modern times)

Vineyards: 20.5ha (11.5ha Chardonnay, 4ha Savagnin, 2ha Trousseau, 1.5ha Poulsard, 1.5ha Pinot Noir)

Visits: Tasting room and shop

Philippe Butin

The restaurateur André Jeunet, a big supporter of Vins Jaunes, used to buy from Philippe's grandfather Eugène and today Philippe is proud to sell his Vin Jaune and Château-Chalon to Jean-Paul Jeunet and other fine restaurants. His parents did not make their own wine, selling their grapes, but Philippe took over their vineyards to create his estate in 1981. The original holdings included a small area in their home village of Lavigny and another of old vines in nearby Pannessières, where his mother, also from a vigneron family, came from. He extended the vineyards in Lavigny and was able to obtain 0.16 ares in the Sous-Roche vineyard of Château-Chalon, including some old vines planted in the 1950s.

Philippe works his vineyards conventionally, but thoughtfully. They are grassed down one in two rows, and he uses an *intercep* to work between the vines in some vineyards, reducing herbicide use. He is particularly careful of pruning methods to help prevent Esca and has an apprentice working with him, Kevin Cesco-Resia, whom he will take on full-time, especially after he won the annual regional pruning competition. Harvesting is by hand, with the same families working year after year.

Since 1999 all the reds have been aged in stainless steel tanks, bottling after 12–18 months, and Philippe makes a particularly enjoyable Trousseau à la Dame from vines planted in the mid-1990s. Some Chardonnay grapes are sold to La Maison du Vigneron and those from older vines are kept for the domaine, also aged in stainless steel, sometimes for several years. Part of the Chardonnay is used for a classic mineral and appley single-varietal wine and the rest is reserved for the biggest-selling wine, Cuvée Spéciale, an excellent deep-flavoured oxidative blend with an unusually high percentage (50–80%) of Savagnin aged *sous voile*.

The Savagnin grown in Lavigny and in Château-Chalon share the same exposition and the same grey marl soil, and the Lavigny vines are the same age as the younger vines in Château-Chalon. They are harvested at the same time and the wines made in exactly the same way, with no *ensemencement*. Barrels are kept full and never washed. Some of the barrels are aged in a loft and the rest in a dry cellar. Both the Côtes du Jura Vin Jaune and the Château-Chalon are wonderfully elegant and fine, sometimes smoky, with curry and a hint of walnuts. There is little difference, Philippe admits. He believes that they age similarly too and are at their best about ten years after harvest.

Most of Philippe's sales are direct to consumers and restaurants, with a tiny amount of Cuvée Spéciale and Château-Chalon exported within Europe. Prices are very reasonable, but in keeping with the market Philippe asks about one-third more for his Château-Chalon than his Côtes du Jura Vin Jaune, yet the latter is more difficult to sell. All I can say is that with *jaunes* of this quality, his grandfather would be very proud.

Showing Philippe Butin's initials, this stained-glass window is in his tasting room.

Philippe Butin

21 Rue de la Combe, 39210 Lavigny

Tel: 03 84 25 36 26

Email: ph.butin@wanadoo.fr

Web: perso.orange.fr/philippe.butin

Map ref: p. 235, C2

Established: 1981

Vineyards: 5.5ha (4.1ha Chardonnay and Savagnin, 1.4ha Trousseau, Poulsard and Pinot Noir)

Visits: Tasting room, visits welcomed by appointment

Caveau des Byards

This cooperative – the only one not to use the name *fruitière* – is the smallest in the Jura and in many ways is run like a large family estate. All 17 members must deliver all their grapes to the cooperative (apart from family use), they all have an equal vote and they are all expected to play their part in decision-making and staffing the tasting room at weekends. Just three votes are shared by two families – the Grandvaux brothers and Franck Vichet (current president of the SVJ), who between them own 30ha or three-quarters of the vineyards. Ninety-five per cent of the vineyards are worked in *lutte raisonnée* and they have a system for storage and safe disposal of vineyard chemicals available for use by all members. Members with small holdings can also benefit from the buying power of the others for vineyard treatments. Member and acting director Denis Grandvaux estimates that they use around 50% less pollutants than the average vineyard run along conventional lines.

Most vineyards are in the village, plus just under a hectare in the Puits St-Pierre vineyards of AOC Château-Chalon, and recently they gained a member with 3.4ha of vines in AOC L'Etoile. Chardonnay is important because, when plans for the *remembrement* in Le Vernois were being discussed (in which the cooperative was much involved), it was realized that there was a growing market for sparkling wines, and indeed today almost 50% of production is Crémant du Jura, bottled, riddled and disgorged at the winery. A new construction from 1998, the winery is impressively well equipped, with a mechanical grape sorting table and gravity flow from presses to mainly stainless steel tanks, all temperature controlled. A mixture of oak is used, although *foudres* are currently being replaced by smaller barrels. There is one full-time winemaker, with an assistant during the harvest period, one other full-time employee and two part-time employees.

Among their four very decent Crémants, standouts are the Brut Prestige, made with 20% Pinot Noir and 24 months *sur lattes*, and a deliciously fruity rosé, with Pinot Noir dominant. In reds, both the Trousseau and the Pinot are well made, slightly lacking in true Jura character, but may well sell better

for that. In whites they make the L'Etoile in a young, fresh style, but better is the Côtes du Jura, aged in *foudres*, which has a real mineral character. The *sous voile* wines are very good indeed, especially the two Vins Jaunes, Côtes du Jura Vin Jaune and the Château-Chalon, but also the good-value Côtes du Jura Savagnin. With decent Vin de Paille and Macvin too, about one-third of production is sold in their very welcoming on-site tasting room, one-third through wholesalers and the rest to restaurants and shops. Even with hardly any exports and prices that are not particularly cheap, business appears good. The members of this cooperative are a real credit to their region and these wines are worth looking out for.

Caveau des Byards
39210 Le Vernois

Tel: 03 84 25 33 52

Email: info@caveau-des-byards.fr

Web: caveau-des-byards.fr

Contact: Denis Grandvaux

Map ref: p. 235, C2

Established: 1953

Vineyards: 40.5ha (25ha Chardonnay, 8ha Savagnin, 3.5ha Pinot Noir, 2ha Trousseau, 2ha Poulsard)

Visits: Tasting room and shop

The Caveau des Byards cooperative cellar in the middle of Le Vernois.

Domaine Hubert Clavelin et Fils

It is no easier to find out the real history behind the Vin Jaune *clavelin* bottle at Domaine Clavelin than anywhere else, even though the famous abbot Paul Clavelin, who ordered these bottles with his name marked on the seal in 1914, was indeed an ancestor, and you can see one of the precious bottles in the tasting room. The family has made wine in Le Vernois for over a century, and currently the company is run by brothers Patrick and Michel Clavelin (sons of Hubert, who started today's winery), together with Patrick's son Romain, who is in charge of the vineyards.

The family has one of the largest vineyard holdings in this part of the Jura. About half of the vines are in Le Vernois, where they benefited from the *remembrement*, and the rest are in Voiteur, including the Perfuzette vineyard, in Mantry and nearby Bréry, with the Les Normois vineyard. There are also small holdings in AOC Château-Chalon in En Beaumont and near Clos Bacchus. They follow *lutte raisonnée* methods and grass down every other row, hoeing everything each autumn. Harvesting is by machine when allowed, and with better machines available today Patrick wishes it could be allowed for Crémant grapes. He estimates that the cost per hectare is approximately one-third of the cost of hand-harvesting.

Vin Jaune and Château-Chalon account for only about 5% of sales, but about 100 barrels a year of Savagnin are aged *sous voile* in locations including two dry loft areas and an old stable, often deemed to give the very best Vin Jaune cellar conditions. They have a policy of keeping back 72 bottles (the amount that fits in a bin) per vintage for personal use and to check how it's ageing. Patrick is the winemaker and his

approach for other wines is technological and modern, including cross-flow filtration and bottling under nitrogen, but there is one major exception. For the Crémants, which account for half of production, this house uses hand-riddling – at any one time there are 12,000 bottles on 100 *pupitres*. It is possible to riddle 10,000 bottles an hour, says Patrick, and his grandfather was an expert riddler, particularly efficient when he had the shakes aged 87.

The Crémants here are good, including the cleverly named Brut-Comté Chardonnay particularly offered to export markets (about 10% of total production is exported). A very pleasant Crémant rosé is made from a 50/50 blend of Pinot Noir and Trousseau, using direct pressing to give a lovely delicate colour and raspberry aromas. Trousseau is the best red, with the Poulsard confusingly labelled rosé, including a back label saying it should be aged, yet it is sealed with a plastic 'cork'. Once again stars here are the *sous voile* whites, culminating in the smoky Côtes du Jura Vin Jaune from Le Vernois and the very elegant and roasted-coffee-like Château-Chalon – nicely different from each other. Patrick is proud of his family business, but evidently worried about the viability of family wineries like his own.

Patrick Clavelin with pupitres *of Crémant du Jura, all hand-riddled at this estate.*

Domaine Hubert Clavelin et Fils
Place de la Mairie, 39210 Le Vernois

Tel: 03 84 25 31 58

Email: gaec.clavelin@wanadoo.fr

Web: clavelin.fr

Contact: Patrick Clavelin

Map ref: p. 235, C2

Established: 1894

Vineyards: 30ha (19ha Chardonnay, 4ha Savagnin, 3ha Pinot Noir, 2ha Trousseau, 2ha Poulsard)

Visits: Tasting room

L'Etoile

The village of L'Etoile is geographically very close to Lons-le-Saunier, yet when you leave the main road to drive the kilometre into the village it seems a world away, nestled below five vine-clad hills. Some believe that these five hills, encircling the village in the form of a star, gave birth to the name L'Etoile, others that it came from the distinctive tiny star-shaped or pentacrine fossils that pepper the vineyards. Starting in the south is the steep hill Mont Muzard, with Château de l'Etoile at its apex at an altitude of just over 350m, then working clockwise are Monterreaux, Montangis, Mont Morin and Mont Genezet, all of which slope slightly more gently and are around 400m at their highest point. Like Arlay to the north, these broke off millions of years ago from what became the Premier Plateau in the big slippage west towards the Bresse plain. The other villages entitled to AOC L'Etoile – St-Didier, Quintigny and Plainoiseau – are located on the other side of these hills.

L'Etoile's marl soils have a little more limestone than the vineyards closer to the Premier Plateau and the topsoil is very stony. They are slightly cooler too – ideal for Chardonnay, for which the appellation is known, and, where there is grey marl, for Savagnin or even Poulsard – the latter allowed in AOC L'Etoile only for Vin de Paille. Much Chardonnay is also grown for AOC Crémant du Jura: L'Etoile has always been well known for its sparkling wines. The few red wines made from grapes grown here must be sold as AOC Côtes du Jura.

Apart from those profiled below, other vineyards in AOC L'Etoile are owned most notably by Domaine Cartaux-Bougaud (see p. 242), owners of Château de Quintigny, but profiled under Arlay, where their main winery is located, and Domaine Geneletti (see p. 253), which also has its winery here but is profiled under Château-Chalon, the main address. There are at least half a dozen estates based elsewhere that own some vines here and make an AOC L'Etoile wine, including Les Chais du Vieux Bourg, that moved its base to Poligny (see p. 220). There was, briefly, a cooperative wine cellar here before the First World War, but today just one grower takes his grapes to the Fruitière Vinicole de Voiteur and another to Caveau des Byards.

Château de l'Etoile

With its traditional, almost aristocratic label, the Cuvée des Ceps d'Or from Château de l'Etoile was one of the first wines I drank from the Jura back in the 1990s. At the time I was convinced it was Savagnin, when in fact it has always been made from old-vine Chardonnay, the variety that is most closely linked with L'Etoile. The mix-up is easily made with the Jura's traditionally made oxidative white wines and this domaine has been run traditionally, handed down from one generation to another since Auguste Vandelle bought the old château in 1883 and planted 3ha of vines on lands below. The family continued as mixed farmers until after the Second World War when Joseph, Auguste's grandson, started farming

Château de l'Etoile is up the hill from the centre of the village.

vines full-time. By the 1990s the estate had over 25ha of vines under Joseph Vandelle and his son Georges, but a family schism at the turn of the century meant that its holdings were split in two, with half going to Bernard Vandelle (George's brother) and his son Philippe, who established a separate estate. Today it is the turn of the fifth generation to run the estate and until 2011 responsibilities were split between Vincent and Alexandre, but now it is solely in the hands of Alexandre.

Château de l'Etoile sits atop Mont Muzard and there appears to have been a castle there for many centuries, but written history is scant. Inevitably there would have been vines on the hillside below – as there are today – forming a circle on the south-, west- and east-facing slopes. The château's vineyards, mostly here with a few parcels elsewhere in the village, are partially grassed down and have been farmed in *lutte raisonnée* since the late 1980s, and Alexandre states that he hopes to give up using herbicide in the coming years. The cellars beneath the castle have been equipped for many years with stainless steel and fibreglass tanks for fermentation, and the thick stone walls give natural aeration for classic *sous voile* ageing in *fûts*.

In the past Château de l'Etoile was reputed above all for its sparkling wines and Crémant du Jura accounts for 40% of production here. Chardonnay is the variety for the basic L'Etoile, aged *sous voile* for a short time, and also for the most consistent wine from the domaine, Cuvée des Ceps d'Or, made from 30–60-year-old Chardonnay vines and aged *sous voile* for three years or more. Keeping up with modern times, Alexandre launched a Savagnin *ouillé* with the 2010 vintage named L'Inattendue ('The Unexpected'), which aims to express the fruit character of each vintage. Réserve

du Mont Muzard used to be a traditional Chardonnay/Savagnin blend but in recent years has become the name for the traditional Savagnin. Vin de Paille has also been reputed from this estate, but recent releases of the range show that for now it is the classic L'Etoile Vin Jaune that is the only real star of this historic estate. The wines are widely sold in supermarkets in France, as well as direct to consumers from the estate and at tasting shows.

Château de l'Etoile
994 Rue Bouillod, 39570 L'Etoile

Tel: 03 84 47 33 07

Email: info@chateau-etoile.com

Web: chateau-etoile.com

Contact: Alexandre Vandelle

Map ref: p. 235, B2

Established: 1883

Vineyards: 15.7ha (9.5ha Chardonnay, 4.5ha Savagnin, 1.7ha reds)

Visits: Tasting room and shop

Domaine de Montbourgeau

Nicole Deriaux is modesty personified about her role as the star producer of L'Etoile. As all good vignerons, she is constantly striving to do better and I fully believe she will, and that these wines, already good, will go from strength to strength. The estate was founded by Nicole's grandfather, Victor Gros, in 1920, who bottled his wines from the start. By all accounts Nicole's father, Jean Gros, who took over in 1956, built up an estate that developed a fine reputation for itself and its appellation, and Nicole follows the same tradition. This remains a very authentic estate. Even though it's not farmed organically, vineyard parcels are vinified separately and each barrel seems as if it's known by name here. Trained in oenology in Dijon,

Nicole approaches things scientifically and practically, but with real care too. Practising *lutte raisonnée* for the vineyards, Nicole says she would like to do more, but has never wanted to be tied to any particular certification programme.

Montbourgeau is a hamlet at the western end of the village of L'Etoile, with the fine country château of Domaine de Montbourgeau located at the end of a classically tree-lined gravel driveway. In the courtyard are other outbuildings where the wine is made and matured and the cellars below the main house are also used for barrel ageing. The vineyards are divided between slopes behind the house below the hill of Montangis, extending around the next hill, and those just to the northeast below Montmorin. Originally this was a classic L'Etoile estate focusing on Chardonnay – Jean Gros never made a Vin Jaune – but after Nicole joined the estate she purchased land specifically to grow Savagnin for Vin Jaune on well-exposed heavy grey marl. Unusually, here Savagnin is made specifically for the traditional Savagnin cuvée rather than being selected from that originally destined

for Vin Jaune. Everything is picked by hand.

Except for the Cuvée Spéciale, wines begin fermentation in stainless steel tanks before being moved into oak, which includes a range of large old *foudres*, *demi-muids* and *fûts* in different locations. Each cellar, Nicole explains, is more or less successful for the *voile* to develop and although all the whites are oxidative, not all develop a *voile* in cask. Several *foudres* have been preserved by adding new wooden fronts with a stainless steel opening with a tap (see photo, p. 69). The basic L'Etoile is a 100% Chardonnay (not marked on the label) showing a baked apple and walnut character, having spent 18 months in a mixture of barrel sizes, with or without *voile*. Since 2007 a small quantity of a cuvée named En Banode is made in some years from a vineyard with heavy marl, co-planted by Nicole's father in the 1970s with about 60% Chardonnay and 40% Savagnin. The flagship white is the intense and very good L'Etoile Cuvée Spéciale from old-vine Chardonnay and a

Nicole Deriaux takes a sample of Chardonnay from one of the large old foudres *in one of Domaine de Montbourgeau's cellars.*

touch of Savagnin, grown on a very stony soil made pretty much in the natural way, although Nicole is far from being part of the natural wine scene. It is fermented in *fûts* and topped up with lees stirring until after the winter, when the malolactic fermentation takes place. Unusually for a wine that is thereafter matured without topping up, allowing a *voile* to form, it is left on its yeast lees and bottled after about four years. No SO$_2$ is added, except possibly before bottling. The Savagnin should not be ignored either, with its lovely elegance and curried flavours.

A very small amount of Côtes du Jura red is made, along with all the Jura specialities, starting with a very Jurassien, appley Crémant du Jura, which is relatively dry and which accounts for around 20% of the estate's production. There is a very good Macvin from Chardonnay with a touch of Poulsard giving a bronze colour and a perfumed edge to the spicy orange flavours, matured before bottling for longer than most; a slightly oxidative and caramelly Vin de Paille from a mix of 60% Chardonnay with 20% each of Savagnin and Poulsard; and, finally, the really beautifully balanced and elegant Vin Jaune in a somewhat lighter style than most. All the wines need time to develop and should age well.

Around 20% of production goes for export, mostly to the USA and Canada, and the rest is sold mainly directly to consumers, who are welcomed at the château, and the wines are also available in good restaurants and some wine shops. Nicole's middle son Baptiste is working with her in the winery while pursuing studies at Beaune and her younger son César has also expressed an interest in joining the estate, so the future looks assured. Until relatively recently Nicole stood out as the only woman to be running a truly successful estate in the Jura and she has set a fine example for others to follow, most particularly with her attention to detail and confident approach to maintaining her domaine's house style.

Domaine de Montbourgeau
53 Rue de Montbourgeau, 39570 L'Etoile

Tel: 03 84 47 32 96

Email: domaine@montbourgeau.com

Web: montbourgeau.com

Contact: Nicole Deriaux

Map ref: p. 235, B2

Established: 1920

Vineyards: 9ha (6.9ha Chardonnay, 1.5ha Savagnin, 0.6ha Poulsard and Trousseau)

Visits: Tasting room, visits welcomed by appointment

Domaine Philippe Vandelle

Philippe is proud of his family's heritage in L'Etoile, always making the point that the vineyards and estate were established in 1883, just as those of Château de l'Etoile, from which he and his father Bernard separated in 2001. They established themselves in a small house and cellar just down the road, but retain separate vinification and some ageing facilities up at the château. Bernard retired soon after they established their own domaine, but Philippe's mother Marie-Rose managed sales and administration until she retired in 2011. Now Philippe employs someone for this, along with two others for the vineyards and winery.

A practical, outdoors person who loves ski touring in the Alps, Philippe is in his element when in the vineyards, mainly on the slopes of Mont Morin, which are farmed in a controlled *lutte raisonnée* method (he is certified by Farre, one of the

Philippe Vandelle outside his busy tasting room.

many controlling bodies for this type of agriculture). He uses a contact herbicide in some places, but otherwise grasses down or works the soil, and for treatments he is rigorous in following the weather station reports, using only what he feels is strictly necessary. Philippe is the vigneron with the harvesting machine in the village, which he operates for himself and his neighbours, except for Domaine Montbourgeau, which harvests by hand. The winery is equipped with stainless steel and *fûts* and vinification is fairly classic, with Philippe having sound technological competence and reasoning for everything he does.

Philippe has occasionally made Chardonnay *ouillé* and a small amount of Savagnin *ouillé* that I have enjoyed, but his clientele favours more traditional Jura styles, something that L'Etoile is reputed for in France. Although he doesn't participate in many tasting shows, he has built up a very good following through his annual stand at the Percée du Vin Jaune festival, from which he sells a significant amount, as the wines are very good value for money. Direct consumer sales account for half of production and he sells to many wine shops and restaurants, plus a small amount of exports.

About a third of production is Crémant, including a very decent white and a Pinot Noir rosé; a little Poulsard red is made along with a very easy-drinking Trousseau, both aged only in tank. The basic L'Etoile Chardonnay is aged for around six months in non-topped-up barrels, but initially the oxidative character shows only a little, emerging later – I find it neither one thing nor the other. However, another L'Etoile Chardonnay named Tradition is aged *sous voile* and has more intensity, with a spicy apple character. Best of all the whites is his Vieilles Vignes from a minimum of 20% Savagnin blended with the Chardonnay, some vinified together, some blended in later. This is elegant and almost curried, with excellent length and ageing potential; this is also true of the Savagnin and the really good Vin Jaune. Chardonnay-dominated Vin de Paille and a Chardonnay Macvin complete this competent range. Philippe Vandelle's wines are what are known in France as a *valeur sûre* – a safe bet.

Domaine Philippe Vandelle
186 Rue Bouillod, 39570 L'Etoile

Tel: 03 84 86 49 57

Email: info@vinsphilippevandelle.com

Web: vinsphilippevandelle.com

Contact: Philippe Vandelle

Map ref: p. 235, B1

Established: 1883

Vineyards: 13ha (7ha Chardonnay, 4ha Savagnin, 0.7ha Trousseau, 0.7ha Pinot Noir, 0.6ha Poulsard)

Visits: Tasting room

671   Conliège (Jura) — Vue générale

B. F., PARIS — Cliché R. Chapuis

AROUND LONS-LE-SAUNIER

In the 19th century the departmental capital of the Jura, Lons-le-Saunier, had a thriving vigneron quarter, and the houses with their distinctive cellar trapdoors can still be seen at the Place de la Comédie near the centre of town. The vineyards, on slopes to the north and east, used to extend to the edge of the town and those within the town limits have long been replaced by the usual urban sprawl of shopping centres and industrial estates. Raising a smile, though, is the La Vache qui Rit cheese factory, owned by Bel, with its distinctive laughing cow logo painted high on a water tower on the ring road.

Above: This postcard from the early 20th century shows the village of Conliège, just outside Lons-le-Saunier in the Vallière Valley. At that time the slope behind was covered in vineyards.

If you are sipping a beer with the name Rouget de Lisle at a bar in town, you might notice that this name pops up all over Lons-le-Saunier on a grand statue by Bartholdi (designer of the Statue of Liberty), on street names and on buildings. Claude-Joseph Rouget de Lisle is Lons' most famous son, a soldier who was also a poet and dramatist, and penned the words of France's national anthem, 'La Marseillaise'. Rather sadly, he died in poverty in Paris. Apart from him, Lons-le-Saunier's biggest claim to fame is its salt mines, which were succeeded by salt baths and a thermal spa, which still exists.

The town of Lons sprawls outwards from the base of some rather impressive cliffs towards the Bresse plain and forms the boundary between north and south

273

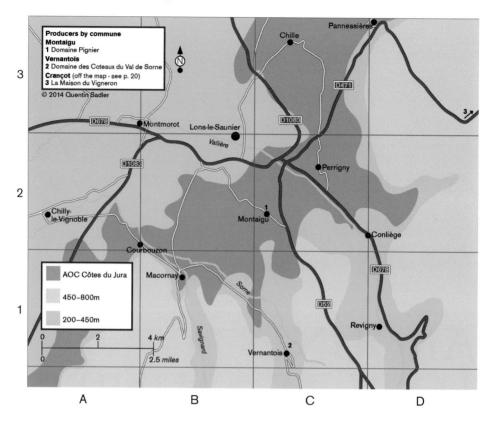

Producers by commune
Montaigu
1 Domaine Pignier
Vernantois
2 Domaine des Coteaux du Val de Sorne
Crançot (off the map - see p. 20)
3 La Maison du Vigneron

© 2014 Quentin Sadler

AOC Côtes du Jura
450–800m
200–450m

Revermont, with their rather different geology. Regrettably, with Arbois having been adopted as the 'capital' of the wine region, no wine bars, restaurants or hotels in Lons could be said to honour the region's wines.

This sector covers the few vineyards (less than 30ha) and wine producers that lie east of the town and begins with a producer based close by that has changed ownership.

Clos des Grives

Based in Chille, just to the north of Lons-le-Saunier, this estate was owned until 2009 by Claude Charbonnier. Established in the 1960s, it was one of the first organic estates. Some very good wines ranging from Crémant through light reds and *sous voile*

whites, including excellent Vin Jaune, were made and sold at very reasonable prices. The vineyards now have Ecocert certification and the label continues under the ownership of the Petite family, owners of the well-known Comté producer Marcel Petite. A full-time manager-winemaker works with contract staff in the vineyards. I have not tasted the range recently.

Vernantois, Montaigu and Conliège

On either side of the village of Montaigu, situated on a cliff about 200m above Lons-le-Saunier, there are two valleys – the most southerly *reculées* of the Revermont, both opening out at the town of Lons. The slopes of these *reculées* were entirely planted with vines before phylloxera hit, and indeed up to the Second World War. Now, even with their soils of marl and fossil-rich limestone with fine expositions, they are virtually abandoned. Historian and vigneron Jean-François Ryon says that in the 1960s and 1970s vignerons thought that Lons-le-Saunier would expand and, as they expected to sell their land for building, the vineyards were neglected.

In the Vallière Valley or Reculée de Revigny (Revigny is the village at the end of the valley) to the east of Montaigu, the only commercial vineyard owner is Domaine Pignier, though there are some isolated privately owned vineyards. To the southwest of Montaigu in the Reculée de Vernantois or the *reculée* of the Sorne river a few scattered vineyards remain, notably those owned by Pignier and Ryon.

Vernantois lies close to the end of the Sorne Valley and is the most remote and quiet of the villages, full of old vignerons' houses and set in truly beautiful surroundings, with a golf course nearby. Beyond Perrigny, now virtually a suburb of Lons, Conliège, in the middle of the Vallière Valley, is just off one of the main roads out of Lons, but it is worth exploring. The 2014 Percée festival was held there and in Perrigny. As well as having some fine viewpoints, the quiet village of Montaigu is a historical gem, complete with vestiges of the town gates and the beautiful buildings that belonged to the Chartreuse, now mainly in the hands of the Pignier family.

Domaine des Coteaux du Val de Sorne

To meet Jean-François Ryon is to discover a somewhat eccentric, original dyed-in-the-wool natural winemaker and organic

Jean-François Ryon in the tasting room of Domaine des Coteaux du Val de Sorne, which doubles as an art gallery.

grower, who still works part-time as a historian and archivist. Jean-François works with his equally single-minded mother, Monique-Rose, who also runs a small art gallery and bed-and-breakfast from her home in the middle of Vernantois – below it is the wine cellar.

When he was growing up in the 1960s Jean-François' parents insisted on buying only organic food and he says that as a child he noticed the change in the local vineyards and the taste of the grapes as chemicals were introduced. In the early 1990s Jean-François started to buy some old parcels of neglected vineyards on the west-facing gentle slopes of Vernantois and to replant, and he continued to plant more parcels in 1997 and 2001, working organically from the start.

All wines are fermented with indigenous yeast and aged in barrel; SO_2 is used in some reds at the maceration stage, but not at all in the whites. In the traditional southern Jura way the white wines are aged oxidatively, but when the *voile* does not form they may be bottled after 12–18 months. Old-fashioned hobby winemaking techniques are used here, including a routine small chaptalization that Jean-François says helps the fermentation to complete. Results are hit and miss, though I have consistently enjoyed the Trousseau, and a Crémant Rosé of 50% Poulsard and 50% Chardonnay is fun. With the pure fruit of organic grapes, Macvin is a success here, and there is a range of fruit spirits as well. The wines are mainly sold through organic tasting fairs, shops and restaurants, plus guests in Monique-Rose's B&B – some people will love them, but they are strictly for the brave.

Domaine des Coteaux du Val de Sorne
8 Rue Lacuzon, 39570 Vernantois

Tel: 03 84 47 17 28

Email: ryonjf@wanadoo.fr

Web: chambresdhotes-vins-jura.fr

Contact: Jean-François Ryon

Map ref: p. 274, C1

Established: 1992

Vineyards: 2.7ha (Chardonnay, Savagnin, Trousseau, Poulsard, Pinot Gris, mainly white)

Certification: Ecocert

Visits: No tasting room, but visits welcomed by appointment

Domaine Pignier

Proud, dedicated, hard-working . . . all these serious adjectives describe the Pignier family, made up of Marie-Florence and her brothers Jean-Etienne and Antoine, the seventh generation of vignerons in their family. One of the earliest Jura estates to be certified biodynamic by Demeter, the siblings have built up the reputation of their estate quietly and modestly, until very recently rarely leaving the hard day-to-day work in the vineyards, cellars and tasting room to woo clients and media. Some say that, more than passion, it is the desire to achieve something through daily hard graft that creates success, and the Pignier family epitomizes this approach.

Broad, steep steps lead down to the Pigniers' magnificently atmospheric 13th-century Gothic cellar, known as the Cellier des Chartreux, in the middle of the village of Montaigu. The property was built as a wine domaine by Carthusian monks from the important monastery Chartreuse de Vaucluse (not the Provence Vaucluse). After the Revolution the domaine and its cellars were sold as 'national property' and in 1794 were purchased by ancestors of the Pignier family, who continued to farm the vineyards. The grandfather of the current generation, Léandre Pignier, turned to polyculture between the wars and owned just 2ha of vines. From 1970 Léandre's son François and his wife Paulette gave up polyculture and increased the vineyards to 5ha. In the 1980s Jean-Etienne, Antoine and Marie-Florence joined the estate and the vineyards were expanded to the current 15ha. The three took it over fully in the mid-1990s when their parents retired.

They have vineyards in both *reculées*. Boivin lies just outside the village on the western side of the Vallière Valley. This is where the monks would have had vineyards and, just as the monks did, they grow Chardonnay for their traditional white Cellier des Chartreux. On the other side of the valley above Conliège is the superbly sited La Percenette, their largest vineyard, obtained by François Pignier in 1990 and planted from 1992. Further vineyards for Trousseau Les Gauthières and Chardonnay grown for Crémant are in the Sorne Valley.

With few neighbours and with their vineyards sited a short distance from the winery, the Pigniers are perfectly placed to farm organically. From the early 1990s they practised a reasoned form of agriculture, grassing down every other row and plough-ing. The three siblings have always taken decisions jointly, and when I first met Antoine Pignier in 2003 they were already in conversion to organics, but he was trying to convince his then somewhat sceptical siblings to commit the estate to 100% biodynamic farming. Antoine had attended some of Pierre Masson's courses on biody-namic farming and wanted to experiment.

Not only were Marie-Florence and Jean-Etienne convinced by Antoine that they should embrace biodynamic methods, they are great evangelists, having seen the improvement in their own wines and their customers' appreciation of them. Certified by Demeter since 2006, the Pigniers are innovative and dedicated to the methods. They have built their own dynamizer to mix their preparations in the middle of the Percenette vineyard and for some years they have limited the use of copper by adding local goats' cheese whey to their sprays. And they have gone further in viticulture, plant-ing Savagnin terraces at the steepest upper section of the Percenette slope on crumbly grey marl, choosing old mass selections of vines when replanting, turning the clock back to co-plant one plot with several varie-ties, and reviving old, almost extinct grape varieties. Jean-Etienne works with Antoine in the vineyards, along with permanent and seasonal workers as needed, and the vine-yards are one of the finest examples in the Jura of biodynamics in practice.

Antoine is in charge of winemaking in the Cellier des Lacuzon, a 17th-century monastery building along the road from the Cellier des Chartreux, which is reserved for white wine ageing. One of the inspirations for turning biodynamic was to preserve the indigenous yeasts from the vineyards and from 2004 Antoine started to use less intervention in the winery, shunning

chaptalization whenever possible and releasing their first sulphur-free red cuvées. He also works with the lunar cycles in the winery. In another big change for an estate that at the time had an ultra-traditional local clientele, they launched their first topped-up white in 1999, Chardonnay à la Percenette. Gradually the winemaking has been refined and this has become one of my favourite Jura Chardonnays, precise and beautifully balanced. A decade later it was joined by Le Sauvageon, a Savagnin *ouillé*, with intense flavours. Antoine constantly experiments with barrel size (they still have large *foudres* alongside standard *fûts* and *demi-muids*) and in 2012 he purchased a 600-litre concrete egg fermenter for Savagnin – destined for Le Sauvageon; early results are good. The most unusual white is the GPS field blend from 40% Chardonnay (the 'G' comes

Marie-Florence Pignier (above) with her brothers Antoine and Jean-Etienne (below) sitting on a rock that was extracted when clearing the land of La Percenette to plant their vineyards.

The atmospheric 13th-century Cellier des Chartreux owned by the Pignier family, where they age their Vin Jaune.

from Chardonnay's old local name, Gamay Blanc), 40% Poulsard (vinified as white) and 20% Savagnin, all vinified and aged together in oak.

The Pignier reds have improved greatly in the past decade and they are highly regarded for their pure-tasting sulphur-free Trousseau Les Gauthières grown on a warm site in the Sorne Valley, aged for a year in oak. The unusual A Table avec Léandre (in homage to their grandfather) is a wild and tasty red blend of Trousseau, Poulsard and Pinot Noir (a local Jura Pinot selection as well as the Burgundy one), along with small amounts of Gamay Noir, Petit Béclan, Argan and Enfariné. The Chardonnay Crémant is delicious and will soon be joined by a no SO₂, zero *dosage* sibling called L'Autre, bottled a year after harvest, using the fermenting must from the newer vintage as the *liqueur de tirage*, and with 24 months' ageing pre-disgorgement. Alongside the traditional *sous voile* whites is a very

fine Vin Jaune, matured in their beautiful 700-year-old cellars.

Their lovely Vin de Paille is from 30% Poulsard, 30% Chardonnay and 40% Savagnin, with occasionally some Trousseau or even one of the rare varieties. The grapes are dried partly in boxes and partly suspended in a loft space above the winery. After a very slow fermentation the barrels are regularly topped up to avoid the oxidative style. Finally there are Macvins and a rather tasty liqueur wine called Anténé, made in homage to their father in the old style from partially concentrated must mixed with Fine du Jura (brandy).

While Antoine usually hides away in the cellars with his teenage son helping him, Jean-Etienne seems to enjoy travel, expanding exports little by little around the world. Marie-Florence manages the tasting room and clients at home and was president of the 2014 Percée festival. The Pignier family has its feet firmly on the once-monastic ground they were born into, and produces a fine range of wines that encapsulates and perhaps honours better than anyone else the historic development of the region right up to the 21st century.

Domaine Pignier
11 Place Rouget de Lisle, 39570 Montaigu

Tel: 03 84 24 24 30

Email: contact@domaine-pignier.com

Web: domaine-pignier.com

Contact: Marie-Florence Pignier

Map ref: p. 274, C2

Established: 1970 (originally 1794)

Vineyards: 15ha (7ha Chardonnay, 3ha Savagnin, 2ha Trousseau, 2ha Poulsard, 1ha Pinot Noir)

Certification: Ecocert, Demeter

Visits: Tasting room

Domaine Voorhuis-Henquet

Based in Conliège, this tiny estate was established by Dutchman Jean Voorhuis in the mid-1990s. He obtained several excellent parcels of old vines in St-Lothain, Voiteur and L'Etoile. The estate quickly made a name for itself, resolutely producing only *ouillé* white wines and blended reds, both of which were more Burgundian than Jura in style. Several cuvées, especially the whites, were top quality and they were listed by Michelin-starred restaurants in Paris and beyond. Jean Voorhuis never integrated with Jura vignerons and found it too difficult to stay in the region. The last vintage produced was 2004.

Crançot

Fifteen kilometres east of Lons, Crançot lies on the Premier Plateau on one of the main roads heading up to the Jura Mountains. It was once known for its limestone quarries; its stones were widely used for building. Just outside the village you will find one of the best plunging viewpoints to the *reculée* of Baume-les-Messieurs. It is home to La Maison du Vigneron, who in their various incarnations have always had their winery here.

La Maison du Vigneron

From the start of the 21st century, in terms of influence, the négociant La Maison du Vigneron has been the most important wine company in the Jura. Every wine region needs big players for the infrastructure of that region to survive, and the more these producers play a quality card, the better it is for everyone. It would be lovely to see this winery, along with its parent company Grand Chais de France (GCF), lead a charge towards organic growing, lower yields, terroir selections and natural yeast, but that would be to live in a dream world. For now, I believe that La Maison du Vigneron plays its part well in keeping the Jura wine region on an even keel.

The winery started out in 1980 as a SICA (a type of grower-owned cooperative) for growers in the Sud Revermont and in 1986 it was the first purchase of the now very large GCF group. Originally named Compagnie des Grands Vins du Jura, from the

La Maison du Vigneron's large winery dominates the village of Crançot.

279

start the company focused on Jura Mousseux (sparkling wine) as the SICA had and, once the AOC was established, Crémant du Jura. As GCV grew nationally in France, so did its Jura subsidiary, which was eventually renamed La Maison du Vigneron. In the meantime it acquired modest estates in the Côtes du Jura and Château-Chalon appellations.

The figures merit examination. Each year the winery produces around 1–1.5 million bottles of Crémant du Jura (about half the total production of the Jura), ages around 1,000 barrels of Savagnin for Vin Jaune (which equates to stocks of around 6,000 barrels *sous voile*) and exports 15–20% of its production, mainly in Europe, making it the region's biggest exporter. It buys grapes from 140 growers (representing 240ha, about 12% of the region) and owns three estates. La Maison du Vigneron also makes over 4 million bottles of non-Jura traditional-method sparkling wine for GCF and employs over 50 people to look after the

winery, vineyards and sales.

The three estates, which lie in the sector between Château-Chalon and Lons, are Domaine de Savagny (12ha), Domaine de Quillot (23ha) and the most recent acquisition, Domaine Durand-Perron (1.5ha of very good vineyard sites in AOC Château-Chalon). The Savagny and Quillot estate vineyards are mainly in Lavigny, Voiteur and Passenans, with some in Menétru and Château-Chalon. They have only around 7ha of red grapes, so there is a dominance of grapes grown for Crémant du Jura and oxidative white wines, especially Vin Jaune.

When the company started, purchased grapes came from the Sud Revermont, but, as the négociant Henri Maire started buying fewer grapes, La Maison du Vigneron's influence spread north, even reaching Arbois. The company uses several brand names around the world aside from

This modern warehouse is a dedicated cave à Vin Jaune *inaugurated by La Maison du Vigneron in Crançot in 2011.*

its domaine names. These include Marcel Cabelier and François Montand (especially in France), Pierre Michel (UK), Léon Palais (USA) and Lachèze (Sweden).

The biggest recent investment by La Maison du Vigneron has been the construction of a huge state-of-the-art Vin Jaune 'cellar', in fact an air-conditioned warehouse. To create the correct ageing conditions, they measured conditions in their other Vin Jaune cellars and have attempted to replicate the annual temperature changes as well as the humidity. Rather curiously, when visiting in 2013, there were not only barrels of Savagnin and Chardonnay aged *sous voile* but some topped-up wines too. Inaugurated in 2011, it will take until 2017 to be full of Savagnin barrels destined for Vin Jaune, because you cannot move wine that is ageing *sous voile*. I sincerely hope that they got the calculations on conditions correct, because up to now I have found the quality – certainly of the Domaine de Savagny Vin Jaune – very decent indeed. Current releases of the Château-Chalon from Domaine Durand-Perron were aged in the original owner's cellar in Voiteur.

There is a range of Jura wines aside from Crémant and Vin Jaune under both the négociant and the domaine labels. My tastings have shown technically correct wines, with an occasional pleasant surprise, but lacking some Jura soul and sometimes over-oaky.

La Maison du Vigneron's biggest expertise is in making and bottling Crémant du Jura, which not only sells in supermarkets around the world but is recommended by critics as extremely good quality for the money. How do they do it? Very simply. Many vignerons, including those who make and sell their own very decent wines, are happy to sell some of their Chardonnay grapes to La Maison du Vigneron (who pay a fair amount and quickly). They insist on clean grapes and the expertise of the winery staff and the well-equipped, modern winery ensure that these grapes are converted into commercially excellent Crémant. The huge volumes they work with mean that they can keep the price down.

The reputation of Jura wine worldwide depends partly on that of its biggest export, Crémant, and the examples from this large company help the reputation enormously. However, being large and powerful inevitably means that La Maison du Vigneron earns respect from those in the region who need the company and disdain from those who don't. The latter are fearful that this négociant might snap up every vineyard and/or domaine that comes up for sale and become too powerful and too influential in how the appellations are controlled and the region marketed. So far they have acted cautiously without investing too much in the region. I think they could take on more, but I would be worried if they grew their estates beyond about 100ha. And I sincerely hope that quality remains paramount and uppermost in their minds.

La Maison du Vigneron
Route de Champagnole, 39570 Crançot

Tel: 03 84 87 61 30

Email: contact@maisonduvigneron.fr

Web: maisonduvigneron.com

Contact: Arnaud Van de Voorde

Map ref: Off the map, see p. 20

Established: 1980

Vineyards: 36.5ha (19.5ha Chardonnay, 10.5ha Savagnin, 3ha Pinot Noir, 2ha Trousseau, 1.5ha Poulsard, representing their domaines only)

Visits: Tasting room and shop open Monday–Friday, shop in Rue de Commerce, Lons-le-Saunier, open Tuesday–Saturday

SUD REVERMONT

As you drive south towards Bourg-en-Bresse beyond the southern suburbs of Lons-le-Saunier, vineyards appear to the east scattered between sleepy villages and pastures below the forest rising up to La Petite Montagne or the Premier Plateau. Known as the Sud Revermont, in the 19th century it would have been fully planted with vineyards between 200m and 400m on the south-facing and westerly slopes. The dramatic decline in both the number of vineyards and producers in the Sud Revermont that continued until recently was more marked here than elsewhere in the Jura for several reasons. It is the furthest from the wine capital, Arbois, it has few tourist attractions, and there is

no traditional cooperative cellar. In 1980 growers joined together to create a SICA (a French legal entity which is a type of cooperative where equipment is shared) that also made and marketed sparkling wines. This enterprise was short-lived, as it was purchased by Grands Chais de France (now La Maison du Vigneron) in 1986.

There have been no vineyards in the historically famous Chilly-le-Vignoble for many years and south of Beaufort only a few remain around Maynal and Augea, with only private vineyards remaining near St-Amour, the southernmost town of the area, which was once planted with several hundred hectares. When the big regional revival project was undertaken in the 1970s only a few here took up the offers of land that were grabbed further north.

Above: Domaine des Miroirs vineyards above the village of Grusse.

Today vineyards are interspersed much more with pastures and crops, creating an attractive patchwork image.

Chardonnay and Pinot Noir do particularly well in these AOC Côtes du Jura vineyards. Indeed soils in the Sud Revermont have more in common with Burgundy, having less of the distinctive marl of the Jura than north of Lons-le-Saunier and more limestone. It is the closest area to Burgundy, and is somewhat warmer than the areas further north, partly due to its position, but also from having more vineyards at lower altitudes than further north.

Since the turn of the 21st century the fortunes of the Sud Revermont area have started to pick up thanks in part to some inspirational producers, such as the Labet family and Jean-François Ganevat in Rotalier and the now retired Richard Delay in Gevingey, and in part to the availability of relatively inexpensive good vineyards for aspiring vignerons to rent or purchase. Today there is a greater proportion of organic/biodynamic producers here than

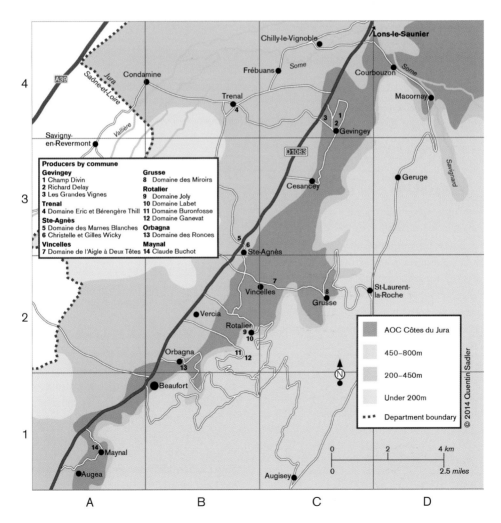

Producers by commune

Gevingey
1 Champ Divin
2 Richard Delay
3 Les Grandes Vignes

Trenal
4 Domaine Eric et Bérengère Thill

Ste-Agnès
5 Domaine des Marnes Blanches
6 Christelle et Gilles Wicky

Vincelles
7 Domaine de l'Aigle à Deux Têtes

Grusse
8 Domaine des Miroirs

Rotalier
9 Domaine Joly
10 Domaine Labet
11 Domaine Buronfosse
12 Domaine Ganevat

Orbagna
13 Domaine des Ronces

Maynal
14 Claude Buchot

AOC Côtes du Jura
450–800m
200–450m
Under 200m
Department boundary

© 2014 Quentin Sadler

0   2   4 km
0   2.5 miles

in any other part of the region, and there seems to be a corresponding accord between growers greater than anywhere else too. Structures have been created to share vineyard and winery equipment and newcomers are encouraged and supported. In 2014 a controversial wine centre, funded by the local municipalities, opened in Orbagna. Some Sud Revermont producers are participating.

The total vineyard area today, stretching from Gevingey to Augea, is around 150ha or 7.5% of the Jura region. The villages with the largest plantings are Rotalier, Vincelles, Gevingey, Ste-Agnès and Cesancey, grouped fairly closely, with several producers who have holdings in more than one. Further south towards Beaufort and beyond to St-Amour is the most deserted vineyard area.

Gevingey and Trenal

Heading down the busy main road from Lons, once out of the suburbs, Gevingey is the first village signposted to the left and it's worth a detour. Set up from the main road, it is a gorgeous little village complete with a 17th-century church and a château that is now a children's holiday centre, but is sometimes let out for wine events, including the organic tasting show, Le Nez dans le Vert, in 2012 and 2014. The main vineyards extend west from the château, and also across the main D1083 road towards Trenal, which is now the base of Domaine Thill, though its vineyards are in Gevingey.

Champ Divin

Down to earth, dedicated and practical is the impression given by Belgian couple

Valérie Closset of Champ Divin bud-rubbing, one of the essential spring tasks for a biodynamic grower.

Fabrice and Valérie Closset, who made the move to the Jura from the Loire Valley with their three children in 2008. There they had farmed 2.5ha of Coteaux du Layon vineyards for two years, and for eight years Fabrice had also worked as a viticultural consultant on organic and biodynamic methods. Valérie consulted on wine exports.

Both Fabrice and Valérie studied agronomy, specializing in soil studies, but a shared interest in humanitarian projects led them to work in Africa. Later they found jobs in the Loire consulting to vineyards and then discovered their real *métier*. At this point there was no turning back, but the Loire was not where they wanted to settle. On a family holiday in the Jura they discovered that Richard Delay's wine estate was for sale, and were attracted by the soils and cooler climate (Belgians like cool weather). With the cost of land significantly cheaper than in better-known wine regions, the deal was sealed and Fabrice gained experience of this very different wine region working side by side with Richard Delay for nine months.

The Clossets immediately set about converting the vineyards to biodynamics and building a winery. Five years on, Valérie has given up her part-time job to work full-time at the estate and the couple are justly proud of what they have achieved.

The winery and main vineyard are in an area known as Fort Champ and originally the Clossets named their estate Champ d'Etoiles (Field of Stars) but soon changed to Champ Divin because of the confusion with the village and appellation L'Etoile. Their vineyards are mainly on ancient limestone deposits with some gravel and flint, but the higher section is marl-based, with Savagnin planted. They work with lunar cycles, but do not stick rigorously to the biodynamic calendar. Otherwise these growers are more than comfortable with biodynamic systems, saying that for them they are 'normal'. In 2013 they purchased a sloping pasture of 2ha with a grey marl subsoil in nearby Cesancey, where they will plant Chardonnay and Savagnin using mass selections.

Fabrice has made the winery building as practical and environmentally friendly as possible. It is built from volcanic tufa bricks, which provide good natural insulation. He uses natural yeasts, making a starter culture in tank first. Second-hand *fûts* and *demi-muids* of varying sizes are used and Fabrice likes to use a little lees stirring.

The Clossets have already developed a niche as one of the few Demeter-certified producers of Crémant du Jura: at 8,000–10,000 bottles a year it represents about 40% of their production. To achieve greater fruit intensity they pick later than most for Crémant and use Demeter-approved yeast for the second fermentation from a strain originally developed by Champagne Fleury. The only part of the process they don't do themselves is disgorgement, but they supply their own *liqueur d'expédition*. Due to demand for the wines they currently age the Crémants for 12–15 months, but their ideal would be to age them for 18 months. Both the Zero Dosage white from a 70% Chardonnay/30% Pinot Noir blend and

their 100% Pinot Noir rosé are delicious.

The still wines are mostly white – they have been hit with low crops of Pinot Noir several years in a row. Keeping the divine or astral theme, their best selections are named Stellaire, with both a pure Chardonnay and blends. Castor is their intensely flavoured *ouillé* blend with equal parts of Chardonnay and Savagnin, with Chardonnay giving the richness and Savagnin the length. Pollux is reserved for a *sous voile* blend. SO$_2$ is added at the press, sometimes after malolactic fermentation and not usually at bottling. They have set aside Savagnin for Vin Jaune ageing from the start and their first will be released in 2015. Their aim is to make accessible wines with a Jura feel and my tastings have shown just that, with thoughtful winemaking and quality shining through.

As both sets of parents did before them on their farms, Valérie and Fabrice also keep bees and make honey. This is a sweet couple indeed: Valérie is a bustling, cheerful soul always with a big smile, and Fabrice too when he's not being serious explaining about the latest improvement he's made in the cellar.

Domaine Champ Divin
39 Rue du Château, 39570 Gevingey

Tel: 03 84 24 93 41

Email: contact@champdivin.com

Web: champdivin.com

Map ref: p. 283, C4

Contacts: Fabrice and Valérie Closset

Established: 2008

Vineyards: 5 ha (2ha Chardonnay, 1ha Savagnin, 2ha Pinot Noir)

Certification: Ecocert, Demeter

Visits: No tasting room, but visits welcomed by appointment

Richard Delay

Richard, who retired in 2008 after selling his land to the Clossets, was particularly known for his Crémant du Jura and his Vin Jaune; he still has stocks for sale of this and some other wines. He regularly presents Jura tastings and judges at regional wine competitions and events and has always been heavily involved in the Percée festival.

Richard Delay
37 Rue du Château, 39570 Gevingey

Tel: 03 84 47 46 78

Email: richard-delay@orange.fr

Map ref: p. 283, C4

Les Grandes Vignes

The story of this family winery, established by Bernard Zanada, who died too young, is one of resilience against the challenges of producing wine in the Jura during the 20th century and I include it here for that reason. A family of masons, the Zanadas came to the Jura from Piedmont in Italy via Switzerland and eventually became mixed farmers. Bernard went to college and in 1973 made the move away from polyculture to create a dedicated wine estate. Sadly, he died in 1999, leaving his wife Françoise, a chef, and their young son Jean-Charles, then 19 and training as a mechanic, to take on the business.

Today the estate sells around half of its grapes to La Maison du Vigneron. The rest is vinified and bottled for sales that are mainly from the old-fashioned tasting room where the ebullient Françoise welcomes individuals and groups. The vineyards are in Gevingey, with a large majority of Chardonnay, and farmed *raisonnée*. Recently large tanks were replaced with smaller ones to give more flexibility. Crémant production is important at 40% and they have their own gyropalettes, using the local service for bottling and disgorging. All their whites are aged *sous voile* and the barrel-ageing cellar is not ventilated, meaning that long ageing is required for the *voile* to take – their Tradition is blended before ageing and stays under the veil for five years. Vin Jaune may mature for up to ten years under the veil.

Although the aromas are attractive, you have to like acidity to enjoy these whites, but this is well covered up in the Crémant, which has plenty of *dosage*. Macvin and Vin de Paille are popular and, as I write, the latter is a non-AOC lower-alcohol version named Sapristi, which means 'Heavens!' in colloquial French. No doubt this refers to the fact that it was refused the appellation. A visit here is like a step back 20 years.

Les Grandes Vignes
2 Rue le Carouge, 39570 Gevingey

Tel: 03 84 47 35 33

Email: lesgrandesvignes.zanada@orange.fr

Map ref: p. 283, C4

Contact: Françoise Zanada

Established: 1973

Vineyards: 11ha (9ha Chardonnay, 1.2ha Savagnin, 0.8ha Poulsard and Pinot Noir)

Visits: Tasting room

Domaine Eric et Bérengère Thill

Eric Thill was brought up surrounded by vineyards, not in the Jura but in Kaysersberg, Alsace. His parents were not vignerons, but his grandfather and others in the family owned vineyards and he declares that he always wanted to become a vigneron. After oenology studies in Alsace and postgraduate studies at the well-respected ENSA in

Montpellier, Eric and his wife Bérengère, who works as a viticulture and oenology consultant, set up home in Trenal, where they had acquired just under 3ha of vines in nearby Gevingey from the Bernard family.

In 2012 they acquired a further 2.5ha, also from the Bernards, who had always farmed more or less organically but without certification. The whole domaine has been certified in conversion to organic farming since 2012. The specificity of the vineyards, planted at various times in the 1970s and 1980s, is that they are spaced widely (wider than Jura AOC rules now allow); however, they are also trained high to compensate for this. They are grassed down every other row, and Eric believes in working the soil at the start of the season but thereafter as little as possible. Organics are important to Eric, he says, in particular since he suffered from cancer, undergoing chemotherapy in 2011. He believes in as little intervention as possible in the vineyard to maintain aromas in the grapes – he says that flowering time is particularly crucial.

The winery is only large enough to vinify just under 3ha and by selling the rest to La Maison du Vigneron it is viable for now. There are no barrels here, just tanks (apart from a couple of barrels for Vin Jaune aged elsewhere), the aim being to bring out the aromatic character of the grape with long, slow pressing and time on lees – the Alsace influence is deliberate here. Eric looks for a direct, fruity style and this certainly comes out really well in both Chardonnay and Savagnin *ouillé* and the character of the terroir is not lost either. So far reds are less successful, but it's early days for this estate, which, with Eric's quiet and thoughtful approach, could be most successful. The range includes Liqueur de Chardonnay, an interesting curiosity – a sweet liqueur wine made as a Macvin but not aged in oak.

Domaine Eric et Bérengère Thill
11 Rue Principale, 39570 Trenal

Tel: 06 89 72 10 33

Email: vinsdujura.ebthill@orange.fr

Web: vinsjurathill.weebly.com

Map ref: p. 283, B4

Contacts: Eric and Bérengère Thill

Established: 2009

Vineyards: 5.35ha (3.15ha Chardonnay, 1ha Savagnin, 0.6ha Pinot Noir, 0.6ha Poulsard)

Certification: Ecocert (in conversion from 2012)

Visits: No tasting room, but visits welcomed by appointment

Cesancey, Ste-Agnès and Vincelles

Either side of the busy main road, these sleepy villages were once important wine centres, and wandering around any one of them you will discover old vignerons' houses with their distinctive cellar openings. Almost all the vineyards lie above the villages on the eastern side of the road.

Eric Thill outside his cellar door.

Domaine de l'Aigle à Deux Têtes

One of the region's outsiders, Henri Le Roy is from Paris but visited the Jura region from a young age. He also knew fine wines, having been educated at one of Paris's *grandes écoles*, the prestigious Ecole Polytechnique, where students were given a generous allowance that Henri and his friends spent on fine dining and wine. Intending originally to study oenology, he ended up studying biology and genetics and worked in industry for many years, but his ambition was to make wine. His wine taste always leaned towards Burgundy rather than Bordeaux, but buying land in Burgundy was too expensive. All he knew of the Jura was that it produced oxidative wines and he presumed that was all that was possible from the terroir. While taking winemaking courses at Beaune he made the move to the Jura and soon met Jean-François Ganevat. Ganevat showed him that from certain terroir *ouillé* wines could be produced with excellent results.

Henri didn't use herbicide on his vineyards initially, but the very steep and stony 1ha En Griffez vineyard, with close-planted old Chardonnay vines in the village of Grusse, has become too hard to weed mechanically. He used conventional chemical sprays at first 'until they ran out' in 2012, when he moved to using only sulphur and copper sprays. His two other plots, Derrière la Roche (0.36ha, also in Grusse) and Les Clous (Vincelles), have been officially 'in conversion to organics' from 2013. On prized grey marl, Les Clous, located behind his house and winery, was just a field when he arrived and in 2008 he started planting with Poulsard and Savagnin, including a few vines of the rare Savagnin Muscaté. Vineyard work obviously fascinates this biologist and he is fastidious about using the right vine-training methods to reduce

Henri Le Roy at work waxing his bottle tops.

the risk of mildew. He has also started using Guyot Poussard to try to avoid Esca attacks.

With the one major exception of *sous voile* wines, Henri started off making all the styles of Jura wines that he could from his three varieties. Now he is dropping Crémant and Vin de Paille, though he continues to make a few hundred bottles of Macvin. He sells in Quebec, the USA, Japan and in particular to top restaurants in Paris, where he says demand is for high-quality terroir-driven mineral *ouillé* whites and that's exactly what he can make from his old plots of Chardonnay in En Griffez and Derrière la Roche. As I write, Le Roy is president of the Côtes du Jura syndicate and he believes there should be a separate AOC for *ouillé* whites to avoid confusion, but he has little support.

His small annual production of Poulsard sells out before he has made it, and in 2011 he produced his first Savagnin, named Les Clous Naturé, an elegant, very dry, stony wine with citrus and herbal notes. The estate currently produces around 8,000 bottles and Henri would like to find another 1ha of land somewhere nearby to increase production of both Poulsard and Chardonnay. These are high-minded wines from a high-minded man.

Domaine de l'Aigle à Deux Têtes
11 Rue Principale 3 Route de Grusse,
39190 Vincelles

Tel: 06 08 09 81 68

Email: Azer7qsdf@laposte.net

Web: domaine-aigleadeuxtetes.com

Map ref: p. 283, C2

Contact: Henri Le Roy

Established: 2004

Vineyards: 2.5ha (1.5ha Chardonnay,
0.5ha Savagnin, 0.5ha Poulsard)

Visits: No tasting room, visits only possible
by appointment

Domaine des Marnes Blanches

This ambitious organic estate was established by Géraud and Pauline Fromont when they were both just 25 years old, and it is certainly one of the rising stars of the region. Both were born in the region, with wine in their blood: Géraud's grandparents had a mixed farm in Buffard in the Doubs, growing some vines from which they made wine for their own consumption. Both Fromonts studied oenology to degree level, Géraud in Dijon and Reims, and Pauline in Dijon.

Returning to the Jura in 2006, the Fromonts took over Domaine Bertrand Millet in Cesancey two years later and subsequently added vines from Domaine Bourgignon in nearby Vincelles and Ste-Agnès, a total of 10ha, quite a substantial amount to begin with. Conversion to organics started right away. The Cesancey vineyards are primarily on white marl – hence the name 'Marnes Blanches' – with stony limestone on top, and in the other vineyards there is mainly red marl with the *calcaire à gryphées* fossil-rich limestone. Vines are up to 100 years old and include some Melon à Queue Rouge

and an old selection of Savagnin Muscaté. Vineyard work includes grassing down and ploughing every other row. At harvest they use successive pickings when possible.

The newly built vinification and ageing cellar, well signposted off the main road in Ste-Agnès, is practical, with every parcel kept separate in stainless steel or oak; most casks are more than five years old. Only natural yeasts are employed, and limited SO_2 – they are making tentative forays into sulphur-free cuvées. They have converted their old stables to incorporate three different levels to age Savagnin barrels *sous voile*, to create different characteristics. The loft area is used to dry grapes for Vin de Paille and they have an attractive tasting room on the ground floor.

The Fromonts offer the whole range of Jura wines, with whites divided in two. The name Reflet is used for the *ouillé* wines, to illustrate that these wines 'reflect' their terroir and grape variety, and Empreinte for the *sous voile* selections to explain the imprint of the ageing method adding to that of the terroir. White (Chardonnay) and rosé (Poulsard) Crémants have a decent length of time on yeast lees; they make single-varietal reds, giving Trousseau and Pinot longer skin contact and some oak ageing, which enables them to have good ageing potential. Their first Vin Jaune from 2008 is due for release in 2015.

Overall there is a lovely purity and cleanness in the wines. There is an enjoyable Trousseau and standouts in the *ouillé* whites include Chardonnay Les Levrettes from very old vines on the *gryphées* limestone and Savagnin Le Jensillard from the old selection of Savagnin Muscaté that gives it a distinctly Gewürztraminer-like nose. Finally, a delicious Chardonnay/Savagnin Macvin shows pure fruit well integrated into the *marc*.

Domaine des Marnes Blanches has a welcoming tasting room.

As well as bringing up a young family, both Pauline and Géraud work together on all aspects of production and sales, with one part-time employee. On their informative website (only in French) a type of mission statement that I've translated states: 'Our ambition is to reinterpret the know-how of our predecessors with the same attention to making the most of our different Jura grapes and terroirs.' I think they are going about it in the right way.

Domaine des Marnes Blanches
3 Les Carouges, 39190 Ste-Agnès

Tel: 03 84 25 19 66

Email: contact@marnesblanches.com

Web: www.marnesblanches.com

Map ref: p. 283, B3

Contacts: Pauline and Géraud Fromont

Established: 2008

Vineyards: 10ha (5ha Chardonnay, 2.5ha Savagnin, 2.5ha reds)

Certification: Ecocert

Visits: Tasting room, visits welcomed by appointment

Christelle et Gilles Wicky

Gilles Wicky was originally a mechanic from Besançon and his wife Christelle is a Jurassienne from the vineyard village of Montaigu. Today they grow vines and apple trees and make wine in rather cramped and chaotic cellar conditions in their old vigneron's house in Ste-Agnès. In conversion to organic viticulture since 2010, Gilles took some short courses in biodynamics, but does not want to use all the methods, though he likes to use plant treatments. Christelle studied viticulture and oenology on a conventional course in Beaune.

The Wickys originally had 7ha of vines, selling most grapes to La Maison du Vigneron, but today they have settled on just over 4ha in two very contrasting vineyards. Just over half is in Gevingey, wide-spaced vineyards taken over from Domaine Bernard with old vines, mainly Chardonnay. The rest are steep, densely planted terraced vineyards above Beaufort that they have sometimes worked by horse.

Of their 12,000-bottle production, up to half is Crémant or Macvin. The latter has been extremely successful, made predominantly from Chardonnay juice and given extra maturity before bottling by blending in a barrel of older Macvin. Winemaking is very simple, following the natural way, but using some SO_2 at crucial stages. A small amount of Poulsard is made into a rosé or light red, but the most successful wine I

Christelle and Gilles Wicky.

have tasted has been their Clos de Jerminy Chardonnay. From 45+-year-old vines grown on the Beaufort terraces – here the soil is stony on top of grey marl, with some little star-shaped-fossils (as in L'Etoile) – it is fermented in 3–4-year-old barrels, kept topped up and bottled after a year.

They used to make more traditional *sous voile* whites and still make a Tradition blend with Savagnin, but demand is growing for *ouillé* wines because their sales are increasingly outside the local area, both in the wider Franche-Comté region and in Paris and Belgium. Becoming Jura vignerons in middle age, it's hard to imagine this couple could ever have been as relaxed and happy as they seem today.

Christelle et Gilles Wicky
13 Rue Principale, 39190 Ste-Agnès

Tel: 03 84 25 10 96; 06 07 59 59 97

Email: gilles.wicky@wanadoo.fr

Web: juraetvin.com

Map ref: p. 283, B3

Established: 2003

Vineyards: 4.7ha (Chardonnay, Savagnin, Poulsard, mainly Chardonnay)

Certification: Ecocert

Visits: No tasting room, but visits welcomed by appointment

Grusse, Rotalier and Orbagna

These villages are set further away from the main road towards the Premier Plateau or Petite Montagne. Grusse is located at the end of a *reculée* and was once an important vignerons' village, with much of its land covered in vineyards. Today less than 10ha survive. Some vineyards owned by producers in this area are technically within the

boundaries of St-Laurent-la-Roche, located up on the plateau. Rotalier, with around 40ha, has the most vineyards in the Sud Revermont and is home to the most important producers too, but the village itself is simple and quiet. To the south, Orbagna, just outside Beaufort, is yet another quiet vignerons' village with a dozen hectares of vines hectares of vines and from 2014 home to a new wine centre.

Domaine Buronfosse

Peggy Buronfosse cannot quite get over the fact that her wines are available in trendy New York wine shops and restaurants. She embraces it, but is humble at the same time. Neither she nor her husband Jean-Pascal set out to be vignerons, but they did fervently wish to put down roots and farm somewhere. They landed in the sleepy hamlet of La Combe below Rotalier. Originally from the cities of Lyon and St-Etienne, today whatever this couple do, together with their children, is a lifestyle choice, and however hard the work is they seem to love the various aspects of producing wine.

Both Peggy and Jean-Pascal trained in agriculture and their plan was simply to find jobs, keep some animals, have a vegetable garden and source as much of their own food as possible. Jean-Pascal worked as a teacher in the Lons agricultural college, and vivacious Peggy (or 'La Peggy' as she's known locally) worked in the vineyards for Domaine Joly and got to know her neighbour Jean-François Ganevat. The vine bug hit her and in 2000 Raymond Pageault, an 80-year-old local vigneron who had heard about her, decided that 'La Peggy' was the one to take over his steep vineyards. He persuaded the couple to rent his parcels of old vines and their challenge started. Although originally Peggy had to use herbicide, that soon changed and she started, with

Jean-Pascal's help, hoeing the vineyards by hand with the aim of being completely organic. Official conversion started in 2007. Now, having taken on a few more vineyards, they have plots predominating in marl, limestone and schist, mainly in Rotalier and St-Laurent de Grandvaux. To fulfil a long-held wish, they are making plans to get a horse for the family and hope to train it to work in the vineyards.

After a struggle at the start, by the 2004 vintage they were beginning to find private clients through wine shows and wine clubs, and the media began to notice as well. Typically for the Sud Revermont, the emphasis is on whites, but inspired more by Ganevat and Labet than by Joly – the modern Rotalier–Burgundian style. They have several stylish *ouillé* Chardonnay cuvées, all distinctly different according to their terroir, plus a blend, Belemnites, and a tangy Savagnin *ouillé* called Entre-Deux; all spend around 18 months in barrel. A first Jaune was released in 2005, there is a tiny amount of red and an exquisite non-approved Vin de Paille named Epicure. Latterly a beautifully pure Chardonnay Crémant has been added to the range.

This is a venture that remains small and will continue to be so. Although Jean-Pascal gave up his teaching job in 2013 and joined Peggy to work on the domaine, they have no wish to expand the vineyards beyond around 4ha. Their beautiful labels are from paintings by Jean-Pascal's brother-in-law and reflect the wines and the terroir. These are smiling, thinking people and it shines through in their wines.

Domaine Buronfosse
2 La Serpentine, La Combe, 39190 Rotalier

Tel: 03 84 25 05 09

Email: buronfossepjp@orange.fr

Map ref: p. 283, B2

Contacts: Peggy and Jean-Pascal Buronfosse

Established: 2000

Vineyards: 4ha (Chardonnay, Savagnin, Poulsard, Pinot Noir, Trousseau, mainly white)

Certification: Ecocert

Visits: Tasting room, visits welcomed by appointment

Domaine Ganevat

In the last book on Jura wines that included detailed profiles of the best producers – *Jura les vins authentiques* (1999) – Domaine Ganevat did not feature. That's how fast this estate has come from nowhere to producing the most sought-after wines in the region. As I write, the 50-something Jean-François Ganevat ('Fanfan' to his friends) would rather, I feel sure, receive our congratulations on the birth of his son Antide in 2013 than the fact that his huge range of wines is available worldwide, but on allocation only and at a steep price.

My first visit to Ganevat was in January 2003 in the snow. The hamlet of La Combe is the epitome of *La France perdue* (hidden France) tucked below the vineyards at the end of a road and as silent as silent can be. Silent that is until you meet Jean-François … I've always been wary of trusting my own

---

Jean-Pascal and Peggy Buronfosse.

palate when it's very cold, the winery is in a fabulous location and I'm in the presence of a potentially deadly combination of adorable dog and a winemaker who talks a lot. My notes from that first visit state: 'He is not a modest man, careful of the hype.' Fortunately I was able to take home samples, and for *Wine Report 2004* selected him as an 'up-and-coming' producer, singling out his Pinot Noir Cuvée Julien Ganevat 2001, priced direct from the cellar at €8.50, already more than the local average. I soon realized that the hype I sensed was partly a little craziness, but mostly sheer dedication.

Jean-François follows several generations of winemakers and can trace his family back to the 17th century. His father moved away from polyculture to focus solely on the vineyards from 1976, expanding from around 3ha to 6ha by 1998 when Jean-François took over. Fortunately his father had kept many old vines, including Chardonnay planted in 1902 and 1919, and an interesting mass selection Pinot Noir brought from his

college in Beaune. After working with his father for several years in the 1980s, Jean-François left the area for formal wine training in Beaune and subsequently worked for ten years for Domaine Jean-Marc Morey in Chassagne-Montrachet, becoming the cellar master. Originally he did not intend to return to the sleepy Jura backwater, but after meeting various winemakers from around France working with biodynamics and low sulphur levels, and knowing his family needed help, he returned determined to do something different. His first vintage solely in charge was 1999.

All the work in the vineyard, the winery and the marketing of the wines is considered plot by plot, depending on the soil, aspect, grape variety, age of vines and eventually how it's made. So a quick rundown of his main holdings: the original 6ha comprised vineyards in La Combe behind

Jean-François Ganevat relaxes with a bottle of the Savagnin he makes from his father's vines.

Keeping fungal diseases at bay, this speaker is rigged up to play music at certain times to Jean-François Ganevat's Pinot Noir vines in his Chalasses vineyard.

the winery, named Sous la Roche ('Below the Rock') and 4ha in nearby Les Chalasses, which includes Les Grands Teppes. To this he added around 2ha in the village of Grusse of vineyards planted in 1991, one of the highest in the Jura at over 400m, and some vines at Champ Bernard in Cesancey.

Jean-François farms his 10ha biodynamically but so far without certification, and he employs eight people full-time, a huge ratio of labour to area. This in no way means that he doesn't work hard in the vineyards himself, quite the contrary. On my last visit he was spray-cleaning the tractor when we arrived and we left him on his tractor working the soil. He told me that this is the hardest and most time-consuming job to do, and the timing must be right; in the wet spring of 2013 he felt that many vignerons started too early.

Working the soil and eliminating herbicide were fundamental to Jean-François and something he set about changing soon after rejoining the family domaine, meaning considerable loss in volumes at the start. His use of biodynamics is well documented and he is someone who continually searches to do better with his individual plots, and especially to care for his old vines. The oldest plots in Les Grands Teppes, planted in 1902 and 1919, are now worked by horse. And in the part of Les Chalasses used to produce his Pinot Noir Cuvée Julien, in 2012 he became the first Jura producer to introduce music into the vineyards through a system provided by Genodics. The theory is that the sound waves strengthen the protein cells in the vines, making them more resistant in particular to Esca, but Jean-François' experience so far is that it helps resistance to fungal diseases in general.

Jean-François is no less experimental in the cellar. When he started at the domaine, the big change was away from the resolutely Jurassien methods used by his father to a more Burgundian style, rigorously topping up barrels, investing in newer oak and using some lees stirring. Indeed he used as much as 50% new oak in those early Pinot Noir selections I tasted and 25–30% in the Chardonnays. Over the years he has invested in different sizes of oak – tronconic vats (shaped wider at the base) for fermentation and *demi-muids* of various sizes, but he rarely replaced the oak barrels that date from his first vintages, so the average age goes up each year, and he has now banished lees stirring.

Jean-François makes wine as naturally as possible, with indigenous yeast and, after reducing sulphur levels each year, he now works very reductively, adding SO_2 only to his two larger-production Chardonnays, Cuvée Florine and Grusse En Billat, and a touch at bottling for some other export wines. Since 2002 he has used whole bunch pressing and now has a large old wooden Champagne press. For reds he has moved from cold maceration to partial carbonic maceration, no punch-downs and no pump-overs. He may seem like a crazy man as you go from barrel to barrel tasting with him, but everything is thought out to the last detail.

The range of wines each year can be upwards of 50, mostly in tiny quantities, including everything from Pet Nat and Crémant to Macvin. His quality reputation has been mainly based on his range of superb, age-worthy, terroir-specific Chardonnays, among which I have a weakness for those from the particularly old vines, especially Les Grands Teppes, though Les Chalasses and Les Marguerites (from Melon à Queue Rouge) are wonderful too. However, he also managed to confound the generally poor reputation of the Sud Revermont for reds, starting with his Pinot Noirs. The Trousseau Plein Sud (from ungrafted vines in Sous la Roche) and the Pinot Cuvée Julien used to be built to age beautifully, but with no SO₂ I am not sure how recent vintages will fare. The ever-more-juicy red J'En Veux ('I Want Some'), a Vin de France from a mixture of rare old varieties, grafted and ungrafted, is only 8.5% alc, yet it tastes like a refreshing 11%, with its fruit balanced by a mineral seam.

When he returned to the Jura Jean-François really did not want to make oxidative wines, but was aware that he should continue with small amounts. Yet he has experimented relentlessly with both *ouillé* and *sous voile* Savagnins and is one of the rare producers who vinifies and matures his

Savagnin Vert and Savagnin Jaune plantings apart, sometimes bottling the wines separately too. He has one extraordinary *ouillé* wine – La Vigne de mon Père ('My Father's Vineyard') – which spends ten years topped up in barrel. His *sous voile* Cuvée Prestige Savagnin is deliberately made to be the opposite of Vin Jaune, less deeply oxidative but showing the intensity of the old vines from Les Chalasses. His Vin Jaune is elegant and smoky, and then there is late-harvest Savagnin and the gorgeous Sul Q, a richly sweet but balanced non-Vin de Paille.

For 15 vintages Jean-François has put his heart, soul and physical toil into working his vines and making a huge range of wines, always without compromise. French bureaucracy drives him mad and he drives importers mad with a random allocation policy. How long can he keep this up, I wonder? Will he allow those who work for him to take some of the burden? At least his sister Anne has joined him to help with administration and tastings and he has moved house away from Rotalier with his new young family to give him some distance. You won't ever see Jean-François at any of the official Jura wine region's activities, but in the past decade his wines have been truly fine international ambassadors for the Jura.

Domaine Ganevat
La Combe, 39190 Rotalier

Tel: 03 84 25 02 69

Map ref: p. 283, B2

Contacts: Jean-François and Anne Ganevat

Established: 1976

Vineyards: 10ha (4.5ha Chardonnay, 2ha Savagnin, 1.5ha Pinot Noir, 2ha Trousseau, Poulsard, rare varieties)

Certification: Ecocert

Visits: Tasting room, but visits possible only occasionally by appointment

Domaine Joly

The family of Claude Joly and his son Cédric, who now runs this domaine, came originally from Champagne, but moved to the Jura several generations ago. Claude's father set himself up in the 1950s as a 'Champagnisateur', a bottling and disgorging service for Jura Mousseux, as sparkling wines were called before Crémant was introduced. Later he became a spirits and beer négociant. He had some vines – around 0.6ha – and this is what Claude started off with when he took over the business in 1964. Claude's original passion was cycling and he almost qualified for the Tour de France. He has now retired and his son refers to him as his 'slave', as he still works as hard as ever, but for no pay. Once Cédric joined his father after wine studies in the 1990s the domaine was expanded, reaching 9ha by 2000, including 2ha in AOC L'Etoile, bought some years ago from Champagne Devaux. The current scaled-down 6.5ha includes the L'Etoile vineyards plus 4ha in Rotalier and the other 0.5ha in St-Laurent-la-Roche, a size that allows the family to work with temporary staff.

Having upgraded the technology, Cédric also provides disgorgement services for the other vignerons in Rotalier, and it's no surprise that around half of Domaine Joly's production is Crémant. Vineyards are run along *lutte raisonnée* lines and the soils are ploughed with every other row mowed. At present herbicide is used under the rows, though an *intercep* tractor attachment that weeds between the vines is on the cards. Cédric harvests partly by machine and likes to pick early, often finishing harvest before his close school friend and neighbour Julien Labet has even begun. He routinely chaptalizes but seeks high acidity, as this, he says, is particularly important for the *sous voile* whites that are this estate's focus.

Cédric Joly in his barrel cellar.

The modern fermentation cellar is equipped for cooling and temperature control and Cédric uses indigenous yeasts except for the Crémant. Red varieties are vinified separately, with fairly short macerations and oak ageing for Trousseau and Pinot. Typically for Rotalier, Pinot is their best red. Experiments with Chardonnay *ouillé* from the Les Varrons vineyard have not yet been very successful in my view, but the *sous voile* whites are exemplary, especially L'Etoile En Mérole (Chardonnay) and the Savagnin grown on warm gravel soil rather than the usual marl. Cédric uses several *sous voile* ageing cellars with different conditions; barrels are filled to the top first and then not topped up as the level lowers. He never uses *ensemencement*. Currently Domaine Joly sells mainly locally, especially from the tasting room, but it is beginning to find export markets.

Domaine Joly
3 Chemin des Patarattes, 39190 Rotalier

Tel: 03 84 25 04 14

Email: cc.joly@wanadoo.fr

Map ref: p. 283, B2

Contact: Cédric Joly

Vineyards: 6.5ha (3.8ha Chardonnay, 1.2ha Savagnin, 1ha Pinot Noir, 0.3ha Poulsard, 0.2ha Trousseau)

Visits: Tasting room

Domaine Labet

Perhaps the greatest unsung heroes of the Jura wine region, and most definitely of Sud Revermont, are Alain and Josie Labet, who retired in December 2012, leaving the estate in the capable hands of their three children, Julien, Charline and Romain. There is always argument, education and laughter in equal measure within this family – it all goes beyond that overused word 'passion'. The family also quietly supports other producers who are starting out and they participate in regional activities, while always ploughing their own furrow in an exemplary way.

Alain Labet's grandfather Albert and father Jean had vines but were mixed farmers and his father ran a small vine nursery as well. Alain inherited some old vines and has managed to preserve many, so that this estate has a large number of vines over 60 years old. He started his dedicated wine estate in 1974 with just 2.5ha and gradually rented or purchased other vineyards in or close to Rotalier. At first he farmed organically but in the rainy years of the mid-1980s, when grass and weeds grew like fury, he used some herbicide as a time-saving measure and sprayed occasionally with chemicals. However, Alain never used chemical fertilizer or insecticides and, unlike most, he never changed to machine-harvesting, preferring to call on a team of local pickers at the last minute to harvest at optimum maturity.

Alain was quite possibly the earliest in the Jura to make and bottle wines from individual terroirs separately. From the 1970s he designated the name Fleurs de Marne for Chardonnays from very old vines of mass selections grown on higher slopes on varying colours of marl soils. In the early 1990s he decided that, to express the terroir better, he needed to make these Chardonnays in a more 'Burgundian' way, by regularly topping up the casks; at the time the wines were aged in *foudres*. In this part of the Jura non-oxidative wines were unheard of during this period and the almost entirely local clientele were initially not happy with this new taste. Undaunted, he courted top restaurants, who did appreciate this new expression of Jura terroir, and this in turn brought some press coverage and export interest. On my first extensive Jura visit I fell in love with the Les Varrons and La Bardette Chardonnays and they remain for me wines that prove that the Jura produces seriously high-quality Chardonnay.

Josie was always involved in sales, administration and serving up tasty meals for family, employees and visitors. I'm not

Alain Labet, though retired, helps with the vineyards, here ploughing in Les Varrons.

sure that I know any other Jura estate where three children of this age (born from the 1970s) have all followed their parents into the business. After studying in Beaune and working with Ramonet in Meursault and Hamilton-Russell in South Africa, Julien, the eldest, returned in 1997, bringing ideas that would shake up the winemaking further. The first thing he did was persuade his father to replace the *foudres* with second-hand Burgundy barrels. Amidst constant argument and debate Alain handed the winemaking over to Julien in 1999. When Julien wanted to go further, eliminating SO_2 if possible and working entirely organically with very low yields, rather than agree his parents helped him to set up on his own with a small estate (named Julien Labet); however, he continued to work at the family domaine. Somehow this dual working partnership succeeded for nine years.

In the meantime Charline, also trained as an oenologist and with experience in Chile, returned home to work closely with Julien, and Romain took on the vineyard work. When their parents retired (although Alain still often works in the vineyard) the three siblings took over, incorporating Julien's own vineyards and wine range.

With the exception of the specialities, the Labets consider each of their wines to be an expression of their individual terroir – as at a typical Burgundy estate – and make six reds in small quantities and 12 whites (one Savagnin, the rest Chardonnay). The main vineyards indicated on labels are Les Varrons, La Bardette, Le Monceau, En Chalasse and En Billat.

Les Varrons is their largest parcel, with 4.5ha on a layer of thick, hard-to-work heavy clay on top of white Bathonian or red Bajocian limestone. It includes 'younger vines' of Chardonnay, clonal selections planted by Alain in the 1970s and 1980s (incidentally, the vines of that era are most susceptible to

Siblings Julien, Charline and Romain Labet in Les Varrons vineyard.

Esca) used in Fleur de Chardonnay and the entry-level Les Fleurs. Here too are some of the much older mass selection vines, used for the potentially superb and age-worthy Les Varrons Chardonnay. The Pinot Noir for my favourite Labet red was also planted in the 1980s.

La Bardette, Le Monceau and En Chalasse are on variations of Liassic marl – each Chardonnay expresses a different character and these form part of the Fleurs de Marne range. From En Chalasse on grey marl comes their fabulous Savagnin *ouillé*, made since the late 1990s, named Fleur de Savagnin. All the whites are vinified and aged in barrel very reductively to avoid any hint of oxidation and to limit or sometimes eliminate SO_2. Every year Julien and Charline work ever harder to achieve just the right balance of wines that will age, be as natural as possible (indigenous yeasts have always been used), express that important terroir, and above all be enjoyable to drink with friends.

Very old Poulsard vines are used for a light red and in some years for their highly respected, often quite delicious Vin de Paille. Except that in recent years it hasn't been Vin de Paille. Alain's Vin de Paille was made the conventional Jura way with some judicious oxidation. Julien dries the grapes on organic straw for longer than most producers, regularly checking and removing any bunches or berries that rot, and has made a lower-alcohol version, named – to the disapproval of the authorities, who are trying to ban the name – La Paille Perdue. It is aged for three years in oak, always topped up, and only the fact that it is lower alcohol than permitted makes it ineligible for the AOC. A late-harvest Savagnin has also been made in recent years.

There is delicious Crémant and good

Macvin too, and of course an oxidative range of whites. Alain Labet's Vin Jaune was revered, and initially Julien did not enjoy making *sous voile* wines, but now he has seized it as a challenge and a chance to experiment. Particularly interesting is the intense, spicy and cooked fruit-flavoured Chardonnay Cuvée du Hasard. From old vines and put in barrel to form the veil, the blend also includes some Chardonnay barrels where no SO_2 was added but the wine had started to turn volatile – these form the veil of yeast incredibly easily when not topped up.

The biggest project for the siblings is to convert the whole estate to organics from 2014. This family forces me to mix metaphors and pile on the accolades. If one can say that salt was once the Jura's white gold, these wonderful people and their wines are the salt of the earth in the Jura and pure gold too.

Domaine Labet
14 Montée des Tilleuls, 39190 Rotalier

Tel: 03 84 25 11 13

Email: domaine.labet@wanadoo.fr

Map ref: p. 283, B2

Contacts: Julien, Charline and Romain Labet

Established: 1974

Vineyards: 13.1ha (8.7ha Chardonnay, 2.2ha Savagnin, 1.1ha Poulsard, 0.78ha Pinot Noir, 0.16ha Trousseau, 0.16ha Gamay)

Certification: Ecocert (with main part in conversion from 2014 vintage)

Visits: No tasting room, but visits welcomed by appointment

Kenjiro and Mayumi Kagami of Domaine des Miroirs in their vineyard above Grusse.

Domaine des Miroirs

If it's a given that all good vignerons are brave to work in the Jura's challenging conditions, surely making a lifestyle change from being a Japanese electronics engineer at Hitachi to running a natural wine estate in the quiet vineyards of the Sud Revermont is doubly brave. However, Kenjiro Kagami, now in his early forties, has three major things on his side: first, that he methodically prepared for his mission by studying the French language and wine production in France and then working with wine estates in Burgundy, the Rhône and Alsace; second, that he has been helped in his venture by several people, notably his previous employers and Jean-François Ganevat; and third, that working alongside him is his ever-smiling wife Mayumi, originally a professional gardener in Japan.

After working for over six years with Alsace producer Bruno Schueller, who works with biodynamics and low sulphur levels, Kenjiro wanted to start his own estate. His preference was for somewhere remote with limestone soils, as in his view this gives wines with both freshness and weight. Having dismissed possibilities in Alsace and Burgundy as either too expensive or with too much concentration of vineyards, he first explored the Loire Valley, as he enjoys Chenin Blanc. In the end he was introduced to Emmanuel Houillon and Ganevat by Bruno Schueller and was impressed by the Jura's interesting grape varieties and high quality potential.

It was Jean-François who helped him find his impressive 3ha plot of vineyards just above the town hall in the village of Grusse, very close to his cellar and home. The sloping vineyards form a wonderful west/southwest bowl with forest just above and some non-chemically farmed vineyards below. These were planted in 2004 by a village collective started by the mayor of Grusse in a bid to revive the village tradition of viticulture. Kenjiro says that the vineyards were not well looked after, but at least they had received very little chemical treatment. When he started farming the vines, which are primarily on limestone, he immediately applied to Ecocert for conversion status and his wines will be officially Ecocert from 2014.

Most of Kenjiro's vineyard and winery equipment consists of second-hand cast-offs from Ganevat and others. He uses both tanks and barrels, and for now adds no SO_2 at any stage, preferring an ultra-natural approach. His first vintage was 2011, when he made four different cuvées of Chardonnay, all in micro quantities, along with a Savagnin and a Poulsard. In the smaller 2012 vintage there will be just two cuvées of Chardonnay, with the other two wines. Each wine has its own cuvée name, such as Ja-Nai (meaning 'yes-no' in Alsace dialect) for the Poulsard to reflect both that Kenjiro was unsure whether it was the best he could do and that it was unusual. Those that I have tasted, mainly barrel samples, have good intensity and finesse, with a resolutely natural edge to them, veering from funky to pure.

Kevin and his father Michel Mazier of Domaine des Ronces.

The Kagamis have already found an eager market back home in Japan, but also in Sweden, Denmark, the Netherlands, local shops and Paris wine shops specializing in natural wines.

Domaine des Miroirs
5 Rue St-Roch, 39190 Grusse

Tel: 06 61 52 00 30

Email: domainedesmiroirs@gmail.com

Map ref: p. 283, C2

Contact: Kenjiro Kagami

Vineyards: 3.1ha (1.5ha Chardonnay, 1ha Savagnin, 0.4ha Poulsard, 0.2ha Trousseau)

Certification: Ecocert (in conversion)

Visits: No tasting room and visits possible only occasionally by appointment

Domaine des Ronces

Thoughtful and understated Michel Mazier runs a typical Sud Revermont estate with a predominance of Chardonnay (some sold to La Maison du Vigneron) and a smattering of other varieties. He makes 13 different wines in a range that is due to enlarge soon, now that his son Kevin is working on the estate. Less than 20,000 bottles are produced and of this 30% is Crémant and 10% Macvin. Around 10% is exported to Belgium and the

rest is sold to private individuals through wine shows and the cellar tasting room. But, for all this ordinary profile, Michel has looked to the future and little by little he has instigated changes, especially in taking care of his vineyards, which are mainly in Orbagna, with some in Vercia, near Rotalier, including the well-known En Chalasse, also farmed by Ganevat and Labet.

From early in the century he started working the soil, stopping herbicide use apart from directly under the vines, and gradually reduced levels of chemical sprays by half. In 2010 he started official conversion to organic farming and has been inspired by the Pignier family and Claude Buchot to use biodynamic practices. He says there is much to learn and clearly enjoys this. A vineyard on grey marl that he has recently grubbed up will be replanted with three types of Savagnin (yellow, green and pink), but only after being left fallow for two to three years. He has practised leaf plucking for several years, especially to give aeration to the vines to avoid the risk of rot, and has never aimed for high yields, so the change to organics is relatively painless in terms of yields.

Michel's father Georges had a mixed farm and in 1950 planted 1ha of vines, selling most of the grapes. Michel, the second youngest of eight children, was originally an electrician, and one of his older brothers was going to take over the vineyards but changed his mind. However, something clicked about vines and wine for Michel and after a short period of study in Beaune he joined his father and became established in his own right in 1986 in order to expand the vineyards. Michel's son Kevin studied at Beaune and took responsibility for winemaking from the 2012 vintage. His father has agreed that Kevin should develop his own range of wines.

The wines are as understated as the family here and thoughtfully made too. An elegant Chardonnay Crémant is made unusually with no malolactic fermentation of the base wine and very low *dosage*. Trousseau and Pinot Noir are aged in old *demi-muids* ranging in size from 350 to 600 litres and the Trousseau is very pretty indeed – these look like improving even more with Kevin at the helm. For now the traditional styles are the most successful whites, with the Cuvée Georges blend of 70% Chardonnay aged *sous voile* for two years and 30% Savagnin for over three years being an excellent example of the style. This is an estate quietly on the up.

Domaine des Ronces
9 Impasse du Rochet, 39190 Orbagna

Tel: 03 84 25 09 76

Email: maziermichel@wanadoo.fr

Web: domaine-des-ronces.sitew.com

Map ref: p. 283, B2

Contacts: Michel and Kevin Mazier

Established: 1986

Vineyards: 6ha (4.2ha Chardonnay, 0.4ha Savagnin, 0.8ha Pinot Noir, 0.3ha Poulsard, 0.3ha Trousseau)

Certification: Ecocert

Visits: Tasting room, visits welcomed by appointment

From Beaufort to St-Amour

Beaufort (not the village famous for its cheese, which is in Savoie) is more of a large village than a town. The mid-point of the Sud Revermont, in terms of vineyards it is almost the southernmost point today. Between Beaufort and St-Amour less than 15ha of vines exist, mainly in Beaufort and Augea, yet in the middle of the 19th century Beaufort alone had 150ha and St-Amour once boasted over 500ha. Technically still included in the Côtes du Jura AOC, St-Amour is now a small, quiet town on the southwestern edge of the Jura department. There are few vestiges of its former wine-producing fame except for some fine cellars and vignerons' houses in both the town and its neighbouring villages, and some patches of privately owned vineyards on the outskirts.

Claude Buchot

One of the very earliest organic vignerons of the Jura, at first Claude Buchot comes over as rather gruff and, like his wines, a little hard to appreciate right away, but give him a little time and a smile will emerge

---

One of the old buildings being restored by Claude Buchot at his estate in Maynal.

– you can't help but like and admire both the man and his very traditional wines. He is old school, but not just old school Jura, Claude is old school organic grower and old school environmental activist. This man may have been born of farming stock but he is a thinker – he studied literature for his Baccalauréat and originally had ambitions to become an intellectual of some sort. He ended up as a vigneron and a big supporter of both his wine region and the environmental cause.

When Claude and his brothers were young his father Xavier bought a plot of land in Maynal known as Bry, and together they cleared it to farm cows. However, when subsidies were available to replant vineyards in the early 1970s Claude decided to join his father in a venture to plant vines at Bry, which has marl soils of varied colours. At the time they planted mainly Chardonnay, using large spacing, but whenever any of the vines – now more than 40 years old – die, Claude replaces them with Savagnin. Almost immediately after planting the Buchots converted to organic farming, something that only three or four small estates practised at the time in the region. As an organic 'militant', converting for philosophical reasons rather than commercial, he did not seek certification until 1998, when customers asked for it.

Claude started using plant sprays such as nettles from 2001 and since 2004 he has worked using mostly biodynamic methods, though not with certification. He started using whey mixed in with his fungicide treatments and since these changes his vines have suffered less from oidium, and he has found more mineral character in his white wines. All the soils have been ploughed at least every other row for many years, and in recent years his steepest Poulsard vineyard has been ploughed by Benoît Royer

with his Comtois mare. Claude also owns another vineyard below the château ruins at nearby Beaufort from where he makes an unoaked fresh Chardonnay, but other than this his whites are aged *sous voile*. The Cuvée Charles Baudelaire blend with 30% Savagnin is particularly good.

There is a surprisingly modern small fermentation room and his oxidative wines are aged partly in an old stable and partly in a traditional cellar. Various buildings arranged around a spacious courtyard have been renovated over the years at the delightful Buchot property in Maynal, and much wine is sold by Claude or his wife from the welcoming tasting room. Claude is a proud man who has found a ready market for his traditional organic wines, which are sold mainly in local organic shops, and a little in Belgium. Today the wines sell easily, but that took a long time to build up. Opened in advance, his wines reveal a clarity and intensity – the Poulsard comes alive after decanting. The couple have one daughter, who has inherited Claude's literary penchant and is not interested in taking over. What will happen to this wine estate, which has been run organically for 40 years?

Claude Buchot
4a Grande Rue, 39190 Maynal

Tel: 03 84 85 94 27

Email: claude.buchot@wanadoo.fr

Map ref: p. 283, A1

Established: 1974

Vineyards: 6ha (4ha Chardonnay, 1ha Savagnin, 0.5ha Poulsard, 0.5ha Pinot Noir)

Certification: Ecocert

Visits: Tasting room

OTHER WINES OF FRANCHE-COMTÉ

Today there are fewer than 120ha of registered vineyards in Franche-Comté that lie outside the AOC boundaries of the Jura, considerably more than just 25 years ago. Most of the plantings are in the Haute-Saône and Doubs departments. There are also small non-AOC areas in the Jura, especially close to Ornans and north of Dole around Offlanges, and there is a minuscule area in the tiny Territoire de Belfort to the northeast of Besançon.

These areas were extensively planted with vineyards until the various crises of the 19th and early 20th centuries. Old vineyard areas were reclaimed by forests, became pastures or were overtaken by housing. It is most particularly in Gy and Champlitte, both in Haute-Saône,

Above: Owned by Pascal Henriot, this typically iso-lated vineyard near woodlands above Champlitte in the Haute-Saône has just been ploughed, revealing the red limestone soil.

that modern pioneers have revived the vineyards. The revival led to the wines being given the designation Vin de Pays de Franche-Comté in 1982, which became IGP Franche-Comté from 2011.

The isolated vineyards close to the Chaux forest near the Loue river and Arc-et-Senans in the Doubs department were mentioned in the chapter 'Around Arbois' (see p. 144), as several young vignerons profiled also make IGP wines from small plots of vineyards there. These plots often contain old vines of Jura varieties or almost extinct grape varieties, providing a wonderful pool of plant material for mass selections. Conversely, in Haute-Saône the Guillaume family, owners of France's largest vine nursery and masters of clonal selection, can be credited with helping the revival of the vineyards there. About 16 producers make wine under the IGP Franche-Comté label.

Gy and Champlitte

From the 11th century until the French Revolution the Château de Gy was the summer residence of the Archbishop of Besançon. The monks cultivated vineyards and also sold the wine widely, shipping it from the port of Gray on the River Saône, just 20km away. Champlitte, even closer to Gray, also had a high reputation for its wines, supplying wine to the bishops of Langres and Dijon. In the 19th century, when Champlitte alone had 600ha of vineyards, terrible frosts ruined the vineyards and led to the emigration of more than 200 of its residents to Mexico.

Considering the proximity to Burgundy (see map on p. 14), it is not surprising that Pinot Noir was grown and it enjoyed a high reputation as early as the 16th century. Chardonnay would also have been grown. Savagnin is mentioned in old texts from the region of Gy, where the château houses a small wine museum. In the revived vineyards of this region by far the most planted varieties are Pinot Noir and Chardonnay.

The proximity of the River Saône warms up what would otherwise be a very cold continental climate. Ripening is usually later here than in Burgundy or the Jura, a blessing or a curse depending on the season. The Champlitte vineyards are on hillsides at around 300m altitude. In 1974 Albert Demard, a local historical museum curator, galvanized a number of individuals into reviving the vineyards of the Coteaux de Champlitte, leading eventually to the creation of a type of cooperative wine cellar that today sells wines under the name of Grand Vignoble Chanitois (GVC) from nearly 30ha of vineyards. His vision spawned the creation of several wine estates.

Xavier Guillaume of Vignobles Guillaume, the wine estate offshoot of the family's important vine nursery in Charcenne.

The vineyard slopes close to Gy are the first foothills of the Jura Mountains, but no higher than 300m, and with more limestone than marl in the soil. It is here that Henri Guillaume first planted commercial vineyards as a sideline to his vine nursery business in 1970. Gy or Coteaux de Champlitte can be added to the label in the IGP Franche-Comté designation.

Vignobles Guillaume

The village of Charcenne, 5km south of Gy, is well known for its *pépinières* – plant and vine nurseries – dominated by Pépinières Guillaume. An offshoot of the nursery is the vineyard and winery run by Henri-Xavier Guillaume (known as Xavier), the largest producer of Franche-Comté wine outside the Jura, roughly a third of which is exported.

Xavier Guillaume's ancestor Albert Guillaume, from a family of vignerons going back to 1732, started grafting vines and selling them in 1895. From the mid-1950s Henri Guillaume, father of Xavier and his brother Pierre-Marie, who runs the nursery side of the business, expanded the business,

On the left Cuvée des Archevêques and Païen, both Savagnins, and on the right IGP Pinot Noir and Chardonnay, all from Vignobles Guillaume.

money and the Collection Réservée wines are fine, though somewhat over-oaked. Traditional-method sparkling wines are another speciality. The Flûte Enchantée ('Magic Flute') is a pleasant commercial sparkler and an Extra Brut 100% Chardonnay, Séduction, is excellent. The base wine is aged for a few months in barrels between two and ten years old and the wines are aged *sur lattes* for at least two years.

Xavier enjoys making a range of other wines, including Gamay, Auxerrois and Pinot Gris as IGPs and others such as Merlot and Gewürztraminer from varieties not incorporated into the IGP rules so sold under the Vin de France (Vin de Table) category. Xavier is a very competent winemaker. He also makes three interesting wines from Jura grape varieties. There is a fun blend of Poulsard and Trousseau named G'PT, which, like all the reds here, could do with less oak input, but gives characteristic red fruits from Poulsard and tannin from Trousseau. Le Païen is an oak-aged Savagnin *ouillé* using the Swiss Valais name for the grape. It is rich with a lovely aromatic character, leaning more towards its Alsace cousin Gewürztraminer than the Jura.

Xavier is both proud and fascinated by the ancient history of his vineyard area. A few years ago the curator of the wine museum at the Château de Gy suggested ageing some barrels there, leaving them untouched as the monks might have done. The result is La Cuvée des Archevêques ('Archbishop's Cuvée'), a Savagnin made exactly as a Vin Jaune. It's a fine wine and a fine tribute to days gone by.

which has grown to become France's largest, and the world's third-largest, vine nursery. Henri was one of the earliest proponents of clonal selection, developing the first Chardonnay clones. According to Xavier, the company sells the highest number of young Chardonnay plants in the world.

There is great synergy between the nursery vineyards and those planted to make wine. The nursery grows a huge range of varieties and several clones of each, and fruit from the mother plants is available for the winery. Making wine allows for small batch testing that can give valuable feedback to the nursery. Xavier runs the wine estate with seven staff. A modern winery with a tasting room was constructed in 1992 and attracts many customers who also buy from the nursery.

Both Chardonnay and Pinot Noir are offered at three levels: a simple varietal wine, a Vieilles Vignes cuvée and the Collection Réservée top-end wine, offered only in some vintages and with longer oak and bottle ageing. All show higher acidity than their equivalents from Burgundy and have little in common with Jura wines. The Vieilles Vignes offers good value for

Vignobles Guillaume
Route de Gy, 70700 Charcenne
Tel: 03 84 32 77 22
Email: vignoble@guillaume.fr
Web: guillaume.fr

Contact: Henri-Xavier Guillaume

Established: 1970

Vineyards: 40ha (14.2ha Chardonnay, 20ha Pinot Noir, 1.1ha Pinot Meunier, 1ha Gamay, 0.6ha Merlot, many small plantings)

Visits: Tasting room, visits welcomed by appointment, shop at the *pépiniériste* (nursery) at 32 Grand Rue

Pascal Henriot

With a prominent and enticing sign on the roadside through Champlitte, Pascal Henriot sells much of the organic wine from his estate directly from his small cellar. After working for GVC and studying in Beaune Pascal cleared parcels of former vineyard land on the nearby hillsides to plant vines and farmed organically from the start. Pascal's vineyards are isolated, which is ideal for organic viticulture, and lie above the town where one can still see many stone walls that originally divided the vineyards.

Normally the vineyards are grassed down one in two rows, but in wet years like 2012 and 2013 the grass has to be removed and the red limestone soil worked entirely, with

the help of an *intercep* attachment. Pascal has one part-time employee, Daniel, who has worked with him for 15 years and is just as dedicated. It is a typical organic routine with animal manure used for fertilizer, Bordeaux mixture for fungal disease and some experiments with whey, silica and plant preparations.

The winery uses gravity flow where possible. Wines are made in a natural way with indigenous yeast and low SO_2, which is added after fermentation or at bottling. One or two 100% sulphur-free wines are made if the vintage allows. Oak input is something that Pascal avoids with most of the wines (although some Pinot may be oak-aged), preferring to offer wines bottled within the year that express the fruit simply. The main range has three whites – Auxerrois, Chardonnay and Pinot Gris – and two reds – Gamay and Pinot Noir. Rosé is made too and sometimes a sparkling Chardonnay, along with a sulphur-free semi-sparkling wine (not tasted), Cuvée des Folains. Just as Pascal has conceived them, the wines taste eminently easy-drinking, fresh, obviously cool-climate styles, with Auxerrois and Gamay being particularly enjoyable.

A roadside sign welcomes visitors to Pascal Henriot's tasting room in Champlitte.

Pascal Henriot
89 Rue de la République, 70600 Champlitte

Tel: 03 84 67 68 85

Email: pascal.henriot2@gmail.com

Web: pascalhenriot.com

Established: 1989 (vineyards in 1985)

Vineyards: 6ha (1.5ha Chardonnay, 1.2ha Auxerrois, 0.35ha Pinot Gris, 2.45ha Pinot Noir, 0.5ha Gamay)

Certification: Ecocert

Visits: No tasting room, but visits welcomed by appointment

THE FUTURE FOR JURA WINE PRODUCERS

Above: Dominique Boivin, a member of the Fruitière Vinicole d'Arbois, works his vines in the Paradis vineyard above Arbois almost entirely by hand, using lutte raisonnée. *How will future generations work?*

Viewed from the outside, after an uphill struggle for three generations Jura wine producers seem to have everything going their way. The world's wine lovers are keen to taste and drink their fascinating wines, wine critics and journalists increasingly seek stories about wine regions with a point of difference and the Jura ticks all the boxes, with its indigenous grape varieties, unusual styles of wine and small, welcoming, family-run producers. The Jura appears to have it all, especially if one adds in the beautiful scenery, famous cheeses and some top restaurants.

Jura wines seem to be just what the wine drinker in the second decade of the 21st century is looking for – fresh styles, not too alcoholic, oaky or over-laden with tannin, food-friendly, drinkable, characterful wines. The word 'authentic' fits the Jura like a glove and the region can even boast one of the highest percentages of certified organic vineyards in northern Europe. Yet, talk to regional officials and many producers, and they are cautious about the future. There are many concerns. Dig a little deeper and the situation seems a touch precarious.

One big issue is that, for such a very small region, the balance of power seems rather unjust. Three producers sell 44% of Jura wine and they have a disproportionate amount of influence over what happens to the region in terms of its relationship with French government organizations and promotional bodies. There are three relatively large family estates up for sale and several smaller ones, so, if the négociant, La Maison du Vigneron (one of the big three) were to buy one of these, the balance would shift even more. The problem of succession for family-owned estates is a constant worry. If there are no children to take over, the estate is put up for sale and its future direction is in question.

The second big concern is even less controllable. The unpredictable weather experienced worldwide can cause extreme effects in the Jura, not least dramatic drops in quantity. Sales volumes have decreased each year for the past six years, simply because of a lack of wine to sell following a run of small harvests (except 2011). This is set to continue following the very small 2012 and 2013 vintages and is a particular problem for producers with successful exports but no stock to sell. Will they retain their customers? The regional bodies supporting the growers, which fund research projects and promotional activities, have less money too because they are partly financed by a levy based on volume.

The growing philosophical and product divide between vignerons working organically, especially those making wine in the natural way, and conventional producers is another concern. The divide has meant that the message from the Jura has become very mixed. There is a huge diversity of wine styles even from traditional producers, but yet more styles emerge from those working in the natural way and some of these producers no longer choose to work within AOC rules.

So what can be done to address these issues to make the Jura wine producers' future as rosy as it seems to the outsider? Like making good wines, the ultimate aim for Jura producers should be to achieve the right balance while maintaining the Jura's authentic character and building a solid long-term future.

This name of this Ploussard cuvée from Raphaël Monnier of Domaine Ratapoil, 'Partout', means 'everywhere'. The modern label includes a state-ment on the side explaining that the wine is a blend from different vineyards, harvested by hand, made using carbonic maceration and indigenous yeasts, and left on its lees. It contains no additives and has not been filtered. It also includes the statutory state-ment that it contains sulphites.

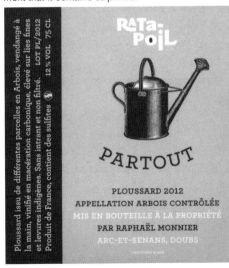

The balance of power risks bubbling over

More than 5% of the Jura's vineyard area is openly for sale and all this is without considering the somewhat precarious situation of Henri Maire. Rumours abound as to whether Verdoso Industries, with its recent Burgundian acquisitions, it is ripe for taking over by a large wine company that may want to turn all its Jura production into making inexpensive Crémant du Jura. Currently a quarter of the Jura's wine production is Crémant and a significant proportion of this is sold cheaply by La Maison du Vigneron, which dominates exports. [Revised 2015: Henri Maire was taken over by the Boisset Group early in 2015.] The Jura's glory is its diversity and if Crémant sales go up dramatically this diversity is at risk. Crémant is a good sparkling wine and can provide an entry into new markets, but it would be wrong for it to become the main wine with which the Jura is associated.

Managing a careful expansion programme

With unpredictable vintages and a laudable tendency for producers to keep yields reasonable in a quest for higher-quality wines, the Jura does not have enough wine to sell. Few in the region have stable enough markets to put prices up to compensate for low volumes. Yet, despite there being plenty of good land available (a mighty 9,000ha of AOC-designated land is not planted – something the Champagne region must envy), no one seems prepared to take the risk of planting new vineyards. In recent years even the annual planting rights of around 20ha have not been fully taken up by Jura producers. It is something the region

plans to address in 2014.

Many quality-minded family-run producers want to remain small so that they do not have to employ costly full-time staff. It is a wonderful 'small is beautiful', self-contained approach, but one wonders whether it is sustainable because it is so dependent on what nature provides in terms of yield and what the market will bear in terms of price – these producers tend to have higher prices. A handful of vignerons are expanding their estates steadily instead, taking on staff to manage different aspects of the business, which allows the owners to travel to market their wines at sensible prices. The Jura badly needs more mid-sized wine producers like these.

High time for more clarity

Keen wine consumers and sommeliers relish the challenge of the Jura's diversity. They welcome each latest release of tiny new cuvées from a select band of small producers, but what of a wine drinker new to the region who would like to try a Jura wine in a restaurant or shop? Often the label gives the consumer no clue about what sort of wine is in the bottle. Jura wine producers sell a large proportion of wine directly to the public, when the vigneron is present to discuss the wines. But otherwise the reality is that these wines have to be explained to stand out from the crowd and attract buyers. This accounts for their success in New York, where wines are traditionally hand-sold, but this does not work elsewhere.

The notoriously unhelpful AOC system meant that until recently grape varieties were not shown on French wine labels and some Jura wine labels still do not reveal the variety. The most confusing issue is the question of whether a white wine is *sous voile*/oxidative or made in the fresh *ouillé* style. A white wine labelled AOC Côtes du Jura often gives no clues. It is time for a new style appellation for *ouillé* wines within existing appellations. An alternative might be compulsory back labels, but they present language difficulties. The Jura cannot afford to continue selling white wines where the content of the bottle is a mystery.

Working in harmony

The rise of organics and biodynamics, as well as increasing numbers of Jura growers using reasoned agriculture (especially those joining the Terra Vitis group) is to be applauded. However, organic/biodynamic viticulture is only for really dedicated, hard-working vignerons, who generally win the battles with nature to secure a decent crop each year. All small producers face problems with rising costs and increased time spent dealing with bureaucracy, but for organic growers there is even more paperwork. It is high time that the region started actively demonstrating support for these producers to avoid a split in the wine community – more than one conventional producer ridicules those working with organics. On the other hand those natural wine producers who have left the AOC system or are considering doing so should remember that it is usually better to fight from within rather than from outside and they should participate more in regional activities to make their voice heard. That way a balance might be achieved.

Marketing and communications

In the 21st century two principal things have helped to spread the word about Jura wine – the ever-successful Percée du Vin Jaune festival and the rise of exports. The Percée revolves around the message of Vin Jaune, yet this legendary wine accounts for only 4% of sales and achieves a price that is hardly worth the effort and the 6+ years it takes to make it. Just compare the price (around €30 from the best producers' cellars) with other top-class, long-lived wines from around the world – Vin Jaune is cheap. So is Vin de Paille, the region's other rarity. To achieve better prices for producers across the range the message from the region needs to convey the incredible value the Jura offers. Producers who export do so to achieve greater return for their investment and hard work, and others want to join them. However, both the regional bodies and the producers themselves must learn to communicate better in English, giving regular, up-to-date, interesting information, especially on-line. This includes information about Jura's *route du vin* (wine route). Apparently a priority for the CIVJ, wine tourism when done well presents a fabulous opportunity to attract worldwide fans for life, yet the Jura offers little geared to foreigners.

Achieving balance for a golden future

It is unlikely that many of my suggestions will be taken up in the short term. Money is desperately short all over France, including the Jura. However, the region can continue to be celebrated by us outsiders for the diversity of its people and its wines, and their authenticity too. Most of the producers profiled in this book are justly proud of what they do. I say to them, please keep on doing the same, but listen to outsiders now and again, and be careful to preserve and build on what your parents and grandparents worked so hard to achieve. Work together and do not compromise on achieving balance for long-term success.

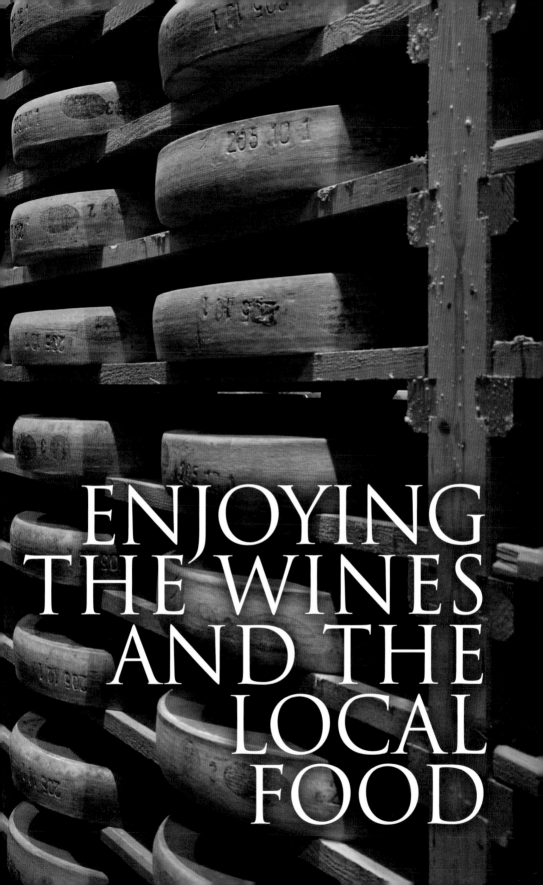

ENJOYING THE WINES AND THE LOCAL FOOD

FOOD AND DRINK SPECIALITIES

As everywhere, it is the nature of the geography that most influences the food and drink traditions of the Jura and Franche-Comté. The diverse landscape of mountains, dense forests, high meadows, vineyards, lakes and the river plain have all shaped what the local population ate and drank. Franche-Comté's gastronomy has much in common with that of Switzerland's western cantons, but there are subtle differences.

Most of the rural population in the mountains and on the plain lived from their dairy cows and pigs, so the principal specialities are the wonderfully rich cows' milk cheeses from unpasteurized milk and tasty pork sausages and charcuterie. The sausages and meats are smoked by hanging in a *tuyé*, a very large pyramidal chimney over the fire, burning wood from conifers.

To these foods can be added lake and river fish and poultry, especially the long-famous Poulet de Bresse. The woodlands provide ample opportunities for finding wild mushrooms and are full of game birds

Previous page: In the 'cathedral' of Comté at Fort St-Antoine, the cellar master of Fromageries Marcel Petite tests the readiness of a 40kg wheel of cheese maturing there. Above: Signs outside the shop of the Fruitière de Plasne-Barretaine, the cheese cooperative above Poligny.

and animals. Vegetables, especially green vegetables, while widely available today, rarely feature on menus as specialities in Franche-Comté – the food tends to be rich in protein and fat, essential to keep hard-working farmers and country folk energized and warm.

Whereas in the south, especially in the Jura, the vine was always prevalent, in the northeast of Franche-Comté towards the border with Lorraine orchards are found, particularly cherry trees. As in nearby Switzerland and Alsace, liqueurs and *marcs* have long been made from various fruits and mountain herbs also flavour spirits. Local beers are making a comeback.

Franche-Comté's best-known AOP (protected appellation of origin) cheeses are all cows' milk cheeses and over 95% of the milk comes from the distinctive brown and white Montbéliarde breed, although the French Simmental breed is also allowed. Each cow must have at least 1ha of pasture for grazing. Farms are still relatively small, rarely with more than 60 cows. A particularity of the region is the prevalence of *fruitières*, the cooperative cheese-making facilities with origins in the 13th century, when farmers found it easier to group together to make large cheeses. *Affineurs* (specialists in cheese ageing) or *caves d'affinage* (ageing cellars) appeared in the area in the late 19th century.

Beginning with Comté, the region's most famous cheese, this chapter summarizes the most important foods and alcoholic drinks, aside from wine, that are prized in the Jura and Franche-Comté. How these are used in gastronomy and how they are matched with the local wines is discussed in the following chapter.

Comté AOP

By far the largest production AOP cheese in France, Comté is made in the departments of the Jura and the Doubs, and to the south in the Ain in the Rhône-Alpes region. It is part of the family of semi-hard Gruyère-type cows' milk cheeses produced primarily in Alpine and mountainous regions. The name Comté appeared only in the early 20th century but farming families have been making very large cheeses that would see them through the winter for centuries. Comté was one of the earliest French cheeses to be protected by the AOC in 1958; this became AOP in 1996.

The pastures lie at between 200m and 1,500m altitude and the cows spend between seven and nine months outside. They are milked twice a day. In addition to grass or hay (in winter) cows are fed a small supplement of cereals (no GMOs are allowed) and vitamins, both summer and winter, but amounts are strictly controlled and no silage is allowed. Each *fruitière* collects milk once a day from around 16 farms within a maximum radius of 25km. The wide range of flowers and herbs in the grass influences the taste of the cheese – each *fruitière* has a different terroir, with up to 200 plants in the pastures.

Cheese is made daily in the *fruitières* under the control of a master cheesemaker. The process is semi-mechanized, but a traditional copper cauldron is still used for the initial warming of the partially skimmed milk. The cheesemaker uses his or her hands to check the consistency of the curd before pouring it into the moulds. Comté is made from unpasteurized milk and is never heated above 55°C. The only additives allowed are the starter culture to acidify the milk and animal rennet to thicken or curdle it; each cheese is given a casein seal on the side. After about three weeks at the *fruitière*,

Montbéliarde cows graze in a pasture high up in the Jura Mountains.

being salted, brushed and turned daily, most of the cheeses are sent to a *cave d'affinage*.

Comté cheese must be aged for a minimum of four months before sale. The average is eight months and many are aged from 12 to 24 months. During this time each cheese rests on spruce wood shelves and is turned, rubbed and salted regularly, a process that has now been robotized. The temperature and humidity of the cellar affect whether holes form and what aromas develop. The best cheeses are aged in a cold cellar (below 14°C) and the two most spectacular ageing cellars are in old military forts. Marcel Petite rented Fort St-Antoine in 1966 and today the company stores around 100,000 cheeses in what it refers to as a 'cathedral of Comté'. The altitude of around 1,100m provides long, slow ageing conditions. At a similar altitude Fort des Rousses is used by Fromagerie Arnaud (Juraflore), storing around 55,000 cheeses.

To decide when they are ready for sale the cellar master at the *cave d'affinage* tests each cheese with a *sonde* – a small hammer that doubles as a device to extract a tasting sample. Claude Querry, cellar master at Fort St-Antoine, likens the production, ageing and testing of Comté cheeses to

winemaking, describing the Montbéliarde cows as the equivalent of Savagnin and the *sonde* as the wine producer's pipette, used to draw samples from barrels. However, he also includes hearing and touch in his testing process – when he feels a cheese it is like using ultrasound, he says.

Each cheese is branded with a code that indicates which farm and which *fruitière* it came from. Under AOP rules each cheese must be tested and given a score out of 20. Those scoring below 12 are rejected as Comté; between 12 and 14 they receive a brown label, and above 14 a green label. Although Comté is sold by age, the time of year when the cheese was made also makes a big difference. Spring flowers in the cows'

Claude Querry, the cellar master at Fort St-Antoine, uses a sonde to take a sample of Comté during ageing.

diet give the most flavoursome cheese. Claude Querry believes age is less relevant than each cheese's history and storage conditions, dismissing buying by age as 'like buying wine by alcoholic degree', but in practical terms age gives the customer more information than anything else unless the cheese purveyor is excellent.

There are said to be 83 common aromas and tastes that can occur in Comté, ranging from lactic notes (cream, etc.) through fruity (including the classic nutty notes), roasted, vegetal, animal or spicy. Beware

Some figures about Comté cheese

- Comté accounts for 26% of French AOP cheese

- There are 130,000 cows in the AOP region

- An average herd has 48 cows

- Each cow requires at least 1ha of grazing land

- Each cow gives 6,000 litres of milk per year

- 400 litres of milk are required for one cheese

- There are 160 *fruitières* and 16 *caves d'affinage*

- Each wheel of cheese weighs 40kg

- A cheese is 60cm in diameter and 10cm thick

- 1.45 million wheels of Comté were made in 2012

- 7.5% of Comté is exported

cheap Comté sold in French supermarkets: it may be AOP, but it is nothing like a fine aged cheese from a top *cave d'affinage*.

Other cheeses

Mont d'Or AOP: Named after a high Jura peak, the raw milk, washed creamy cheese Mont d'Or can also be called Vacherin du Haut-Doubs and is made primarily around Pontarlier. It used to be known as Vacherin Mont d'Or, but the name Vacherin on its own can now be used only for the Swiss equivalent, which is made from thermalized (between raw and pasteurized) milk. It was traditionally made in the winter months when farmers could not pool their milk to

Above: Mont d'Or cheese in its spruce box. Below: The three main Franche-Comté cheeses: Comté (left), Morbier and Bleu de Gex (front).

make a large cheese. Today it can be made only between 15 August and 15 March and offered for sale from 10 September to 10 May. After 21 days' ageing, Mont d'Or is packed in spruce boxes ranging from 480g to 3.2kg; some sappy flavour comes through from the box. Although unctuously rich when eaten cold, the cheese can be heated in its box, when it is delicious scooped out on to potatoes. The rind is good to eat too.

Morbier AOP: Named after the town of the same name in the high Jura, Morbier is a semi-soft cheese with a distinctive blue-black line in the middle. Originally farmers who did not have enough milk from the morning's milking would cover the curds with a layer of ash (taken from heating the cauldron) to protect it, before adding the curd from the evening's milking on top. These days Morbier is made from a mixture of morning and evening milk. The curd is cut in two and a layer of vegetable charcoal is placed on one half. The two halves are then pressed together for several hours. The cheese is aged for a minimum of 45 days and weighs 8–10kg. Many cheese shops sell a younger, milder version and a more mature, slightly harder Morbier with a stronger taste.

Bleu de Gex AOP: Also known as Bleu du Haut-Jura or Bleu de Septmoncel, Bleu de Gex is a soft blue cheese, made by only four producers in a delimited area of the departments of Jura and Ain. Roquefort penicillin is added to the milk and, when the cheese is ready for ageing, it is pierced to facilitate the mould spreading. Bleu de Gex weighs 6–9kg and is aged for three weeks before sale. It is a mild blue cheese and it is possible to eat the soft rind.

Cancoillotte: This runny cheese was always made by farmers' wives, who were responsible for most cheese-making, as a by-product of butter. Easy to spread on bread or toast, or served hot over potatoes, it was revived in the 2000s and is now made by several producers. There are flavoured versions, using everything from garlic to morel mushrooms or even absinthe, Savagnin or Vin Jaune.

La Vache qui Rit: The Vache qui Rit ('Laughing Cow') brand of processed cheese dates back to 1921 and is owned by Fromageries Bel. The main factory and a museum celebrating the brand are in Lons-le-Saunier. It is made mainly from hard cheeses, which are melted, emulsified and pasteurized. Its success, along with other local competitors, was very important in stabilizing the local dairy industry.

Sausages and charcuterie

Saucisse de Morteau IGP: Made originally in the Doubs and always from Franche-Comté-reared pork that is traditionally raised on small farms and often fed partly with the whey from cheese-making, the producers of Morteau sausages received IGP (protected geographic indication) status in 2010. The dense, uncooked, thick amber-brown sausages of at least 40mm

Morteau sausages with tags indicating that they are approved by the Label Rouge (red label) certification organization.

diameter are made from a mixture of lean and fatty chopped pork with a natural pork casing. They have a strong smoky character from around 48 hours smoked in a *tuyé* or its modern equivalent, fuelled with conifers and juniper. The texture when cooked is soft rather than chewy. Jésu de Morteau (or Jésus de Morteau) is a fatter and more irregularly shaped version.

Montbéliard sausage: This sausage is produced anywhere in Franche-Comté (and producers are also applying for IGP) in a similar way to Morteau. A Montbéliard sausage is smaller (25mm diameter) than Morteau, made from a larger pieces of chopped pork and smoked for around 24 hours. It is usually flavoured with pepper, cumin and other spices.

Charcuterie: Two smoked hams made from local pork have protected names and are particularly prized: Jambon Fumé du Haut-Doubs is a wonderfully textured smoked ham and Jambon de Luxeuil, a tasty ham made in Haute-Saône, is steeped in red Arbois wine before being dried with spices and flavourings such as juniper berries and then lightly smoked. Smoked, dried and flavoured pork *saucissons* (salami-type sausages) are widely found. The only non-pork speciality is an air-dried beef called Bresi (sometimes Brési) from the Doubs, made since medieval times, smoked in a *tuyé* and tasting similar to Swiss air-dried beef from the Grisons.

Other food specialities

Poulet de Bresse AOP: Highly prized in France for its rich flavour, tender pink flesh and bright yellow fat, the Bresse chicken was the first livestock of controlled origin in the world, receiving its AOC in 1957. Much very good poultry comes from the vast

Sign outside a restaurant indicating that it serves Poulet de Bresse.

Bresse area, but AOP Poulet de Bresse has a set of specific rules. The AOP region covers much of the departments of Ain (Rhône-Alpes), Saône-et-Loire (Burgundy region) and the western part of the Jura near Lons-le-Saunier. Only five breeders were left in the Jura in 2012. The chickens, with their distinctive white feathers and blue feet, are the small Gauloise de Bresse Blanche breed. The male has a red crown. The chickens are given a much wider area to roam than most free-range birds, and feed and production conditions are highly controlled. The result is a very expensive chicken, but with superb texture and flavour, used in the iconic dish of the Jura, *Poulet de Bresse au Vin Jaune et morilles* (Bresse chicken cooked with Vin Jaune and morels).

Lake and river produce: *Truite* (trout), *perche* (perch), *brochet* (pike), *sandre* (pike-perch or zander) and *omble-chevalier* (related to the Atlantic char, similar to large salmon trout) are the most common freshwater fish; some may be farmed. To these can be added *écrevisses* (crayfish) and – much prized in season – *grenouilles* (frogs). There is a tradition of catching and eating whole young red frogs (*grenouilles fraîches*) in a short one-month season from mid-March. Technically they are not farmed, but caught and 'looked after' before being sold to restaurateurs. Recently, inferior green frogs imported from Asia have invaded the market and 'producers' of the real thing are grouping together to protect their original frogs. Purists say they are best fried in butter – eating them is a messy process.

Wild mushrooms: The damp climate of Franche-Comté provides a good choice of mushrooms in spring and autumn. The famous *morilles* (morels) are found in spring in orchards and on sandy river banks – their flavour, reminiscent of truffles, is accentuated when dried. *Girolles* (chanterelles), another variety of spring mushroom, are found in woodlands. In the autumn *trompettes de la mort* (black trumpets) and *bolets* (ceps) are particularly prized. All are available from markets in season (but one is never sure whether they are locally picked) or bottled or dried out of season.

Cerises de Fougerolles: The village of Fougerolles in Haute-Saône, on the border with Lorraine, has been known for its cherry orchards since the 19th century, when a number of distilleries were established to make Kirsch. The cherries (*cerises*) are a wild cherry called *guigne*, a small, very sweet but tart cherry used for jams and syrups as well as distillation (see 'Other *marcs* and liqueurs' below). Griottines is a name registered by the Peureux distillery for a tasty mix of imported cherries soaked in Kirsch de Fougerolles.

Spirits and beers

Marc du Jura AOC: In 2014 Marc du Jura will be ratified as an AOC. Up to now it had to be labelled Eau de Vie de Marc de Franche-Comté, a spirit sold by many Jura wine producers. It is made by distillation of the *marc*, the residue of the grapes (skins, pips, etc.) left over after pressing. All the permitted Jura grape varieties can be used

KIRSCH de Fougerolles AOC

After receiving AOC designation the distillers of Kirsch de Fougerolles revived a special bottle called the 'Bô Fougerollais', based on an 18th-century design.

and wine producers can produce *marc* only from their own grapes, distilled in the region. About 90% of *marc* made in the Jura is used in the blend for Macvin du Jura and this must be aged for at least 14 months in wood. Crucially, for the new AOC Marc du Jura label the spirit must be aged in wooden barrels for at least 24 months. There are some very fine examples around – a few wine producers even make a special Marc du Jura from the pressings of Vin de Paille.

Fine du Jura: Like a brandy, this is distilled from wine rather than grape residue. There are no rules for ageing and it tends to be an inferior product to Marc du Jura. Several non-Macvin liqueur wines are made using Fine in the blend, but it is also sold as a spirit in its own right.

Other *marcs* and liqueurs: Kirsch de Fougerolles AOC, an *eau-de-vie* or clear spirit, is produced by four distilleries in the village of Fougerolles in Haute-Saône, distilled from the local *guignes* (wild cherries). Apart from a plethora of other fruit *eau-de-vies*, other commonly found liqueurs from the mountain areas are Sapin, made with local fir tree buds, and Gentiane, a bittersweet herbal liqueur made from the root of the yellow gentian.

Absinthe and aniseed spirits: Absinthe may have first been produced in Switzerland, but production became just as important on the French side of the Jura Mountains in the 19th century. Henri-Louis Pernod (yes, that Pernod) was the first to open a distillery in Pontarlier and the town became the centre for absinthe production with, at its peak, 22 distilleries. Based on the bitter herb wormwood (*Artemisia absinthium*), the drink, considered a tonic, became popular and highly fashionable. Known as the 'green fairy', it was immortalized by writers and artists. As its price dropped, consumption increased and it was banned in France in 1915, ostensibly for health reasons, though in reality it was banned under pressure from the wine industry, which was threatened by its success. Aniseed-based spirits took the place of absinthe, but only two distilleries survived in Pontarlier, Distillerie Les Fils d'Emile Pernot and Distillerie Pierre Guy, producing a range of spirits. The latter, still family owned, battled hard to prove scientifically that distillations from the wormwood plant were not poisonous, and eventually the ban was repealed in France in 2011. Both distilleries make a range of absinthes, in which distilled spirit is infused with a mixture of aniseed, wormwood and other plants.

Beer: As in the rest of France, there has been a resurgence of small breweries in Franche-Comté, including two well known in the Jura. Brasserie La Rouget de Lisle in Bletterans, which was founded in 1994, offers a range of styles, including the flavoured beers popular in France. Flavours include local products such as Griottines de Fougerolles. In 2008 two musician friends started La Franche in La Ferté, near Arbois, which offers a range of styles, graced by funky labels. There are several other microbreweries across the region.

A tasting line-up of absinthes at Distillerie Pierre Guy together with baskets containing the plants used to make them. The decanter dispenses water, dripping it over a spoon holding a sugar lump to sweeten the absinthe.

SERVING JURA WINES

Many people believe that wine should be quite simply opened, served and enjoyed without fuss, with or without food. It's a sentiment that I agree with in principle, yet in my experience, much more than other wines, Jura wines express themselves so much better when served at the right temperature, when they have been opened well in advance and to accompany

Above: The ultimate Jura combination: Comté and walnuts with Vin Jaune.

well-chosen food. If not, the dominant acidity, minerality and often a somewhat surprising reductive note in many wines have a tendency to mask great complexity and a wealth of other flavours.

Like so many aspects of Jura wines, much appears contra-indicative in terms of serving. Many reds need to be served cooler than whites; they are traditionally served before whites; and indeed they age less well than whites. Yet, with the many different styles of whites, for example, it becomes hard to draw up a set of simple rules for serving them at their best. This chapter gives advice on getting the most out of Jura wines.

The chapter also includes an overview of the most recent vintages and, because good Vin Jaune ages so magnificently, I list some of the best vintages of the past century. Vin Jaune merits special attention not only in terms of service but also in food matching. It is beyond the scope of this book to provide recipes or detailed food and wine matching advice, but some classic local pairings are included along with some broad concepts on how to match Jura wines with food.

Temperature and decanting

If you have the chance to buy Jura wine to age, normal cellar conditions should be observed as for any wine – a constant temperature, or one with slow fluctuations, ideally around 12–13°C but anything between 10°C and 18°C is fine. Relatively high humidity of 70–75% is also ideal, with as little light as possible. If you purchase wines made in the natural way with little or no added SO$_2$, it is essential that their storage temperature should never exceed 16°C – even for a week. If you do not have the right conditions, arrange for storage with your wine merchant or cellar storage service, or buy them at the last minute.

Temperature of service

Bear in mind that wines warm up fast once opened and in a warm room, so consider serving the wines 2–3°C cooler than the temperatures recommended below, which are the best drinking temperatures.

Sparkling wines: Serve at whatever temperature you enjoy Champagne, preferably not too chilled, to allow the flavours to emerge. 5–10°C.

Red wines: For those Poulsards made with full or semi-carbonic maceration, and for all Poulsards in summer, serve lightly chilled. In winter the more traditional Poulsards can be served somewhat warmer, as should both fruit-forward Trousseau and Pinot Noir reds, but still at a cool cellar temperature, say 11–13°C. The more structured Trousseaus and Pinot Noirs can be served a little warmer, up to 16°C.

Ouillé (topped-up) white wines: Apart from the few really fruity examples for drinking young, do not chill these wines. In the Jura producers and sommeliers serve good Savagnin *ouillé* and Chardonnays at around 12–15°C. However, if you are accustomed to chilled white wines, you may prefer them a little cooler than this, especially on a warm summer's day, but if you over-chill them you will miss out on the real character of these wines.

Oxidative Chardonnay and blends: Serve at 14–16°C or a little cooler if you prefer.

Vin Jaune and *sous voile* Savagnin: Never be tempted to chill Vin Jaune. It is much better served at a cool room temperature. Even if it creeps up to 18°C it will taste better than at 10°C. What is ideal depends on your taste and the season, but 14–17°C is a good rule.

Vin de Paille: With 70–110g/l of residual sugar, even a traditional Vin de Paille needs to be served cool at 8–10°C. Sweeter (often non-official) Vins de Paille can be served cooler than this.

Macvin: Serve chilled at 6–8°C.

Opening and decanting

If the bottle has a wax top the best method of removing it is to insert the corkscrew very gently directly into the wax. As you screw in the corkscrew the wax will gradually break up around it. Try to avoid any wax pieces falling into the wine as you draw the cork out. Once the cork is removed, gently chip the remaining wax from the open mouth of the bottle, but leave it on the sides. Jura producers and sommeliers do not recommend chipping the wax off the top of the bottle before pulling the cork, as it is laborious and can damage the bottle.

Both red and white wines from the Jura benefit from opening an hour or more before drinking, even if conventional wine wisdom asserts that there will be very little air contact with the wine if it is not decanted. Nevertheless, with Jura wines there is a marked improvement and real evolution of the wine if the bottles are opened and left at a cool room temperature (15–18°C). Perhaps the most surprising wines to benefit from opening in advance are the *ouillé* Chardonnays that have been made in Burgundian fashion, fermented and aged in *fûts* or *demi-muids*. Chardonnays from the classic Jura marl terroirs really benefit from

Decanting a young Vin Jaune is highly recommended, not because there will be a deposit but to aerate it.

at least two hours open. If you drink part of the bottle and keep the remainder cool, you will find a marked improvement in the wine's expression the following day or even two or three days later.

If there is no time to open in advance, decanting is a faster way of aerating. This is recommended for wines made highly reductively with little or no added SO_2. A modern trend is for sommeliers to vigorously shake the decanter for natural wines and this has some merit, but you need to be sure that it is a reductive wine. Take advice about the specific wine before doing this.

Young Vins Jaunes, including Château-Chalon, should be opened at least 12–24 hours ahead. If this is not possible, it is well worth decanting a Vin Jaune, especially a young one (less than ten years old). Although these wines are already oxidative, in the reductive environment of the *clavelin* bottle they close up. Once opened and kept cool with a cork in, a partly consumed *clavelin* of Vin Jaune remains as fresh as a daisy for a week, a month or sometimes longer. The biggest change occurs in the first 48 hours; thereafter development is slow and after a month some of the wine's character simply ebbs away. Only a poorly made Vin Jaune would seem maderized and that is usually noticed right away on opening, so the contact with air will make no difference. There is no need to decant an old Vin Jaune (25 years or more), but, if you do, open it a few hours beforehand and decant it just before serving.

Glasses

There is no definitive glass for any style of Jura wine. In the region the better establishments serve Vin Jaune in a good, decent-sized white wine glass. Vin de Paille is usually served in a smaller glass.

A guide to vintages

The following is a brief guide to Jura vintages since 2000. Bear in mind that these are generalizations and will inevitably go out of date.

2013: 'Catastrophe' was the word most vignerons used. Quantities were around 50% of an average year. A very cold, late, wet spring caused poor flowering of Savagnin, Trousseau and Poulsard; after much rain a hot, dry spell in July and August relieved the pressure. However, in September intermittent rain brought rot and the late harvest was rushed. Quality is good, but not great, with reds better than whites.

2012: Before 2013 this was thought to be the hardest vintage for many years and quantities were around 60–70% of an average year. Intermittent rain throughout the growing season gave rise to poor flowering, especially for Poulsard, and mildew problems. Selection was the key but there is good quality, particularly in whites.

2011: This was one of the few prolific vintages in recent years, and one of the earliest. Good-quality wines have been made in all styles, as long as producers were selective and kept yields down.

2010: Fine autumn weather saved the harvest though much selection was needed, especially in reds. Quantities were small, but there is good quality overall, particularly Chardonnays. The little Savagnin produced promises well for Vin Jaune.

2009: The very warm, dry summer and autumn gave a richness to the wines, but Chardonnays in particular were somewhat lacking in acidity. However, the reds were excellent, with good colour and fruit, and there should be fine, if rather rich, Vins Jaunes.

2008: Not an easy season, but another vintage when a fine autumn saved the harvest. White wines are better than reds and Vin Jaune is likely to be good.

2007: Fine autumn weather dried out rot after a difficult summer. Savagnin was good, giving elegant Vins Jaunes.

2006: Difficult for reds; whites, though much better, were rather soft. Due to the low acidity Vins Jaunes should be drunk relatively early.

2005: The top vintage of the 2000s so far, excellent for all wine styles with a perfect balance between ripeness and acidity. Vins Jaunes will age for many years.

2004: High quantities gave rather mixed quality, though Savagnin did best, giving good Vins Jaunes for mid-term drinking.

2003: The year of the heatwave, with the earliest harvest since the 19th century (starting mid-August). Very low quantities, but good concentration in the reds. Surprisingly pleasant Vins Jaunes to drink relatively early.

2002: A very good vintage across all styles, giving wines of structure, including Vins Jaunes, built to age well.

2001: A difficult, small vintage, but the end of the season was fair. No Château-Chalon but other decent Vins Jaunes.

2000: High quantities gave some lack of concentration and selection was the key.

The best years of the 20th century for Vin Jaune/Château-Chalon: 1999, 1996, 1995, 1990, 1989, 1988, 1985, 1983, 1979, 1976, 1969, 1966, 1964, 1959, 1955, 1952, 1949, 1947, 1945, 1942, 1934, 1929, 1921, 1911.

Macvin tends to be served in a variety of glasses, depending on when it is served during the meal.

Jura wines with food

How Jura wine is enjoyed in the region and how it is enjoyed across France and around the world appear to be quite different. Vin Jaune has been prized for centuries by top French chefs and sommeliers, both to use as a luxury ingredient in cooking and to serve as an accompaniment to classic creamy-rich dishes. It is also served with Comté either as a cheese course or as part of a cooked dish. In recent years certain Jura wine styles, such as the pale Poulsard reds and *ouillé* whites, have caught the imagination of wine lovers and sommeliers around the world, to drink on their own or with more or less any food accompaniment.

Restaurants in the region are divided between traditional and innovative. The latter often create dishes specifically to match the local wines and use modern interpretations of traditional dishes with a focus on seasonal food. Top chefs around the world, notably in the USA, Denmark and Japan, have been inspired by them. Whether oxidative or *ouillé*, white Jura wines are driven by a combination of crisp acidity, stony minerality and spicy notes. With good weight and intensity of flavours they can stand up well to a range of spicy foods, including Asian foods that are not over-spiced with chilli, as well as dishes with exotic fruits. These ideas are at the heart of innovative food matches.

Crémant is most often enjoyed as an aperitif and in the Jura Macvin is also regularly offered as an aperitif. Both are also served with dessert. Serving Crémant in the *brut* style is a peculiarly French habit that I don't think works with sweet dishes, but Macvin can match desserts well. Innovative matches are also endless with Vin de Paille, but more often than not this is best sipped on its own.

Matching Jura wine with classic regional foods and dishes

Poulet au Vin Jaune et morilles (sometimes *coq au Vin Jaune* or *Poulet de Bresse au Vin Jaune*): Chicken, cock or Bresse chicken cooked in a Vin Jaune sauce with morels. Top chefs in the region mostly use a more inexpensive *sous voile* Savagnin or oxidative white blend, only adding a glass of Vin

Poulet de Bresse with morels in a Vin Jaune sauce, the iconic dish to go alongside Vin Jaune.

Typical local dish of slices of Morteau sausages with melted Cancoillotte cheese. A Poulsard or Trousseau red wine would make a perfect pairing.

Jaune towards the end of cooking to ensure the flavour really reveals itself. The obvious accompaniment is a Vin Jaune or a great Savagnin. Other dishes with a similar sauce offered are *truite au Vin Jaune et morilles* (trout with Vin Jaune and morels) and *croûte aux morilles* (morels in a Vin Jaune sauce served in a puff pastry case).

Morteau or Montbéliard sausages: These tasty sausages are usually cooked simply in water, accompanied by boiled potatoes and melted cheese, often Cancoillotte. The classic match here is a traditionally made Poulsard or Trousseau. Charcuterie also works extremely well with Jura's indigenous reds.

Pork, rabbit and game casseroles: Many versions of rich casseroles are made with these meats, providing a perfect foil for the underlying tannins of Jura Trousseau and Pinot Noir.

Cheeses: Comté, Morbier and Bleu de Gex are all used to create dishes, as well as being served as the cheese course. In the regional restaurants cooked cheese classics such as fondue (made usually from a mix of local cheeses), *raclette* (from the local Raclette or

Morbier) or *boîte chaude* ('hot box', referring to Mont d'Or) are offered and it is very much personal preference which of the local wines to match with them, since the high acidity does a great job cutting through the cheese. Choose any white or one of the lighter reds. As far as non-cooked cheese is concerned, in general, whereas Comté matches sublimely with Vin Jaune and oxidative whites, Morbier is better with an *ouillé* white wine or a Poulsard red. Bleu de Gex is a relatively mild but quite acidic blue cheese and the best match is a Vin de Paille.

Matches with Vin de Paille and Macvin: Vin de Paille and Macvin are used in the region in a range of inventive dishes, both as ingredients and accompaniments. The sweetness and spiciness of Vin de Paille can go with anything from spiced pastries to fruit tarts and chocolate. The spirity character of Macvin makes it wonderful poured over ice-cream or sorbet; indeed it can be used, as can Vin de Paille, to make ice-cream or sorbet.

Planning a Jura wine tasting

Due to the variety of wine styles from the Jura, planning the order for tasting is always challenging. My recommendation for a tasting is a slight variation on how the wines are offered for tasting in the Jura. Start with Crémant, then reds, starting with the lighter ones, continue with *ouillé* whites, followed by oxidative or *sous voile* whites, including Vin Jaune. Finish with Vin de Paille, then Macvin. For a Jura wine dinner it depends on what the dishes are, but do not be afraid to go back and forth between reds and whites.

VISITING THE REGION

The Jura wine region is beautiful to visit any time from spring to autumn. In midwinter it can be very cold and damp and many hotels, restaurants and shops are closed from around Christmas to early February or later. Most visitors to the wine region choose to be based around Arbois, as there is a greater choice of accommodation, restaurants and shops in this lovely little town. However, the choices further south are increasing and a base near Poligny or Château-Chalon is central for producers in all Jura areas. For the main access routes into the region see p. 18. If you are travelling independently it's essential to have a car to get around the Jura – there is no public transport and taxis are scarce.

This chapter lists suggestions of where to stay and eat, along with recommended wine, food and drink shops, museums and other attractions. I have visited all of them at least once. The list is divided into the same geographical sections as Part 3, running roughly north to south and alphabetically within the same town or village. A guide to Jura's main wine festivals and key tourism websites is given at the end. To plan wine producer visits, see Part 3. There is advice on arranging visits on p. 139.

Above: At the end of the Reculée de Baumes-les-Messieurs, the Cascade des Tufs waterfall in springtime.

The symbol 🛏 is used for accommodation, 🍴 for restaurants, 🛏 🍴 for hotel-restaurants, 🛍 for shops and 🏛 for museums and other attractions. Map references refer to approximate location on the producer maps.

For each accommodation and restaurant recommendation I have given a very basic three-star rating as follows:

★★★ Classy/expensive   ★★ Good quality/mid-price   ★ Decent/inexpensive

The accommodation includes hotels, *chambres d'hôtes* (bed-and-breakfasts) and self-catering *gîtes* (cottages, villas or apartments). The bed-and-breakfasts and *gîtes* have been selected as being most suited for international travellers, with Wi-Fi and modern facilities.

Around Arbois

Château Mont Joly ★★ 🛏 🍴

6 Rue du Mont Joly, 39100 Sampans

Tel: 03 84 82 43 43

Email: reservation@ chateaumontjoly.com

Web: www.chateaumontjoly.com

Map ref: See main Jura map, p. 20

Just north of Dole, this comfortable small hotel in a refurbished classical château has a restaurant with imaginatively prepared cuisine by one-star Michelin chef-owner Romuald Fassenet. The good list of fairly traditional Jura wines is selected by Romuald's wife Catherine, sister of vigneron Marie-Pierre Chevassu-Fassenet (see p. 249).

La Chaumière ★★ 🛏 🍴

346 Avenue du Maréchal-Juin, 39100 Dole

Tel: 03 84 70 72 40

Email: lachaumiere.dole@wanadoo.fr

Web: lachaumiere-dole.fr

Map ref: See main Jura map, p. 20

Just south of Dole's centre, less than half an hour from Arbois, this comfortable hotel is an ideal stop before or after a visit to the Jura, but is also close enough to act as a base. Chef-owner Joël Cesari has a well-deserved Michelin star and offers a selection of Jura wines that is inspirational, mainly from small organic producers.

La Saline Royale – The Royal Saltworks 🏛

25610 Arc-et-Senans

Tel: 03 81 54 45 45

Web: salineroyale.com

Map ref: p. 141, B5

A UNESCO World Heritage site, this fascinating collection of buildings, designed by architect Claude Nicolas, was originally built as a concept for 'ideal living', incorporating a factory and a village. Today it is an excellent museum, covering the history of salt production in the area and Claude Nicolas' architecture and vision.

Hotel l'Edgar ★★ 🛏

10 Rue Edgar Faure, 39600 Port-Lesney

Tel: 03 84 73 82 97

Email: contact@ledgar.fr

Web: ledgar.fr

Map ref: p. 141, C4

This small, slightly eccentric hotel has been tastefully converted from a 19th-century inn. Breakfast is served in the delightfully decorated Bar Edgar, which also operates as a bar, occasional restaurant and even music venue.

Château de Germigney ★★★ 🛏 🍴

Rue Edgar Faure, 39600 Port-Lesney

Tel: 03 84 73 85 85

Email: germigney@relaischateaux.com

Web: www.chateaudegermigney.com

Map ref: p. 141, C4

In a fabulous park this sumptuous Swiss-owned Relais et Châteaux hotel offers fine accommodation and dining in a beautifully converted hunting lodge. Michelin-star chef Pierre Basso Moro is known for his inventive cuisine, with a Jurassien touch. Experienced local sommelier Christophe

Menozzi and his team offer a fine wine list and advice – food and wine matching menus are available.

Bistrot de Port Lesney ★★ ⑪

Place du 8 Mai 1945, 39330 Port-Lesney

Tel: 03 84 37 83 27

Email: contact@bistrotdeportlesney.com

Web: bistrotdeportlesney.com

Map ref: p. 141, C4

Owned by the Château de Germigney, this delightful restaurant with its red-checkered tablecloths and traditional French *bistrot* decoration offers a wide menu of classic *bistrot* and local standards, with a decent wine list. Close to the Loue river, it has a large terrace.

La Maison Salines ★★★ ⑂

8 Rue de la République, 39110 Salins-les-Bains

Tel: 03 84 37 81 97

Email: contact@lamaisonsalines.com

Web: lamaisonsalines.com

Map ref: p. 141, D3

Gîte. In this fine town house there are two very comfortable apartments accommodating 4–14 people available for weekends or longer stays. Normally offered on a self-catering basis, part or full service is available on request. There are four small studio apartments, each for two people, available in the garden wing of the house.

Hotel Charles Sander ★★ ⑂

26 Rue de la République, 39110 Salins-les-Bains

Tel: 03 84 73 36 40

Email: residencesander@wanadoo.fr

Web: residencesander.com

Map ref: p. 141, D3

Located in the middle of the small town of Salins-les-Bains, this modern hotel offers 14 spacious modern rooms, including some studios with kitchenettes. Breakfast is available and half-board deals are with nearby decent hotel-restaurant Les Deux Forts.

Le Gîte des Flâneurs du Jura ★★ ⑂

102 Grande Rue, 39600 Villette-lès-Arbois

Tel: 03 63 40 90 55

Email: arboisgite@gmail.com

Web: gite-jura-arbois.com

Map ref: p. 141, B3

Gîte. This large village house 3km from Arbois has been converted into two adjoining apartments, one for up to five people and the other up to ten. It is well equipped and very comfortable with just one drawback: the bathrooms are not close to the bedrooms. Huge terrace.

Restaurant La Balance Mets et Vins ★★ ⑪

47 Rue de Courcelles, 39600 Arbois

Tel: 03 84 37 45 00

Email: contact@labalance.fr

Web: www.labalance.fr

Map ref: p. 141, B2

Thierry Moyne and his restaurant have become the go-to place for wine visitors to Arbois. The menu is innovative and modern, with several set menus with different wines for

Bistrot des Claquets in Arbois.

each course. There is a classic *coq au Vin Jaune* and, most unusual for rural France, a tasty vegetarian menu. The wine list features several excellent vignerons.

Closerie Les Capucines ★★★ ⑂

7 Rue de Bourgogne, 39600 Arbois

Tel: 03 84 66 17 38

Email: accueil@closerielescapucines.com

Web: closerielescapucines.com

Map ref: p. 141, B2

Bed-and-breakfast. Patricia Chatelain has refurbished this town house in the middle of Arbois to create what for the Jura is a luxurious place to stay. With a pleasant garden and pool, it is within easy walking distance of restaurants and shops.

Hotel Les Caudalies ★★ ⑂ ⑪

20 Avenue Pasteur, 39600 Arbois

Tel: 03 84 73 06 54

Email: contact@lescaudalies.fr

Web: lescaudalies.fr

Map ref: p. 141, B2

A fine town house close to the centre of Arbois, with the garden stretching down to the Cuisance river, Les Caudalies has nine practically furnished rooms of different sizes. The restaurant is recommended and offers the right sort of mix of well-prepared food to show off the very good wine list put together by the sommelier-owner, the aptly named Philippe Troussard.

Hotel des Cépages ★ ⊨ ⸾⸾

5 Route de Villette, 39600 Arbois

Tel: 03 84 66 25 25

Email: contact@hotel-des-cepages.com

Web: hotel-des-cepages.com

Map ref: p. 141, B2

With 33 rooms, this simple hotel is useful in midwinter when most of the other nearby hotels are closed. Aimed mainly at business people and groups, the owner and his staff are unfailingly helpful and polite. There is a basic restaurant open on weekdays.

Bistrot des Claquets ★ ⸾⸾

Place de Faramand, 39600 Arbois

Tel: 03 84 66 04 19

Map ref: p. 141, B2

This is where you should bump into a famous vigneron or two. With a zinc-topped bar and traditional small *bistrot* feel, it is ideal for lunch (no food in the evenings). There is one menu, with a small buffet entrée, one or occasionally two main

courses and a cake or tart for dessert, all very much home-cooked style, tasty and filling, only for meat lovers.

La Cave de Comté ⸾⸾

44 Grande Rue, 39600 Arbois

Tel: 03 84 66 09 53

Map ref: p. 141, B2

Primarily a cheese shop, excellent hams and local sausages are also available, along with a range of local preserved goods and delicatessen items. A few tables are available for lunch from a small menu of simple but hearty open sandwiches, salads and a couple of hot dishes, together with a selection of good local wines.

La Finette ★ ⸾⸾

22 Avenue Pasteur, 39600 Arbois

Tel: 03 84 66 06 78

Email: info@finette.fr

Web: finette.fr

Map ref: p. 141, B2

Open all year, the large La Finette restaurant was founded by Henri Maire (see 'History', p. 120) but is now privately owned. The menu offers filling Franche-Comté food with well-executed cooked cheese and sausage dishes, more typical of somewhere in the Jura mountains. The traditional list of local wines reveals one or two good finds. The walls are covered with Henri Maire and Jura wine memorabilia.

Fruitière du Plateau Arboisien ⸾⸾

1 Rue des Fossés, 39600 Arbois

Tel: 03 84 66 09 71

Email: contact@comte-arbois.com

Web: comte-arbois.com

Map ref: p. 141, B2

A useful shop near Château Béthanie, home to the Arbois Fruitière, where you can buy Comté, other cheeses produced by the cooperative and a range of local food and drink products. The cheeses are very good value.

Hirsinger Chocolatier et Pâtissier ⸾⸾

38 Place de la Liberté, 39600 Arbois

Tel: 03 84 66 06 97

Email: contact@hirsinger.com

Web: chocolat-hirsinger.com

Map ref: p. 141, B2

Third-generation Edouard Hirsinger is one of the most famous *chocolatiers* in France. All the delicious chocolates are made on the premises with some very inventive recipes; there are also chocolate works of art and a fabulous range of cakes and pastries. Under the arches there are a few tables where you can enjoy a pastry snack or light lunch with coffee or a glass of wine.

Les Jardins de St-Vincent ⸾⸾

49 Grande Rue, 39600 Arbois

Tel: 03 84 66 21 75

Email: contact@lesjardinsdestvincent.com

Web: lesjardinsdestvincent.com

Map ref: p. 141, B2

Owned by Stéphane Planche, former chief sommelier for Restaurant Jean-Paul Jeunet, this shop offers an eclectic selection of Jura wines from

Musée de la Vigne et du Vin 🏛

Château Pécauld, 39600 Arbois

Tel: 03 84 66 40 45

Email: museevignevin@wanadoo.fr

Map ref: p. 141, B2

A small museum where you can learn all about the wines of the Jura, in particular Vin Jaune. There is a display of old vineyard and cellar tools, and some particularly good black and white photographs of vignerons. Wine-related art exhibitions are held here regularly too.

Bistrot de la Tournelle ★ ‖

5 Petite Place, 39600 Arbois

Tel: 03 84 66 25 76

Email: domainedelatournelle@wanadoo.fr

Web: domainedelatournelle.com

Map ref: p. 141, B2

Hard to categorize or give a star rating, the delightful *bistrot* by the River Cuisance run by Evelyne and Pascal Clairet (see 'Producers', p. 195) is open from around 20 June to 1 September. It has to close when it's raining, as all the tables are in the garden. At lunchtime and in the evening delicious small plates of food are served with their own wine and a few others from friends across France.

smaller, mostly organic vignerons who are sometimes hard to visit. There are usually several wines open to taste and it doubles as a wine bar offering small plates.

Hotel-Restaurant Jean-Paul Jeunet ★★★ ⊨ ‖

9 Rue de l'Hôtel de Ville, 39600 Arbois

Tel: 03 84 66 05 67

Email: reservation@jeanpauljeunet.com

Web: jeanpauljeunet.com

Map ref: p. 141, B2

For many years this has been the top local restaurant and remains the only two-star Michelin restaurant in Franche-Comté. Jean-Paul Jeunet (see 'History', p. 122) and his wife Nadine have created a lovely ambience in which to eat the exquisitely prepared food. The wine list is large and spectacular, with a focus on organic producers and with many old vintages available, including Vin Jaune. The hotel is rather pricey for the size and style of rooms but the annexe down the road in Jean-Paul's mother's house is cheaper and more homely.

Maison de Pasteur 🏛

83 Rue de Courcelles, 39600 Arbois

Tel: 03 84 66 11 72

Map ref: p. 141, B2

This little house by the river was Pasteur's home. His private apartments and laboratory can be visited with a guided tour. A fascinating visit. The Académie des Sciences has plans to extend this museum over the coming years.

Vins et Vinaigres 🍷

16 Grande Rue, 39600 Arbois

Tel: 06 07 03 25 08

Email: ph.gonet@wanadoo.fr

Web: philippe-gonet.fr

Map ref: p. 141, B2

Philippe Gonet has been the only producer of vinegar in Arbois for over 15 years, most particularly from Vin Jaune. He sells a range of extraordinarily good vinegars as well as carefully selected oils, including local walnut oil. He also sells a few local wines under his own label.

Le Grapiot ★★ 🍴

Rue Bagier, 39600 Pupillin

Tel: 03 84 37 49 44

Email: julieetsamuel@legrapiot.com

Web: www.legrapiot.com

Map ref: p. 141, B2

Having bravely extended this restaurant, the young owners, Samuel and Julie Richardet, do a wonderful job in the kitchen and the interconnecting dining rooms, offering friendly and efficient service. This could be the best-value restaurant in the region and has an ever-growing wine list showing off the best of Pupillin and beyond. If you don't want to drive, Pupillin has several simple bed-and-breakfasts, all within easy walking distance.

Around Poligny

Epicurea 🍷

5 Place des Déportés, 39800 Poligny

Tel: 03 84 37 16 05

Map ref: p. 217, D3

With a focus on organic wines and top-class Comté and other cheeses, this shop in the middle of Poligny is owned by Philippe Bouvret, whose cheese-ageing business Essencia also has a shop at 5 Place Notre Dame. Working with local organic vignerons, he has created his own Jura wine label. There is a small bar with a few wines available by the glass.

Les Jardins sur Glantine ★★ 🛏

30 Grande Rue, 39800 Poligny

Tel: 03 63 86 50 78

Email: l.bindernagel@gmail.com

Web: jardinsurglantine.natidees.com

Map ref: p. 217, D3

Bed-and-breakfast. The middle of Poligny has no hotel worth recommending, but there is an unusual alternative. Nathalie Eigenschenk and vigneron Ludwig Bindernagel of Chais du Vieux Bourg (see p. 220) restored this handsome old vigneron's house and offer two large suites, each with two bedrooms, and a gorgeous garden. The couple are very happy to provide tastings and excellent meals on request.

Les Logis du Théâtre ★★★ 🛏

17 Rue du Théâtre, 39800 Poligny

Tel: 03 84 37 09 27

Email: jennifer.russell@free.fr

Web: homeaway.co.uk/p1137058

Map ref: p. 217, D3

Gîte. Despite being in the centre of Poligny this comfortable, recently refurbished *gîte* is very quiet, with a pleasant garden. Well equipped, it offers four bedrooms, each pair sharing a bathroom. Two practical little studios are available June–August. Owned by an Anglo-French couple, long-term residents of Poligny, who could not be more helpful in sharing local advice.

Fruitière Les Délices du Plateau 🍷

1 Route de la Fied, 39800 Plasne

Tel: 03 84 37 16 67

Email: delicesduplateau@wanadoo.fr

Web: www.comte.com/plasne

Map ref: p. 217, C2

This village cheese cooperative is on the Premier Plateau directly above Poligny. It has a high reputation for the quality of its Comté, the principal production, and the shop sells a range of cheeses and other local products. At 9am each day in summer, and by reservation at other times, you can watch the cheesemakers at work and hear the process explained in French.

Le Bistrot de la Mère Simone ★ 🍴

84 Rue de l'Asile, Place du Village, 39230 Passenans

Tel: 03 84 44 38 99

Email: bechinard@hotmail.fr

Web: www.bistrot-mere-simone.fr

Map ref: p. 217, B2

This brightly decorated little café-*bistrot* in the heart of Passenans provides an ideal

---

and very pleasant place to stop for lunch on a day of vineyard visits, with generous portions of home-made food and friendly service. Also open evenings.

Domaine du Revermont ★★ ⌂ ⊺⊺

Route du Revermont, 39230 Passenans

Tel: 03 84 44 61 02

Email: contact@domaine-du-revermont.fr

Web: domaine-du-revermont.fr

Map ref: p. 217, B2

Close to Passenans' vineyards, this is the largest hotel in the area and somewhat impersonal, but offers good-quality rooms and a good breakfast, as well as a decent-size outdoor swimming pool. It is very conveniently situated for visiting vignerons and local sites of interest. The restaurant has a good local wine list to go with well-prepared simple cuisine.

Château-Chalon, the Upper Seille and L'Etoile

Hotel-Restaurant La Fontaine ★ ⌂ ⊺⊺

D 1083, Montchauvrot, 39230 Mantry

Tel: 03 84 85 50 02

Email: contact@hotel-lafontaine.fr

Web: hotel-lafontaine.fr

Map ref: p. 235, B4

Set back from the main road,

this budget hotel is fine for a short stay and is very well situated. It also has the great advantage of being open all year, with the surprisingly good restaurant open daily.

Château d'Arlay 🏛

2 Route de Proby, 39140 Arlay

Tel: 03 84 85 04 22

Email: chateau@arlay.com

Web: arlay.com

Map ref: p. 235, B3

This historic 18th-century château and wine producer (see 'Producers', p. 237) is well worth a visit. From May to October the vast park is open to visit and from June to mid-September the interior of the château and cellars can be toured, along with beautiful innovative gardens.

Hostellerie Saint Germain ★★ ⌂ ⊺⊺

635 Grande Rue, 39210 Saint-Germain-lès-Arlay

Tel: 03 84 44 60 91

Email: reservation@hostelleriesaintgermain.com

Web: hostelleriesaintgermain.com

Map ref: p. 235, B3

This restaurant, in a refurbished 18th-century coaching inn, offers the best food in this part of the Jura wine region, with seasonal menus that work well with the wines on the extensive local wine list. There is an especially good selection of Vins Jaunes. Both the restaurant and the hotel were extensively renovated and the hotel was enlarged in 2013 to create 12 modern rooms and suites.

Restaurant Au Petit Victorien ★ ⊺⊺

Rue de Beaumont, 39210 Voiteur

Tel: 03 84 44 18 63

Map ref: p. 235, D3

At the foot of the Château-Chalon vineyards, the restaurant is in a large, newly built wooden chalet-farmhouse with a sizeable terrace. There is a big choice of menus or à la carte, with excellent-value local wines and friendly, efficient service. The owners offer a basic but convenient gîte next door.

Les 16 Quartiers ★★ ⊺⊺

Place de l'Eglise, 39210 Château-Chalon

Tel: 03 84 44 68 23

Map ref: p. 235, D3

This small, cosy restaurant next to the church is simply decorated and has a large, sunny terrace. If you stop for lunch, be prepared – even in this touristy village only full meals are served, not snacks, so allow plenty of time. The food from the small menu is very good and the wine list highlights excellent local vignerons.

Fromageries Vagne 🧺

Le Chalet, Rue St-Jean, 39210 Château-Chalon

Tel: 03 84 44 92 25

Email: fromagerievagne@orange.fr

Web: comte-vagne.com

Map ref: p. 235, D3

Excellent cheese shop in old Comté maturation cellars, with some of the best Comté available. Other local cheeses, foods and a few wines are also available.

Maison de la Haute Seille 🏛

Place de l'Eglise, 39210 Château-Chalon

Tel: 03 84 42 76 05

Email: infos@hauteseille.com

Web: tourisme-hauteseille.fr/en/the-maison-de-la-haute-seille.htm

Map ref: p. 235, D3

In the middle of Château-Chalon this old renovated house has been converted into a fascinating museum and information centre. It provides a great way to discover more about the region. The vaulted cellar shows a film about the making of Vin Jaune.

La Maison Vincent ★★ 🛏

Rue de la Tour, 39210 Château-Chalon

Tel: 03 84 44 60 48

Email: berthet-bondet@orange.fr

Web: berthet-bondet.net/en/holiday-cottage.htm

Map ref: p. 235, D3

Gîte. Vignerons Jean and

Vagne cheese shop in Château-Chalon.

Chantal Berthet-Bondet (see p. 246) restored an outbuilding next to their grand manor house to create this large *gîte* with four bedrooms, unusually each with an en suite bathroom. It is a very comfortable choice.

Le Relais des Abbesses ★★ 🛏

36 Rue de la Roche, 39210 Château-Chalon

Tel: 03 84 44 98 56

Email: contact@relais-des-abbesses.fr

Web: relais-des-abbesses.fr

Map ref: p. 235, D3

Bed-and-breakfast. Owners Agnès and Gérard Vidal restored this large, perfectly situated Château-Chalon house, which has four guest rooms of reasonable size, all with private bathrooms. A decent *table d'hôte* dinner is available on request.

Le Grand Jardin ★ 🛏 🍴

6 Place Guillaume de Poupet, Rue des Grands Jardins, 39210 Baume-les-Messieurs

Tel: 03 84 44 68 37

Email: contact@legrandjardin.fr

Web: www.legrandjardin.fr

Map ref: p. 235, D1

Bed-and-breakfast and restaurant. A real find in the centre of this idyllic village: in the small restaurant you will find fresh décor and ingredients and a warm welcome. The menus are well balanced and there is a good little selection of local wines. The three large rooms are simple.

The site of Baume-les-Messieurs 🏛

39210 Baume-les-Messieurs

Map ref: p. 235, D1

A visit to this ancient village deep in its *reculée* should not be missed. In summer you can visit the abbey and church in the middle of the village and in winter simply wander around the abbey courtyard. It is also well worth driving to the end of this blind valley to see the pretty river and waterfall, and to gaze up at the steep cliffs. In summer the *grottes* (caves) are open to visitors. There are also several spectacular viewpoints from above.

Le Relais de la Perle ★★ 🛏

184 Route de Voiteur, 39210 Le Vernois

Tel: 03 84 25 95 52

Email: contact@lerelaisdelaperle.fr

Web: lerelaisdelaperle.fr

Map ref: p. 235, D2

Bed-and-breakfast. Conveniently situated by the road running from Lons-le-Saunier to Voiteur, this former vigneron's house has five comfortable bedrooms in the refurbished winery. Nathalie offers a good welcome and a tasty breakfast in the main house.

Around Lons-le-Saunier

Hotel Parenthèse ★★ 🛏 🍴

186 Chemin du Pin, 39570 Chille

Tel: 03 84 47 55 44

Email: reservation@hotel-jura.com

Web: hotel-jura.com

Map ref: p. 274, C3

A modern, quiet three-star hotel, the Parenthèse has rather quirky individually designed rooms, but it makes a good base for touring the vineyards. The restaurant is decent if unexciting, but with advice offered about the wide choice of local wines. Outdoor swimming pool.

Le Cèdre Bleu ★ 🛏

198 Route de Montaigu, 39000 Lons-le-Saunier

Tel: 03 84 43 99 36

Email: gisele.ehrlich@orange.fr

Web: www.lecedrebleu-lonslesaunier.com

Map ref: p. 274, B2

Bed-and-breakfast. On the edge of Lons on the road towards Montaigu, this fine rambling town house has five guest rooms of varying sizes with small bathrooms. The rooms are basic, full of old furniture and very fancy soft furnishings, but everything functions well and the welcome is sincere, with a typical French breakfast.

La Comédie ★★ 🍴

65 Rue de l'Agriculture, 39000 Lons-le-Saunier

Tel: 03 84 24 20 66

Email: resto.lacomedie@orange.fr

Web: www.restaurant-la-comedie.fr

Map ref: p. 274, B2

Located by the delightful historic vignerons' square, this is the only restaurant of real note in the middle of Lons-le-Saunier. You will find a small choice of typical French fare here with a twist of Jura, and fish is a speciality. The wine list is short but carefully chosen.

Hotel Val de Sorne ★★ 🛏 🍴

39570 Vernantois

Tel: 03 84 43 04 80

Email: resa@ghrvds.com

Web: valdesorne.fr

Map ref: p. 274, C1

Less than ten minutes from Lons in the beautiful Sorne Valley outside the village of Vernantois, this hotel offers facilities not available elsewhere in the Jura wine region – top golf course, outdoor pool, sauna and fitness room. Rooms are comfortable, the service friendly and the restaurant more than decent.

Sud Revermont

La Maison du Revermont ★ 🍴

23 Route Nationale, 39190 Beaufort

Tel: 03 84 25 12 82

Email: maisondurevermont@orange.fr

Web: restaurant-lamaisondurevermont.com

Map ref: p. 283, D4

At the Percée du Vin Jaune in Ruffey-sur-Seille in 2011. The Sunday morning procession of the Ambassadeurs des Vins Jaunes, carrying the barrel to church for the blessing.

Located in a mini-shopping mall by the main road, this is the only really reliable restaurant in the Sud Revermont. It offers a good refuge and avoids having to go back to Lons-le-Saunier or St-Amour to find something to eat. Local and classic French cuisine is simply presented.

La Renouée ★★ 🛏

5 Rue de la Mairie, 39190 Maynal

Tel: 03 84 44 46 99

Email: reservation@larenouee.com

Web: larenouee.com

Map ref: p. 283, A1

Bed-and-breakfast in a recently refurbished house. The four en suite bedrooms are small but bright and this is a life-saver if you want to visit wine producers in the Sud Revermont, south of Lons-le-Saunier. An ample breakfast is provided and a simple dinner of local dishes is available on request.

Festivals

In summer there are many festivals in the wine region that may include wine tastings, some linked with concerts. The following, including two in winter, are the key wine festivals that take place every year.

La Pressée du Vin de Paille

Arlay on the Sunday closest to 22 January.

This small but growing festival is linked with the festival of Saint Vincent celebrated by the vignerons and residents of Arlay, whose church's patron saint is Saint Vincent. The festival celebrates the pressing of the grapes to make Vin de

Paille and twice a day there is a demonstration using an old press, with the juice offered to taste. A handful of vignerons have tasting stands and there are some food stands too.

La Percée du Vin Jaune

Takes place in a different town or village each year on the first weekend of February.

Web: percee-du-vin-jaune.com

The most important wine festival in the Jura, La Percée du Vin Jaune (see 'History', p. 126) attracts up to 40,000 people over the two days, but despite the crowds it is hugely enjoyable. The festival celebrates the release of the 'new' vintage of Vin Jaune (6 years and 3 months after the harvest) and the main ceremony and processions are on Sunday morning. An auction of old wines takes place on the Saturday afternoon. From midday each day around 70 wine producers offer their wines for tasting and sale in the cellars of houses in the village. Food and street entertainment are also on site. Shuttle buses are laid on from designated parking areas.

Fête du Biou

Arbois on the first Sunday of September. Pupillin on third Sunday of September.

The Biou festival in Arbois has an ancient history and the town has applied for it to be recognized by UNESCO. The main procession and blessing in the church celebrate the biblical story of the return of the Israelites from Canaan (the land of plenty) carrying the Eschol, a huge bunch of grapes, known in French as the Biou. It is worth arriving by 9.30am to join

the locals supporting the many well-known vignerons, dressed uncharacteristically in suits and ties, who accompany the four men carrying the Biou from the Maison de Vercel opposite the Maison du Pasteur to the Eglise St-Just, where the Biou is hung from the rafters. The vignerons make the Biou the previous day (go to the Maison de Vercel in the afternoon), stringing together bunches of white and red grapes. There is a big town parade after the church service, followed by a free aperitif offered by the vignerons, who line up their wines along the Rue de Bourgogne. Other events take place on the same weekend in Arbois, such as an interesting wild mushroom exhibition and a funfair. The event is more low key in Pupillin, and latterly four women vignerons have carried the Biou to the church.

Tourism websites

The official tourist sites provide the latest information about events and festivals and give more details about places to visit in the Jura and Franche-Comté.

Jura tourism: jura-tourism.com

The official Jura tourism site – multilingual.

Franche-Comté tourism: franche-comte.org

Regional tourism portal – multilingual.

Wine Travel Guides: winetravelguides.com

On-line guides to visiting the Jura, including GPS codes and interactive maps, written by Wink Lorch.

APPENDIX 1:
ESSENTIAL RULES FOR THE APPELLATIONS (AOCS)

The following rules have been extracted from the *cahier des charges* (specifications) for each AOC. They are the ones that I believe to be the most essential, and those that are specific to the region rather than general throughout France. These rules expand on those outlined in the chapter 'The appellations', pp. 21–5, which also includes a summary of the IGP and Vin de France categories. Not included are the rules for testing. Those for AOC Château-Chalon are outlined on p. 22.

General rules applicable to all Jura AOCs but note exceptions and specific rules below

1) The communes (villages/towns) with vineyards entitled to AOC Côtes du Jura, AOC Crémant du Jura and AOC Macvin are in the following list. Those eligible for AOC Arbois are marked (A), AOC Château-Chalon (C) and AOC L'Etoile (E):

Abergement-le-Grand (A), Abergement-le-Petit, Aiglepierre, Arbois (A), Arlay, Les Arsures (A), L'Aubépin, Augea, Aumont, Balanod, Baume-les-Messieurs, Beaufort, Bersaillin, Blois-sur-Seille, Brainans, Bréry, Buvilly, Césancey, Champagne-sur-Loue, La Chapelle-sur-Furieuse, Château-Chalon (C), Chazelles, Chevreaux, Chille, Chilly-le-Vignoble, Conliège, Courbouzon, Cousance, Cramans, Cuisia, Darbonnay, Digna, Domblans (C), L'Etoile (E), Frébuans, Frontenay, Gevingey, Gizia, Grange-de-Vaivre, Grozon, Grusse, Ladoye-sur-Seille, Lavigny, Lons-le-Saunier, Le Louverot, Macornay, Mantry, Marnoz, Mathenay (A), Maynal, Menétru-le-Vignoble (C), Mesnay (A), Messia-sur-Sorne, Miéry, Moiron, Molamboz (A), Monay, Montagna-le-Reconduit, Montaigu, Montain, Montholier, Montigny-les-Arsures (A), Montmorot, Mouchard, Nanc-lès-Saint-Amour, Nevy-sur-Seille (C), Orbagna, Pagnoz, Pannessières, Passenans, Perrigny, Le Pin, Plainoiseau (E), Les Planches-près-Arbois (A), Poligny, Port-Lesney, Pretin, Pupillin (A), Quintigny (E), Revigny, Rotalier, Ruffey-sur-Seille, Saint-Amour, Saint-Cyr-Montmalin (A), Saint-Didier (E), Saint-Germain-lès-Arlay, Saint-Jean-d'Etreux, Saint-Lamain, Saint-Laurent-la-Roche, Saint-Lothain, Sainte-Agnès, Salins-les-Bains, Sellières, Toulouse-le-Château, Tourmont, Trenal, Vadans (A), Vaux-sur-Poligny, Vercia, Vernantois, Le Vernois, Villeneuve-sous-Pymont, Villette-lès-Arbois (A), Vincelles, Voiteur.

2) Permitted grape varieties for white wines are Chardonnay and Savagnin (and additionally Pinot Noir, Poulsard (Ploussard) and Trousseau). Permitted grape varieties for rosé and red wines are Pinot Noir, Poulsard (Ploussard), Trousseau (and in addition white varieties).

3) Before planting, vines must have been treated with water at 50°C for 45 minutes.

4) The minimum vine-planting density is 5,000 vines/ha except for vines planted on terraces.

5) Permitted pruning systems: Single or Double Guyot or Cordon de Royat. Buds limited to 20 per vine.

6) The height of the leaf canopy must be at least 1m and at least 0.6 times the distance between rows (this is particularly relevant for those seeking derogations for wide-spaced vines with fewer than 5,000 vines/ha as in 4) above).

7) There must not be more than 20% of dead vines in any parcel.

8) Cultivation rules since 2009 to protect the surrounding environment: new plantings must have a grassed-down turning area at the end of each row of at least 3m for rows longer than 30m and at least 1m for shorter rows. Vine rows on slopes of more than 15% must be no longer than 70m unless there is a system to collect water runoff.

9) The maximum average yield of grapes per parcel of vines is set at 11,000kg/ha.

10) The start of harvest is fixed by a local mandate.

11) The maximum base yield for white wines is set at 60hl/ha (with a maximum ceiling granted according to the year at 72hl/ha) and 55hl/ha for rosé and red wines (with the ceiling at 66hl/ha). For grapes from terraced vineyards with higher-density vines a calculation is applied to work out the maximum yield.

12) The minimum must weight for white grapes is 161g/l and for red grapes 153g/l.

13) The minimum natural potential alcohol (before chaptalization) must be 10.5% for white wines and 10% for rosé and red wines. The maximum after chaptalization is 14% for white wines and 13.5% for rosé and red wines. (However, note that chaptalization is limited by EU rules according to climate zone, so grapes picked at a potential of 10.5% would never become a wine of 14%.)

14) Residual sugars (glucose and sucrose) may not exceed 3g/l (except for Vin de Paille).

15) Specific oenological practices: use of oenological carbon in the making of rosés is not permitted; the use of oak chips is not permitted; concentration techniques are allowed for musts for making red wines – partial concentration is limited to 10%.

Rules specific to individual AOCs in addition to the general rules above

Specific rules for AOC Côtes du Jura (see below for specific rules concerning the production of Vin Jaune and Vin de Paille)

1) Still white, rosé and red wines may be made, as well as Vin Jaune and Vin de Paille.

2) As an *aide-mémoire* (not specifically stated in the rules), note that wines may also be sold under AOC Côtes du Jura in these circumstances: when only some of the grapes for a cuvée have been grown within AOC Arbois; for all styles of wines apart from Vin Jaune from AOC Château-Chalon; and for rosé and red wines made from grapes from AOC L'Etoile.

Specific rules for AOC Arbois and AOC Arbois-Pupillin (see below for specific rules concerning the production of Vin Jaune and Vin de Paille)

1) Still white, rosé and red wines may be made as well as Vin Jaune and Vin de Paille.

2) AOC Arbois-Pupillin may be used only for wines from vineyards in Pupillin. Wines from these vineyards may choose to use AOC Arbois instead.

Specific rules for AOC L'Etoile (see below for specific rules concerning the production of Vin Jaune and Vin de Paille)

1) Only Chardonnay, Savagnin and Poulsard (for Vin de Paille) may be used for wines made under this AOC.

2) White wines only may be made, including Vin Jaune and Vin de Paille.

Specific rules for Vin Jaune (AOCs Arbois, Côtes du Jura, L'Etoile and Château-Chalon)

1) Only Savagnin may be used for Vin Jaune.

2) Vin Jaune must be aged in oak barrels, without topping up, until 15 December of the sixth year after the harvest, including at least 60 months *sous voile*.

3) Vin Jaune can be sold only after 1 January of the seventh year after the harvest.

4) Vin Jaune must be bottled in a *clavelin* bottle containing 62cl.

Specific rules for AOC Château-Chalon (in addition to those above for other Vins Jaunes)

1) AOC Château-Chalon is reserved for Vin Jaune.

2) The maximum base yield is 30hl/ha (with a maximum ceiling granted according to the year at 50hl/ha). Special rules apply for grapes from vines on terraces.

3) The maximum average yield of grapes per parcel of vines is set at 8,000kg/ha.

4) The minimum natural potential alcohol (before chaptalization) must be 12%. The maximum after chaptalization is 14%.

Specific rules for Vin de Paille (AOCs Arbois, Côtes du Jura, L'Etoile)

1) Only Chardonnay, Savagnin, Poulsard and Trousseau may be used for Vin de Paille.

2) Grapes designated for Vin de Paille must be hand-harvested.

3) The maximum yield for grapes for Vin de Paille is 20hl/ha, whatever the conditions.

4) Grapes for Vin de Paille must be dried on straw or in boxes, or suspended from rafters, for a minimum of six weeks in a well-ventilated room without heating. The use of a fan is permitted.

5) At pressing the Vin de Paille must have minimum 320g/l sugar and a maximum of 420g/l.

6) Vin de Paille must be aged until at least 15 November of the third year after the harvest, with at least 18 months of that period spent in barrel.

7) The final Vin de Paille wine must be minimum 14% (with a minimum 19% total potential alcohol, including residual sugar).

8) Vin de Paille may not be sold before 1 December of the third year after the harvest.

Specific rules for AOC Crémant du Jura

1) AOC Crémant du Jura is white or rosé sparkling wine from base wine harvested from vineyards in the communes listed for other Jura AOCs, subject to the same cultivation rules.

2) Grape varieties allowed include Pinot Gris in addition to the standard five Jura varieties. White Crémant must be from base wines made from a minimum of 70% Chardonnay, Pinot Noir and/or Trousseau. The base wine for rosé Crémant must be from base wines made from a minimum of 50% red or *gris* grapes.

3) Vineyards must be declared as being specifically designated for Crémant by 1 June before the harvest.

4) The maximum average yield of grapes per parcel of vines is set at 14,500kg/ha.

5) The maximum base yield for grapes for Crémant is set at 74hl/ha (with a maximum ceiling granted according to the year at 80hl/ha).

6) Harvest must be by hand.

7) The minimum must weight for white grapes is 144g/l.

8) Base wines must be from musts where a maximum of 100 litres has been extracted from 150kg.

9) The minimum natural potential alcohol (before chaptalization) of the must is 9%. The maximum alcohol following disgorgement must not exceed 13% if the base wine was chaptalized.

10) For white Crémant whole grapes must be pressed.

11) The press must not have a central screw or chains.

12) The traditional method is used, with second fermentation in the bottle and rules following those for all Crémants, which include: the base wine must not be bottled before 1 December following harvest; the wine must undergo a minimum nine

months of lees contact before disgorgement; at disgorgement the minimum pressure must be 3.5 atmospheres.

13) Crémant du Jura may not be sold until at least 12 months after bottling.

Specific rules for AOC Macvin du Jura

1) AOC Macvin du Jura is white, rosé or red fortified wine made from grape juice of any of the five Jura grapes and subject to the same cultivation rules as AOC Côtes du Jura with the same yield requirements. It is mixed with *marc* from the producer's own production.

2) At harvest the grapes must have a minimum sugar content of 170g/l.

3) There are certain rules about the addition of the *marc* (fortification). The must may not be chaptalized or enriched

with sugar. It must not be concentrated and it cannot be filtered. It should have a potential alcohol of at least 10%. The must may have begun fermentation but it must have a minimum of 153g/l sugar at the point of fortification. This must take place around harvest time. Musts should not be stored for later use.

4) The *marc* used for fortification must have been distilled from grapes from the same producer. It must be 52% alc and aged in oak barrels for a minimum of 14 months before being added to the Macvin.

5) The final Macvin blend must be aged for a minimum of ten months in oak barrels.

6) Macvin for sale must be of minimum 16% alc and maximum 22% alc.

7) Macvin may be sold from 20 September the year following the harvest.

APPENDIX 2:
ABBREVIATIONS, CONVERSIONS AND PRONUNCIATIONS

Abbreviations and conversions

This book uses the metric system as used in France. The following gives the abbreviations used, if any, and conversions when possible.

Temperature

°C degrees Celsius (official conversion when temperature above freezing: $°C × 1.8 + 32 = °F$) Examples: 5°C = 41°F; 10°C = 50°F; 15°C = 59°F; 20°C = 68°F.

Volume/weight

1 litre (0.22 imperial gallons or 0.264 US gallons)
g/l grams per litre
mg/l milligrams per litre

Area/yield

ha hectare (2.47 acres)

hl/ha hectolitres per hectare (conversion is not exact, as other measurements use weight of grapes rather than volume of grape juice) Example: 50hl/ha is approximately 7 tonnes/ha or 3 tonnes/acre

Distance

km kilometre (0.62 miles)
m metre (3.28 feet)
mm millimetres (0.039 inches)

Pronunciation guide

This pronunciation guide is for key Jura names and the most commonly used technical wine terms used in the Jura. The hyphen indicates a new syllable or slight pause.

Arbois [arr-bwa]
Château-Chalon [shat-oh-shalon]
clavelin [cla-ver-la(n)]
Comté [kor(n)-tay]

Côtes du Jura [coat doo zhew-rah]
Crémant du Jura [kremon doo zhew-rah}
L'Etoile [letwaal]
Jura [zhew-rah]
Lons-le-Saunier [lawns-le-sewn-e-ay]
Macvin du Jura [mack-van doo zhew-rah]
marc [marr]
Montigny-les-Arsures [mont-ee-nyee-lays-arse-ure]
ouillé/ouillage [oowee-yay/oowee-yarge]
Ploussard [ploo-ssar]
Poulsard [pull-ssar]
Pupillin [poop-y-an]
Savagnin [sav-a-nyan]
sous voile [sooh vwahl]
Trousseau [true-so]
Vin Jaune [van zhown]
Vin de Paille [van der pie-y]
voile [vwahl]
Voiteur [vwa-ter]

APPENDIX 3:
WINES INSPIRED BY THE JURA

As we saw in Part 1 'All about the wines', Vin Jaune and other oxidative wines have a certain amount in common with the other great oxidative wines of the world – Sherry and Tokaji. Additionally, it was mentioned that two of Jura's indigenous grapes, Savagnin and Trousseau, have been grown for many years under other names elsewhere in Europe, notably as Traminer, Païen or Heida for Savagnin, and as Bastardo or Merenzao for Trousseau. Poulsard is also grown in the Bugey area to the south of the Jura. It is beyond the scope of this book to discuss wines that have overlaps with Jura wines, but this brief appendix focuses on a handful of New World wines inspired by the wines of the Jura.

Savagnin from Australia:

That Savagnin is grown in Australia is the result of a wonderful accident. Several growers there, interested in making wines from grapes beyond the well-known varieties, had planted Alvarinho (the Portuguese variety, known as Albariño in Spain) and were making a fresh white wine, inspired by the wines made from this grape in Galicia, northwest Spain. According to the book *Wine Grapes*, mislabelling or misidentification of vines in Galicia, subsequently perpetuated in France and Australia, led to some of what was thought to have been Alvarinho/Albariño being actually Savagnin.

After this was discovered through DNA testing in 2005, confirmed only in 2009,

the majority of Australian producers making 'Albariño' were forced to relabel their ranges as Savagnin or its other name Traminer, something they were initially not happy about, as Albariño wines were fashionable at the time and Traminer was often used as the name for Gewürztraminer. With the recent rise in interest in Jura wines in Australia, a few of these producers have seized the opportunity to make a Jura-inspired Savagnin, *ouillé* in the majority of cases, but a few are experimenting with *sous voile* Savagnin too.

The only wine that I have tasted is the 2011 *sous voile* Savagnin from Crittenden Estate in Victoria, the first the winery had made (before it made only a topped-up version, called Tributo). One barrel was made and aged for around two years, not topped up. From a cool year giving plenty of natural acidity, the wine is called Cri de Coeur Savagnin Sous Voile and the 2011 showed classic lemon characteristics with an attractive oxidative character, not that dissimilar to a young Savagnin pulled out early from Vin Jaune ageing.

Savagnin from Canada: The
long-established Château des Charmes winery in the Niagara Peninsula, owned by the originally French Bosc family, has grown Savagnin since 1993 and made its first icewine from the variety in 2006. It was made not at all as a *vin de glace* might have been in the Jura in days gone by (simply the term for making a wine picked after the first frost): the Château des Charmes icewine is made from

properly frozen grapes and ends up with 9% alcohol and over 250g/l of sugar, but with great balancing acidity. Quite delicious.

A handful of other wineries in Niagara have Savagnin too, including the boutique John Howard Cellars, which makes a very small amount of Savagnin in an *ouillé* style under its Megalomaniac label. A tasting of the 2011 showed it to be a little over-laden with oak and showing a warmer style than from the Jura, but with that trademark lemony character.

Trousseau from the USA:

Since early in the century Trousseau has been grown in a warm area of California, Lake County, under the name of Bastardo, planted by grape farmers who believed it might be purchased by winemakers to use in a blend for a Port-style wine. Arnot-Roberts winery in Sonoma specializes in making small lots of French-style wines from purchased grapes and the owners happen to be big fans of the Jura. When they discovered that Bastardo (aka Trousseau) was available, they determined to buy some and make a wine as close to the Jura Trousseau style as they could. Despite the warmth of the area, somehow, using old oak maturation of course, they have managed to make an extraordinarily successful attempt at a California version, with the trademark light colour and a backbone of earthy fruit and tannin. They have inspired others to plant in California and Oregon, so there will be more in the future.

APPENDIX 4: GLOSSARY

The terms below are defined as they specifically apply to Jura wines.

acetaldehyde/ethanal formed by the action of oxygen on alcohol. Exists in all wines but is present in greater quantities in **Vin Jaune** and **oxidative** wines of the Jura; it forms a vital part of the distinctive character of the wines. Also in Sherries aged under **flor**, such as Fino.

acetic acid acetic bacteria react with alcohol in the presence of air to produce acetic acid or vinegar. Also known as volatile acid.

acid the chief acid in wine is tartaric acid. It is also the most common acid added in acidification (very rare in the Jura). Other important acids in wine are malic and lactic acids. See **malolactic fermentation**.

acidity provides freshness and balance. Whereas most of the world measures acidity in g/l of tartaric acid, in France it is measured in g/l of sulphuric acid. An alternative measure of acidity is **pH**.

alcohol refers to ethyl alcohol or ethanol, produced by the conversion of sugars through the action of **yeast** during fermentation.

AOC (Appellation d'Origine Contrôlée) controlled appellation of origin. The strictest level of regulated appellation in France. See also **AOP**.

AOP (Appellation d'Origine Protégée) protected appellation of origin in the European Union (EU) for agricultural products. Replaces **AOC**, but AOC can also be used for wines in France.

biodynamic philosophy of organic farming and wine production, originally based on the teachings of Rudolf Steiner. The use of dynamized spray preparations to nurture both the soil and the plant feature, as well as working according to lunar and astral calendars. Certification body is Demeter. See **organic**.

Botrytis cinerea noble rot, desired grape fungus that appears on ripe grapes in autumn resulting in a concentration of sugars, acids and flavours.

carbon dioxide/CO$_2$ gas produced during process of fermentation. A small amount remains dissolved in the wine and helps protect juice and wine from **oxidation**. May be deliberately retained or even added at bottling. Dissolved carbon dioxide forms the bubbles in sparkling wine.

carbonic maceration a method of red wine fermentation where uncrushed whole grapes undergo intracellular fermentation in the presence of **carbon dioxide**. Produces a fruit-forward wine with virtually no discernible **tannins**. In **semi-carbonic maceration** the grapes are partly crushed so that both an intracellular and exterior fermentation take place.

cave à Vin Jaune dedicated location (cellar, not necessarily underground) for ageing barrels of **Vin Jaune**. Usually with ventilation to encourage temperature variations.

chaptalization sugar added to grape **must** before fermentation to increase alcohol content, levels controlled by law.

CIVJ (Comité Interprofessionnel des Vins du Jura) regional wine organization for Jura wine producers, responsible for promotional activities and recording sales.

clavelin name for the 62cl bottle that must be used for **Vin Jaune** and Château-Chalon.

clonal selection process of selection for vines chosen for their particular characteristics and subsequently propagated. See **clone**.

clone genetically identical vine cultivated from cuttings from the same original vine plant.

corail name sometimes used in the Jura for pale red wines, usually from a blend of varieties.

coulure disease that affects vines due to poor weather conditions (usually cool or wet) during or just following flowering, resulting in poor berry set and fruit development.

Crémant du Jura sparkling wine made by the **traditional method**.

cultured yeast see **yeast**.

cuvée used to denote a particular selection from a winery's range, e.g. a producer might have three Arbois Chardonnay cuvées, each from a different **terroir**.

demi-muid size of barrel that varies from 350 to 800 litres – larger than a *fût* and smaller than a *foudre*.

disgorgement/disgorging removal of **yeast** deposits following *remuage* in the making of **Crémant du Jura**.

dosage amount of sugar mixed with wine to make the *liqueur d'expédition* added immediately after **disgorgement** of **traditional-method** sparkling wines. The amount of *dosage* affects the style and taste, e.g. *brut*.

dzi/guillette Jura colloquial terms for the small tap in a barrel allowing a sample of wine to be withdrawn from beneath the *voile*.

ensemencement/ensemencé inoculation of laboratory **yeast** cultures, in the Jura normally for Savagnin to encourage the veil of yeast to form in order to make **Vin Jaune**.

Esca vine trunk disease that is fungal in origin and kills individual vines. No cure at present.

ethanal see **acetaldehyde**.

ethanol see **alcohol**.

flor see *voile*.

floral term used in the Jura to denote a white wine made without the influence of the *voile* and without exposure to oxygen. See also *ouillé*.

foudre large oak cask or vat varying in size from 2,000 to 12,000 litres.

fruité fruity, also term used in the Jura as an alternative to *floral*.

fruitière cooperative for cheesemakers or vinegrowers.

fût oak barrel or cask of 228 litres. Also known as a *pièce*.

goût du [Vin] Jaune the typical taste of **Vin Jaune**.

guillette see *dzi*.

Guyot cane pruning system widely used in the Jura that can be Single or Double Guyot.

gyropalette pallet holding sparkling wine bottles that may be turned manually or in an automatic system for automating the process of *remuage* or riddling.

IGP (Indication Géographique Protégée) Protected Geographical Indication (PGI) for agricultural products. More flexible and deemed lower quality than **AOP** or **AOC**.

INAO (Institut National de l'Origine et de la Qualité) French National Institute of Origin and Quality, a publicly administered establishment under the Minister of Agriculture, Food and Forestry that regulates **AOC** and **AOP**.

indigenous grape varieties that are native to a winegrowing region; for the Jura the most important are Poulsard (Ploussard), Savagnin and Trousseau. See also **yeast**.

intercep tractor attachment used to weed mechanically between each individual vine.

Jurassien term applied to people or methods of the Jura region.

lieu-dit literally a named place, usually referring to a specific area of vineyards.

liqueur d'expédition wine mixed with sugar added after **disgorgement** of **Crémant du Jura**. See **dosage**.

liqueur de tirage blend of sugar and **yeast** added to the base wine before bottling to initiate second fermentation for **Crémant du Jura**.

maceration (time) contact of grape skins with the fermenting juice to extract colour, **tannins** and flavour. Usually refers to red wines, but skin maceration is also possible with white wines, especially in amphorae. See also **carbonic maceration**.

Macvin (du Jura) liqueur wine only produced in the Jura from a mixture of grape juice and Marc du Jura.

maderized see **oxidation/oxidized**.

malolactic fermentation bacterial conversion (usually starting naturally) of harder malic acid into softer lactic acid, deemed essential for red wines and generally desirable for whites too in the Jura.

marc distilled grape skins, pips, etc. Part of the blend to make Macvin and also sold as a spirit, Marc du Jura. A *marc* is also an *eau-de-vie*.

mass selection/massal(e) selection selection and propagation of specific (often old and/or rare) vines from existing vineyards.

méthode ancestrale sparkling winemaking method using a single fermentation in the bottle. See also **Pétillant Naturel**.

mildew fungal diseases affecting the vines. Most prevalent is downy mildew or peronospera (called *le mildiou* in France) provoked by humidity. Controlled through chemical preventative sprays or Bordeaux mixture. See also **oidium**.

mildiou see **mildew**.

millerandage berry shot, or 'hen and chickens'. Uneven berry development within the bunch, resulting in tiny and full-sized grapes together. May follow on from *coulure*.

mistelle generic term for fortified wine made from unfermented grape **must** mixed with spirit.

must juice from crushed or pressed grapes before or during the start of fermentation.

natural way phrase used in this book to describe producers (usually **organic** or **biodynamic**) who make wine with minimal or no intervention or additives, in particular with low or no additions of **sulphur dioxide**.

natural wine unregulated term for wines made in the **natural way**.

noble rot see *Botrytis cinerea*.

oidium also called powdery mildew, fungal virus disease.

organic method of agriculture avoiding use of chemical fertilizers or treatments. Certification body is Ecocert. The term 'organic wines' has recently been controlled by the EU with criteria that are different to those elsewhere. See also **biodynamic**.

ouillé/ouillage topped up/ topping up. The act of replacing the evaporated wine in barrel (mostly) or tank to ensure no oxygen contact. As a term *ouillé* is used in the Jura to differentiate white wines made in this way from those that are aged **oxidatively** or *sous voile*.

oxidation/oxidized wine that has been over-exposed to air has unpleasant flavours and ages prematurely. Maderized is an extreme form. It is chemically the opposite of **reduction**.

oxidative and non-oxidative 'oxidative' is a term denoting a white wine that has been deliberately exposed to oxygen, usually by not topping up the barrels regularly. All *sous voile* wines are oxidative, but not all oxidative wines have been aged *sous voile*. Non-oxidative wine has been protected from exposure to air for clean, fresh fruit characters.

Pétillant Naturel sparkling wine made in a similar method to the *méthode ancestrale* with a single fermentation that completes in the bottle.

pH measure of **acidity** level in soils, grapes, grape **must** or wine.

reculée blind valley.

reduction/reductive reduction is the opposite of **oxidation**. Wines may be made in a reductive manner, avoiding any contact with oxygen. A wine that shows or suffers from reduction may have developed undesirable flavours. Bad notes of reduction may disappear on decanting or aerating a wine. Wines from the Poulsard grape are prone to reduction or having reductive flavours.

remuage **(riddling)** turning and shaking bottles of **Crémant du Jura** to move the sediment to the neck of the bottle before **disgorgement**.

residual sugar sugar remaining in wine after fermentation is complete. Amounts are usually given as g/l (grams per litre).

rubis name in the Jura sometimes used for red wines.

Saccharomyces principal wine **yeast** strain for alcoholic fermentation and the *voile* for **Vin Jaune** and other **oxidative** whites.

semi-carbonic maceration see **carbonic maceration**.

sotolon a type of aldehyde that develops during the ageing process of **Vin Jaune**, most particularly after bottling. Partly responsible for the flavours of **Vin Jaune**.

sous voile see *voile*.

sulphites/sulphur/sulphur dioxide/SO$_2$ the most important additive in wine, present naturally in very small quantities following fermentation. Acts as an antioxidant, antibacterial and antimicrobial substance, protecting the wine from being spoilt. It may be added in various forms at various stages to protect the grapes at harvest, and/or the wine during production and before bottling. The amount is subject to strict controls. It is noxious in quantity and a few asthmatics are allergic to it, hence a warning label 'contains sulphites' is compulsory.

sur lattes the period of time following bottling **Crémant du Jura** for its second fermentation and before it is riddled and disgorged is known as the time *sur lattes*, referring to the wooden slats the bottles are traditionally laid down on.

SVJ (Société de Viticulture du Jura) organization that works with and for the wine producers of the Jura, as well as with the **INAO**, to ensure rules are followed and also to research and advise producers on all production aspects of general concern. See also **CIVJ**.

tannin deriving from the grape skins, pips and stalks as well as to an extent from oak barrels (especially new), tannin is a particularly important component of red wines.

terroir can be used in many senses, most often to describe the geographical features of a piece of land or vineyard, incorporating site position, climate, geology and soil.

topped up/topping up see *ouillé*.

tradition non-legally-defined term used on some Jura wine labels. In whites it indicates a single varietal or blended **oxidative** wine; in reds, usually a wine from a blend of grape varieties.

traditional method sparkling wine method used for Champagne and **Crémant du Jura**. Involves a second fermentation in the bottle and a period of at least nine months *sur lattes*, followed by removal of **yeast** through *remuage* (riddling) and **disgorgement**.

typé typical, also the term used in the Jura to denote white wines that have been made **oxidatively** or *sous voile*.

ullage the space between the level of wine and the top of a vessel, which could be a barrel or a bottle.

Vin de France/Vin de Table lowest quality classification of wine in France with the fewest restrictions.

Vin Jaune Savagnin white wine that is matured under a veil of **yeast** – see *voile*. Bottled only in *clavelin* bottles and released from the seventh year after vintage.

Vin de Paille sweet wine made from grapes that have been dried. The wine is matured in oak for at least 18 months. Sold in half-bottles no earlier than three years after vintage.

voile or *veil* layer of **yeast** that forms on the surface of wine in an unfilled barrel, essential and actively encouraged for the

making of **Vin Jaune**. Similar to **flor** in Sherry. A wine aged *sous voile* is an **oxidative** wine aged under the veil, but not necessarily for the length of time required to make a **Vin Jaune**.

volatile acidity/volatility see **acetic acid**.

working the soil mechanical weeding, turning the soil or ploughing, used as an alternative or in addition to

grassing down, planting cover crops or using herbicide.

yeast microscopic organism responsible for the conversion of sugars in grape juice into wine during fermentation. Yeast also forms the *voile* in **Vin Jaune**. Indigenous yeasts occur naturally in the vineyard and in the cellar. Cultured yeasts, also known as selected yeasts, are grown in a laboratory.

BIBLIOGRAPHY

Books

Berthet-Bondet, Jean and Roulière-Lambert, Marie-Jeanne (2013) *Le Château-Chalon*, Mêta Jura

Bétry, Philippe (2012) *Le Vin de Paille du Jura*, Aréopage

Boulanger, Sylvaine (2004) *Le vignoble du Jura*, Grappes & Millésimes, Presses Universitaires de Bordeaux

de Brisis, Bruno, de Brisis, Christian and de Brisis, Eric (1992) *Vins, vignes et vignobles du Jura*, Cêtre

Campy, Michel et al. (2011) *La parole de Pierre*, Mêta Jura

Campy, Michel and Bichet, Vincent (2009) *Montagnes du Jura*, Néo Editions

Chevrier, Pierre (2009) *Le vin d'hier*, Editions Slatkine

Friol, Jean-Paul and Bertaud, Michel (1999) *Jura – Les vins authentiques* (self-published)

Gibey, Roger (1999) *Les travaux de Pasteur sur le vin*, Pasteur-Patrimoine Arboisien

Gibey, Roger (2002) *Pasteur et le Vin Jaune*, Pasteur-Patrimoine Arboisien

Gibey, Roger (ed.) (2008) *Bulletins de la Société de*

Viticulture et d'Horticulture d'Arbois

Goode, Jamie and Harrop, Sam (2011) *Authentic wine*, University of California Press

The green guide Burgundy Jura (2011) Michelin Apa Publications Ltd

Grosjean, Olivier et al. (2013) *Tronches de vin*, Les Editions de l'Epure/Marie Rocher

Groupe d'Etude du Vin Jaune (2002) *L'Arbois Jaune de 1774 dix ans après*, GEVJ

Jefford, Andrew (2002) *The new France*, Mitchell Beazley

Liem, Peter and Barquín, Jesús (2012) *Sherry, Manzanilla, Montilla*, Manutius

Raffenoux, Jean-Pierre (2010) *A la découverte des vignerons du Jura*, JP Raffenoux

Robinson, Jancis (2006) *Oxford companion to wine*, 3rd edition, Oxford University Press

Robinson, Jancis, Harding, Julia and Vouillamoz, José (2012) *Wine grapes*, Allen Lane

Rouget, Charles (1897) *Les vignobles du Jura et de la Franche-Comté*, Auguste Côte

Waldin, Monty (2004) *Biodynamic wines*, Mitchell Beazley

Waldin, Monty (2013) *Best biodynamic wines*, Floris

Wilson, James E (1998) *Terroir*, Mitchell Beazley

Conference papers

Campy, Michel and Barnéoud, Christian (Nov. 2007) 'Terroirs et cépages du vignoble Jurassien: un mariage réussi', conference paper presented to Société d'Histoire Naturelle du Doubs

Levaux, Jacques and Berthaud, Olivier (Feb. 2011) 'Installation du voile dans les fûts de veillissement', paper at Levons un Pan de Voile conference, Percée du Vin Jaune

Magazines

The Art of Eating (2006), no. 72

La Revue du Vin de France

Le Rouge et Le Blanc (2006) no. 81, (2009) no. 92, (2009) no. 93

Internet sites

Le Blog d'Olif by Olivier Grosjean: leblogdolif.com

La Passion du Vin forum: lapassionduvin.com

Verre de Terre by Florence Kennel: verre2terre.fr

Wine Terroirs by Bert Celce: wineterroirs.com

INDEX

Useful websites

CIVJ: jura-vins.com

CIVJ blog in English: blog-jura-vins.com/en

SVJ: sv-jura.com

Jura wine, food and travel (by Wink Lorch): jurawine.co.uk

Comté cheese: comtecheese.co.uk or comte-usa.com

KICKSTARTER ACKNOWLEDGEMENTS

In April 2013 I ran a successful Kickstarter campaign to raise funds to help finance the publication of this book. Rewards, the most popular of which was the book, were offered to those who pledged. Particularly generous were Mimi and Ken Lamb, who I will be guiding on a trip around the Jura wine region in 2014, and Stephan Bauer, Joëlle Nebbe-Mornod and Carol Whitehead, whose rewards will be tutored tastings of Jura wines. There were a further 360 people who pledged generously towards the project and they are listed here. My thanks to everyone.

Kate and Warren Adamson
Pedro Martinez Aguado
Luiz Alberto
Aitor Alegría Alonso
William Allen
Alexandra Alznauer
Marlene Angelloz
Jane Anson
Scott C Arellano Borges
Mark Armstrong
Terry Armstrong
Benoit Badoz
Talia Baiocchi
Jimena Ballestero
Richard Bampfield
Yacov Bar-Haim
Jesus Barquin Sanz
Sophie Barrett
Andrew Barrow
Karl Michael Baymor
Eli Beate
Paul Belbusti
Martin Berggren
S Berkowitz
Liz Berry
Chantal and Jean Berthet-Bondet
Mariëlla Beukers
Ian Black
Claire Blackler
Neville Blech
Hal Blumberg
David Bolomey
Jon Bonne
Laine Boswell
Carolyn Bosworth-Davies
Bill Bounds
Céline Bouteiller

Anna Catarina Bovik
Gab Bowler
Sue Boxell
Lucy Bridgers
Graeme Broom
Emil Broome
Julie Brosterman
Daniel Brown
Hans Brunold
Sue Bryant
Bill Bucklew
Jim Budd
David Bueker
John Burke
Francisco Javier Calzadilla
Manuel Aguinaga Cano
Erin Carr
Mark Carrington
Alfonso Cevola
Nicholas Cheek
Victoria Christodoulopoulou
A Cibej
André Cis
Cameron Clark
David Clawson
Laura Clay
Nicolas Clerc
David Coffey
Kelly Coggins
John Comyn
Andres Conde Laya
Susie Conley
Frankie Cook
Oswaldo Corrêa da Costa
EJ Cory
Neil Courtier
Wendy Crispell

Sid Cross
David Crossley
John Cruse
Giles Cundy
Sean Curry
Duarte Da Silva
JB Danvin
Arnaud Daphy
Michael Davidson
Anthony Davies
Mark Davis
Paul Day
Michael De Alessi
Luca De Carli
Steve De Long
Fernando de Luna
Ward De Muynck
Julio Defez
Quentin Delille
Tom DeLorme
Carson Demmond
Erica Dent
Leonard R Dest
Carlos Diaz Alfaro
John Dickinson
Alison Dillon
Joseph P Doherty
Audrey Domenach
Sergio Domingo
Steve Donigan
Heather Dougherty
John Ducker
Helen Duddridge
Richard Dudley
Gavin Duley
Geoffrey Durbin
Sue Dyson
Kevin Ecock
Donald Edwards
Trevor Elliott

David English
Sarah Jane Evans
Jack Everitt
Laine Fabien
Tom Fiorina
Wong Sao Fong
Susanna and James Forbes
Gunnar Forssell
M Foulk
Christy Frank
Vivienne Franks
E. Fremont
David Friedmann
Andrea Frost
Micaela Frow
Junichi Fujita
Emmanuelle Galdin
Rosemary George
Kate Gewehr
Peter R Gibson
Stacey Gibson
Ricardo Sanchoyarto Gil
Ginny Gilmore
Thomas Glasgow
Malcolm Gluck
Marcy Gordon
Gill Gordon-Smith
Nick Gorevic
Simon Grant
Hilary and Andrew Green
Gareth Groves
Elisabeth Gstarz
Steve Gurevitz
Luis Gutierrez
Victoria Gutierrez
R Hargreave
Morgan Harris
Tom Harrow

Simon Hayward
Jon-David Headrick
Susan Hedblad
Gunther Hein
James Helman
John Hemsley
Mark Henderson
Caroline Henry
Cathy Henton
Oscar Hernandez
Lars Heskjaer
Roger High
Douglas Hillstrom
Ed Hodson
DR Hole
Mike Holliday
Erik Hooijmeijer
Meg Houston Maker
Emilie Hsu
Trevor Hughes
Caroline and Patrice
    Hughes-Béguet
Michael Igdaloff
Anne-Catherine Jack
Tom Jarvis
David Johansen
Andrew Johnstone
Jaume Jordà
S Jordan
Jakub Jurkiewicz
Bronwyn Kabboord
Marisa Kalf
Nathan Kandler
Robert Kania
Daniel Keller
Harry Kendall
Florence Kennel
Leah Kirkland
Tom Kisthart
John Kline
Roger Kolbu
BJ Kole
Ilona Koren-Deutsch
Gregory Kozar
Anne Krebiehl
Henri Kujala
John Lamond
Cesar LaTintoreria
Matthew Latuchie
Xavier Lavoipierre
Family Lawton
Nathan Lee
Tim Lemke
Pascaline Lepeltier
Valérie Leveque

Matthew Levin
Michael Lewis
Peter Liem
Amy Lillard
Michael Lim
Peter and Barbara Linton
Jannae Lizza
Ignacio Lopez-Amor
Dave Lorch
Gwen McCann
Daniel McCurdy
Jen Macdonald
Robert McIntosh
Carole Macintyre
VJ Madden
Bob Madill
Matthew Maguire
Howard Mahady
Hampton Mallory
Richard Manley
Tim Martin
Keith Mattrick
Sarah May
Daniel Mayer
Charles Metcalfe
Duncan Arnot Meyer
Fiona Monaghan
Dawn Montgomery
Alexis Montpeyroux
Frank Morgan
Jasper Morris
R Kat Morse
Colin Muddimer
Ken Munno
Gregory Murphy
Judy Musa
Bill Nanson
Ágnes Németh
Gray Newman
Mark Newman
Ryan O'Connell
Eduardo Ojeda Cebrián
Marcel Orford-Williams
Piotr Orlov
Rachel Ostrowski
Chris Parker
Lyn Parry
Sharon Parsons
Harold D Partain
Tim Patterson
Leanda Pearman
Stuart and Barbara
    Pemble
Tom Perry
J Persson

Grant Phillips
Tao Platón González
Randall Pollard
Juliette Pope
Eduardo Porto Carreiro
James Prettitore
Jonathan Pryse
Bob Rabin
Magdalena Rahn
Edward Rand
Amy Ray
Hugo Read
Angela Reddin
Alex Redfern
Phil Reedman
Chita Reijmer
Magnus Reuterdahl
Nicolas Rezzouk
André Ribeirinho
Roy Richards
Thomas Riley
John Ritchie
Luis Rivera
Greg Roberts
Justin Roberts
William Roberts
Stephen Robins
Isabel Rodero Baños
David J Rodriguez
Michal Rosenn
Pieter Rosenthal
Zachary Ross
Joyce Rothenberg
Zev Rovine
JH Rudolph
Erich Sachse
Liz Sagues
Lorenzo Alconero Sainz-
    Rozas
Nicholas Sapirie
Tony Saracino
Helen Savage
Ronan Sayburn
David Schildknecht
Richard Schnitzlein
Janet Scollay-Lorch
Peter Scudamore-Smith
Bernardo Silveira M
    Pinto
Linda Simpson
Ole Jacob Skagen
Robert Slotover
Colin Smith
Jesus Soto
Hans Staal

Gregory Staple
Jeff Steiner
Toni Stern
Leon Stolarski
Sue Style
David Sugarman
M. Sweet
Julian S Talaveron
Patricio Tapia
Rupert Taylor
Rob Tebeau
James Thomas
Arthur Wellesley
Paola Tich
David Tietz
Graham Tigg
WR Tish
Cathrine Todd
Mike Tommasi
Caroline Tunnell-Jones
Anna Tyack
Lauri Vainio
F Vandenberg
David Vareille
Max Veenhuyzen
José Vouillamoz
Monty Waldin
Arnold Waldstein
Nick Walker
Christine Walliman
Onne Wan
Stuart Warmsley
Ian Westcott
Christopher Wheaton
Colin Wills
Will Wilson
June Winters
Michael Wising
Magnus Wold Ueland
Jonathan Wood
Simon Woolf
Stephen Worgan
Deb Worton
Doug Wregg
Tim York
Andrew Zachary
Anna Zell
Krystof Zizka
Edgar Znutins

IMAGE CREDITS

Principal photographers

Mick Rock/Cephas

3, 4, 5, 10 (top), 12, 16, 18, 24, 25, 26, 28, 36, 38, 39, 43, 45, 46 (top), 48, 50, 51, 52, 57, 58, 59, 60, 62, 63, 65, 66, 69, 70, 73, 75, 79, 81 (top, middle) 83, 84, 96, 102, 103, 106, 109, 111, 114 (top), 116, 123, 127, 132, 134, 140, 148, 150, 152, 153, 156, 157, 159, 161, 162, 165, 166, 168, 169, 172, 176, 179, 180, 185, 186, 190, 192, 195, 196, 198, 203, 206, 207, 213, 216, 219, 230, 234, 236, 237, 238, 241, 246, 247, 252, 256, 257, 262, 263, 266, 268, 270, 272, 277, 278, 279, 280, 282, 284, 292, 293, 294, 297, 298, 300, 306, 308, 312, 314, 316, 317 (bottom), 318, 319, 322, 324, 328, 332, 335.

Brett Jones

8, 10 (bottom), 21, 32, 40, 53, 55, 124, 131, 143, 145, 154, 170, 178, 182, 189, 197, 199, 201, 215, 221, 222, 223, 225, 226, 232, 233, 243, 244, 249, 259, 261, 264, 265, 267, 275, 287, 288, 290, 296, 301, 302, 304, 305, 307, 317 (top), 320, 321, 327, 330.

Xavier Servolle

37, 41, 76, 92, 128, 147, 171, 188, 205, 208, 212, 231, 240, 251, 253, 255, 260.

Other images

Henri Bertand: 93; **Courtesy of Raymond Blanc:** 6, 7; **Philippe Bruniaux:** 81 (bottom), 110, 115, 117; **Collection Philippe Bruniaux** (from *Arbois, miroir du temps*): 98, 112; **Jean-Pierre Calame:** 125; **Gaël Delorme/SVJ:** 46 (bottom); **Courtesy of the Fruitière Vinicole d'Arbois** (from *1906–2006 Un siècle de passion*): 19, 54, 86, 100, 174; **Courtesy of Jean-Paul Jeunet:** 122; **Wink Lorch:** 133, 193, 336; **Collection Wink Lorch:** 88, 142, 273; **Courtesy of Domaines Henri Maire:** 118; **Serge Moreau:** 130; **Collection Musée d'Art Hôtel Sarret de Grozon, Arbois:** 113; **Puget/Amarante-photogalerie:** 326; **Serge Reverchon:** 114 (bottom); **Courtesy of Marie-Christine Tarby:** 120; **Kevin Tessieux:** 187.

Thanks are due also to **Michel Campy** for permission to adapt his diagrams, which feature on pp. 30, 31, 46 and 99.